ALSO BY LILIA MORITZ SCHWARCZ

The Spectacle of the Races

THE EMPEROR'S BEARD

The Emperor's Beard

DOM PEDRO II AND

THE TROPICAL MONARCHY OF BRAZIL

Lilia Moritz Schwarcz

TRANSLATED FROM THE PORTUGUESE BY JOHN GLEDSON

Hill and Wang

A division of Farrar, Straus and Giroux

New York

Hill and Wang
A division of Farrar, Straus and Giroux
19 Union Square West, New York 10003

This work is published with support from the National Book Department of the Brazilian Ministry of Culture's National Library Foundation.
Obra publicada com o apoio do Ministério da Cultura do Brasil/Fundação Biblioteca Nacional—Departamento Nacional do Livro.

Grateful acknowledgment is made to the following for permission to reprint previously published material: "The Emperor's New Clothes," from *The Complete Fairy Tales and Stories* by Hans Christian Andersen, translated by Eric Haugaard, copyright © 1974 by Eric Christian Haugaard. Used by permission of Random House Children's Books, a division of Random House, Inc.

Library of Congress Cataloging-in-Publication Data
Schwarcz, Lilia Moritz.
[Barbas do imperador. English]
The emperor's beard : Dom Pedro II and the tropical monarchy of Brazil /
Lilia Moritz Schwarcz ; translated from the Portuguese by John Gledson.—
1st American ed.
p. cm.
Includes bibliographical references and index.
ISBN-13: 978-0-8090-4219-7
ISBN-10: 0-8090-4219-3 (hc : alk. paper)
1. Pedro II, Emperor of Brazil, 1825–1891.   I. Title.

F2536.P37 S3913 2003
981'.04'092—dc21
[B]   2002038839

Designed by Jonathan D. Lippincott

www.fsgbooks.com

1   3   5   7   9   10   8   6   4   2

This book has been dedicated from its inception to two important people: my children:

For Pedro, who always wanted to know if the research involved was an homage to his name, or the other way around. There's no need to decide.

For Júlia, who, as well as having read the thesis from beginning to end, gave me the best gift of all. Not long ago she looked at me in the way she has and said she wanted to be a historian.

There's nothing better than the future.

There was only one thing the great monarch didn't do during all his happy reign: shave his beard.
— Mendes Fradique, *History of Brazil by the Confused Method*

During a recent session of the New York Linguistic Circle . . . someone reminded us of the etymology of the word for "uncle" in certain Romance languages: the Greek word theios *produced in Italian, Spanish, and Portuguese* zio *and* tio; *someone else added that in some areas of Italy, uncles were called* barbas (beards). *The "beard," the "divine uncle"— how suggestive these words are.*
— Claude Lévi-Strauss, *Structural Anthropology*

Contents

Dom Pedro II, Father of the Whites

Caricatures of Dom Pedro II. MMP

When the Gê-Timbira Indians tell the story of the origins of the white man, they tell about the adventures of Aukê. This is an indigenous myth that has several variants:

> A young girl called Amcukwéi was pregnant. One day when she was bathing together with many other girls, she suddenly heard a cry: "Cavy! [guinea pig!]" Surprised, she looked all around her but could not discover where the sound had come from. Soon it came again. Going back home, she lay down on her wooden bed and heard the cry for the third time; now she realized the sound came from inside her own body. "Mother, are you already tired of carrying me?" "Yes, my child," she replied, "come out . . ." Amcukwéi began to feel the birth pangs and went alone into the forest. Putting palm leaves on the ground, she made a promise: "If you're a boy, I'll kill you, and if you're a girl, I'll raise you . . ." A boy was born, and Amcukwéi did as she had said: she dug a hole, buried her son, who was still alive, and went home. Her mother asked after the baby and, when she learned what had happened, berated her daughter: she should have brought the boy back because she, the grandmother, would bring him up. Not content with this, Amcukwéi's mother disinterred the child, bathed it, and brought it home. Amcukwéi didn't want to suckle it, but the grand-

mother breast-fed it. Then little Aukê said: "So you don't want to raise me?" Amcukwéi was very shocked and said, "Yes, I'll raise you."

Aukê grew quickly. He had the power to turn into any animal . . .

Then, one day his uncle decided to kill him. The child was sitting on the ground eating, and his uncle hit him hard on the back with a truncheon and then buried him behind the house. Next morning, however, the boy came back, covered with earth . . .

His uncle decided to get rid of Aukê in another fashion: he called him to come with him to fetch honey . . . Coming to the crest of the third mountain range, the uncle grabbed the boy and threw him into the abyss. But Aukê turned himself into a shriveled leaf and fell slowly, in spirals, to the ground . . .

The uncle soon conceived a new plan to kill Aukê: sitting on a mat, he gave him food . . . Then he knocked him down with a truncheon and burned him. They abandoned the village and moved to a faraway place.

Sometime later Amcukwéi asked the chieftains and the councilors to order Aukê's ashes to be brought . . . When the two men reached the place, they found that Aukê had been transformed into a white man: he had built a plantation house and was now raising black men . . . The lad called the two messengers and showed them his plantation. Then he called Amcukwéi to come and live with him. *Aukê is now the emperor Dom Pedro II, father of white men.*[1] (my italics)

Any story allows room for several ways of telling it, of course, and innumerable interpretations.[2] In the context of our interests in this book, the myth of Aukê helps us to understand the Brazilian monarchy as an experience seen from many different viewpoints and subject to many kinds of reconstruction and reinterpretation. In this version, Aukê becomes the white man *par excellence*, lord and distributor of wealth, and is identified with Dom Pedro II. The myth speaks of a situation of inequality, but in its mixture of cosmologies it seems to have had a preexistent meaning. The monarch appears simultaneously to attract different types of representation. In the Gê version of the myth, he is father of all the whites; in another version, a transplantation of a Portuguese myth, he is King Sebastian of Portugal in the tropics; sometimes he is a king who divides his royalty with a Prince Obá who walks the streets of Rio de Janeiro; or he is a parody of the king of Congo and his queen Ginga. In the nineteenth-century readings Dom Pedro II is a "monarch with many crowns." Honored in some festivals as a king of kings, in others he is a forgotten or subordinate character. Sometimes the parade passes right in front of him to pay him homage; at others it scarcely heeds him, and he plays at best a secondary role.

Dom Pedro took his title as Emperor of the Divine Holy Spirit from the Festival of the Divine Holy Spirit,* and he made a deal with a culture in Brazil that, while Europeanized by his very presence, was essentially mulatto, black, indigenous—and unequal. The internal dynamics of the process by which this culture emerged was to elaborate and create many new images and rituals.

How are we to explain the continued existence in nineteenth-century Latin America, for almost seventy years, of a monarchy encircled on all sides by new republics? How are we to understand that a royal family of the Bragança dynasty (also Bourbon and Habsburg) took root in Brazil's tropical environment, surrounded by Native Americans, blacks, and mulattos? We must appreciate the peculiarity in a situation that Brazilian textbooks present as quite natural. On the one hand, far away from the luxurious courts of Europe, in 1838 the capital of the Brazilian monarchy had about 37,000 slaves in a total population of 97,000 and in 1849 79,000 bondsmen and -women in a population of 206,000. Moreover, 75 percent of the slaves were Africans, a statistic that underlines the importance of the black component in the city of Rio de Janeiro.[3] On the other hand, indigenous peoples, living far from the capital and going through a process of fairly systematic destruction, were turned into a symbol of the monarchy! Distant in reality, they took on a new representational life in paintings and allegories, in sculptures and in the titles of Brazil's nobility.

The court and its palaces seemed like islands of would-be Europeans in a tropical, above all African, sea. Witnesses of the time spoke of how Rio's streets and public places were filled with blacks—slave and free—engaged in the most diverse occupations, and showing their distinctive gestures, colors, and expressions. "If I didn't know it was in Brazil, it could be taken without much exercise of the imagination for an African capital, the residence of a powerful black prince, in which a population of pure white foreigners goes completely unnoticed. Everything looks black," said the German doctor and

---

*At the suggestion of José Bonifácio, the virtual architect of the Brazilian Empire. Bonifácio preferred the title *emperor* to *king* precisely because of its association with the Festival of the Divine Holy Spirit.

travel-writer Robert Avé-Lallemant in 1859.[4] Dom Pedro II—emperor, great
monarch, and "father of the whites"—often appeared among other divinities.
After all, African kings and princes "pepper the history of the slaves brought
to America," as a Brazilian historian has put it, and they had the right to insist
that people kiss their hand or bow to them, as the French painter Jean-Baptiste
Debret noted in 1835 when he witnessed the funerals of African princes in
Rio de Janeiro.

The Funeral of a Black King, Jean-Baptiste Debret, 1834. CGJM

   Both official and unofficial relations between Brazil and Africa had been
characterized for centuries by extensive exchange. They were at opposite
ends of the trade in human beings that had been organized by Portugal, but
links developed between the two continents that were more than economic.
According to the historian Alberto da Costa e Silva, "Africa received and
Africanized the hammock, manioc and corn, while Brazil adopted *dendê* oil,
the red-pepper bush, and the type of cloth peculiar to the [West] African
coast."[5] People on both sides of the Atlantic knew about these two-way ex-
changes. It is no accident that two African kings—Obá Osemwede of Benin
and Ologum Ajan of Eko, Onim, or Lagos—were the first to recognize the independence of Brazil in 1822.
   And when African kings and nobles for reasons of war or in other disputes
had been sold as slaves and exiled because of the "shameful trade," they tried
to reconstitute the political and religious structures of their distant home-
lands in the heart of Brazil. A famous case is that of Nan Agotiné, mother of
King Guezô, from Danshomé (Dahomey), sold by slave-traders, who is supposed to have set up her altars and her court in the Casa das Minas, in São
Luís do Maranhão. Other Africans in Brazil went back home, like Prince

Fruku, who lived in Brazil for twenty-four years and returned to Africa with the name of Dom Jerônimo, disputed the throne of Danshomé, and only just lost it to Agonglo. As the Africanist Pierre Verger says, "Africans in Brazil and Brazilians in Africa [were the] unforeseen consequence of the ebb and flow of the slave traffic."[6]

Apart from true African princes, there lived in Brazil allegorical kings—of the *congada* dances, of cavalcades and drum sessions—who represented the highest authority for the brief time when festivals were celebrated. And there were also native tribal chieftains. This intimacy with so many imaginary and real kings allowed Brazilians to have different understandings of royalty and even a somewhat positive receptivity to the idea of monarchy. "There was a monarchist mentality, so to speak, that circulated among blacks and that seems to have been a re-creation of African concepts of leadership, reinforced in a colony, later a country, governed by crowned heads. Also, Dom Pedro II's popularity among the *carioca* [residing in Rio de Janeiro] blacks is well known . . . The ideal of the king as the fount of justice . . . was equally strong in [Latin] America, even among the slaves."[7]

As royalty was common to different cultural universes, various monarchies could encounter one another during rituals, despite the total absence of social and political freedom otherwise. The "kings" who lived in Brazil had nondemocratic but at least frequent contact: King Balthasar, the king of the Congo, and the viceroy of Portugal came to pay homage to the Emperor of the Divine Holy Spirit as to the Three Kings on Epiphany. These "majesties" also honored Portugal's Dom João VI on the occasion of his 1816 coronation. Then, in 1822, with Brazil's independence, "King Charlemagne and the Twelve Peers of Gaul" paid homage to Dom Pedro I with shows of horsemanship. Nor should we forget King Obá, who in the last years of Brazil's empire went to the palace every Saturday to kiss the hand of Dom Pedro II.

These kings communicated not only with one another but also with the saints; in Brazil religion and royalty were linked in a very individual fashion. No magical or transcendental powers were attributed to kingship (as in the classic French cases studied by the great historian Marc Bloch in *Les rois thaumaturges* [*The Royal Touch*]), but still, local rituals gave substance to the rather pallid ceremonials of the Braganças. In Brazil emperors were anointed and consecrated, in an attempt to give the prestige of holiness to a tradition whose inspiration was ancient but whose practical realization was already outdated. In a reciprocal movement, while monarchs gained in holiness, the saints, when objects of adoration, gained in royalty. The Divine Holy Spirit

"His Majesty the African prince Dom Miguer Manoer Pereira da Natureza." *O Besouro*, 11 May 1878. MMP

was given an empire in Brazil, and the god Momus, years later, became King Momus in Carnival. Imperial mantles coexisted with saintly ones, and Brazilian Catholicism was strongly affected over time by royal imagery, just as scenes of royalty fueled a series of popular festivals, like Carnival, with its empires and its stories of kings and queens.*

Given so many crowns and saints in Brazil, it is better not to interpret them according to the standards of European royalty and its traditions, but above all to understand, with new kinds of interpretation, how royal authority and hierarchy were retranslated and newly understood in the Brazilian environment.

The Brazilian historian and anthropologist Gilberto Freyre concluded that the monarch adopted local forms of ritual at different moments of the empire.[8] With his green cloak, echoing the color of the nation itself, his crown, and his

---

*In the Carnival parade in Rio de Janeiro in 1995, for example, the *samba-enredo* of the Imperatriz Leopoldinense samba school dramatized the misfortunes of Dom Pedro II, who tried to replace Brazil's well-adapted donkeys with camels brought from the Middle East. Its signature samba, "I'd rather have a moke that'll have me on its back / than a camel that'll give me flak," won the first prize, and its whole spectacle was full of empresses, kings, princesses, and courts. The Viradouro samba school, from Niterói, had as its theme the famous events surrounding Dom João's flight with his court to Rio de Janeiro in 1807, when Napoleon threatened Portugal. Imperial symbolism in the imagery of Rio's Carnival is well known and often recurs. Elements alluding to the monarchy and the nobility can be seen in the formation of the samba schools themselves.

"An African King and Queen in Brazil." *A Ilustração Luso-Brasileira.* MMP

cape of toucan breast-feathers, like a tropical Louis XIV, Dom Pedro II was in dialogue with his subjects, appearing as they reimagined him according to their own ways of understanding. Without forgetting the asymmetrical power relations between masters and slaves, we can see in this dialogue between different cultural categories the presence of common elements, if not in content, at least in forms, that allow us to understand the creation of a particular, local repertoire of images of monarchy. The term *empire* not only referred to the extent of Brazilian territory* and paid homage to Napoleon (the greatest influence on Dom Pedro I, according to his biographers) but also alluded to the Emperor of the Festival of the Divine Holy Spirit. We are in the presence of a regime that from the first had entered into a dialogue with local cultures and created new meanings for ancient traditions.

To cite only some isolated instances: What does it mean to invent a royal court on Western Hemisphere soil, drawing its rules from an authentic European medieval tradition but adopting indigenous names and titles? How are we to explain a prince who dresses with the majestic formality appropriate to the great courts of Europe but adds a cape of toucan breast-feathers like a Native American chieftain and a mantle embroidered with coffee-bush branches

---

*According to the French political scientist Maurice Duverger, the term *empire* is connected with the idea of a vast territory containing many peoples; also, an empire is a monarchy, a political system in which supreme power is assumed by a single titular head chosen by heredity and hallowed by his sacred nature. This classic definition is purely formal, since several empires have not met the three qualifications—royalty, extensive territory, and the coexistence of different peoples within its bounds.

and tobacco leaves? What are we to say about the famous Santa Cruz plantation, seized from the Jesuits when they were expelled from Brazil in 1759 and
protected by the monarchs who lived in Brazil, where countless slaves sang
sacred music? How are we to understand an emperor who appeared at the
Brazilian stands at the Universal Exhibitions—those late-nineteenth-century
celebrations of capitalism's technological and industrial accomplishments—
and exhibited his crown alongside indigenous products and traditional popular
artifacts?

Each of these themes, which I treat in separate chapters of this book, raises
issues concerning Brazil's "tropical monarchy"—an exception in the local
context, and exotic in relation to its European counterparts. The South American republics, for which a monarchical regime and its continued existence
were difficult to understand, eyed Brazil mistrustfully. Even taking into account Simón Bolívar's cherished dream—he leaned toward a monarchy himself and noticed the fidelity of most Latin Americans to the crown[9]—or
General Agustín de Iturbide's advocacy of a constitutional monarchy in Mexico in 1822, or the fragile empire of Jean-Jacques Dessalines in Haiti in 1804,
or the short, dramatic imperial experiment in Mexico of the Austrian archduke Maximilian (Dom Pedro II's cousin), shot in 1867 after Napoleon III
withdrew his support, the fact is that, as the historian Francisco Iglésias has
written, monarchical experiments in American territory have an "almost
tribal, anecdotal character, when they aren't tragic farces, as in the Mexican
case."[10] With the promulgation of the Monroe Doctrine in the United States
in 1823—"The American continents, by the free and independent condition
which they have assumed and maintained, are henceforth not to be considered as subjects for future colonization by any European powers . . . [Euro-
pean intervention in the Western Hemisphere cannot be viewed] in any other
light than as the manifestation of an unfriendly disposition toward the United
States"—monarchy became associated with Europe, and North American attempts to inhibit the rise of royalist systems in the Western Hemisphere increased. Although there are no instances of reprisals taken by the United
States against Brazil's monarchy, its recognition of Brazilian independence
was slower (it took a year) than with the other Latin American nations.

Surrounded by republics, the Brazilian monarchical model had other obstacles to its recognition: it was boycotted by other South American nations,
and European nations mistrusted the close relationship it continued to maintain with Africa and with the slave trade. Thus, even after Great Britain and
Portugal had recognized independent Brazil, there was a need to distance the

Brazilian monarchy from the idea of anarchy—so commonly associated with South America—from the "traffic in souls," and from the long-lived, widespread slave-based system on which its society and economy were structured. This is why from the very first there was a clear investment in spreading the image of this distant empire, at once familiar and strange. It was familiar in the European aspect of its monarchy—related to the Braganças, Bourbons, and Habsburgs—and in its civilizing character, its enthusiasm for new technologies and ideas of progress. And it was strange inasmuch as the Atlantic separated it from Europe and a whole social and geographical reality made Brazil distinctive. Brazil was well known in Europe from travelers' accounts, always identified as the place with lush, Edenic flora but also as the country with an extreme degree of racial mixture, with Indians, and with slavery. There was no way that the tropical realities of the young empire could be disregarded.

In their efforts to create a new nation, recently separated from the Portuguese "fatherland," and to establish guarantees for it, the elites in Rio put their trust in royalty and in elaborate local rituals. To them monarchy seemed the only system that could assure the unity of Brazil's vast territory and prevent the nightmare of dismemberment that so many of Spain's former colonies had suffered. The monarchical system became an essential symbol and a means of counteracting the fragility of the situation. The symbolic representations of imperial power, transcending the human person of the king, evoked images of "long duration" (Fernand Braudel's famous concept) that associated the sovereign with ideas of justice, order, peace, and stability. José Bonifácio wrote:

> Some accuse me of having implanted the Monarchy. Rightly, because I saw that there was then no other way; because I observed that the customs and character of the people were eminently aristocratic in nature; because it was necessary to capture the interest of the old families and the wealthy men who detested and feared demagogues . . . Without Monarchy there would be no center of strength and unity, and without this unity we would be unable to resist the Portuguese parliament and achieve National Independence.[11]

In the dynastic continuities and breaks, the continuations and updatings of ritual, sacred and profane values were both involved: European origins were not abandoned but combined with a new and untried environment.

Understanding this symbolic dimension of the representation of Brazil's royalty, we can see aspects of Brazil's past that are little studied yet fundamental to models of social life that are still part of the national life today. The Brazilian monarchy was fated to follow a course that was at the same time sui generis and similar to others, that corresponded to the essence of an imported culture but also was adjusted to local sensibilities. Here, it seems, was an "original copy": a culture constructed on continual borrowings that it incorporated, adapted, and redefined.

Perhaps this is why the legitimacy of the republic's symbols were initially problematic, for in 1889 the country was still attached to effective and widespread royal emblems. That the most successful icons of the republic—like the national anthem and the flag—are in some ways linked to royal symbols shows that the effect of republican "invention of traditions" was slight and that imperial symbolism had penetrated beyond official political limits.[12]

The historian José Murilo de Carvalho has shown that the very same elite that helped to overthrow the Brazilian monarchy struggled to establish a specific symbolism for the new republican state, but it did not succeed in imposing a new system of images. The story of the national anthem is significant: despite a hurried competition for a new composition to be chosen by 20 January 1890, Francisco Manuel da Silva's old hymn, which had not even been a candidate, ended up winning. "I prefer the old one!!!" Marshal Manuel Deodoro da Fonseca, the first president of the republic, is supposed to have said, discarding the candidate that had won first place (Leopoldo Miguez's anthem, with words by Medeiros e Albuquerque) and making it the Anthem of the Proclamation of the Republic. So the national anthem stayed the same, in spite of the suspicion that Dom Pedro I himself had composed it. (In fact, after Dom Pedro I abdicated in 1831, Francisco Manuel da Silva composed the melody, with words by Ovídio Saraiva de Carvalho e Silva, and it was first played as the imperial family left for Europe. In 1841, at the coronation of Pedro II, it was played again, with new words whose authorship is unknown. During Pedro II's reign it was played on solemn civil and military occasions but without words; it had been adopted by consensus and with no official act of recognition. It was also played abroad, as, for example, at the opening of the Philadelphia Universal Exhibition, on 9 May 1876, in the presence of Dom Pedro II and President Ulysses S. Grant.)

As for the national flag, despite innumerable a posteriori explanations for its design—about the greenness of the jungles and the golden yellow of Brazil's mineral wealth—it too has its links with imperial tradition: green is the heraldic color of the Portuguese royal house of Bragança; yellow is the color of the imperial Austrian house of Habsburg. The republican design also adopted the imperial flag's diamond (Dom Pedro I's homage to Napoleon) and merely removed the royal shield with its imperial arms and introduced the Positivist motto "Order and Progress."[13]

This redefinition is typical of Brazil's process of cultural development: traditional elements of European heraldry, with their precise and ancient meaning, have superimposed on them a form taken from a revolutionary French flag, the whole now interpreted as expressive of Brazil's physical reality. This republican flag, accepted for generations as the authentic expression of Brazil's characteristics, "seems to have been born from transpositions, substitutions and inventions, which gave Brazilians the idea of making it symbolize the things they have which are most specific to them."[14]

True, they were not freely chosen icons and in that sense popular; but it is also true that the acceptance of the flag generated a consensus that, in the end, claimed to see in them images or representations of Brazil. So the issue is not so much the failure of republican symbols but the continuing power of monarchic imagery, still present today not only in elements of patriotic rhetoric but in a whole conception of Brazilian society, which is still imbued with the mystique of noble titles, honorific orders, and rituals of consecration: "The image of our country, which lives as a project and an aspiration in the collective consciousness of Brazilians, has never been able to distance itself far from the spirit of imperial Brazil; the conception of the state embodied in this ideal is not valid simply for the whole life of the nation: it is still not possible for us to conceive our projection on the international scene in any other fashion."[15]

In this battle over symbols waged between republic and monarchy, we should rethink the importance of the cultural dimension. Following clues suggested by the scholar Bronislaw Baczo, who emphasizes the importance of a society's symbolic systems, we can see that every regime has at its base a "social imaginary" made up of utopias and ideologies, of myths, symbols, and allegories; these powerful elements help to shape its political power, especially when they gain popular acceptance. And the creation of symbols is neither gratuitous nor arbitrary; it does not take place in a social vacuum. Symbols are re-elaborated under the influence of their cultural context; the degree of success in manipulating them is directly linked to a "community of meanings." For us to understand how certain symbols succeed in times of change while others do not, we must pay heed not only to how they are coined but also to how they are received and transmitted.

In the Brazilian case, we can see on the one hand that the elite make an almost deliberate use of the figure of the king; they intend—and say so—to construct a representative national figure by creating rituals, giving them official sanction, and encouraging their use, by building monuments and a "past" in order to have a temporal continuum that culminates in the empire. On the other hand, in the reinterpretation of this figure at popular festivities, we see a mythic image of a sacred, religious king who is not limited to any particular place and time.

So meanings develop *in context*, but we also must emphasize their cultural particularity and allow for a synchronic analysis that gives adequate weight to the specific repertoire of each culture. This perspective, on the border between history and anthropology, allows us to see continuums and reinterpretations—of mental structures—and thus to think about the reasons for the success or failure of this or that set of manipulated symbols.

There are many signs of the use of an extensive symbolic language in Brazil's tropical monarchy, but we find them perhaps most obviously concentrated in its iconography and in its original rituals: the traces of a dialogue with external reality retranslated in local terms. As we shall see, this story does not begin with the emperor Dom Pedro II, but it is he who is surrounded by the greatest number of images and representations, as if the "body of the king" mediated these two forces: the political and institutional monarchy on the one hand, and the mythic figure in the popular imagination on the other.

From 1840 to 1889 Dom Pedro II's life was marked by dramatic events both public and private. The first monarch to be born in Brazil, Pedro de Alcântara was compared to the Child Jesus in the Portuguese Christian tradition, seen again as the Emperor of the Divine Holy Spirit of Brazilian ritual, and understood as a new King Sebastian by the last believers in the prophecies of the seventeenth-century Jesuit missionary António Vieira. A scion of the Bragança and Habsburg families and closely related to the Bourbons, Dom Pedro was recognized as a little European god, surrounded by mulattos. He lost his mother when he was a year old and his father when he was eight, became emperor at fourteen and was exiled at the age of sixty-four: it's difficult to see, in this career, where the mythic language of memory begins and political and ideological discourse ends; where history begins and where metaphor can be found.[16]

We must go step by step along the various paths of events in which the figure of the emperor was involved. From the nation's orphan he becomes a king in majesty; from emperor in the tropics and patron of the Romantic movement he turns into a citizen-king; he is finally immortalized as an exiled martyr and as a myth after his death.

This work does not pretend to be a complete, detailed biography of Dom Pedro II, or a political history of the Brazilian empire. Rather, its purpose is to focus on and understand certain important moments in—and aspects of—the construction of the emperor's public image. So while some of the chapters are chronological and biographical, other, more "vertical" ones concern specific aspects of the imperial presence throughout Dom Pedro's reign. Our aim is to recover not so much his story as his memory or, better, a collection of national memories. This, at least, is the course that the images in this book invite the reader to follow.

The official, institutional line about Dom Pedro II has not always gone hand in hand with the more popular imagining of him, which did not discard certain references that predated Brazil's independence or even the arrival of Dom João. But during Pedro II's reign and even in the "retranslation" of his exile in Europe, it is possible to see how the "body of the king" gave substance to symbolic battles of different kinds.

True, Dom Pedro II did not make all the imperial decisions; nor did he even participate in all the empire's political maneuverings. Often he was a mere bit player in the larger drama and not its author. That is why it is relatively unimportant to know if he was more or less cultivated, very intelligent or not at all gifted. Rather than personalizing the issues, it is better to look at how this state myth, this monarch of the tropics, was constructed.

Imperial Brazil was fertile in the production of a wide spectrum of images, and outstanding as a creator of national icons—hymns, medals, emblems, monuments, poetic maxims, and escutcheons—and it concentrated its efforts in carefully assembling an image of the monarch who seemed to symbolize the nation. My intention is to recover the means and processes whereby the great "production" of Dom Pedro II and the Brazilian Empire was effected. I shall try to follow not only the larger instances of this process but also the smaller, daily measures. The official iconography reveals aspects produced by the political elite in Rio de Janeiro, but other rituals and celebrations point to other, more popular interpretations. The figure of the emperor stands right at the center of both, and we shall follow his life story, highlighting the moments when and places where it was put together, noting how certain episodes were recounted while others were forgotten.

The chapters are composed on the basis of unpublished documents, the iconography of the period, and the vast bibliography about Dom Pedro II.

This last material was very useful, but it had to be negotiated with care: often overly laudatory and in some cases (just after the proclamation of the republic) openly hostile, the biographies were written in a spirit of praise or contempt, and they construct a character with no context. Reading them, it is difficult to see where history begins and myth ends. Turned into a myth when he was still quite young, Dom Pedro is always older than his father in official images—which even today confuses Brazilian schoolchildren, but that also tells us of a political iconography that history created, remembering a few things and forgetting a great deal, keeping certain images in its memory and erasing others.[17]

THE EMPEROR'S BEARD

ONE

"The Emperor's New Clothes"

REFLECTIONS ON ROYALTY

The royal mantle as depicted in *O Antonio Maria*, 1880. MMP

Once the reading ends, the Peris—who don't know exactly where Brazil is—go silent and don't know what to say. But both are crushed, and their faces show none of their previous hostility; any king, whether king of the pygmies or the cannibals, has an aura and power that impose themselves. —Rubem Fonseca, *O selvagem da ópera*

The Emperor's New Clothes

Many, many years ago there was an emperor who was so terribly fond of beautiful new clothes that he spent all his money on his attire. He did not care about his soldiers, or attending the theater, or even going for a drive in the park, unless it was to show off his new clothes. He had an outfit for every hour of the day. And just as we say, "The king is in his council chamber," his subjects used to say, "The emperor is in his clothes closet."

In the large town where the emperor's palace was, life was gay and happy; and every day new visitors arrived. One day two swindlers came. They told everybody that they were weavers and that they could weave the most marvelous cloth. Not only were the colors and patterns of their material extraordinarily beautiful, but the cloth had the strange quality of being invisible to anyone who was unfit for his office, or unforgivably stupid.

"This is truly marvelous," thought the emperor. "Now if I had robes cut from that material, I should know which of my councilors was unfit for his office, and I would be able to pick out my clever subjects myself. They must weave some material for me!" And he gave the swindlers a lot of money so they could start working at once.

They set up a loom and acted as if they were weaving, but the loom was empty. The fine silk and gold threads they demanded from the emperor they never used but hid them in their own knapsacks. Late into the night they would sit before their empty loom, pretending to weave.

"I would like to know how they are getting along," thought the emperor; but his heart beat strangely when he remembered that those who were stupid or unfit for their office would not be able to see the material. Not that he was really worried that this would happen to him. Still, it might be better to send someone else the first time and see how he fared. Everybody in town had heard about the cloth's magic quality, and most of them could hardly wait to find out how stupid or unworthy their neighbors were.

"I shall send my faithful prime minister over to see how the weavers are getting along," thought the emperor. "He will know how to judge the material, for he is both clever and fit for his office, if any man is."

The good-natured old man stepped into the room where the weavers were working and saw the empty loom. He closed his eyes and opened them again. "God preserve me!" he thought. "I cannot see a thing!" But he didn't say it out loud.

The swindlers asked him to step a little closer to the loom so that he could admire the intricate patterns and marvelous colors of the material they were weaving. They both pointed to the empty loom, and the poor old prime minister opened his eyes as wide as he could; but it didn't help, he still couldn't see anything.

"Am I stupid?" he thought. "I can't believe it, but if it is so, it is best no one finds out about it. But maybe I am not fit for my office. No, that is worse, I'd better not admit that I can't see what they are weaving."

"Tell us what you think of it," demanded one of the swindlers.

"It is beautiful. It is lovely," mumbled the old prime minister, adjusting his glasses. "What patterns! What colors! I shall tell the emperor that it pleases me ever so much."

"That is a compliment," both the weavers said; and now they described the patterns and told which shades of color they had used. The prime minister listened attentively, so that he could repeat their words to the emperor; and that is exactly what he did.

The two swindlers demanded more money and more silk and gold thread. They said they had to use it for their weaving, but their loom remained as empty as ever.

Soon the emperor sent another of his trusted councilors to see how the work was progressing. He looked and looked just as the prime minister had, but since there was nothing to be seen, he didn't see anything.

"Isn't it a marvelous piece of material?" asked one of the swindlers; and they both began to describe the beauty of their cloth again.

"I am not stupid," thought the emperor's councilor. "I must be unfit for my office. That is strange; but I'd better not admit it to anyone." And he started to praise the material, which he could not see, for the loveliness of its patterns and colors.

"I think it is the most charming piece of material I have ever seen," declared the councilor to the emperor.

Everyone in town was talking about the marvelous cloth that the swindlers were weaving.

At last the emperor himself decided to see it before it was removed from the loom. Attended by the most important people in the empire, among them the prime minister and the councilor who had been there before, the emperor entered the room where the weavers were weaving furiously on their empty loom.

"Isn't it *magnifique*?" asked the prime minister.

"Your Majesty, look at the colors and the patterns," said the councilor.

And the two old gentlemen pointed to the empty loom, believing that all the rest of the company could see the cloth.

"What!" thought the emperor. "I can't see a thing! Why, this is a disaster! Am I stupid? Am I unfit to be emperor? Oh, it is too horrible!" Aloud, he said, "It is very lovely. It has my approval," while he nodded his head and looked at the empty loom.

All the councilors, ministers, and men of great importance who had come with him stared and stared; but they saw no more than the emperor had seen, and they said the same thing that he had said: "It is lovely." And they advised him to have clothes cut and sewn, so that he could wear them in the procession at the next great celebration.

"It is magnificent! Beautiful! Excellent!" All of their mouths agreed, though none of their eyes had seen anything. The two swindlers were decorated and given the title "Royal Knight of the Loom."

The night before the procession, the two swindlers didn't sleep at all. They had sixteen candles lighting up the room where they worked. Everyone could see how busy they were, getting the emperor's new clothes finished. They pretended to take the cloth from the loom; they cut the air with their big scissors and sewed with needles without thread. At last they announced: "The emperor's clothes are ready!"

Together with his courtiers, the emperor came. The swindlers lifted their arms as if they were holding something in their hands and said, "These are the trousers. This is the robe, and there is the train. They are all as light as if they were made of spider webs! It will be as if Your Majesty had almost nothing on, but that is their special virtue."

"Oh yes," breathed all the courtiers; but they saw nothing, for there was nothing to be seen.

"Will Your Imperial Majesty be so gracious as to take off your clothes?" asked the swindlers. "Over there by the big mirror, we shall help you put your new ones on."

The emperor did as he was told; and the swindlers acted as if they were dressing him in the clothes they should have made. Finally they tied around his waist the long train that two of his most noble courtiers were to carry.

The emperor stood in front of the mirror admiring the clothes he couldn't see.

"Oh, how they suit you! A perfect fit!" everyone exclaimed. "What colors! What patterns! The new clothes are magnificent!"

"The crimson canopy, under which Your Imperial Majesty is to walk, is waiting outside," said the imperial master of court ceremony.

"Well, I am dressed. Aren't my clothes becoming?" The emperor turned around once more in front of the mirror, pretending to study his finery.

The two gentlemen of the imperial bedchamber fumbled on the floor, trying to find the train which they were supposed to carry. They didn't dare admit they didn't see anything, so they pretended to pick up the train and held their hands as if they were carrying it.

The emperor walked in the procession under his crimson canopy. And all the people of the town, who had lined the streets or were looking down from the windows, said that the emperor's clothes were beautiful. "What a magnificent robe! And the train! How well the emperor's clothes suit him!"

None of them were willing to admit that they hadn't seen a thing; for if anyone did, then he was either stupid or unfit for the job he held. Never before had the emperor's clothes been such a success.

"But he doesn't have anything on!" cried a little child.

"Listen to the innocent one," said the proud father. And the people whispered among each other and repeated what the child had said.

"He doesn't have anything on. There's a little child who says that he has nothing on."

"He has nothing on!" shouted all the people at last.

The emperor shivered, for he was certain that they were right; but he thought, "I must bear it until the procession is over." And he walked even more proudly, and the two gentlemen of the imperial bedchamber went on carrying the train that wasn't there.[1]

This well-known story, written in the mid-nineteenth century by Hans Christian Andersen, is a good starting point for a reflection on elements that define modern royalty: its theatricality, the symbolic dimension of its political power. Though any political system has this dimension, the use of symbols and rituals as foundations of power is strongest with a monarchy.

Let us return to the story: In what kind of regime would the power of the emperor's theatricality allow the farce to go on for so long? Would ritual take on such importance that only a boy, immune to its effect, could denounce the nonsense and no one else say a word? Only in a monarchy does etiquette become so important that in its complex game reality and representation are confused. In a monarchical system ritual is found not only in customs but in the laws themselves, and etiquette is not a secondary but a fundamental part of the system. What matters is *seeing* what the monarch *sees*. What works the miracle is the king looking; the consensus around ritual power clothes nakedness. Andersen's story makes clear that etiquette is a fundamental part of the structure of a royal state, and no mere ornament. Norbert Elias has written on the close relationship of the court to its rituals: "The social structure of the court . . .

alone can make the isolated phenomenon of luxury comprehensible." Understanding court society means entering the logic of royalty, of a life centered on the king, of a daily routine that insists on constant self-affirmation and exhibition. In each gesture a symbolic economy is present, a "prestige-fetish." Elias argues, indeed, that behind the ritual lies a profound conception of etiquette that guarantees a certain stability; it is the visible sign of invisible relations. In "The Emperor's New Clothes" we see the etiquette game: the procession goes blindly onward, and the nobles admire what the king too claims to admire; like a dramatic plot, etiquette itself becomes an integral, essential part of the courtly state.[2]

Andersen's story reveals a still deeper understanding of the mythical penumbra around the very concept of royalty. The "king's two bodies," as Ernst Kantorowicz has put it, his dual forms of power, join, in a unique way, the human and transitory element to the mystical one: this is the eternal, hidden basis of monarchy. Mortal man as divine king is subject to the rituals of consecration, coronation, funeral, procession, and other court ceremonies. This king, as understood according to medieval juristic theology, is gradually detached from the church and becomes secularized yet retains the attributes of a mystical body.

Kantorowicz suggests that Shakespeare's *Richard II* is the text that transformed what was only a metaphor into a structure of meaning. In this play a fundamental transgression occurs, a usurpation of the crown followed by regicide; two figures of the king then fight it out—a divine king incarnate and a physical person who exercises power. The symbolic system behind the dramatic action highlights in an almost didactic fashion the divine right and the personality of this mortal king. Shakespeare makes of the king and his power "the fulcrum of the symbolic relationships between the lifeblood, the sap, the earth; between man, plant-life, and nature."[3] Richard II, as a guilty king, is reduced to his singularity as a man. The king who never dies is thus replaced by one who dies every day, who suffers moral anguish. Removing himself from the realm of the miraculous, Richard becomes less a king every day, like Andersen's monarch who, when seen naked, stops being a king and is transformed exclusively into his weaker element: his perishable humanity.

But this is not the logic of royalty in its classic form, which is the model for many theories, as the great French historian Marc Bloch showed. In *The Royal Touch* he examined the place of the marvelous in politics, the magic power of royalty, and tried to understand the curative power ascribed to French and English kings between the twelfth and eighteenth centuries. Far from proposing a rational explanation, Bloch suggested that effective belief in the king's thaumaturgical power was the result of a desire for the miraculous, which led the sick to credit any eventual recovery of health to the monarch: "This . . . was all the faithful subjects of the French or English kings asked for. No doubt there would not have been this readiness to proclaim a miracle unless there had been the predisposition to expect no less from the hand of royalty." Bloch considered belief in the miracle of the royal cure to be a "collective error"; he found evidence of its importance in "the popular mind" and concluded that "what created the faith in the miracle was the idea that there was bound to be a miracle."[4] Obeisance to the royal will, which the French historian Jean Barbey called the "founding secret of royalty" because of its "superhuman" origins, seems to have been common not only in royal regimes in the ancient world but also in the classic monarchies of the West: "Monarchy changes, but the mystery stays the same."[5]

This, then, is the territory of a political culture whose efficacy is symbolic, not exclusively rational. The miracle is based on the desire for the miracle, on the phenomenon of belief in a power different from and superior to that of humanity itself. The parallel with Claude Lévi-Strauss's famous discussion of the effectiveness of the magician in "The Sorcerer and his Magic" is plain: Lévi-Strauss concludes that what explains the shaman's cure is not his songs and potions but the fact that a great shaman is the work of a consensus: "Quesalid did not become a great sorcerer because he cured his patients; he cured his patients because he had become a great sorcerer."[6] There is no reason to doubt the dedication of monarchs—and/or sorcerers—to their mission, but in both cases the logic of belief in a miracle clearly precedes, and is stronger than, the miracle in itself, since it is based on a collective and symbolic consensus.

The origin of Western divine monarchy can be dated, but the search for the marvelous is a different matter: it leads to linking a man to a nation symbolically and attributing to him a power that separates him from other mortals. Sir James Frazer, in *The Golden Bough*, called attention to the recurrent notion in the literature of antiquity of a "man-god," of beings endowed with divine and supernatural power. As gods incarnated in men, these sacred kings were supposed to regulate the course of nature for the good of their societies, and they were often blamed for bad harvests or other kinds of misfortune.*

*Frazer's object, in his chapter on "priestly kings," seems to have been to link divine monarchy to certain stages of civilization. In spite of its dated presuppositions, his work is still valuable because of its wide range and wealth of material. It is no accident that Lévi-Strauss got material from Frazer for his structural model.

There is, then, a certain structure, repeated and reproduced, as if it were possible to find many versions of this mythical monarchy, varied examples and individual instances of these "gods who appeared in human form."

But in the modern period (or beginning about halfway through the Middle Ages), with Europe's absolute monarchs "form is given to the marvelous," as Barbey has put it, and rituals surrounding royalty are homogenized. Two complementary realities are affirmed: consecration and the principle of heredity. Heredity, a guarantor of the mystique of the king's sacred body, was made official in consecration rites, which dramatized and made visible the monarch's holiness. A spiritual aura surrounded the power of the king and made him a ruler distinct and distant from his subjects.

Based on a kind of universality, charismatic royal power—which, again according to Kantorowicz, lasted for more than two hundred years in half a dozen countries—justified and ordered its existence by means of stories, insignias, ceremonies, and formalities that were often inherited but sometimes new. Thus Andersen's story did not simply show the king's ostentation, vanity, and luxury but showed that they were a fundamental part of the process of making his power effective.

By means of ritual used officially—and daily—the king multiplied his image, extended his power, and imposed his image on others. "The intense focus on the figure of the king and the explicit construction of a cult around him—which would become a complete religion—make the symbolic character of the domination so palpable that not even Hobbesians and utilitarians could ignore it," the anthropologist Clifford Geertz has written. In his analysis of the social structure of Bali, Geertz found a "theatre-state," in which politics was symbolic action: "The state ceremonials of classical Bali were metaphysical theatre: theatre conceived to express a vision of the fundamental nature of reality and, at the same time, to mold the existing conditions of life to harmonize with reality." In this great ritual, in which representation and reality were inseparable, the king and his court appeared as living facsimiles of an imagined order, and at the same time, through them, the general structure of that society was produced and reproduced. In the ritual the king is transformed into a master image that never dies.[7]

As a person and a myth, then, the king is above all a ritual object, an obvious image of power. Monarchy is a kind of "constructed state," marked particularly by a high degree of artifice, as the Brazilian philosopher Renato Janine Ribeiro shows, and by a particular ethics linked to a particular aesthetics: "Not many societies can have so emphasized those moments in which life is offered up to inspection from outside, for the eyes and ears of all; not many cultures can have seemed so transformed into theater, both in the way it made itself into a spectacle and in the way it consciously accepted itself as representation, as contrived and artificial."[8]

European monarchs of the seventeenth and eighteenth centuries surrounded themselves with extraordinary pomp, which was the extension of their body: "palaces to lodge their court, their ministers, their mistresses; avenues along which to parade with carriages and retinues; theatres for their amusement; factories to increase their income; churches in which to submit themselves to their God," as the historian Jean Starobinski has put it. They were people with "unlimited needs." The narcissistic relationship of the prince to his works was transmuted into a public act and a display of sovereignty, and it produced a habit of spectacle. The divine right of the prince was inscribed by means of this ceremonial, a great simulacrum, that caught the spectators in a dazzling game. If it were not for a small unforeseen detail, the emperor's clothes of Andersen's story would really be the most beautiful of all the elements, outshone only by the beauty of the entire spectacle.

Peter Burke has underlined this notion of spectacle in his consideration of modern monarchs as the inventors of political marketing. He reflects on the strategies of Louis XIV and his court, on the preoccupation with promulgating the prince's public image and constantly revising it, and analyzes how the king was celebrated and glorified by the painters, sculptors, tailors, wigmakers, dancers, poets, choreographers, and historians who worked to persuade the public of his greatness.[9]

How did the king's subjects incorporate these images of royalty, change them, emphasize, reduce, select, or omit them? The central issue is not just the means and instruments of propaganda but the different social groups. It matters little in Andersen's story to know why the king accepted the farce of putting on clothes he couldn't see; it is more interesting to know how his community believed, or wanted to believe — just as he did — in the miracle worked by those clever tailors.

Cultural analysis has much to contribute to our understanding of this issue. The anthropologist Marshall Sahlins has called attention to the cultural circularity in encounters among different cosmologies: "It is only when appropriated by and through a cultural schema that an event acquires historical meaning." Sahlins underlines the importance of anthropology in reinterpreting the practical function of meanings in action with his idea of the "structure of the conjuncture" — the realization of cultural categories in a specific context, and their expression in the actions of historical agents—and he sheds new light on the dangerous terrain of "symbolic risks" and cultural resignification. Obviously there was a sometimes predictable intention underlying the theater of court life, and it is also true that it allows of many interpretations, which depend on the context. "The problem now," says Sahlins, "is to explode the concept of history by the anthropological experience of culture." This means we must highlight the cultural dynamics and the circulation of ideas.*

It is in this circular relationship, the product of reciprocal influences going from the top down and from the bottom up, that culture is made. It is not enough to imagine a simple, passive cultural reception on the part of popular elements in society, or their total alienation from official culture. Culture is dynamic, always in movement, animated by the continuous play of events.

Andersen's little story, then, is a good beginning for this book, in which I reflect on the ways in which the public figure of Dom Pedro II was symbolically constructed. In Brazil as in other countries, the monarchy invested in ritual and theatrical self-affirmation, with titles, corteges, processions, manuals of correct behavior, paintings, history, and poetry. It was an effort to occupy, through memory and monumentality, a space in the representation of the nation. The Brazilian Empire produced many images that were fundamental to putting this process into practice.

The time has passed when those of us who do research on social questions believed in the tradition that allotted exclusive value to the written word (called by Jacques Le Goff "the imperialism of written documents"). We adopt a perspective that allows us to incorporate many other types of material, above all iconographic ones. But we should not limit these to a decorative function, tacked on to the explanatory structure. To recover the intricate network of relationships that each work contains, to seek out its internal logic, is a much more difficult analytic enterprise.

For my purposes, it matters little to reflect on the quality of the images or the artistic worth of, for example, works produced in Brazil's Imperial Academy of Fine Arts. For me, it is more interesting to find out what these documents or artworks can tell us as representations of an epoch.

---

*This is the issue that separates art historians like Aby Warburg and his followers, for whom the work of art is of central importance as a source for historical reconstruction, from those identified more with the school of Ernst Gombrich, who pay attention to the direct communications established among works of art and who believe that pictures owe more to other pictures than to the direct observation of reality.

The origins of much of the material used in this book are revealing in their own right. In 1890, soon after Dom Pedro II was banished, he decided to "donate to Brazil" his private collection, and he gave it in the name of his wife who had recently died: the Teresa Cristina Maria Collection contains more than twenty thousand photographs, portraits, oil paintings, woodcuts, and lithographs, which were spread around the public institutions of Rio de Janeiro: the National Library, the National Archive, the Brazilian Historical and Geographical Institute, and later the Imperial Museum at Petrópolis. An important part of this material is still in the process of recovery and classification. Hundreds of portraits of the imperial family; landscapes and images of national institutions; evidence of the emperor's journeys and his visits to expositions and learned establishments; records of his scientific experiments; marks of the Paraguayan war kept only on military uniforms—all these comprise a collection that is an effort to construct and perpetuate a certain national memory. It also demonstrates how short was the distance between the monarch's few intimate moments and his official life. In addition, the collection contains images of great nineteenth-century themes—in arts, urban development, archaeology, biology, botany, mining, public health—and of the most important events of the time, and of the Brazilian people. It shows us what the emperor saw and, in what is missing, what he did not see or wanted to forget. (For example, slavery is absent, like an actor hidden in the wings.) A certain civilization is represented as it remembers one thing or recollects another.

Like any collection, this one has its method of classification. It is not enough, however, to grasp its original logic; we can interpret the allegories, discover the alterations that were made, and bring them into a dialogue with the appropriate contexts. The images can be categorized by their technique—woodcuts, lithographs, oil paintings, watercolors, ink or pencil drawings, cartoons, and, from the 1860s on, photographs (daguerreotypes, ferrotypes, and ambrotypes)—and by their dates. But in the many official portraits and the images made to be seen outside Brazil, and among the bare sketches and intimate scenes, we find recurrent issues that only the material seen as a whole reveals to us. More than six hundred Pedros observe us as we observe him, witnessing not only the character's chronological growth but distinct moments in his evolution as a symbol of the state.

That is why I have chosen for this book pictures in which the role and presence of Dom Pedro are plainest. In the first chapters—concerned with the arrival of the royal family and the emperor's childhood—the treatment is less detailed; and later it becomes more sustained, when the Brazilian court, strongly organized in a program of festivals and rituals, made ample use of monarchy's symbolic representations, evoking ancient historical factors, associating the king with ideas of justice, order, peace, and stability. This was deemed a suitable model to oppose to the image of the South American republics, with their civil wars and anarchy, a model for the imposition of a civilized "European" image.

In this symbolic dimension, showing how the memory of Dom Pedro's monarchy was constructed, we find something new in his story: the magical and sacred terrain of a monarchy that brought royal tradition up to date and brought it into dialogue with Brazilian representations ("intellectual models") that predated its establishment.

"Political Theaterology." *O Besouro*, 8 August 1878. Dom Pedro, center stage, in the pagan theater of Brazilian politics. MMP

TWO

An Empire Is Born in the Tropics

The Entrance into the Bay of Rio de Janeiro. Rugendas, 1835. CGJM

"There was a country called Brazil, but, unquestionably, there were no Brazilians."
—Auguste de Sainte-Hilaire

Historians have tried to understand the originality of the Brazilian monarchy by associating it with the arrival of the Portuguese royal family in Brazil in 1808. And it is indeed unusual to have a colony become the seat of an imperial capital. The installation in Brazil of the Portuguese court, in flight from Napoleon's troops, was no mere chance or accident: it was a key moment in both Portuguese and Brazilian national history, and it came when Brazil was in the process of a unique emancipation. Whether it was a simple flight or a political coup, the fact is that, along with Dom João and his family, the Portuguese court itself—a group estimated at fifteen thousand, and this when the population of Rio was only sixty thousand—and several important Portuguese institutions were transferred (with British help) to Brazil. This was not all: British and French merchants, Italian artists, and Austrian naturalists came along with the luggage. It is difficult to imagine a greater cultural shock.

Already by 1815 virtually coequal with Portugal in a United Kingdom, Brazil slowly moved away from its old colonial status and enjoyed relative autonomy, which it had never previously known vis-à-vis Portugal. The humili-

ated, persecuted, and transplanted Portuguese state reproduced its administrative apparatus in Brazil,[1] and from Rio de Janeiro the regent, also known as
the king of Brazil, governed his empire. At that point Rio de Janeiro became
the capital of Portugal and of all its possessions in Africa and Asia. Brazilian
ports were opened to British trade, according to an agreement made with the
British crown, which had guaranteed the safe transport of the court across the
Atlantic in exchange for this commercial accord.

The court's program of celebrations and system of royal etiquette became,
in these lands below the equator, even more colorful. With the Portuguese
bureaucracy came Te Deums, thanksgiving masses, embassies, and great
court ceremonies. Monuments, triumphal arches, and processions disembarked with the royal family, which tried to improve on its unfortunate circumstances by placing the court theater in a new setting and instituting a
new "logic for spectacles." This had, among other aims, the intention of creating a memory of monarchy and giving visibility and grandeur to the paradoxical situation. A good example is the coronation of Dom João VI in 1816.
The architect Auguste Grandjean de Montigny built grandiose monuments
for the occasion, but the most intense expectations were about the night of 13
May 1818, when an allegory in four acts that sang the praises of the Portuguese
monarchy was staged, accompanied by a large painting in which the French
artist Jean-Baptiste Debret mixed gods of classical mythology with figures
from Portuguese history. (Montigny and Debret were members of a French
artistic mission that came to Brazil in 1816 and founded the Academy of Fine
Arts some years later.) Dom João VI in royal uniform was seen borne by figures symbolizing the three united nations—Portugal, Brazil, and Algarve,
along with Hymen and Love and portraits of the royal prince and princess.
Debret and Montigny outdid themselves in giving the decadent Portuguese
court a grand and solemn air, trying with pomp and ritual symbolism to link
a defeated empire to heroic antiquity.

With this dramatization of history and a wealth of spectacle meticulously
staged by the king's representatives, local groups and the newly arrived Portuguese finally encountered one another; in the streets the brilliance of the
rituals delighted the people, who were already accustomed to baroque processions with allegorical monarchs. This time, at last, Brazil had a real king.

It is worth emphasizing that the coming of the royal family to Brazil was a
fundamental factor in the monarchy's taking root in Brazil and in guaranteeing its territorial unity. The events surrounding Dom Pedro I's declaration of
Brazil's independence on 7 September 1822 seemed more like a reply to the

The backdrop for a historical ballet put on in the court theater in Rio de Janeiro on 13 May 1818 for the acclamation of Dom João VI and the marriage of his son, the heir apparent Dom Pedro I. Greek gods are depicted together with the Portuguese royal family. Jean-Baptiste Debret, 1834. CGJM

Cortes in Lisbon, with its attempts to recolonize Brazil, than an expression of a nationalist or separatist will. According to the historian Maria Eurídice de Barros Ribeiro, "national feeling in Brazil was not necessarily linked to separatist intentions." Still, the presence of the court in Brazil did not guarantee that the monarchist solution would be viable. Emancipation from Portugal would have come with or without the monarchy, which was only one option among many.

The local elites had two fundamental political problems: to maintain political unity and to guarantee social order, and the symbolic power of a king reigning above local, private disagreements solved both. Fears that Brazil might disintegrate were for a while very well founded. "The decision to achieve independence with a representative monarchy, to keep the ex-colony united, to avoid giving the armed forces predominance, to centralize public income, et cetera, were some of the political options," concludes José Murilo de Carvalho, and he notes that Brazil's political elite at the time was quite homogeneous, basically educated in Portugal and in the habits of a monarchical regime.[2]

Recourse to an imperial form juxtaposed new and old elements. Dom Pedro I had the recent examples of Napoleon and of Francis II of Austria, his father-in-law. And closer to the Brazilian context there was Mexico, where in 1822, in an attempt to contain Spanish attempts at recolonization and to withstand republican, nativist rebellion, the upper echelons of the Mexican aristocracy proclaimed General Agustín Iturbide emperor. Beyond these contemporary examples, the Brazilian Empire also represents the return and prolongation of the millenarian desires of the Reconquest and the years of Portuguese expansion, when Portugal enjoyed its greatest period of power and conquest. This nineteenth-century empire heralded the coming of a new age, sung in verse and prose since the time of Dom Sebastian in the sixteenth.

As a symbol of union, royalty seemed to the local elites and landowners the best possible way to prevent an excessive autonomy and possible separation of Brazil's provinces; only the figure of a king could keep this vast territory, with its profound differences, together. They opted for monarchy, hoping that the young king would be a convenient puppet. But politics was not exclusively in their hands. Great Britain recognized Brazil's independence and negotiated the treaty signed with Portugal, but it also increasingly opposed the Brazilian presence in Africa and the plan to make Angola independent of Portugal and to incorporate it into the Brazilian Empire. Beyond Brazil's own territory and frontiers, its emancipation produced a reaction in several African regions in its export area. In Guinea, Angola, and Mozambique groups of African merchants proposed to join the rebels of Rio de Janeiro. No coincidence that the kingdom of Dahomey was the first to recognize the independent Brazilian Empire.

Brazilian independence was won, then, by using these intercontinental links. It was vital to the new country to guarantee continuation of legal trade with the United States and Europe, as well as the importation of African slaves, the "infamous trade" that, in spite of British pressure, would not be abolished until 1850.

The originality and firm independence of Brazil's monarchy were not easy achievements, either internally or externally: they were the result of many hard-won agreements. The figure of José Bonifácio de Andrada e Silva—the future tutor of the emperor's children—was central; together with the elites of southern and central Brazil who gravitated around the new court, he dedicated himself to ensuring the territorial unity of the Brazilian Empire, wanting to keep the example of Spanish America from being repeated. This is how, in formerly Portuguese America, measures were taken to avoid the republican alternative, even though it was then thought to be the "natural vocation of the Americas." And it is why, soon after the declaration of independence in 1822, so much was invested in the ceremonial of Brazilian royalty and in establishing a certain kind of memory.

Dom Pedro I was acclaimed emperor on 12 October 1822—a date at first

thought more important than 7 September, when he had uttered the famous
"Cry of Ipiranga"—"Independence or Death!"—the day on which Brazilian
independence is now commemorated. In an effort to break with Portuguese
customs, and influenced by Napoleon's consecration and coronation in 1804,
he took part in an important religious ceremony; it was claimed to have biblical origins and was carried out according to the details given in Book I of the
old Roman *Pontifical*, a document that established that sovereigns should be
anointed and consecrated in a solemn pontifical mass (a custom the Portuguese kings had long since abolished). The ceremony took place on 1 December in the then imperial chapel. The chief chaplain, Dom José Caetano
da Silva Coutinho, consecrated the new emperor and anointed him with
holy oil. Jean-Baptiste Debret's painting shows the ritual's rigorous, exacting
nature. It was intended to emphasize the coming of a new history, based on
different suppositions from those of Portugal.

The new empire entered into a dialogue with tradition, but it also introduced elements of local culture. From now on a Brazilian imperial culture
was developed on the basis of two elements of emergent nationality: "the
monarchical state, vessel and impulse behind the civilizing project; and nature, the state's material and territorial basis."[3]

The coronation of Dom Pedro I by the bishop of Rio de Janeiro. With its lavish setting and
elaborate detail, it marked the official establishment of a new public memory. Oil on canvas, Jean-Baptiste Debret, 1828. MI

Also in 1822 the same artist, who had already been responsible for creating Dom João VI's official images, elaborated an allegory specially for the front curtain of a theater piece celebrating Dom Pedro's coronation. Debret, a "through-and-through neoclassicist" and a disciple of Jacques-Louis David, found it hard to adjust to a context so different from that of his own revolutionary France. The praise of virtue and other exemplary qualities had to be shown in an ideal form with figures of neoclassical heroism, but given the daily reality of slavery and of a transplanted court, it was not easy to translate these "formal idealizations into a reality completely foreign to its presuppositions," as one scholar has put it.[4]

In this case, the allegory had to be pleasing: the empire of Brazil had to appear in all its pomp but also in all its originality. "In these circumstances," Debret observed, "the director of the theater felt more than ever the need of replacing his old curtain, representing a Portuguese king surrounded by kneeling subjects. As a theater painter, I was charged with the new curtain, a sketch of which showed the universal fidelity of the Brazilian population to the imperial government, seated on a throne covered by a rich tapestry stretched between palm trees."[5]

The painting passed inspection and was approved by the emperor and José Bonifácio. We can do no better than to quote the revealing description of it made by its creator:

> The imperial government is represented on its throne by a seated, crowned woman, dressed in a white tunic and the imperial Brazilian

Curtain for the court theater. Jean-Baptiste Debret, 1834. CGJM

mantle with a *green background* richly embroidered in gold; she carries on her left arm a shield with *the emperor's arms* on it and with the sword in her right hand holds up the tablets of the *Brazilian constitution.* A group of uniforms placed at the base of the throne is hidden in part by a fold in the mantle, and a cornucopia overflowing with *the fruits of the country* occupies a large space at the center of the steps to the throne. In the foreground at the left is seen a boat tied up and laden with *sacks of coffee and bundles of sugar cane.* To the side, on the beach, *the fidelity of a black family* is manifested by the little black boy, armed with an agricultural implement, who accompanies his mother who, with her right hand, vigorously holds the ax destined to fell the virgin forests and defend them against usurpation, while with her left hand she holds on her shoulder her husband's rifle; he has been conscripted and is ready to leave . . . Not far off a *white indigenous woman,* kneeling at the foot of the throne and carrying her oldest child on her back *in the manner of the country,* presents two recently born twins, for whom she pleads the help of the government . . . On the other side, *a naval officer* . . . behind, *an old paulista* [from the province of São Paulo], leaning on one of his young sons who carries a rifle slung over his shoulder, protests his loyalty; behind him, other *paulistas* and *mineiros* [from the province of Minas Gerais], just as dedicated and enthusiastic, express their feelings, sabers in hand. Just behind this group kneeling *caboclos* [part-indigenous, part-European] show by their *respectful attitude the first step on the way to civilization that brings them closer to their sovereign.* The waves of the sea, breaking at the bottom of the throne, are an indication of the *geographical position of the empire.*[6] (my italics)

Debret's allegory obviously represents "the state incarnate on the imperial throne, accomplishing its mission to subject another, different one to its dominion."[7] But we should not limit ourselves to an exclusively political analysis. We are in the presence of a "great inauguration," a more or less formalized representation of a monarchy being installed in Brazil, trying to translate itself into tropical terms. With the picture and Debret's description of it, we can see how the theater curtain condensed fundamental elements of Brazil's new identity in a single scene. The throne, at the center, ensures that our eyes will go directly to the emperor—with the P and the crown above the figure: the image of the woman holding the Constitution, the greatest symbol of Western progress.

The painted curtain is about the idea that a new civilization is being installed in the tropics. Faithful blacks share the scene with an indigenous (white) woman, who carries her child "in the manner of the country." Savages at the back, with their arrows, declare their loyalty, along with more conspicuously placed people of mixed backgrounds. *Caboclos* occupy the "level of civilization" they can reach. The fruits, palm trees, and other vegetation are tropical, which adds to the exoticism. Finally, the waves of the sea beat at the base of the throne, just as the Atlantic separated Brazil from and united it to "civilization." Brazil's new symbols had an inaugural character, as if all of history were beginning with this newly independent nation. United and conjoined in a royal figure — the woman seated on the throne with the text of the basic law in her hands — a mixed-race nation arms itself to defend constitutional monarchy, made legitimate by the loyalty of "its people." In spite of the profusion of details in Debret's image, there is "a stiffness that is ill resolved, the result of a somewhat naïve grandiosity, faithful, perhaps, to the hesitant spirit of the Brazilian monarchy but very limited in its achievement as a painting."[8]

There was no way of forgetting the slaves, which made the Brazilian monarchy unique. At the time more than 45 percent of 79,321 people in Rio de Janeiro were slaves, which gave the streets an atmosphere of their own. In this empire the world of work was limited to that of the slaves. Peddlers, black women selling sweetmeats, hired slaves offering themselves as bricklayers, barbers, tailors, tinsmiths, and carpenters could be seen everywhere in Rio's streets.[9]

Yet the liveliness of the streets did not correspond to the social structure, which was hierarchical, violent, and unequal. Here was the great contradiction: how could the civilized, constitutional image of this monarchy be affirmed, given this reality? Nevertheless, in official images the mixed element gave vivacity to the new, recently emancipated nation. A hundred years later an anonymous artist showed how powerful the images of these inaugural moments were: a popular reinterpretation from the early twentieth century, Dom Pedro I appears with José Bonifácio and Debret; it is a new version of Brazil's emblems, but what is interesting is the grouping of the characters; a black slave woman and a Native American with a thoughtful expression observe the great scene — a beautiful image of reconciliation.

A painting inspired by the work of Eduardo Sá, *The Foundation of the Brazilian Nation*, anonymous. Different Brazilian types and skin colors are emphasized. The white man is the painter Debret; a Native American warrior and a black woman kneeling in submission observe the scene. Dom Pedro I and José Bonifácio appear as the true protagonists of independence. CEA

THREE

The Nation's Orphan

"GOD'S WILL BE DONE"

Dom Pedro de Alcântara, Jean-Baptiste Debret, 1826.
Detail. MI

In the early morning of 2 December 1825, the court at Rio de Janeiro awoke to the thunder of salvos from the fortresses and ships in the bay. At two-thirty in the morning the heir apparent had been born, center of all the hopes of the nation, or at least of the Brazilian elites, haunted as they were by fear of the nation's disintegration.

Pedro de Alcântara João Carlos Leopoldo Salvador Bibiano Francisco Xavier de Paula Leocádio Miguel Gabriel Rafael Gonzaga was his name, as large as the aspirations focused on this "little prince," twenty-three inches long: the first to be born on Brazilian territory. Like his father, the heir to the throne carried in his name an homage to his patron saint, Pedro de Alcântara. The House of Bragança was devoted to certain saints, among them this saint of Spanish origin who was associated with the sick and was canonized soon after the Counter-Reformation. But the emperor was born before the child, or, to paraphrase Roberto DaMatta, "D. Pedro II was not born, he was founded; he became a national heritage, an autochthonous king."[1]

Even before Pedro II's birth, orders were given for the procedures to follow in announcing the news and celebrating the birth of the new Brazilian prince. Three salvos of fireworks would announce the arrival of a boy; if it was a girl, only two. On the days until the christening, there would be festivities with the ringing of bells, gun salutes, and fireworks. It would be impossible for anyone not to know that the monarchy planted by the Portuguese on tropical land—recently liberated from its colonial yoke by the Portuguese prince himself—had been reinvigorated, emerging to a new eternal life. Though he was born into a constitutional monarchy, the heir apparent to the crown was shown to the nation with the divine support of mythical angels.

The empress, Maria Leopoldina of Habsburg, archduchess of Austria and daughter of Francis I, emperor of Austria, and Dom Pedro I, eighth duke of Bragança, already had four daughters and had "implored heaven" to be granted a son, whom they dearly wanted. The hopes for the continuity of the recently founded empire were invested in him. It was thought that many blessings would flow from his person, who all his life would be surrounded by a mystical aura, the result of a concept of divine monarchy inherited from medieval Europe but above all from the local political and cultural context. On his father's side, the imperial prince descended from kings and illustrious forebears immortalized in Portuguese literature and linked to the Capetian kings of France. On his mother's side, he was grandson of Leopold II (brother of Marie Antoinette, wife of King Louis XVI), and descended also from Francis Joseph, duke of Tuscany, husband of Empress Maria Theresa. His genealogy, like that of all monarchs, went a long way back: to Saint Stephen, king of Hungary; to Philip II and Philip IV; to the kings of Aragon, Castile, and France.

With this inheritance from Bourbon, Habsburg, and Bragança, the imperial prince's baptism was surrounded with rare magic. The ghosts of many kings, emperors, and adventurers, of enlightened, romantic, or melancholy princes would surround the life of this prince. The journalist Pedro Plancher, of the *Spectador Brasileiro*, quickly linked the birth of an heir apparent to a glorious destiny: "Anarchy died in France on 2 December; Charlemagne's crown avenged on that day the terrible insults directed at the grandchildren of Henry IV. God's will be done!"

Already in his early childhood, a manner of portraying the "orphan of the nation" began to be suggested. While in the first months following independence Dom Pedro I had been acclaimed for his illustrious lineage, for his youth (he came to the throne at the age of only twenty-four), and even for his virility (confirmed by stories of his love affairs), the situation soon changed. The Brazilian Empire was not in good health, among other reasons because of the young emperor's headstrong nature. Echoes of the imposition of the Constitution in 1824 made themselves felt, above all Article 98, which created the executive, legislative, and judicial powers, and along with them a fourth, the "moderating power": "The moderating power is the key of the

The only image in which Dom Pedro appears in the lap of a black nanny, or a slave of any kind; in fact, some authors question the identity of the baby, saying he may not be the future emperor. Attributed to Jean-Baptiste Debret. MMP

whole political organization and is exclusively delegated to the emperor as supreme chief of the nation, and its highest representative, so that he may constantly keep watch to maintain the independence, balance, and harmony of the other political powers." Contradicting the maxims of the time, which said that "the king reigns but does not govern," Dom Pedro was invested with a greater, almost absolute power, above that of others. As Article 99 said: "The

Angels bestowing their blessings on the future emperor, sketch in honor of the recognition of Dom Pedro II as the future prince. A. do Carmo, 1825. MMP

person of the emperor is inviolate and sacred. He is not subject to any kind of responsibility."

Strongly influenced by Benjamin Constant and by his *Principles of Politics*, the text of Brazil's Constitution was explicit about the division of powers. Legislative power was concentrated in representative assemblies, with the monarch's sanction; executive power in the ministers; judicial power in the courts. The emperor, for his part, stood in the middle of the three—in Constant's definition, as "a kind of neutral power."

Though Article 100 laid down the originality of the Brazilian royal title—"Constitutional Emperor and Perpetual Defender of Brazil—and he is to be addressed as Imperial Majesty"—the rest showed how limited were democratic practices in the country, in view of this fourth power. Above all, Article 101 detailed the activities and attributes of the monarch, who could nominate senators, call an Extraordinary General Assembly, sanction its decrees and resolutions, temporarily suspend resolutions of the provincial councils, prorogue or delay general assemblies, dissolve the Chamber of Deputies, freely name ministers of state, suspend magistrates, and give amnesties in urgent cases. In Brazil, then, the king reigned *and* governed, as Article 126 of the Constitution clearly stated when it said that he "physically and morally directed those he governed. He thought, ordered and acted like the captain of a ship, who issues orders and has them carried out."[2]

Faced with this imposition of the figure of the king, the parliamentary history of the empire's early years was marked by political tension and by the fear of a restoration of Portuguese colonial rule. In Pernambuco, on 2 July, there erupted the Confederation of the Equator, a first reaction against the new constitution from the northeastern provinces: Pernambuco, Paraíba, Rio Grande do Norte, Ceará, Piauí, and Pará. The execution of the Confederation's leaders caused discontent, and a new nationalism arose, increasingly mixed with obvious displays of anti-Portuguese feeling. And when he signed the 1825 treaty with Portugal, which recognized the independence of Brazil in exchange for the concession of unfair financial advantages to Portugal, and above all because he held on to his position as heir to Portugal's throne, Dom Pedro I began to disappoint Brazilian politicians, who distrusted him and feared a union of the two kingdoms.

The antiliberal policies of the first emperor were not limited to internal matters. In external affairs he continued Portugal's expansionism, aiming to extend Brazil's southern frontier to the mouth of the Rio da Prata. The result was a bungled Cisplatine war with Argentina, from which only Britain benefited. In 1827 the Cisplatine province became the independent nation of Uruguay, and the two contenders were both defeated. In fact, Britain was in general a great beneficiary of Dom Pedro I's policies.

In the private sphere, things were also tense. At the time of Dom Pedro II's first birthday, 2 December 1826, his mother was ill; she died nine days later. As if this were not enough, suspicions surrounded the cause of the empress's death. This was the time of Dom Pedro I's great love affairs, and there was plenty of talk of Leopoldina's sorrow, of her having been "assassinated" by the jealousy she felt for her husband's innumerable mistresses: "infamous women, like Pompadour and Montespan, if not worse, for they lack education."[3] The emperor, known for his impetuous character, had progressively abandoned the empress and made his affairs public, as on 12 October, when he made the marquesa de Santos a viscountess. (The marquesa de Santos went down in history as Dom Pedro's "mistress," but in popular memory she had a more ambiguous position as the "good-hearted prostitute," protector of the wayward but also "benefactress." Even today, in the Consolação cemetery in São Paulo, her grave has tributes from anonymous admirers, flowers, and a notice saying that photography is not permitted.) The fact is that Pedro II's mother died during a miscarriage, and this truth only contributed further to the popular image of the baby as the "nation's martyr" whose mother "died of sadness" as a consequence of her husband's ill treatment.

Isolated in the palace and forgotten in the political turbulence and because of his mother's death, Pedro de Alcântara was a little symbol, the memory of a "genuinely Brazilian" monarch with a promising future. There are very few images of this phase of his life: one or two portraits of the future emperor lying on green cushions, the color of the flag and of the nation, or drawings in which Dom Pedro appears dressed in a clumsy bonnet, or, finally, the only image of Dom Pedro on his mother's lap, with his sisters Dona Maria da Glória, Dona Januária, Dona Paula, and Dona Francisca Carolina.

Perhaps the best-known depiction of his childhood shows Dom Pedro seated beside an imposing drum. The official setting superimposes itself on the family and the personal aspects: the monarchy's emblems on all sides— on the drum; on the child's jacket; and in the green of the emperor's coat. Yet in spite of all the national icons, this is probably the only painting of the time that shows the prince in an intimate context, with his toys, and even with a timid smile on his lips.

Many attempts were made to find a new wife for Dom Pedro I. It seemed that the Brazilian emperor's bad reputation prevented him from aspiring to the hand of a princess of good European lineage. After three years, he finally married Dona Amélia de Leuchtenberg, princess of Bavaria, sixteen years old, whose beauty, so the documents said, calmed the king's bad tempers.

It was a brief lull. Already by 1828 a grave crisis surrounding the succession to the throne in Portugal had begun. Dona Maria da Glória, daughter of Dom Pedro I and legitimate heir, had been prevented from coming to the throne by her uncle Dom Miguel, who had abolished the Constitution and established himself as an absolute monarch. In Brazil, meanwhile, the excesses of Dom Pedro I's willfulness ended up forcing him to abdicate on 7 April 1831. As if he were a mere instrument put on the throne by the elites, he was also removed by them. The monarch then left for Portugal, with the fixed aim of recovering the Portuguese throne for Dona Maria da Glória and leaving behind the prince, Dom Pedro, little more than five years old, and the imperial princesses Dona Januária and Dona Francisca, all in the care of a tutor: José Bonifácio de Andrada e Silva, who had in recent years become his political enemy. (No explanation has been found for Dom Pedro's choice: he brought José Bonifácio

The beautiful Dona Amélia. FMLOA

out of an exile he himself had decreed. Everything points to the hypothesis that Dom Pedro saw no inconsistency in keeping both kingdoms and believed the dynasty was above needing the monarch to be actually present. José Bonifácio's time as tutor was short, however, and in 1834 the tutorship passed to the marquis of Itanhaém, a member of a family with wealth in both Rio de Janeiro and Minas Gerais. The strong influence of Napoleon on Dom Pedro I is also paradoxical: after all, the French emperor had been responsible in the first place for the flight of the Portuguese court to Brazil.)

Two images depict the departure of Dom Pedro I and the acclamation of his son, but they show us two different settings. In the first Dom Pedro leaves with Dona Amélia and Dona Maria da Glória in a scene filled with submissive blacks and slaves. In the other Debret again transformed the acclamation of the young Dom Pedro into an idealized, celebratory moment. And again the practical aims of this ritual are in dialogue with the popular acclamation, which makes the young emperor the realization of such prayers and prophecies.

Thus began the Regency of Dom Pedro II and a new phase in Brazilian history. The historian Caio Prado Jr. was the first to emphasize the importance of popular participation in the revolts of this period, which according to him signified a reaction on the part of the intermediate classes, above all in the cities, to the oligarchic policies of the great landowners. José Murilo de Carvalho, in turn, saw these rebellions as clear expressions of the difficulties

Departure of Dom Pedro I, Dona Maria da Glória, and Dona Amélia for Portugal. From Jorge Caldeira, *Mauá*.

Dom Pedro II's Acclamation. Jean-Baptiste Debret, 1834. CGJM

in establishing a national power system based on a monarchy. On the other hand, as far as Dom Pedro was concerned, the fiction of the six-year-old boy, still under the guidance of his directors and tutors, was beginning. Once more an orphan, the "ward of the nation" had to be placed, frightened, on a little bench so that he could watch the multitude acclaiming him.

In the lives of kings, separations between them and their children always represent solemn moments. In a little gold snuffbox made at this time, the drama of the moment becomes a moment of glory: Dom Pedro I gives the Brazilian crown to his son and holds his hand out over Dona Maria da Glória, future queen of Portugal. The serene character of the occasion sums up the official image of the departure of Dom Pedro I and his firm intention of keeping his hold on both his kingdoms.

As if by magic, reality becomes myth and myth reality. This is what the more traditional biographies hint at, when they describe Dom Pedro I's departure as taking place in an atmosphere of great emotion and underline the phrases uttered by the young stepmother, Dona Amélia, as with tears she begged "Brazilian mothers to look after her boy, as they might look after their own children," or declared, "Good-bye, dear emperor; you are the victim of your greatness before you even come to know it."[4]

In spite of the conspiracies preceding it, Dom Pedro I's abdication assured the monarchy's continuity, and little Dom Pedro II was acclaimed in the press as the consolidator of national independence, the monarch born on Brazilian soil who would look after the country's interests. The reactions to this "bloodless revolution" speak of hopes that a constitutional monarchy would be established, free of the abuses of an authoritarian emperor linked to the interests of the Portuguese state: "Fellow citizens! We now have a fatherland; we have a Monarch who is the symbol of your unity, and of the integrity of the Empire, who, educated among us, will receive almost from the cradle his first lessons in American Freedom and will learn to love the Brazil that witnessed his birth."[5]

However, the nine years of the Regency were very disturbed ones, with a series of rebellions breaking out in several parts of the country. The propaganda press was divided, according to their owners' views and the trends of the particular moment, and swung back and forth between plans for centralization and decentralization. The foundation in 1833 of a newspaper entitled *Dom Pedro I*, soon followed by the creation of *Dom Pedro II*, which argued for all to unite against the restoration of the first emperor's rule, is an interesting symptom. The young emperor was giving his name to a cause that he symbolized, but knew little of—Brazilian independence.

Allegory of Dom Pedro passing
the realm of Portugal to his
daughter Dona Maria da
Glória. FMLOA

Almost nothing is known of the second emperor's childhood. If we did not have accounts of the monotonous daily life of the young Dom Pedro and his sisters and the descriptions of his mediocre teachers, we might well think that the future ruler was sleeping the sleep of the just, waiting for a great awakening.

In a letter of 8 May 1838, Dom Pedro writes to his sister Dona Maria da Glória, the Portuguese queen: "My dear and most beloved sister. We are taking advantage of the journey to Paris of Sr. Antônio Carlos de Andrada, our tutor's brother, to send you news. For some time we have heard nothing of you or of our beloved mother . . . Here we are trying to follow her example: writing, arithmetic, geography, drawing, French, English, music, and dance divide our time; we are making constant efforts to acquire knowledge, and only our hard work brings some solace to us, as we miss you so much."[6] Far from one part of his family, what was left to him were his studies, which Dom Pedro took seriously, as a good heir to the throne.

In his dutiful exercises in calligraphy, the king was learning his lessons: to do good, maintain the right, fear God, or to find his own name in a pattern made up of isolated letters. In witnesses' accounts, in the testimony of many documents and biographies, everything seems to form a chain, as if Dom Pedro were waiting for the right moment when the happy ending that everyone expects finally arrives.

What is most striking is the young heir's tedious daily routine and the strict rules, followed with clocklike precision, which kept Dom Pedro distant from his subjects: an early rise, clear soup at meals, baths always in cold water, and visits with fixed beginnings and endings. Here are the palace's rules for 1834: "His Imperial Majesty wakes at 7, breakfasts at 8, break at 9, lessons till 11.30, recreation till 13.30, dinner at 14.00 precisely (with the doctor and the steward), recreation at 16.30 and 17.00 in summer, 18.30 bath, 20.00 supper, 22.00 to bed."[7] He met his sisters only after dinner, for an hour, and the rest of the time he stayed with the servants, who were allowed to address him only when he spoke to them.

During the Regency Dom Pedro II was above all an image carefully manipulated by Brazil's local elites. Significant in this context was the impasse produced on 24 September 1834, with the death in Lisbon of his father. From now on (given the earlier death of Leopoldina) the question arose of who should have the responsibility for the choice of the boy's tutor: Dona Amélia, or the General Assembly (which had previously ratified the tutorial appointments of José Bonifácio and Itanhaém). The political stakes were high.

In spite of a commitment from Dona Amélia that she would claim

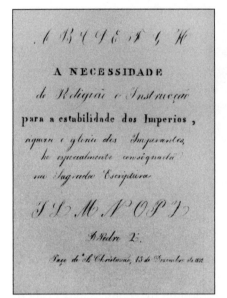

The "necessary" stability of the empire was a subject for the young heir's writing exercises. MMP

Calligraphy: the future emperor's homework. MMP

guardianship of the children only if they left Brazil, in 1836 groups opposed to the then regent Padre Diogo Feijó tried to use the imperial tutorship as a political pretext for his removal. But the situation began to stabilize when the strong-minded Padre Feijó was replaced by Pedro de Araújo Lima, marquis of Olinda, and Itanhaém was kept in his post as tutor. Also, Dona Mariana de Werna (known as Dadama), who had been removed because of disagreements with José Bonifácio, and her daughter Dona Maria Antônia were both recalled. Both women were highly esteemed by Aureliano Coutinho and Paulo Barbosa, the two men who dominated life in the palace and everything concerning the imperial children. Transformed into a "national institution" long before he had any possibility of effective rule, Dom Pedro had already become a political symbol, jealously guarded by the local elites.

The teachers, the strict hours, the customs, the loneliness, and the advice he received almost solely from Dadama, from the chief steward, Paulo Barbosa, and the influential Aureliano Coutinho formed the unhappy reality of a person gradually being molded as a monarch who was to be completely different from his father in character, education, and above all personality. For that reason, only the most official dates could be used as pretext for celebration.

One can hardly find any descriptions of the young prince without one or

```
ODNUGESORDEPMODOMPEDROSEGUNDO
DNUGESORDEPMODRDOMPEDROSEGUND
NUGESORDEPMODRORDOMPEDROSEGUN
UGESORDEPMODRODORDOMPEDROSEGU
GESORDEPMODRODADORDOMPEDROSEG
ESORDEPMODRODARADORDOMPEDROSE
SORDEPMODRODARERADORDOMPEDROS
ORDEPMODRODAREPERADORDOMPEDRO
RDEPMODRODAREPMPERADORDOMPEDR
DEPMODRODAREPMIMPERADORDOMPED
EPMODRODAREPMIOIMPERADORDOMPE
PMODRODAREPMIOAOIMPERADORDOMP
MODRODAREPMIOAVAOIMPERADORDOM
ODRODAREPMIOAVIVAOIMPERADORDO
DRODAREPMIOAVIVIVAOIMPERADORD
RODAREPMIOAVIVAOIMPERADORDO
ODRODAREPMIOAVAOIMPERADORDOM
PMODRODAREPMIOAOIMPERADORDOMP
EPMODRODAREPMIOIMPERADORDOMPE
DEPMODRODAREPMIMPERADORDOMPED
RDEPMODRODAREPMPERADORDOMPEDR
ORDEPMODRODAREPERADORDOMPEDRO
SORDEPMODRODARERADORDOMPEDROS
ESORDEPMODRODARADORDOMPEDROSE
GESORDEPMODRODADORDOMPEDROSEG
UGESORDEPMODRODORDOMPEDROSEGU
NUGESORDEPMODRORDOMPEDROSEGUN
DNUGESORDEPMODRDOMPEDROSEGUND
ODNUGESORDEPMODOMPEDROSEGUNDO
```

TABOA DE MULTIPLICAR

Portuguese and math, subjects given particular importance in the emperor's education. In the first, a small game—finding his own name (O imperador Dom Pedro Segundo) in the mass of lettering. MMP

Paulo Barbosa da Silva, the famous and
influential chief steward. MIP

more references to the three principal figures in the palace. Dona Mariana
de Werna, the future countess of Belmonte, was chief stewardess and looked
after the organization of the palace's daily round; Paulo Barbosa attended to
the finances and the official rituals involving Dom Pedro; and Aureliano
Coutinho, future viscount of Sepetiba, acted as a kind of political overseer,
even involving himself in the regent's decisions. The interference of this
group was so obvious that there was talk of a "court faction," a "camarilla," the
"Joana club" (the group met near the Boa Vista, where there was a stream of
that name), and of the decision-making power of this "palace group" in relation to the young, inexperienced, apathetic monarch.

The few portraits of the time repeat the image of a boy "born to be king"
taken up with his official duties. Already he is associated with a certain sacred
quality. In one idealized image from 1839 he floats above clouds. The splendor
of a child who rises up above the mundane world of his subjects seems to have
become the established way of representing him. It was, in fact, in perfect con-
sonance with his minimal involvement in the immediate destiny of Brazil.

In the diary of the prince of Joinville, future husband of Princess Francisca,
the twelve-year-old child is described thus on 3 January 1838: "The emperor
has a great deal of the Austrian family about him, but his manners are those of
a man of forty." One notes not only the necessary strategic representation of
the monarch's precocious maturity but also the young adult's learning. Espe-

Dom Pedro II in a conventional official image, this time in the clouds. Graciliano Leopoldino dos Santos, 1839. MMP

cially after José Bonifácio's replacement as tutor in December 1833 and the death of his father in Lisbon in September 1834, the pictorial reproductions of the future monarch gather intensity: Dom Pedro II appears as an heir conscious of his responsibilities, whose image is being put together both within and outside Brazil. A new group of images shows a feature that was to become an essential part of the representation of Dom Pedro for the rest of his life: dissimulation. True, a sideways look and a serene, impassive expression are marks of royal portraits in general, but in Dom Pedro's case this characteristic became a part of his very personality.

In images that show him as a boy, it is difficult to divine any particular feeling. Sometimes wearing military uniform, sometimes in civilian clothes, surrounded by various icons of power (uniforms, decorations, or escutcheons) or symbols of the country (like coffee and tobacco), the expression is repeated: Dom Pedro never looks at the observer; the king looks out, but not to a reciprocating gaze. In coins already circulating during the Regency, the child shines out, surrounded by stars. A theater of politics imposed itself and became confused with reality.

Even when portrayed with his sisters, the official image does not disappear. Dom Pedro wears the sash and gets to be in the middle of the canvas. If the siblings' black clothes can be interpreted as a sign of mourning for their dead father, on the other hand the relative scarcity of elements making up the picture seems to indicate an austere, ordered atmosphere, a study room appropriate for the education of a national leader.

Few accounts of the future emperor endow him with any humanity: he usually appears in a serious, solemn attitude, engrossed in his studies. Yet occasionally the mischievous child is seen, as in the story of one of his daily visits to his sisters' room, which Pedro de Alcântara recounts to the chief steward: "At 8 I breakfasted. Then I went to the schoolhouse to see my sisters. It so happens that my sisters were not paying attention, I criticized them, and they turned their backs on me: I hit them without meaning to, and they burst out crying. I left, and soon after Dona Mariana came to me saying that my sisters were crying and that I should make it up with them. I wouldn't do it. What a lie!"[8]

Another interesting image from this period comes from an almanac published in 1837. The little prince appears right in the middle—with his sisters placed at the top right and left—and surrounded by scenes of Rio de Janeiro and of the tropics. This document repeats the soon frequently repeated theme that associates the monarchy with the tropics. But our attention is caught by the allegory at the top center: next to distant goddesses among palm trees and

Dom Pedro with his sisters Francisca and Januária in São Cristóvão Palace. Drawing by Félix Emílio Taunay, c. 1837. MMP

The young Dom Pedro after his father's abdication, always portrayed with the symbols of his kingship. FBN

pineapples stands a small character who, with an imperial escutcheon, takes in the calm scene. In the midst of the disturbing years of the Regency, marked by rebellions and insurrections, an idyllic panorama emerges in which nature's perfection combines with the sanctified and supposedly stable character of the monarchy, which was in fact still confined to the silence of the palace. Once again the secrecy of the monarchy gave it a sacred quality.

In the scarce iconography of the period, we can see how the image of an eternally old king began to be molded. The images are of a prince quite different from Dom Pedro I, almost his antiportrait: responsible already as a young man, placid, and well behaved. The future monarch was not expected to display the same enthusiasm as his father, nor his "bad image" as an adventurer, of which Dom Pedro I never freed himself. The new emperor was a myth before he became a reality: he would have been deemed just even if he had not been, cultured even if he had no creative intelligence, of high morals even if he had had mistresses. Like Andersen's king, Dom Pedro II was being meticulously dressed, and the limits between the visible and the invisible were disappearing into thin air.

Separated from the world of politics, Dom Pedro did not imagine that he would soon be called to his royal mission. Quite the contrary, the Regency was settling in, for the Additional Act of 1834 guaranteed a certain decentralization of power and established a single, elected regent: Padre Feijó was elected on 7 April 1835. Rio de Janeiro, too, had changed a great deal. In 1836 the population reached 200,000, with people "rubbing elbows with one another in the central rectangle of the city" and new customs molding the city's way of life.[9] Fashion and commerce could be found on the Rua Direita, new hotels opened their doors, the habit of eating out proved attractive to more and more people, and in 1835 an Italian, Basini, introduced into Brazil a new sweet adapted to the heat of the tropics: ice cream.

People also left their houses more. Aside from going to mass on Sundays and holy days, attending religious festivals, processions, and official ceremonies or receptions in the imperial palaces, the principal social activity now was visiting, and the whole family went along, even the obedient slaves. Men's fashions also changed: it was the end of short breeches, replaced by long trousers, whose color matched that of the frock coats. A gentleman normally had four of these: a black one for funeral masses or solemn acts; a green one with yellow buttons for official ceremonies; a blue suit for visiting; and a snuff-colored one for strolling along the Rua Direita.

In this straightforward and unpretentious milieu, the little emperor lived and studied. But if tranquillity and control seemed to reign in the palace, the situation was quite different in the corridors of the legislature, in the press, and in the political clubs, where factions competed for power. In several provinces rebellions broke out that, though different in their local character, had one similar objective: decentralization. The Balaiada in Maranhão, the Sabinada in Bahia, the Carneiradas in Pernambuco, and the Cabanagem in Pará revealed the imminent danger of Brazil's disintegration.

Folhinha Nacional Brasileiro, 1837. More and more the Brazilian monarchy is linked to the tropics. MIP

FOUR

The Little Big King

An official portrait of
Dom Pedro II for his
coronation. FBN

The idea of bringing forward Dom Pedro's accession to the throne, which
the Constitution had decreed should be in 1843, when he was to be eighteen,
began to be discussed in 1835, encouraged by the Rio elite. In 1838 newspapers in the capital were freely commenting on the emperor's future coronation: "Gone are the days of true monarchy, in which royalty were thought of
as the symbols of divinity on earth. Nowadays there is no respect for anything.
See for example: the tutor wants to make the emperor simply into a citizen-
king . . . If the young monarch, object of our love and of our dearest hopes, is
nothing but a citizen-king like the present king of France, what is to become
of us! . . . the palace is thought of simply as the emperor's home. What a disgrace!!"[1]

If the plan to anticipate the emperor's majority was at first no more than a
simple political maneuver, little by little the measure took on an air of "national salvation." The Liberal Party, in 1840, with the creation of the Majority
Club, gave substance to the notion; but the task was not really difficult. Even
those on the government side seemed to favor ending the system of an elected
regent. Neither the regent Pedro de Araújo Lima, the marquis of Olinda; nor
Padre Feijó; nor the two Andrada brothers Antônio Carlos and Martim Francisco; nor Eusébio de Queirós; nor Bernardo Pereira de Vasconcelos—none
of the most influential politicians of the time were convinced that the Regency ought to continue. Even Olinda, whom the Liberals wanted to remove

from power, did not directly oppose the plan. The instability of the political order and the apprehension caused by the many rebellions, north and south, led them to bury the regime before it was dead.

When disagreements in the Chamber of Deputies and the Senate had been resolved, a commission was set up that went to the palace to solicit the formal acquiescence of the monarch, who was then fourteen. Early biographers claimed that when Dom Pedro was consulted, he said that "the business should be carried out by the Andradas and their friends." But later a new version came to light, which reveals how completely the lad was estranged from the political struggles going on around him. In an account dated March 1840, Pedro de Araújo Lima, a man trusted by the palace, told of a conversation he had with Dom Pedro on the subject of his majority. When he explained the situation to the prince and inquired as to his opinion, the boy only replied: "I haven't thought about it." Surprised, Lima said: "Your Majesty hasn't thought about it?" "Yes," he deigned to reply. "I've heard talk of it but haven't thought about it."

However, according to official chroniclers of the empire, Dom Pedro was quite prepared to take on the role for which he had been prepared and, when consulted in 1840, said, "*Quero já!*" (I want to now!). This suggests a sense of his own mission and even an emotional maturity that is hard to imagine in someone of his youth and small experience. Already the legend that was to accompany the monarch to his death was being forged: his impassive mien, his care in choosing his words, his enigmatic, unemotional character. To all accounts, were it not for his thin legs and high-pitched voice—a voice that was mimicked and mocked until his death—Dom Pedro was the incarnation of a sacred European monarch removed from "mundane matters." Of the Habsburg type— prominent chin, very blue eyes, smooth, somewhat blond hair—Dom Pedro stood out in a population made up in good part of mestizos and mulattos.

Let's return to the coup. The historian Oliveira Lima was to write that the coronation of Dom Pedro in advance of his majority was no more than "a rebellion of the instinct of self-preservation." Nobody thought of asking about his merits as a king. Once again the symbol imposed itself on the person. The image and the prestige of the institution would "save the nation." An elegant adolescent was portrayed, sometimes in official garb, infrequently in less formal clothes, but always wearing icons of his place and position. Dom Pedro was becoming a useful, necessary image for newspapers, government offices, paper money, even the lithographs that were beginning to be distributed, like presents, at court.

The serious, absorbed look hardly went well with Dom Pedro's young face, high voice, and smooth skin. The "emperor's beard" caused much debate and great apprehension from the early years of his adolescence. When it appeared, it would be extensively portrayed; the beard went white immediately after the Paraguayan war and became almost stiff in his funeral portrait. At the beginning, it was badly needed, even though it did not disguise the emperor's callow youth. A similar concern to age the boy prematurely is

Portraits of the young monarch distributed throughout the empire at the time of his consecration and thereafter. FBN

shown in newspaper articles of the time, which never tired of praising Dom Pedro's prodigious qualities: his education, his intelligence, his culture, his familiarity with languages living and dead, as well as the arts of riding and fencing: "If we didn't know that the intellectual development of this prince is beyond his age, and reveals such penetration and discernment for such a youth, they would do honor to more than one statesman used, by experience and study, to the difficult study of men."[2] Many articles covered up the emperor's youth by exalting his "precocious maturity" and "prodigious intelligence."

The expectation that an emperor would be able to guarantee security and stability to Brazil was so powerful that Dom Pedro, in one of his first proclamations, which was to the rebels in Rio Grande do Sul, in August 1840, spoke like a father but with all the authority of a fourteen-year-old—or rather, he repeated, authoritatively, a speech written by others: "If, however, you continue deaf to my voice, the time for clemency will end, and much against my wishes, the hour of punishment will come . . . Come, Rio-Grandenses, lay your fratricidal arms down at the foot of the throne; come to the arms of your monarch who, like the sun, brings light to his deluded child."[3]

Uniting his anointed authority to the powerful metaphor of the Sun King, the little monarch was growing in stature before his subjects' very eyes. He was taking part in a play being staged in which the emperor began his civic life surrounded by his precocious maturity, itself like a sumptuous theater. His adult clothes, his mature gestures, his advanced lessons, his fame as a philosopher, all this contributed to making him seem exceptional, a stranger to his own self. And the moment when this was most clearly seen was the rite of his consecration and coronation, in 1841.

The decentralizing impulse that had marked the Regency had not sat well with the Rio elites, who favored the monarchical principle. The first election of 1840 became known as the "cudgel election" (an expression also used for the first election in which the Liberals won, immediately after the "coup of the majority"). The central government appointed new provincial presidents, removed judges and police chiefs, and suspended the higher officials of the National Guard, replacing them with others. Then, with the coup making Dom Pedro II the emperor before his majority, the boy incarnated his empire, and unity and continuity were guaranteed. This was the culmination of a period of conservative reaction (1836–40) marked by the retreat of liberal policies and decentralizing measures; it sealed the fate of the monarchy in Brazil.[4] All that was needed was to deal with the monarch's youth: it became a mere detail in the context of a great, elaborate ritual.

On 18 July 1841 Rio de Janeiro awoke once again to a day of celebration. It had been said that Dom Pedro should reign like his relative Louis Philippe of Orleans, who in 1830, when he allied himself with the bourgeoisie and swore to uphold the Constitution of France, became known as the citizen-king. But his consecration was closer to the Napoleonic model, or to the more elaborate rituals of earlier European monarchs, than to an exaltation of "modernity." The courtiers in full court dress awaited the greatest ritual ever prepared in Brazil.

A booklet printed at the time and distributed around the court, *Arrangements for the Consecration of His Majesty the Emperor*, wonderfully demonstrates the intentions to display the grandiosity of a monarchical state and to create a tradition. "Program number 1" dealt with the rules for the entrance of the emperor into the capital of the empire in a grand cortege, going from the São Cristóvão Palace, located a few miles outside Rio, to the City Palace. Set to begin at noon on 16 July, it involved hundreds, even thousands, of people, who were specified to join it at precise moments in its progress, in positions and attitudes that were minutely described: guards, coaches, marches, carriages, archers, fireworks, cannons, and salvos of gunfire would thunder

This is perhaps the only somewhat realist picture we have of Dom Pedro at the time of his coronation. Not only does he look childlike, but the disproportionately large mantle drags at his feet, and the scepter is too tall, details that were adjusted in official images of the ritual. FBN

out at prearranged moments. Everything was calculated to fix the attention, to attract, to seduce, and—why not?—to intimidate.

"Program number 2" concerned the consecration, on 18 July; it regulated the formation of the procession to accompany young Pedro to the imperial chapel and all the wonders of the long ceremony. Signs and symbols abounded: insignias held high with pomp and ostentation arose from the ranks of the empire's great men, the gentlemen, and notable officials. There were plenty of them: the mantle of the founder of the empire, the imperial sword of Ipiranga, the Constitution, the offerings, the imperial globe, the ring and gloves, the emperor's own mantle, the hand of Justice, the scepter, the emperor's sword, the crown—a whole arsenal of symbols. Still to come were the standards, canopy, arms, and flags, and the anthems, of independence and of the emperor, the bows, the Latin chants.

Then came the banquet—and here we might notice one curious detail among others: the emperor's hands were not "washed" by the water that a gentleman handed him at a precise moment, but rather his hands were "purified," which in Portugal had not been done for a very long time. All the

Official images from Brazilian and foreign newspapers in 1841 of Dom Pedro II as emperor. FBN

complex gestures, full of meaning, laid out in the *Arrangements* directed the aesthetics of the spectacle so that it would reach certain emotional and spiritual heights. The Constitution itself was treated as a sacred sign, to be unrolled with an air of suspense after the "Vivas" were shouted, following the coronation, and placed next to a missal.

"Program number 3" established the calendar for the days following: a day to receive congratulations, an evening for fireworks, a visit to the Theater of São Pedro de Alcântara, a ball. Finally came the general arrangements, to make quite sure that nothing went wrong.[5]

With such a full schedule, the public finances were bound to be severely strained, but the whole show seemed to be above material interests. In truth, the coronation of the young prince was needed as a strategy to relieve the fear that Brazil might be dismembered. A year before, when the deputies and senators had announced that it would happen, a song expressed a certain expectation:

> Let young Pedro come to the throne
> And all the nation rejoice
> The heroes, the fathers of the nation
> Have approved with one voice.

> Let him wear silk, put on the purple
> And all the nation rejoice
> The heroes, the fathers of the nation
> Have approved with one voice.

> The camarilla's gone
> That we all hated
> The heroes, the fathers of the nation
> Have approved with one voice.

Other verses were also heard in the streets, less optimistic sometimes: "We want Pedro II, / Even if he's not old enough, / Let the nation waive the law, / And long live the majority." Others were not so flattering: "No reason for the people to rejoice / Because Pedrinho's on the throne; / It can't be a good thing / If he's ruling with the same people." And finally, this one: "When you put the government / In the hands of a child, / You put gobbledygook / In the mouth of a jaguar."[6]

Work went on for the coronation for six months, using the highest-quality materials and best professionals: wood, cloth, glass, paint, ironwork; carpenters, painters, directors of the fireworks displays, seamstresses, respected artists, and apprentices. The plan was supervised by the architect and painter Manuel de Araújo Porto Alegre, who received a monthly fee of 250 mil-réis. He himself painted the most important works of decoration and directed the work of a group of subordinates. Marc Ferrez got twice this amount for sculptures he made for the occasion. Crystal chandeliers, wall lights, lamps, lanterns and reflectors, dozens and dozens of different-colored glasses, good-quality flooring, gold and silver for gilding and silvering, molds, inscriptions, carvings, embroideries, fringes, bugle beads, cords, silk thread—everything made of fine gold; paper for the walls, gilded metals, velvets, damasks and silks, gold tassels and trimmings, gold and silver cloth, rich tapestries, huge numbers of lights and other objects made from the finest crystal . . . these are words that strike the eye on reading the accounts, and the description of the famous Veranda.[7]

The Veranda was a temporary building constructed in the square in front of the palace, amply proportioned and filling the space between the palace and the imperial chapel, to which it was joined. It was divided into three principal parts: a central temple and two pavilions, one on each side, with connecting galleries.

Symbols and allegories abounded in the decoration of the Veranda, beginning with the word *temple* itself, which plainly connotes a religious cult, a divine revelation. The names of the side pavilions, Amazon and Prata, gave homage to the giant rivers that determined Brazil's borders, as immense as

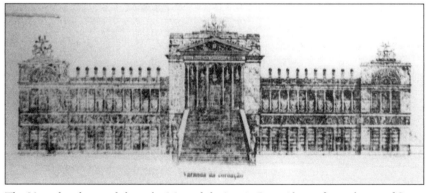

The Veranda: plans and decor by Manuel de Araújo Porto Alegre, future baron of Santo Ângelo, who was to become a famous set designer for Rio's theaters. MIP

the empire itself, and were represented by two colossal statues: "The Amazon seated, leaning back on an alligator, carrying a cornucopia full of the fruits of Brazil in his left hand . . . and the statue of the Rio da Prata, with the same attributes." The ceremony's sacral importance was emphasized, but the monarchy was decidedly American.

Two magnificent lions—strength and power—were to be found at the bottom of the stairs leading from the Rio da Prata Gallery to the imperial chapel. On the topmost floor of the pavilions were triumphal carts and carriages; at the top of the temple four horses pulled a triumphal cart carrying the genius of Brazil, who was holding the imperial scepter and crowned with laurels. The imperial staircase that led from the temple to the square ended with statues of Justice and Wisdom and the inscription: "God protects the emperor and Brazil."

At the top of the central temple was the throne room, whose

> aspect . . . is truly magnificent . . . where all the perfection and luxury of the arts can be found, all the decorative pomp . . . surprises the observer, befitting the high aim it is destined for. Two things most strike the eye: first the imperial throne, because of its elegance and opulence, the first that Brazil has seen with so much richness; the second the ceiling, whose central picture represents the emperor Dom Pedro I giving to two of his children the crowns of Portugal and Brazil, and being himself crowned by Brazil and Portugal with a halo of stars, the symbol of immortality.[8]

There is more. On the Brazilian side was a golden standard with the sphere representing its arms; at Portugal's feet the laurels of its ancient glory put forth new shoots, surrounded by stars symbolizing the provinces of the empire and the signs of the zodiac for the new emperor's dates of birth and accession (Sagittarius and Cancer), all on a blue background. Giving added strength to the image and tradition of the predestined sovereign, large medallions represented Charlemagne, Francis II, Napoleon, and Peter the Great. And, of course, the arms of Portugal and Austria, origins of the Brazilian imperial house, were displayed. On the arch over the throne could be seen the profiles of Pedro I and Dom João VI and, behind, a genius led by an eagle—symbol of royalty—with a palm frond in one hand and a crown in the other; both looked toward the emperor.

Lastly, in the same throne room, was the great apotheosis foretelling the historical destinies of Brazil:

> At the sight of the emperor invested with his constitutional right, the vices, calamities, and crimes that tore the empire apart during the abnormal, anarchic time of his minority, flee terrified back to the hell they came from. Some give up already; it is notable that vanity is the one with greatest strength, and will be the last to give way to the wisdom and virtue of the new regime. As the vices withdraw, sciences, arts and civic virtues take their place and work, under the protection of the throne, for the prosperity and glory of the empire and the monarch.

In the galleries and pavilions, tributes and portrayals of historical events were selected to give continuity to an imperial narrative—the celebrated day of 9 January 1822, when Dom Pedro I refused the Portuguese order to return to Lisbon, and said instead, "I'm staying," "*Fico*," and the day of independence, 7 September 1822. Names of illustrious patriots were engraved on the moldings atop the columns—where one also sees some indigenous names: Caramuru, Araribóia, Tibiriçá. The foundations of a new official history were laid, with the monarchy right at its center.

The mobilization of resources, people, and expenses for the ceremony seems to have known no limits. Details of the norms, regulations, and arrangements for the smooth running of royal spectacles were usually printed by the National Printing Press and distributed to the court some time ahead so that, like good actors, people could prepare themselves for the roles and be sure to make no mistakes. For the great act of the consecration and coronation of Dom Pedro II, the count of Valença received polite invitations—more exactly, summonses—printed on fine *canson* paper and signed by Cândido José Araújo Viana:

> His Majesty having determined to make His solemn entry into the Capital of the Empire, in full state, on the 16th day of July next; and The Same August Lord deeming it good that Your Excellency should accompany him not only in this Act, but also in that of his Consecration and Coronation, which will take place on the 18th of the same month: I thus inform Your Excellency, sending you a copy of the Pro-

grams, which should be observed, and should rule your actions. God
save Your Excellency.   *Palace, 22 June 1841*

His Majesty the Emperor designated the 19th day of this month to receive, at one in the afternoon, in the City Palace, Congratulations for
the happiest of motives, that of His Consecration and Coronation; and
The Same August Lord deeming it good that Your Excellency should
accompany him in this Act: I thus inform Your Excellency for your
cognizance. God save Your Excellency.   *Palace, 9 July 1841*

The countess of Valença merited a personalized invitation, since her role differed from her husband's:

Since His Majesty the Emperor has commanded me to invite Your
Excellency to be present, on the 18th day of July next, at the Act of his
Consecration and Coronation in one of the tribunes of the Imperial
Chapel: I thus convey his orders, and send Your Excellency a copy of
the Programs, which should be observed. God save Your Excellency.
                                                   Palace, 22 June 1841

Yet another invitation, printed on card and with the stamp of the empire, was
sent to the countess—a witness of some confusion in the preparations—this
time signed by the chief steward Paulo Barbosa and inviting her to sit at one
of the windows of the City Palace to watch the ceremonies.[9] Little slip-ups
like this did not detract from the grandeur of the event.

   With the scenery and actors ready, the great moment came.

   For his part, the poor frightened lad, fifteen years old, could hardly hide
his fear under his bulky, clumsy costume, the heavy crown, specially made
for the occasion, the long scepter with a snake, sculpted at its tip, symbol of
the Braganças,* the green mantle with branches of coffee and tobacco that
dragged along the ground because the boy was so short, and the mantelet of
feathers of cock-of-the-rock, created in his father's time as an homage to

---

*This snake has the body of a crocodile, bat's wings, and an eagle's head. It is usually called the
"winged serpent." On the Portuguese escutcheon it symbolizes vigilance and good moral values. The
crown came from Charlemagne's ritual; the Byzantine sovereigns also wore a golden circle adorned
with pearls and precious stones, symbolizing the religious virtues of its wearer. The holy oil lifted the
monarch above his subject.

Commemorative coins for the emperor's coronation: a Native American crowns Dom Pedro and crushes underfoot a snake representing barbarism, and a Native American with his tools represents the Brazilian nation. 1841. MMP

Brazil's birds and Indian chiefs. The monarchy was "tropicalizing" itself. It was said at the time that a merchant had specially ordered the cock-of-the-rock mantle from a group of Tirió Indians as a present for the emperor. This article became a vital part of the costume of Brazilian emperors; it was replaced in the 1860s by another of toucan breast-feathers. The color of this second mantelet was more vivid, and its manufacture required more skill.

In the sequence of images of the consecration, one or two show the monarch looking a little like himself—a boy tangled up in clothes too big for him—but in most of them we see only a representation of Dom Pedro, saluted in several languages as the great new emperor, with his crown on his head. (Only later did Dom Pedro place the crown by his side, on a green cushion, as was required by the ceremonial of the Bragança kings, who were acclaimed but not crowned.) In the official images the Brazilian emperor looked more like a French Bourbon or Austrian Habsburg, for the Brazilian monarchy had reintroduced the ritual of consecration that had been abolished in Portugal a long time before. Borrowing an age-old European rite, Brazilian politicians had laid the groundwork for a truly grandiose ceremony. The coronation ritual initiated the emperor into the exercise of sovereign power; all its elements were full of meaning and employed according to a precise choreography.

The economical Portuguese ritual was made more elaborate in Brazil.

The solemn coronation of the emperor. The two imperial princesses stand out on the Veranda; in the center, in profile, stands the corpulent figure of Chief Steward Paulo Barbosa. A study by Manuel de Araújo Porto Alegre, c. 1843. MHN

The emperor was acclaimed, crowned, *and* consecrated, as if the perfection of the event compensated for the uncertainty of the political moment, as if the unexpected coup, in a burst of enthusiasm, put an end to lack of confidence. And although the coronation and consecration of Pedro II took place in a church, he was named "Dom Pedro II, Constitutional Emperor of Brazil, by the Grace of God and the Unanimous Acclamation of the People." In the blending of old and new rituals, the consecrated and anointed king became a constitutional monarch.

Still, the spectacle leaned more toward being a marvelous transfer of power than a bureaucratic exercise. We can begin with the insignia, a fundamental part of the whole production. The efficacy of the new symbols—the sword, the scepter, the mantle, the crown—guaranteed the strength of the recently invented "imperial tradition." A good proportion of the clothes were specially designed and made for the occasion (except the suit, which had belonged to Francis I, Pedro II's grandfather). The mantle of green velvet with embroidered border, sewn with gold stars, dragons, and spheres, and lined with yellow satin, recalled the colors and emblems of the houses of Habsburg and Bragança and is supposed to have been put together in thirty days by ladies of the elite. The choice of American green was also in homage to the New World; the same was true of its "poncho" form, a reference to local forms of dress. The sword of gilded silver, which had belonged to Dom Pedro I, had the Portuguese arms engraved on both sides of its blade.

The tray on which the sword was carried also bore a copy of the Constitution of the empire in book form, bound with a green velvet cover, the ribbon of the Imperial Order of the Southern Cross on top. Armillary spheres decorated the corners of the pages, and the text was written out in elegant calligraphy.

The imperial globe, the indispensable insignia for emperors, was a silver armillary sphere with nineteen gold stars on its ecliptic, divided by the cross of the Order of Christ: a European symbol adorned by a Brazilian sky. The ring, worn on the right hand, encrusted with diamonds, had at its center two dragons with their tails entwined. The monarch's silk gloves were embroidered with the arms of the empire. The scepter was of solid gold and measured eight feet, long for a boy of fifteen. Two diamond eyes stood out on the image of the snake, a Bragança symbol in a Brazilian ceremony. The "hand of Justice," modeled on the emperor's right hand, was made in plaster by Marc Ferrez soon after the consecration, and copies were distributed to the chief courtiers to display in their houses as a symbol of their belonging to "good society." The emperor's sword had a Teutonic cross enriched with large diamonds and "D. Pedro II" engraved on the handle. On the commemorative coin a Native American (in fact, a virtual European with a headdress) crowns the little monarch, precariously balanced on his throne.

Lastly, the crown, specially made for the occasion, had a gold circle as its base and eight imperial bands, also gold, meeting at the top, with a golden sphere topped by a cross. Its sixteen-inch height made it heavy for the little emperor's head. The base of the crown was adorned with pearls and diamonds (part of them taken from Dom Pedro I's old crown because, so it was said, of necessary speed and lack of money). Everything was "new," just as the Second Reign (Dom Pedro II's reign) itself was to be new, and a new beginning: an empire that would be "genuinely Brazilian, unified by culture."

The great cortege, as it pressed its way through the Rua Direita, left the crowd ecstatic. In the imperial chapel the court awaited the king for the usual ceremony of kissing the hand and the beginning of the ceremony.[10] (The custom of kissing the king's hand had come from Portugal, and Dom João VI had incorporated it into Brazilian ritual: every night, at about eight, except on feast days and Sundays, the emperor received the public in a room set aside for this purpose, in São Cristóvão Palace. Dom Pedro was to abolish the practice in the 1870s.) It was said that, because there were so few French coiffeurs and they couldn't attend to all their clients in time, some ladies who had had their hair done on the previous day had slept fully dressed, leaning back on cushions, so as not to spoil their elaborate hairdos.

Following the recent model of King Charles X, at whose coronation in 1824 the old oath had been superseded by a full commitment to uphold the new French constitution, the archbishop next anointed the sovereign on the wrists, the right hand, and the shoulder blades. The order of ceremony was adhered to strictly, and it looked like an authentic version of the most traditional of European consecrations. (The ceremony lasted from eleven-thirty in the morning to two in the afternoon of 18 July.)

José Martiniano de Alencar, official orator of the Senate and father of José de Alencar, the Indianist novelist, gave a speech in praise of the king.

> If in the succession of events, one stands out above all the others, so that from it we reckon the duration of others . . . in the life of a monarch; this event, this act, is without doubt his consecration and coronation. The intervention of religion seems to establish a kind of contract between God and the consecrated monarch, who renews his alliance with the people; God comes to instill in him the powerful help of His grace, so that he may fulfill the high functions conferred on him. Then the Chosen One, the Beloved of the people, becomes the chosen of God, Anointed of the Lord. These are the salutary effects of the act of religion we have enthusiastically witnessed . . . The Senate hopes that Your Imperial Majesty will accept the feelings of commitment and loyalty to your Sacred Person . . . and trusts with religious hope that Divine Providence will bless your glorious Reign and make it happy.[11]

The coronation celebrations went on for nine days, ending on 24 July with a gala ball in the City Palace. At five in the afternoon the first of the twelve hundred guests began to arrive. The emperor appeared at eight, together with his sisters and palace dignitaries. Dinner was served at midnight, and in each pavilion of the Veranda a table with eighty places was set, where the guests took their turns. The ball ended at two in the morning. Baron Daiser, the Austrian ambassador, left a vivid impression in a letter to Prince Metternich:

> I must say, in truth, that the court showed a wealth of equipages, liveries, and furniture of all kinds, truly astonishing in this country, where resources are very limited, where not long ago everything was lacking, and where there is so little, or, really, no precedent; for everything that had been done in the time of Dom Pedro was nowhere near what we have seen this time, whether in terms of wealth, good taste, or dignity . . . The sight at the moment when the emperor appeared to the people on the balustrade of the Veranda was magnificent, perhaps incomparable because the nature of the setting . . . the sun was dazzling, and the sea calm and beautiful, with a heavenly velvet color.[12]

Perhaps the consecration of Dom Pedro II represents the first moment in which two trends came together: one favored a calculated ritual devised by the elites to put back the emperor as symbol of the nation and as the institution that would arbitrate their quarrels; the other, with its richness of ritual and intensity of publicity surrounding it, led to an explosion in the popular imagination, reinterpreting the mystique of this little Brazilian king as "sacred and enchanted."

Medallion commemorating the coronation of Dom Pedro II; the image looks medieval and European. J. Sturz, 1841. MMP

Let us look more closely: there was no doubt about the quality of the ritual concerning a Brazilian monarch at once both constitutional and sacred. These were novelties to be transplanted and perfected in the New World: the public figure had to be flexible and capable of adaptation. Bells rang out, cannons boomed, and the multitude saluted the new emperor. With the heavy crown on his head, dragging his long mantle behind him, and with his feather mantelet giving him the naïve look that kings had in celebrations of the Divine Holy Spirit, Dom Pedro mounted the steps to the throne and looked back at the crowd at his feet. Small as he was, he was more like an allegorical figure, and the allegory could hardly disguise the boy with his bewildered look.

The wealth of insignias and the strictness of the ritual of consecration awed and dazzled the public, and people were enchanted by the grandiose spectacle. Indeed, the coronation and consecration seemed to affirm a real past, an imperial tradition that really did look consolidated and prosperous. Forget the sovereign's age, the haste in producing the ritual, the falsity of the scenery. The real impression was that the political difficulties of the Regency had vanished at a touch. It occurred to no one to shout that the king was, in fact, wearing no clothes.

FIVE

The Great Emperor

Dom Pedro II in his
costume for the Gala Days.
FBN

The years from 1841 to 1864, the year the Paraguayan war began, represent an important phase in the consolidation of the Brazilian monarchy. Rebellions in Bahia, Pará, and Maranhão during the Regency had been overcome with the help of General Lima e Silva (he received the title of baron of Caxias for services rendered*). At this moment, too, the cabinet, which included Antônio Carlos and Martim Francisco de Andrada, gave symbolic amnesty to those rebels who gave themselves up to the authorities; this helped greatly to bring calm and reduce misgivings. The Farrapo war in Rio Grande do Sul, however, was still a matter of critical importance in the first few years. And in this troubled political atmosphere, with parties taking turns in power, attempts to stifle rebellion became the great theme of the empire, while the imperial regime placed itself above party divisions.

Meanwhile, far from public affairs and the governance of the state, Dom Pedro II was finishing his education, interested more in science and literature than in politics. Everything seemed to suggest that Dom Pedro would limit himself to "reigning" and dedicate himself to the arts, culture, and science; politics and economics produced no enthusiasm in him. The "great em-

*In Chapter 8 more detail is provided on the logic of titles in imperial Brazil. Here it needs only to be noted that the baronetcy was for life and was not hereditary. After the Paraguayan war Caxias was made a duke.

peror" was a mere representation of himself, carrying out official duties according to a pompous, elaborate ritual intended to show him as a monarch only in certain symbolically important moments.

Paulo Barbosa, his chief steward, was perhaps the only person who kept him in touch with reality and minimally informed, at least, of palace activities and expenses. In a note of 1842, Dom Pedro asked him, "What is the herald's name? What is the name of the master of ceremonies? Which posts have no place in the army? How do I find the first assistant of the master of ceremonies? How many servants of the bedchamber are there, and what are their names?" Or again in 1863: "I don't know exactly how much is spent on the stables. I don't know if any reduction in the service is possible . . . The allotment of money for the kitchen is the third in size, is that right?"[1]

Still beardless, the emperor, in a haughty posture, hardly looks like himself in his new portraits; he is much older, and his face is strange, to say the least, compared to previous portraits. Removed from day-to-day troubles and isolated in his palace, the young sovereign looks like a European monarch, a replica of Old World models—distinguished as a Brazilian only by the ornaments proper to the Brazilian imperial house.

Pictorial images were important in depicting a monarch who was otherwise invisible in the daily life of most Brazilians. Dom Pedro II remained isolated in the palace and existed only in these pictures showing a secure, young, strong king.

In a series of portraits from the 1840s, Dom Pedro still looks like an idealized king. With a distant look, his mantelet half-hidden, his legs less thin than they actually were, the emperor seems merely to correspond to models composed elsewhere. At a time when everything seemed to presume he was a perfectly functioning puppet, nothing was better than this fixed image: perfect for making copies. Even the beard has suddenly grown, which did not go unnoticed by his contemporaries: "His Majesty has a different appearance, and even his beard is more or less grown."[2] The beard was part of a political iconography, just like the mantelet and the mantle.

It is worth stressing the production of many more or less identical portraits. If it were not for different objects depicted—which though they appear accidental are calculated—we could say that they all are the same picture. Whether the throne is there or not, the scepter, the crown, the sword, or the Constitution; whether the face looks right or left, the expression is always the same, with no trace of emotion. Following the characteristic vogue for portraits of this time, the images project a model type that combines individual

Coronation of Dom Pedro II, 18 July 1841. In this lithograph we see an older monarch. FBN

Dom Pedro in his imperial robes, looking quite different, 1841. FBN

Dom Pedro at twenty, without the beard. FBN

Dom Pedro II in the late 1840s. The telescope is a reference to the monarch's taste
for astronomy. FBN

A portrait based on the telescope portrait in
which Dom Pedro II appears as a constitutional monarch, by a table with the Constitution of Brazil. Lithograph by Krumholz.
FBN

traits with a formal expression that puts one in mind of universal qualities
such as wisdom and kindness.

We see the technique developed in a collection of portraits that, like a
game of "spot the difference," show small variations (in the glove, shoes, sash)
in more or less the same scene, though the image of the monarch does not
change, as if it were necessary to repeat over and over again the artificiality of
the situation. The young emperor is in a theater, surrounded by all his props.
In public buildings, in the Brazilian and foreign press, in celebrations in Rio,
on kerchiefs and coins, Dom Pedro's face is "spread around." Only in this way
does it become real.

After Dom Pedro actually achieved his majority, the rituals became more
fixed. The complete dress ensemble—a "gala" dress uniform—was used only
at civic celebrations: his birthday; the anniversaries of the "Fico," the adoption of the Constitution, his coronation, the proclamation of independence;
and the opening and closing of the legislature. "Half-gala" dress, including a
military uniform, was reserved for less official occasions, and *pequena gala*
(small gala) was used for "half-mourning." The pictures are still similar: the
facial expression is identical and only the clothes vary. An image of a more

mature monarch is repeated to the point of exhaustion. The aim was to reach not only the whole immense area of Brazil but also "civilized" nations elsewhere. Inside Brazil the distribution of the portraits in the press and by other means was part of the attempt at unification. The *Almanak Laemmert*, for example, which announced the feast days, customs, and calendar of the imperial court, also issued portraits of Dom Pedro II.* Outside Brazil the press and almanacs specializing in European royalty were all curious about Dom Pedro. In the *Almanach de Gotha*, for example, he was constantly portrayed, the older the better. As the press said in 1843, "At last, our monarch has a beard."[3]

The time had come for the emperor to marry, for his adult image to be given substance. The Portuguese had always adhered to the tradition of "marrying well," at least as far as ceremonial was concerned, and the effort invested in triumphal entries, the kissing of hands, thanksgivings, and the building of new monuments was always redoubled with a royal wedding; it would be no different in Brazil. Dom Pedro was approaching eighteen, and finding a good match was difficult for a king and empire that were so distant and exotic. The biographers differ in their dates, but most of them say that even before his coronation, negotiations for his marriage were already in progress, though they would come to fruition only years later. It was said that Dom Pedro, who was shy, blushed at the idea of marrying; still, the treaties would be made without his participation, as happened in European courts.

In a letter from the influential Pedro de Araújo Lima to Paulo Barbosa, Dom Pedro's attitude to marriage was commented on:

I asked him if he gave authorization to begin a negotiation in which I did not want to take a single step without his consent, because this matter touched his person and would influence his domestic happiness. He had the goodness to tell me that I could do as I thought fit. I made myself explicit to the point of asking him for the appropriate permission, which he had the goodness to give me. I then asked him if he had any European royal house in mind for this marriage, and he said he could not think of any and that I could choose what I thought best.

*The *Almanak Laemmert* gradually became the great reference work for the court. In 1839 Eduardo Laemmert founded his *Folhinha* and, five years later, the *Almanak*, which continued under the republic. Until 1902 it continued to publish a list of "Brazilians decorated by the honorific orders of the late empire."

Then I explained that it would be well for the marriage to take place as soon as possible, so that he would be enabled to enter into the exercise of power . . . The emperor was quite content with this information . . . This happened toward the end of 1839.[4]

It is plain that marriage between monarchs is really an affair of state. A list of single, young princesses had to be drawn up in the early 1840s, and Bento Lisboa was entrusted with the task. There were, after all, possible candidates: Dona Maria, archduchess of Saxe; Princess Alexandrina, daughter of the king of Bavaria; the Infanta Luisa, cousin of the queen of Spain . . .

For Dom Pedro, too, his "domestic happiness" was not the issue. What mattered were the needs of the wider public: the marriage meant making his majority a practical reality. What Araújo Lima calls his "goodness" was nothing more than a complete lack of personal view on his part; the king was completely removed from the great political issues. Still, a marriage is a kind of mediation between the public and private spheres: public because kings never marry the person they simply want to or because they want to; private because children will result (yet they too are heirs of the nation, and again the public wins out over the private).

Whether Dom Pedro willed it or not, negotiations proceeded involving three marriages at the same time: those of Dom Pedro and his two sisters, the emperor's being strategically the most important.

In 1842 Araújo Lima sent his subordinate Bento Lisboa to Europe. His task was to find "an as yet unengaged Habsburg." This was not easy, however, for Dom Pedro, emperor of a far-off, unknown land, was also thought of as being poor. In Viennese court circles, the Brazilian representative was mocked, as was "his American emperor." It is said that after a year, giving up the idea of finding a princess in the highest royal ranks, Bento Lisboa ended up consoling himself with the prospect of a Habsburg relatively far removed from Vienna: the sister of King Ferdinand II of the Two Sicilies.

On 23 July 1843 the attaché, José Ribeiro da Silva, arrived with the contract and a small portrait of Teresa Cristina Maria, princess of the Two Sicilies. Teresa was a Bourbon by three of her grandparents and a Habsburg by one grandmother. Her family was not very wealthy, and her dowry was modest. Moreover, she was four years older than Dom Pedro. But it was said that she was a good singer, and she was the niece of Marie Amélie, queen of the French, and sister of Fernando II, king of Naples. This very Catholic king satisfied the requirements of Brazilian conservatives: he had

Two portraits of Teresa Cristina that were sent to Dom Pedro II. In the first the slope of Mount Vesuvius is in the background. MMP and MIP

forbidden the use of beards, alleged to be a symbol of republicanism, in his country.

Dom Pedro had to judge the portrait. In spite of his usual moderation, the monarch claimed he liked the image, which in fact improved on Teresa's physical qualities. She appeared as a young woman with a slight smile, with her hair beautifully arranged, curls framing a plump face. Behind her is Vesuvius, proof of her origin.

The marriage was celebrated by proxy, in Naples, with the presence of the diplomatic corps of the two countries. After the ceremony Teresa Cristina faced a long journey—it took about eighty days to get to Brazil. And this was after having waited for a long time for the vessel to arrive from Brazil. In fact, a lack of white sailors was the reason for the delay: a crew whose "color might cause surprise" was not wanted. The cost incurred by the Brazilian government was not trifling. In total, 3,555 mil-réis* was spent for the emperor's portrait, a gift for the future empress (a ring of rubies and amethysts surrounded by diamonds), and gold ingots.

*The mil-réis was at this time the Empire's standard unit of currency. Also in use were a larger unit, the conto, which consisted of a thousand mil-réis, and a smaller unit, the réis, worth one-thousandth of a mil-réis.

On 3 September 1843 the frigate *Constituição* arrived back in Rio de Janeiro bay. Everything was ready for the ceremony, as always minutely planned and regulated. His Majesty, in an admiral's uniform, was to board the imperial launch, crowned with the golden dragon of the Braganças, and its twenty-four oarsmen, carrying white ribbons with the arms of the Two Sicilies, were to salute the sovereign with three cheers; the *Partênope* would let off a cannon salvo to starboard. Three other vessels would bear the ministers. The emperor would give a brief greeting, and only then would he go to the empress's quarters, where he would also meet her maids of honor and her brother, the count of Áquila (future husband of Dom Pedro's sister Dona Januária).

At eleven o'clock the royal couple would disembark and go in a royal carriage to a Te Deum and to the ritual kissing of hands. Afterward the detailed itinerary included celebrations, a gala dinner at the São Cristóvão Palace, and dances in the parish churches, in which the slaves were allowed to perform in homage to the empress, "mother of the Brazilians."[5] It was an exotic ritual, with this mixture of so many different customs.

The information he had received concerning the empress's virtues notwithstanding, Dom Pedro could see only her defects: Teresa Cristina was small and fat; worse, she was lame and ugly. Disappointment was imprinted on the young monarch's face, and it is said that he wept in the arms of the countess of Belmonte, Dadama, his governess.

> In the early days the disappointed young man no longer had that self-possessed and laconic temperament, and he openly bewailed his fate: first, in Dadama's lap, then on Paulo Barbosa's shoulder . . . He did not lack comfort and encouragement, however: "Remember the dignity of your position," the steward said to him. "Do your duty, my son," the countess of Belmonte said hesitatingly.[6]

The two imperial princesses had better luck. Dona Francisca, the "lovely Chica," as she was called, married the prince of Joinville, son of Louis Philippe of France, in 1843, making the links between the two monarchies still closer. And Dona Januária married the count of Áquila, Teresa Cristina's brother, in the same year.* In this way the ties binding the Brazilian monarchy to other European royal families were reinforced.

---

*The marriage of Dona Januária was not, so the biographers tell us, as happy as her sister's. Disagreements between husband and wife began in the first year, when Áquila insisted on returning to Naples. In years to come, Dom Pedro would have to pay for many debts contracted by his brother-in-law; his sister's reputation mattered a great deal to him.

The imperial couple at the time of their wedding. To create this montage an image of the emperor from the time of his consecration has been used. Lithograph by Gati e Dura, 1843. MMP

Looking at that first picture that was given to the emperor and the later ones done after the empress's arrival in Brazil, one would hardly know that she is the same person. In state affairs, personal preferences count for little, and in the official images, the couple appear contented, as was required.

The biographers tell us that in spite of all the ritual and the commemorative medallions, it took a while for the marriage to take on real substance in the intimate sphere. In 1845 the couple's first son, Dom Afonso, was born: he died on 11 June 1846 of yellow fever. In 1846 Teresa Cristina gave birth to a daughter, Isabel, and in 1847 to Leopoldina. Dom Pedro Afonso, the couple's fourth child, would also die at the age of one, on 10 January 1850 at the Fazenda de Santa Cruz. The papers said that "the sad fate of the few male children of the House of Bragança" had again befallen the Brazilian imperial family.

With the 1850s new images of the monarch were produced. In them we can see the emperor's age, but the same style continues: in official portraits,

The princesses Isabel and Leopoldina out riding. Engraving by S. A. Sisson, c. 1855. MMP

the model is still European. Except for the crown placed on a cushion at his side, the whole setting is foreign to Brazil itself, as if Dom Pedro were living in a theatrical set that had already been mounted. The portraits oscillate between an emperor now older, now younger, and this may be for political reasons. In spite of his personal travails, Dom Pedro II was taking large steps toward maturity, even though he was still only twenty-two.

The emperor was indeed taking more and more cognizance of the affairs of state. In fact, Dom Pedro went in the opposite direction to that taken by other kings. In Europe 1848 was marked by a wave of revolutions that began in Paris with the overthrow of the monarchy on 24 February and passed through Germany, Bavaria, Austria, Hungary, and Milan, finally reaching Sicily. In a short time over a vast area, "hundreds of small kingdoms, dukedoms and principalities were unceremoniously removed from power."[7] Dom Pedro's own sisters felt the effects: Francisca was obliged to go into exile from France in England; Januária only just managed to escape from the kingdom of Naples.

Meanwhile Dom Pedro II lived in the best of all possible worlds. With the recent political and financial stability obtained by the entry of Brazilian coffee onto the international market, he became the center of attention: master of the cultural scene, holding the scales in which political decisions were measured. He took on an active role in forming the Brazilian Historical and Geographical Institute and also set out to form a generation of intellectuals and artists of his own age. This is the period that saw the romantically inspired exaltation of Native Americans, the grandiose canvases displayed in the Imperial Academy of Fine Arts. Little by little the emperor was becoming a "tropical monarch." An enamel and gold box, showing an empire that reconciles opposing symbols, admirably expresses this: Dom Pedro II is in the middle, with on one side a Native American, and on the other civilization.

Rio de Janeiro was also changing. It was larger and more varied and was becoming the center from which fashions and habits spread out over the Brazilian Empire. There the imperial family became the center of almost everyone's attention.

Commemorative coins for the royal wedding, showing the insignia of the two nations. MMP

SIX

Life at Court

POLITE SOCIETY

Fashionable Brazil, on the Rua do Ouvidor in Rio
de Janeiro. H. Fleiuss, in *A Semana Ilustrada*, 1862.
MMP

The year 1850 is a milestone in the history of the Second Reign. An unambiguously conservative ministry had been in power since 1848: its main figures were Pedro de Araújo Lima, Eusébio de Queirós, Paulino José Soares de Sousa, and José Joaquim Rodrigues Torres. The Chamber of Deputies was of the same persuasion, with one Liberal for every 110 Conservatives. These were the men who had to legislate on fundamental issues of agriculture and land ownership, incentives to immigration, and, finally, the thorny question of the slave trade.

The fight against traffic in slaves had begun in 1807, when Great Britain prohibited its own subjects from engaging in it, and a long campaign started to eliminate it in countries open to Britain's influence. Various treaties regulating the trade—in 1810, 1815, and 1817—had been imposed on Portugal, and thus Brazil, too, felt the pressure. In 1826 a treaty was signed whereby the slave traffic was deemed to be piracy. Until 1830 all the Brazilian government did was resist these pressures, signing treaties it knew it would not honor. But between 1839 and 1842 the capture of slave ships increased. Finally in 1850 the external pressure against Brazil became inescapable. This was a period of great expansion in world trade, and London laid down more and more distinctions between countries in which slavery was permitted and those where it was officially prohibited.[1] Though the Brazilian state connived at the trade, its prohibition would be fundamental to the process of legitimating the nation's political autonomy. Maintaining the trade placed Brazil in the group of "barbaric nations," the exact opposite of the civilized image the empire tried to promulgate.

It was not easy to persuade the people in Brazil's agricultural interior, who were very dependent on slave labor, that it was right to abolish the trade. Between 1841 and 1850, 83 percent of the total number of Africans transported to the Western Hemisphere came to Brazil (12 percent went to Cuba, and the rest divided between Puerto Rico and the United States).[2] The trade brought not only people to Brazil but, as its organization spread over three continents, huge profits for the traders. The problem of slavery was central, and if it is not taken into account, Brazil's new laws cannot be understood.

The Land Law, the abolition of the transatlantic slave trade, and the reform of the National Guard were all interconnected. The controversial Land Law of 1850, first proposed in the legislature in 1843, was an attempt to prepare Brazil for the eventual end of slave labor, and it was approved a few days after the traffic was finally abolished; debate, and resistance on the part of the big landowners, continued for decades before slave labor itself could be abolished, too. The centralization of the National Guard was an effort to strengthen the government's position vis-à-vis the landowners, whose reactions both to the end of the slave trade and to attempts to regulate land ownership were predictably negative.[3]

An unexpected visitation was added to the list of the important events in 1850: the first large yellow fever epidemic ravaged the capital of the empire; deaths were in the thousands. And finally, the publication of the Commercial Code in that year was an attempt to regulate the tidal wave of business ventures flooding Brazil after the liberation of capital previously tied up in the slave trade. Massive resources were suddenly freed up. A good deal was invested in the country's infrastructure, above all in transportation. Between 1854 and 1858 Brazil's first railways were built and its first telegraph lines and shipping routes established; gas lighting arrived in cities, and the number of educational establishments grew. With the end of investment in the slave trade, imports grew 57.2 percent in only two years: great news for a government that lived primarily off import taxes.[4]

The end of the slave trade also coincided with a rise in the coffee price on foreign markets. The coffee trade, which had made no profits between 1840 and 1844, from 1845 on had become extraordinarily lucrative. Sales rose 23 percent between 1850 and 1851, and optimism was the order of the day. Brazil's financial situation really had changed. In 1831, just after Dom Pedro I's abdication, the empire's total receipts were calculated at 11,171,520 mil-réis; in 1840 they rose to 16,310,571 mil-réis; in 1862–63, to 48,343,182 mil-réis. This period, with its large investments in finance and industry, became known as the "Mauá era," after Irineu Evangelista de Sousa, viscount of Mauá, the greatest entrepreneur of the time, and as the "railway epoch." And at the same time, in 1851, the success of foreign policy in the Rio da Prata area, with the defeat of the Uruguayan leader Manuel Ceferino Oribe, ended the territorial issue that had been one of the causes of Dom Pedro I's abdication.

Partly as a consequence of the unsuccessful Land Law and the abolition of the slave trade, for the first time Brazil developed a policy to attract European immigrants. But it was not in a strong position to compete with other countries, especially not with the United States, which could offer greater opportunities to acquire land, had a better transportation system, and in a large part of the country had no slaves. For this reason, as an alternative to European labor, Brazil laid plans to import Chinese workers; some came as early as 1856. The immigration policy remained unsuccessful, however, particularly after the revolt of Nicolau Vergueiro's sharecroppers in 1856, followed by the Prussian government's prohibition of emigration in 1859.[5] When the government started financing *European* immigration, though, and with the in-

The opening of the Dom Pedro II Railway in 1858, by L. A. Moreau. More than ten thousand kilometers of railways were built in the empire between 1854 and 1889. FBN

troduction of Swiss and Germans to the coffee plantations, the empire not only changed its image but "whitened" itself. In spite of the imminent end of slavery, people did not forget the foreboding expressed in scientific circles about the future of countries with mixed populations, or the fear of "the example of Haiti" in a country in which the greater part of the labor force were slaves. In 1849, out of a total population of 250,000 in Rio de Janeiro, as many as 110,000 were enslaved.[6]

The 1850s were associated above all with financial stability and peace, and the emperor's popularity grew. In the trips he took to different parts of the country, he was warmly received, and on every occasion the "theater" of the court was restaged: as we have seen, it was a basic element in strengthening royal power. Pictures of his visit to Recife in 1859, along with the processions and kissing of hands, testify to his visibility. With trips like these, not only was the emperor seen more but symbolically he was taking possession of his vast territory. "Seeing and being seen" was the new logic, and one consequence was the unification of Brazil.

The effects of the end of the transatlantic slave trade were most immediately felt in Rio de Janeiro, where capital began to be invested in new buildings and in elegant city shops. Rio went through a truly revolutionary process of urbanization. The model was bourgeois, neoclassical Paris, but the contrast between elegant neighborhoods and the streets where slave labor dominated was still enormous. In sections where access was easy, majestic palaces, monumental buildings, and wide avenues were constructed. The Academy of Fine Arts and the Palace of Commerce stood out, along with the major avenues leading to the São Cristóvão Palace, which were opened a little later, and the first public gardens: the Campo de Santana and the Quinta da Boa Vista.

Rio had other improvements: trees were planted (from 1820), streets were cobbled (1853), gas lighting was put in (1854), a sewage system was built (1862), and piped water for domestic consumption was installed (1874); the first mule-drawn trams appeared in 1859, taking over from the old carts, sedan chairs, and litters carried by slaves. Even so, new problems appeared: people had to be wearing shoes if they wanted to ride the trams, and the animals, even though domesticated, could sometimes be stubborn and refuse to go in the right direction.

On the new, better-paved avenues, faster and cheaper cabriolets replaced the tilburies: they cost a thousand réis to rent. Joaquim Maria Machado de Assis wrote in his "Anedota do cabriolé":

The crowd in the Rua do Colégio in Recife, during Dom Pedro II's visit. *Monitor das Famílias*, 1859. FBN

A salon in the palace in Recife; the ceremony of kissing the monarch's hand. *Monitor das Famílias*, 1859. FBN

The return to the capital, "Paris in the Americas," 1860. FBN

"Cabriolet here, massa," said the black man who had come to São José Church to call the priest to give extreme unction to two young people. The younger generation didn't witness the coming of the cabriolet to Rio de Janeiro, nor its departure. They won't remember the time when the *cab* and the *tilbury* joined the cast of our public and private forms of transportation. The *cab* didn't last long. The tilbury, the first of the two, seems fated to last until the destruction of the city.

New consumer habits, and the fashion of walking and promenading along the public avenues, began to develop. For the more up-to-date high-class commerce, the area around the Rua Direita, with its mixture of fashionable shops, small grocers, and other establishments, no longer seemed enough. The narrowness of the streets, the stink from the sewers, the slaves carrying out their tasks, and the smell of the mud at low tide all contributed to the downfall of this area. "The mystique of the Rua do Ouvidor began: one after another, French fashion shops, florists, jewelers and tobacconists opened."[7] Commerce increased by leaps and bounds: afternoon visits to town, tea in the polite cafés, and elegant attire, with English textiles and French styles, came into fashion. Women went to town in wide, long dresses, Indian silk shawls, and little hats. Seamstresses with foreign names took care of fashion, while coiffure was the province of the popular salon of M. Charles Guignard. The Desmarais perfumery made sure that the tropical heat and lack of baths didn't bring on a "natural" smell.

The most popular patisserie was the Carceler, which served ice-cream cones for 320 réis—rather expensive, when one considers that a pair of ladies' leather boots cost 8,000 réis. Everything has its explanation: the hides were Brazilian, but the ice-maker came from the United States.[8] There were many cafés, the Alcazar, Belle Hélène, and the Café de la Paix being the most fashionable. A coffee cost 60 réis and a soft drink 200. Local restaurants also offered menus for varied palates and pockets. A good lunch cost from 1.5 to 2 mil-réis, a more modest one only 600 réis.[9] Lunch was eaten at ten; dinner, at four in the afternoon, was usually a large meal, with soup, meat, rice, chicken, spinach, quince jam, and fig dessert. A "substantial clear soup" (made of vegetables and boiled fowl) finished off the meal; apart from the port, bananas, orange pudding, or sweet rice with cinnamon that completed a good repast. After all this there was a little space for supper, eaten in general at home, at about eight at night. Even a superficial analysis of this list is revealing. Bananas and port wine, soup with rice, and cinnamon . . . tropical spices and fruits in a city influenced by French fashion.

While the habit of eating out was becoming established, the same cannot be said of the habit of staying out. Rio's hotels were still few and uncomfortable. The best were the Hotel França and the Hotel dos Estrangeiros, where the daily rate was 6 to 12 mil-réis. Although less celebrated, the Hotel Aurora (in Tijuca, a resort outside the city) charged more than double that, and asked for half the payment in advance "unless the person is known to the management or has been recommended."[10]

The glamour of Rio was completed by the Garnier and Laemmert Brothers' bookshops, and bathhouses like the Pharoux, which had this tempting slogan: "Go take a running jump into the Pharoux baths: just what you need."

The Rua do Ouvidor became the favorite symbol of the new lifestyle, for it imitated the mores in the European capitals, with their recently constructed boulevards. Horácio, one of the main characters in José de Alencar's novel A pata da gazela (The Gazelle's Foot) (1870), is a perfect example of the masculine ideal of the time: he is "king of the salons," concerned only with his own elegance, "one of the princes of fashion, one of the dandies of the Rua do Ouvidor," "the dandy most admired by the belles of Rio, the Attila of the Casinos, the Genseric [chief of the Vandals] of the Rua do Ouvidor."[11] In Alencar's descriptions, at times almost sarcastic, the capital itself was like Horácio and the Rua do Ouvidor: frivolous, artificial, and futile.

Some of Machado de Assis's stories give the same impression. The most significant in this regard is perhaps "Fulano" (1884), which tells the story of a simple man whose social and political rise brings about profound changes in his habits. One new habit is "showing himself in the Rua do Ouvidor"; another, consoling himself for his wife's death in a way that we can only call original: "Our friend shared his pain with the public, and if he buried his wife without ostentation, this didn't stop him from ordering a magnificent mausoleum to be sculpted in Italy, which the city of Rio admired when it was put on show in the Rua do Ouvidor for almost a month."[12]

The Rua do Ouvidor was a stage for many productions:

Someone called the street the queen of fashion and elegance; someone else baptized it the exclusive "Forum" where all questions of politics, business and literature, the arts, and above all fashion are debated; "the sympathetic nerve of the population, whose pulse can be felt all over the huge city." It exploded in 1862 with the big shops—Notre

A shop on the Rua do Ouvidor during a sale. H. Fleiuss, in *A Semana Ilustrada*, 1865. MMP

Dame de Paris, Wallerstein et Masset, Desmarais, Bernardo Ribeiro . . . Here groups of fashionable women pass by, elegantly dressed, with all the care of the most beautiful Parisian women, alighting like butterflies on the windows filled with flowers, jewels, silks, garlands.[13]

But the Rua do Ouvidor was not the only focus of local attention. Rio de Janeiro, seat of the imperial court, was a center from which habits, customs, and even languages radiated out into the whole country. Marriageable girls all over Brazil dreamed of the amusements in the capital, while the great plantation owners in the interior provinces feared their children's entry into the "delights of the *carioca* Babylon," as José de Alencar put it in *O tronco do ipê* (The Trunk of the Ipê-tree) (1871). He contrasted the unaffectedness of girls from the plantation houses with "certain customs imported by the ladies of the capital; with affected French manners, concerned only for their fashions and their toilette." "Everyone to his own taste," Adélia says in the same novel, "yours must be better than mine, because you live in Rio and I'm only a country girl."[14]

Political factions hardly mattered in this context. Education, career, title, and personal relations were what was needed to establish a place among those who formed the social strata

closest to the centers of power . . . solemn faces and identical dark clothes make the differences between the Saquaremas and the Luzias [conservatives and liberals] disappear. But the more they look like each other, the more they tend to look different from the other parts of "polite society," whose privileged representatives they are . . . They themselves emphasize their marks of distinction, most perfectly displayed in the monopoly they have over discourse, beginning in the home, polished in law school, and exercised in formal and informal tribunals, in salons, and in the legislature.[15]

This was the time when the great coffee planters built sumptuous residences in the interior of Brazil but also sometimes in the city. These were the *solares*, "large constructions whose most obvious characteristics were their size, their spaciousness, the number of their windows; in these houses they resided for part of the year, and from time to time they offered a ball, or prided themselves on offering hospitality to an important personage: the emperor, or the president of a province."[16]

Meanwhile in the capital, in the years between 1840 and 1860 a feverish round of dances, concerts, parties, and entertainments became the norm. Rio highlighted the contrast between itself and the provinces, taking on the job of informing everyone of the most civilized customs, which were linked to British and French imports. At home the men played omber, backgammon, chess, and whist, and the boys at seeing who got the short straw. The women amused themselves with games—forfeits, charades, and many others.

The picture was completed in the theaters, where people went to see and be seen. The most important, the Teatro São João, opened on 12 October 1812; here at every performance the city showed off its wealth. Good plays could also be seen at the Teatro Lírico Fluminense in the Campo da Aclamação, or at the Teatro Lírico, also called the Provisório because its construction was never completed. It was at the Lírico that Carlos Gomes put on

The public promenade in Rio de Janeiro. Drawing and lithograph by Bertichen. From Pinho, *Salões e damas*.

his first opera, *A noite do castelo* (The Night in the Castle), as a birthday tribute to the emperor on 2 December 1861. Many musicians from abroad, as well as Brazilians like Francisco Manuel da Silva and Henrique Oswald, played in these theaters.

Some of Luís Carlos Martins Pena's comedies, mounted at this time, offer important evidence of current habits and idioms. The trivial aspects of life in Rio and its slavish imitation of French fashion appear in many of his works. In this excerpt from *Os dois ou O inglês maquinista* (The Two, or the English Engineer) (1841), Pena satirizes the mania for studying French:

CLEMÊNCIA: Júlia's teachers are very happy with her. She's very advanced. She
    speaks French, and in two years she won't know how to speak Portuguese.
    It's a very good school. Júlia, say hello to the gentleman in French.
JÚLIA: Oh Mummy . . .
CLEMÊNCIA: Don't be so silly!
JÚLIA: *Bonjour, Monsieur, comment vous portez-vous? Je suis votre serviteur.*
JOÃO: *Oui,* she's very advanced.
CLEMÊNCIA: What's the French for table?
JÚLIA: *Table.*
CLEMÊNCIA: Arm?
JÚLIA: *Bras.*
CLEMÊNCIA: Neck?
JÚLIA: *Cou.*
CLEMÊNCIA: Good God! Mind your mouth! [In Portuguese, *cu* means something quite different.]

The Italian Adelaide Ristori was the first actress to become famous in Brazil. Hansen and Weller, 1869. FBN

JÚLIA: It is *cou*, Mummy, isn't it, cousin? Isn't *cou* the right word?
CLEMÊNCIA: All right, that's enough.
EUFRÁSIA: These French people are filthy. Fancy that, calling the neck such
  a dirty name: why, it's right next to your face.[17]

The elite's mania for imitating foreign fashions and their excessive love of
imported goods are regular butts of Martins Pena's fun. In *Um sertanejo na
corte* (A Hillbilly in Rio) (1837), the yokel Tobias can't understand what a piano is, or what it's for, and insists on calling it a "peon, a peon, whatever you
want." In *O caixeiro da taverna* (The Barman) (1845), Francisco complains:
"It's a mania; everyone goes along with it; if it's foreign, that's good enough.
All you can find in this city are French tailors, American dentists, English engineers, German doctors, Swiss clockmakers, French hairdressers, foreigners
from all six continents." The British, whom Pena often calls "misters yes,"
also come out the worse for wear in *As casadas solteiras* (The Single Wives)
(1845). Jeremias says: "Who are these two? They look English . . . They must
be, they must be . . . Not the kind of stuff we need over here. They don't like
Brazil. *Brésil non preste!* But they still keep coming, just to make money." But
Pena's most frequent target is the "French mania." Fashion and local reality
are out of step, he thinks:

FIRST GYPSY: That's the fashion in Paris.
TOBIAS: In what?
FIRST GYPSY: Paris.
TOBIAS: Who's that?[18]

Still, even when seen in a satirical light, Rio was presented as the most entertaining place in Brazil, the more so when compared to life in the countryside. Aninha, in *O juiz de paz na roça* (The Justice of the Peace in the Country)
(1838), says: "Isn't Rio lovely? You can have fun there. Theater, magic shows,
dancing horses . . . All kinds of things! I want to go to Rio!" When Marcelo complains of the Rua do Ouvidor, in *O diletante* (1844), Antônio promptly replies:

MARCELO: The Rua do Ouvidor is just a confused mass of people going up
  and down, making such a racket you feel quite dizzy.
JOSÉ ANTÔNIO: You should enjoy all these things before you start complaining. No point in burying yourself in the sticks. Go to the theater, to
  Norma, Belisário, Ana Bolena, Furioso.[19]

Though the theaters were one of the capital's main activities, the greatest entertainments were the balls and parties. The historian José Wanderley de Araújo Pinho precisely defined the skills to be polished in a salon: "appreciating or preparing a friendly, stimulating atmosphere; cultivating humor and the arts of conversation; dancing a waltz or singing an aria, declaiming or inspiring poetry, criticizing others wittily and without indulging in slanderous gossip, showing off female beauty by wearing the latest fashions." According to the same author, these balls reached their peak during Dom Pedro's reign and before the Paraguayan war. Of course it had all started with the arrival of the court of Dom João, which brought with it new clothes, adornments, and even hairdos, but it was in Dom Pedro II's time that the salons took on social and political weight. True, Brazilian salons were less literary than French ones (partly because literary men preferred to meet in pastry shops, cafés, and theaters), but at least they were original in bringing men of opposing political parties together. According to Pinho, they fostered debate and, ultimately, conciliation between the parties. "Politics can't work without canapés," said the baron of Cotegipe, and Nabuco de Araújo seemed to be of the same opinion: in 1851 and 1852, when he was president of the province of São Paulo, he brought both Saquaremas and Luzias (conservatives and liberals) to his house for balls, receptions, and parties.[20]

Donizetti, Rossini, and Verdi were the favorite composers at concert-parties, above all those at which their imperial majesties were present. Yet, while it is part of the function of a king and his family to establish the tone of social life, in the Brazilian court Dom Pedro II's "social reign" was a short one. In the first years of his marriage, the emperor took a lively, active role in social life in the capital and in his journeys to the provinces. With time, however, he became increasingly averse to social functions. The last dance in the palace took place on 31 August 1852, when the legislature adjourned for the year. It was well attended: there were 548 ladies and 962 gentlemen, and his majesty took part in nineteen contredanses, twenty quadrilles, four schottisches, and six waltzes. (The emperor danced more than his wife, whose lameness made her less mobile.) But parties were not Dom Pedro's forte. At the São Cristóvão Palace dinner was taken en famille at five o'clock. Afterward, if the weather was good, there was a walk in the garden, followed by tea. Then the princesses played the piano, looked at photographs, and played forfeits. Everything finished at half-past nine.[21]

With or without the emperor at the helm, Rio dominated fashionable life in Brazil. Elegant dresses for the ladies often included padding, which performed miracles in rounding out shapeless parts of the body. A posy in the ladies' hands, a cigar for the men, balls in the casinos, with silk and wool grosgrain, tulle, fans made of ivory, mother-of-pearl, tortoiseshell, or sandalwood . . . a language for a whole new life of polite society was being discovered. The *dernier cri* of Paris fashion came to the tropics. But, as we can see in Martins Pena's satires, rules for different dances sometimes led to confusion. In *A Hillbilly in Rio*, Tobias gets Inês up to dance, and when she proposes a *galop*, the poor plantation owner replies: "Oh, my! That's a good one! So my horse knows how to dance and can come to this thing too!"[22]

We shouldn't delude ourselves into thinking that Rio de Janeiro was like Paris. It was a small island in a sea of countryside, and slavery was everywhere. The adopted European elegance lived cheek by jowl with the smell of the streets; commerce was still on a small scale, and the tiny court was marked by African colors and habits. In his bleak story "Father Against Mother" (1906), Machado de Assis recalls "the professions and gadgets left by slavery": the masks, the neck rings, and the unhappy profession of slave-catchers—escaped slaves were the subject of innumerable advertisements in the daily newspapers. Cândido Neves, the main protagonist, looks for runaways and is proud of his métier. Threatened with having to give up his own newborn son for adoption, he catches a pregnant mulatta, who has a miscarriage. "Not every child can make it," says Neves, as if he wants to exorcise the ghost of slavery from his mind.[23]

From the court's point of view, though, the world of the slaves and of work ought to be neither seen nor heard. This was in flagrant contrast to the actuality. Slaves made up anything from 40 to 50 percent of Rio's inhabitants in the nineteenth century. According to the *Almanak Laemmert* for 1851, Rio had 110,000 slaves out of 266,000 inhabitants: the largest urban concentration of slaves since the end of the Roman Empire. In the nine parishes of the central city, the slave proportion was less but the impact of the black presence still greater. This was the heart of the capital, with its principal public buildings, squares, and most important commercial establishments. Out of a total of 206,000 inhabitants of this area, 79,000 (38 percent) were slaves.[24]

The historian Eduardo Silva tells us that right near the palace there was a "kingdom of Obá" made up of Africans, Brazilian-born blacks, and mulattos, who might be slaves, freedmen, or free colored people.[25] According to the 1849 census, one out of every three inhabitants of this area, known as Little Africa, came from Africa: 74,000 free and enslaved Africans lived in the heart of the empire.

Advertisement for an escaped slave.
Almanak Laemmert, Rio de Janeiro. FBN

By dividing up the city's space, the polite society of the Rua do Ouvidor tried to make slavery invisible. Nevertheless, it could be found right in the middle of the capital and throughout the extent of the empire: a constant menace to the stability of the monarchy, a glaring contrast to its civilizing gloss.

Slavery was not the only issue to cast a shadow over the empire's ambitious aims; we should not forget the isolated nature of the capital and of Brazil's few other cities. The population of the principal cities of the empire in 1823 was less than 9 percent of the total population, 10.41 percent in 1872, and 9.54 percent in 1890. And about half of these people were concentrated in only three cities: Rio de Janeiro, Salvador (Bahia), and Recife (59 percent in 1832, 48 percent in 1872, and 58 percent in 1890).[26] We can see, then, that Rio was not only a center from which civilization spread but also an exception. Fashion was for the few.

Politics, too, was an occupation for the few, especially after the 1850s, when the country became financially and politically more stable.

The political struggles that began in the Regency ceased in 1845, with the end of the Farrapos war, and then finally in 1849–50, when the Praieira revolt in Pernambuco was suppressed. After the death of Dom Pedro I in 1834—when most of his supporters joined the ranks of the monarchists, then called conservatives—two parties had taken turns in power. The conservatives won the elections of 1836 and ruled from 1837 to 1840; then the liberals won, taking over in alliance with some conservatives and remaining in power until 1841; it was the conservatives' turn from 1841 to 1844, the liberals' in 1844–48, and the conservatives' again in 1848–53. In 1853 began the "conciliation," a new direction in imperial policy that mixed representatives of both parties.

The coalition lasted only five years, but it revealed not only the fragility of the two parties but also the potential room for Dom Pedro II to intervene. "In the absence of a powerful middle class able to regulate social relations by the mechanisms of the market," one historian writes, "it would fall to the state . . . to take the initiative, by taking measures to unify markets, destroy feudal privileges, consolidate national leadership, and provide economic protection." The ruling elite was marked by homogeneity in both ideology and training; a bureaucratic sector, initially dominated by magistrates and military officers, was gradually taken over by members of the liberal professions and lawyers: the famous *bacharéis* (bachelors of law) of Dom Pedro II's reign.[27]

This Brazilian elite could be fairly characterized as "an island of men of letters in a sea of illiterates."[28] Education was its distinguishing mark, in a country in which, as the census of 1872 was to show, only 16 percent of the population could read and write. (This did not take the almost entirely illiterate slave population into account.) A good part of the elite chose to be educated in law: before independence at Coimbra, in Portugal, and after 1828 in the two provinces where law schools had been founded: São Paulo, and Olinda, Pernambuco (later, in nearby Recife). The educational system of the Brazilian elite was quite predictable. Wealthier families hired private tutors, who prepared their pupils for entry into the *liceus* (grammar schools) like the Botafogo for girls and the Atheneu and Vitória for boys and, if possible, to the Colégio Pedro II, created in 1838, which guaranteed a degree of bachelor of arts and was the sure route to the coveted law schools. Its graduates then went either to Europe or to one of the two schools of law or one of the two medical schools (in Rio de Janeiro or Bahia). For the sons of less well-off families, the choice lay between the church, the army, or engineering. The law schools trained jurists and advocates but also deputies, senators, and diplomats: the entire state bureaucracy, in fact. There was a surfeit of *bacharéis*, however, and an eager search for jobs in the civil service (Machado de Assis satirizes this in his stories). It reinforced the centralizing role of the state and the orientation of the imperial bureaucracy to its clientele.[29]

Bacharel gradually became a symbolic term that meant more than that one had a simple qualification. In theory, the *bachelor* was a man with a degree in law—from Brazil or abroad—though young men trained in literature or sciences could also sport the title and compete for the diminishing number of vacancies in the civil service. Silvio Romero, in his *Doutrina contra doutrina* (Doctrine Against Doctrine), caricatured this group of fellows in frock coats begging for some job or other, if possible a sinecure requiring little personal effort—lawyers with no clients, doctors with no patients, writers with no readers, magistrates with no courtrooms, who had made their diploma into a badge, a stable, easy way of gaining a living.

Though a host of lesser mortals also hoped to get the plum jobs, Brazil was not an absolute state, with all the patronage centralized around the emperor. Most of the nation's major political decisions were made by representatives of the executive and legislative powers as well as by councilors of state, by ministers, senators, and deputies.

At the summit of the imperial elite was the Council of State, the "brains of the monarchy," created in 1823 and abolished in 1834, then restored in 1841 and lasting until the end of the empire. Its members were the "emperor's men"; the post was for life, although the monarch could suspend a member for an indeterminate period.

The ministers, according to the imperial Constitution, represented the executive power, but the emperor had total liberty in choosing them. After 1847, with the introduction of the post of president of the council, Dom Pedro appointed only the president, who in his turn chose the other ministers.[30] The emperor's intervention and veto power, along with the particular way that Brazilian ministries were formed, meant that the life of each cabinet was very short. Before 1861 there were six, and after that date seven more. The most important ministry was finance, a kind of school for future presidents of the council. Presidents of the provinces, who did not have to be linked to the province they represented and of which they were the highest authority, were also of central importance.

In the imperial hierarchy, senators came next. Again, it was the emperor who chose them according to strict conditions out of a list of three elected candidates: the candidate had to be at least forty and have an annual income of at least 800 mil-réis per year. The senators' great power came from the fact that their posts were for life: some of them held power for more than thirty years. It was in this "lifelong" Senate that the emperor, even when still a boy, met some of the political chiefs of the nation. Some were associated with his father's reign and with the period of the Regency, like Barbacena (the diplomat who negotiated Brazil's independence), Paranaguá (president of the Senate), or Padre Feijó, the great leader and regent in 1835 but already an old man. Alongside them were politicians of a younger generation, like Francisco de Abrantes; the marquis of Olinda; Bernardo Pereira de Vasconcelos; Paula Sousa; José da Costa Carvalhu, marquis of Monte Alegre; and Candido José Viana, marquis of Sapucaí. The senator who held his post for longest was Viscount Sousa Queirós, who was appointed in 1848 and stayed in office until 1889 and the proclamation of the republic. After him came the viscount of Suaçuna, who was appointed in 1839 and died in 1879.[31]

On a lower step in the hierarchy of power were the deputies, more numerous and less powerful, but still taking a vital step on the way to more important posts. To be eligible, candidates had to be at least twenty-five and have an income of 400 mil-réis. Many of these younger men had been law students, and they stayed with the emperor to the end of his reign: Francisco de Sales Torres Homem; José Tomás Nabuco de Araújo; Wanderley Pinho, future baron of Cotegipe; José Maria da Silva Paranhos, future viscount of Rio Branco; Pedreira, future viscount of Bom Retiro, Dom Pedro's childhood friend and perhaps his only confidant; Carvalho Moreira, baron of Penedo; and José Antonio Saraiva.

This, then, was the political elite that, in the 1850s, watched the emperor as he matured. At that juncture, he was only one part of the structure, a symbol; surrounded by more or less experienced politicians, he was not the master of the scene. With time, however, and armed with the "moderating power," which gave him power of veto in several contingencies, Dom Pedro II began not so much to reign as to govern. Gradually he became the arbiter, tipping the scales in one direction or another. It was common, by mid-century, to hear it said that there was nothing more like a Saquarema (the nickname of the conservatives, because their principal leaders owned plantations in the region of that name, in the north of the province of Rio) than a Luzia (as the liberals were known) once he was in power. The politician Afonso Celso, a well-known critic of the empire, said: "Liberals and Conservatives spend time in government, but when they leave, there is no way to distinguish between them. To any observer looking at them from a historical distance, they look completely alike. One can hardly notice the alternation in power. The mainspring of all these struggles, the central theme of all government programs, is, 'Get out of the way so I can take your place.'"[32] Machado de Assis, in his famous story "Education of a Stuffed Shirt" (1882), lists the good advice a devoted father gives his son. When the latter asks if he should avoid any profession, like politics for instance, the father replies: "Not even politics. It's only a question of abiding by certain rules and performing certain simple duties. You can belong to any party you please, liberal or conservative, republican or ultramontane, the only condition being that you do not link any special idea to these terms."[33]

We might, however, question this cliché about the complete sameness of the parties in the Second Reign. According to Rohloff de Mattos, though it has come down to us as a useful way to underline the lack of a real program and the similarity of the political parties, there were important shades of difference. Between the end of the Regency and the end of the Praieira revolt in 1849, after which the party until then known as Luzia took the name Liberal, one can identify the liberals with a policy of decentralization of power in the direction of the provinces.[34] The political defeats they suffered after 1842 were imprinted on the nickname of their party, since Luzia was the name of a battle they lost in the 1842 revolt in Minas Gerais. On the other hand, they were also known for adopting the policies of their adversaries when they returned to government.

The name Saquarema speaks of the conservative leaders' power base,

Bordalo Pinheiro satirizes the "politics among peers" of the Second Reign: "The opening of the Chambers: The Robinsons are open. Let the Robinsons speak. Let the Robinsons make the laws." *O Besouro.* MMP

where many of their families lived. Use of this label spread rapidly during the time of liberal predominance in 1844–48, as Mattos notes, and it carried a negative connotation, referring to the family members the conservatives protected or favored and seeming like revenge for the nickname Luzia, since liberals hated the stigma attached to it and dared to associate Saquarema with the idea of *sacar* (to take, to rob). Saquarema was especially associated with "a holy trinity" of conservatives from the province of Rio de Janeiro: José Joaquim Rodrigues Torres, future viscount of Itaboraí; Paulino José Soares de Sousa, future viscount of Uruguai; and Eusébio de Queirós.

Only after the Regency did the two political parties truly come into being. According to Carvalho, the Conservative Party was formed by a coalition between former moderates and supporters of the restoration of Dom Pedro I; under the leadership of Bernardo de Vasconcelos they argued for changes in the laws favoring decentralization, while proponents of decentralization came to be called Liberals.[35] But this political division can only be inferred from political speeches and legislative debates on the question of decentralization, since neither party had yet presented an official program: the Conservative Party never did. Also, "The Conservative Party represented the alliance of the bureaucracy with big business and large-scale export agriculture, while the Liberal Party brought together the urban liberal professions and agricultural interests producing for the home market and in areas of more recent colonization."[36]

The Luzias and Saquaremas were not mirror images, then. Indeed, in Mattos's opinion, there was even a hierarchical relation between the two, for after the Liberals' failure in 1848, the Conservatives virtually dominated the political scene of Dom Pedro II's reign.[37]

People at the time made fun of the parties' lack of explicit programs, the sycophancy surrounding the emperor, and the indulgence in the "politics of spectacle" in the worst sense. Afonso Celso tells us that the legislators were past masters of posing and groveling to the press, which published their speeches and pronouncements. For others, "being a deputy is a hobby. They are married, but they leave their wives in the provinces and lead a riotous bachelor life in Rio, going to the theater and other more questionable places."[38]

The legislature, the stage on which the ritual of politics was played out, became the favorite place for giving long speeches to small audiences.[39] Afonso Celso considered their great length to be a serious political defect:

It was commonly thought that speeches lasting less than an hour, and in certain debates, less than two hours long, were no good. Thus, orators avoided concision, diluted their ideas, piled one digression on another, and used all kinds of tricks in order to carry on speaking. They spoke with their eyes on the clock, trying not to fall short of the time allotted. They loved interruptions and points of order, which gave them the excuse to prolong what they had to say.[40]

The origins of the highfalutin Baroque manner and the overuse of quotations in Brazilian political speeches lie in this period.

Dom Pedro II and the politicians around him, meanwhile, did not know at first exactly how to use the moderating power specified in the Constitution. Yet as time went on, he came frequently to use this "fourth" power, his and his alone. The strengthening of his public persona, which followed from the temporary reconciliation between the parties and the consolidation of the empire, aided him in this respect.

In his own annotations to the book-length poem of 1856 by Domingos José Gonçalves de Magalhães, A Confederação dos Tamoyos (The Alliance of the Tamoios, an Indian tribe), dedicated to Dom Pedro II, we can read the author's homage to the monarch, and his reply.[41]

> Sire! This book is inspired not by any desire to benefit from any special favors from Your Imperial Majesty, but from a deep feeling of patriotism and the inspired recognition of the prosperity of our country, owing to the sovereignty, love, and justice that shine so brightly in the Throne of Your August Person . . . Your Majesty wishes to be loved for his *public and private virtues*, which edify our whole country . . . Public education, complete freedom of the press, religious toleration . . . all this makes Brazil a nation, and gives to the world a *perfect Prince*. (my italics)

Dom Pedro, in turn, scribbles on page eleven that two great enterprises remained to be accomplished: "to organize the nation morally, and to form an elite." The monarch, who has hardly involved himself in his nation's politics and culture, now devotes himself to these two tasks of the ruler: shaping an official, national culture, and creating a local nobility. His civilizing plans meant thinking of Brazil in international terms, as one of the concert of nations. It was time to found a national project with a distinct culture, far removed from anything that might remind one of slavery.

SEVEN

"A Monarch in the Tropics"

THE BRAZILIAN HISTORICAL AND
GEOGRAPHICAL INSTITUTE, THE IMPERIAL ACADEMY
OF FINE ARTS, AND THE PEDRO II SCHOOL

The allegorical figure in the center gives light to the tropical empire. *A Ilustração Luso-Brasileira*, 11 August 1858. MMP

Brazil's whole economic and political scene seemed favorable to Dom Pedro II: he shone at its center, an effective symbol of it all. The magazine *Ilustração Luso-Brasileira* well expressed this positive evaluation of the monarchy in 1858:

> His immense empire, divided by vast, copious rivers and eternally covered by wondrous vegetation, looking out over the ocean . . . is now considered the central point of *New World civilization* . . . safe from the anarchy that is slowly devouring the other states of South America . . . Here on its virgin soil there flourishes a new, transplanted branch of the ancient tree of the Braganças . . . Its first years were not happy. Brazil was too uncultured to understand the nobility of the place it was to occupy among civilized nations . . . it was the Emperor Dom Pedro II who gave it peace, and the prosperity that can now be seen in this magnificent empire whose destiny is, more than that of other nations, linked to that of its monarch.[1] (my italics)

On virgin soil, then, the transplanted tree of the Braganças was flowering. With the revolts of the Regency over, Brazil saw itself as an oasis in the confusing desert of Latin America; a monarchy with European lineage and a European style that seemed to guarantee peace and, by extension, civilization.

And, after a time of relative isolation, Dom Pedro was beginning to appear in the public eye. The removal of Paulo Barbosa, when he was sent to Europe on leave, and the end of Aureliano Coutinho's tutorship contributed to this new attitude. Also, the creation, in 1847, of the post of president of the Council of Ministers helped to give the emperor more power of intervention. No longer a child absorbed in his lessons and controlled by the so-called court faction, Dom Pedro at the age of twenty-four was ready to exert his influence on the cultural politics of his country.

A monarch in the middle of the American continent naturally inspired mistrust, and internally, too, there had always been a need to develop a clear Brazilian identity. The hurried creation of two law schools in 1827—in Olinda and in São Paulo—the reorganization of the two schools of medicine in 1830, and the foundation of an establishment dedicated to "Brazilian letters" should be understood in this context. Modeled on the Institut Historique founded in Paris in 1834 (by, among others, Monglave and Debret, who were well known in Brazil), the Brazilian Historical and Geographical Institute in 1838 brought the *carioca* economic and literary elite together. (Lisbon's Royal Academy of Sciences, founded in 1779, was also an important influence.) It was this establishment that protected the Brazilian Romantic artists and writers in the 1840s and onward, and the young monarch became its dedicated supporter and frequented its meetings. By the 1850s the Institute had become an active center of study, encouraging literary work, stimulating intellectual life, and linking that life to the world of officialdom. So this young king, a supposed marionette, in fact became increasingly popular as a statesman and patron of the arts, from the age of about twenty.

The Institute soon became Dom Pedro's favorite place. Right at the start he was asked to be its "protector," and in 1839, under Paulo Barbosa's influence, he "offered" one of the rooms in the imperial palace in Rio for the Institute's meetings. In 1840, on his birthday, a medal was coined with, on its reverse, "Auspice Petro Secundo. Pacifica Scientiae Occupatio." In 1842 the emperor became a member of the Institut Français and in the next years set up prizes for the best works submitted to the Brazilian Institute. But he was still primarily a figurehead.

The Institute was composed mostly of the court elite and some selected literary gentlemen, who met on Sundays to debate topics agreed upon beforehand. Its purpose was to create a history of Brazil, taking as a model the story of great figures who had always been honored as national heroes. In the words of its secretary, Januário da Cunha Barbosa, the members did not want "to

leave the task of writing our history to the speculative genius of foreigners."
They wanted to establish a single, continuous chronology, as part of an enterprise that one could call the "foundation of a nationality." By direct financial support, incentives, and assistance given to poets, musicians, painters,
and scientists, Dom Pedro helped with a project that not only strengthened
the monarchy and the state but helped to unify Brazil. It was also, inevitably,
a cultural matter. At the outset the state contributed 75 percent of the Institute's funds; from 1840 onward Dom Pedro II was almost always present at its
meetings in the imperial palace. It became a kind of secure haven, an official
base for the young monarch's experiments; he seemed determined to mark
the nation's culture with a clearly Brazilian character. And he took a personal
interest, presiding over a total of 506 meetings between December 1849 and
November 1889 and absenting himself only if he was traveling. In contrast, he
appeared in the Chamber of Deputies only at the beginning and end of the
year, to open and close the proceedings.

In one of his first direct participations in the Institute, in 1849, Dom Pedro
chose to debate the following question: "Does the study of the Romantic poets favor or hinder the development of a Brazilian national poetry?" He and
the political elite of the court concerned themselves with recording and per-
petuating a certain kind of memory of Brazil but also with consolidating an
essentially Romantic project, the shaping of a "genuinely Brazilian" culture.
His involvement was to give him a reputation as a Maecenas, a wise emperor
of the tropics. Following the example of Louis XIV, the monarch formed his
court and at the same time chose historians to formulate a national tradition,
painters to glorify it, and writers to devise the characters and images that
would symbolize it.

The comparison with great European monarchs was a recurrent theme at
the Institute, where the importance and history of kings in their nation's
greatness was continually underlined: "the protection given to letters is the
most valuable attribute, and the most precious jewel in the crown of princes;
that is how Louis XIV and the Medici in Italy made themselves great, when
they gave a welcome to the scientific and artistic achievements that had survived the ruins of the Greek empire."[2] In every speech and at each solemn
occasion, the association of the Brazilian emperor with other great princes
was reaffirmed: "It is fitting that we should see that the munificence of Augustus in Rome, of Louis XIV in France, of Dom Diniz, Dom João V, and
Dom José in Portugal also shines forth in Brazil, welcoming learned men,
who in every age have glorified the names and deeds of great princes, engen-

dering the respect and admiration of the world." Parading the "finest flowers" of European royalty, the Institute tried to legitimate a monarchical model whose examples went back to antiquity—to Philip and Alexander of Macedon; to Augustus, Trajan, and Marcus Aurelius in Rome; and to the writings of Aristotle, Xenocrates, and Sextus Empiricus—and found inspiration in more modern kings, like Charles II of England, Louis XIV, Cristina of Sweden, Leopold and Joseph of Austria, Peter the Great and Catherine the Great of Russia, and the Popes Leo X, Sixtus V, and Benedict XIV.[3] There was no lack of models.

But the copy had a certain originality. Romanticism seemed to be the most favorable route to self-expression for a recently founded nation, because it left room for ideas that affirmed individual qualities, and Brazil's individuality in contrast with Portugal's classical tradition. Without forgetting the official, royal origins of the movement, Romanticism was admirably suited to the desire to show off the young nation's specific qualities to advantage and to break with the canons inherited from the mother country.

The literary project had already taken shape in 1826, when Ferdinand Denis and Almeida Garrett called the attention of Brazilian writers to the need to use local features in place of conventional classical motifs. Brazilians should concentrate on describing their country's natural setting and customs, and above all on emphasizing native Americans, the country's primitive and most authentic inhabitants, according to Denis. Later Romanticism became associated with a nationalist project, a change hastened by the conversion of a group of young Brazilians resident in Paris in the 1830s. Welcomed by French intellectuals who had lived in Brazil and were members of the Institut Historique, they published in 1836 two issues of a journal, Niterói, that had as its motto "Tudo pelo Brasil, e tudo para o Brasil" ("Everything from Brazil, and everything for the sake of Brazil").

This nativist program was plain in the magazine's name, as Domingos José Gonçalves de Magalhães (1811–82), soon to be one of the emperor's protégés, announced in the first issue. Niterói was named for the place in Brazil first discovered by a sixteenth-century French traveler and mapmaker, André Thevet, and in using it they meant to suggest that Brazilians ought to find inspiration for their new literature in indigenous culture, which coexisted with slavery. Thevet's discovery was used to contribute to a representation of the American continent that—in maps, illustrations, or, on a larger scale, in comparison with other continents—always emphasized Native Americans and their exotic practices of cannibalism, polygamy, nakedness, and "lack of religion." In *Niterói* the pattern varied. Its editors advocated a modern spirit that "would consist of changing Brazil's subordination to Portugal, and promoting the triumph of a national literature, which in the Brazilian case ought to take into account the poetic abilities of the Indian."[4] The group's characteristic moderation, favoring reform rather than revolution, worked in favor of the project's being accepted in the prevailing culture of the time. Using the ideas of autonomy and patriotism, the group proposed a smooth, almost imperceptible move to a kind of academic neoclassicism.

Along with Magalhães, the principal figures included Manuel de Araújo Porto Alegre (1806–79), who was known less for his literary career than for his work in the Academy of Fine Arts. Joaquim Norberto de Sousa e Silva (1820–91) was another. A great admirer of Magalhães, Sousa e Silva also participated in an important project of historical reconstruction concerning the Inconfidência Mineira, a Brazilian movement for independence that had arisen in the 1780s. Joaquim Manuel de Macedo (1820–82) secretary of the Institute, is remembered above all for A *moreninha* (The Dusky Little Beauty) (1844), a Romantic novel set among the *carioca* upper classes, the first really popular work of Brazilian literature. Macedo was also a dramatist, poet, and newspaper columnist. Later, he wrote *Vítimas e algozes* (Victims and Executioners) (1869), which deals with slavery. Antônio Gonçalves Dias (1823–64) was considered by the literary critic Antonio Candido to be the only writer of real quality in his generation. And Francisco Adolfo de Varnhagen (1816–78), founder of Brazilian historiography, was another important figure in the group linked to the emperor. Varnhagen did original research in primary sources, discovered unpublished documents, and wrote, between 1854 and 1857, the two-volume *História geral do Brasil* (General History of Brazil), in which he developed a model according to which Brazilian history could be thought of as a whole. Unlike most of the others in the group, Varnhagen had an anti-Romantic concept of the Indians, whom he depicted as savage and cruel. In his opinion, their lack of characteristic human beliefs justified the pitiless actions of the colonizers. Other writers, like Álvares de Azevedo, Casimiro de Abreu, Fagundes Varela, Almeida Seabra, and Castro Alves also took part in the Institute, but without having a close relationship with Dom Pedro.

These writers used the Institute's *Review*, which began in 1839, as their preferred medium for spreading their ideas. The Institute's official respectability helped to get the group and their project for literary renewal accepted, above all because of the constant presence of Dom Pedro. But while the emperor gave stimulus and support, he also generated a certain conform-

America. Anonymous engraving from the book of Arnoldus Montanus, 1671. CGJM

(below) America is represented by the figure in the hammock (suggesting sloth), nudity, and, in the background, cannibalism. The colonizing power arrives with its symbols of modern engineering. Engraving by Theodore Galle and Jan van der Straet, 1589. In Belluzzo, 1994.

ity, inhibiting more rebellious, less conventional initiatives. And he tended to select certain members and openly pushed others aside. As a result, Brazilian Romanticism became an official, nationalistic project.

Thus began Brazil's study of "local original characteristics." Very little was known about the Native Americans who had lived in Brazil before the coming of the Europeans, but now epic novels about them began to appear that put heroic Indians and chiefs into action or described passionate love affairs—all with the "virgin jungle" as background. The old dictionaries of Brazilian native languages compiled by the Jesuits became newly important, for native terms could be found in them to use in new poetry. Dom Pedro himself, inspired by this fashion, proposed new grammars and dictionaries and began to study Tupi and Guarani (this turned out to be useful to him during the war with Paraguay in the 1860s), which gave him a kind of leadership in the Romantic movement.* But basically the Indian policy during his reign was based on the idea of spreading Christianity and civilization by conversion, education, and painless assimilation. The educational plans were clear: conversion by work, and a pragmatic assimilative process. (One settlement, in Paraná, where this policy was tried out was in fact named after the emperor's saint: Saint Peter of Alcântara.)[5]

The image of the wise patron was already being molded. Dom Pedro gave support particularly to research on documents relevant to the history of Brazil, both at home and abroad. In different ways he helped the work of scientists like Carl von Martius and the research of Peter Lund, Henri-Claude Gorceix, the naturalists Louis Couty, Emílio Goeldi, and Louis Agassiz, the geologists Orville Derby and Charles Hartt, the botanist Auguste Glaziou, the cartographer Christian Seybold, and the many naturalists who visited Brazil. He also financed lawyers, agronomists, an aviator, teachers in primary and secondary schools, engineers, pharmacists, doctors, soldiers, musicians, priests, and many painters. It is no accident that a phrase he used at the Institute, echoing Louis XIV, "A ciência sou eu" (Science is me), should have become famous.

It was the job of the new Brazilian history to assemble a pantheon of national heroes, create a past, and search for historical continuities, but it was in literature that Dom Pedro's role was clearest. Under the monarch's direct protec-

---

*In the 1880s and after Dom Pedro went into exile, some cartoonists and critics questioned the emperor's knowledge of Tupi. Records of the Paraguayan war tell of a conversation he had with a Paraguayan prisoner who spoke it.

tion, a movement grew to promote the autonomy of Brazilian literature. Once again the project was cast in a Romantic mold and used Indianism as its main vehicle. *Guanabara*, a journal founded in 1850 by Manuel de Araújo Porto Alegre, Antônio Gonçalves Dias, and Joaquim Manuel de Macedo, among others, highlighted Dom Pedro's support in its first issue, where the bases of a "policy for literature" were set forth. This was the context in which Magalhães wrote A *Confederação dos Tamoyos* (1856), financed by Dom Pedro and awaited, after many years in preparation, as the great document that would demonstrate the "national validity" of the Native American theme.

Going back, in a way, to the model of Rousseau's "noble savage," Magalhães had written, to order, what was to be the great national epic poem, centered on indigenous heroes, with their acts of bravery and sacrificial gestures. In his efforts to mix "romantic eccentricity with historical research," he believed one could overcome regional specifics and lay down a foundational myth for the nation.[6] But the results were disappointing; the book was important only because of its institutional links, which were clear enough. The book opened with a declaration to "Your Imperial Majesty," in which Magalhães expounded on the "patriotic feeling" and "profound admiration" for the emperor that had inspired his work, "the perfect prince, who dedicates all his efforts to promoting the good of his people."

The book's plot pits wicked Portuguese colonists against bold, naturally courageous natives—material inspired by an article by Baltasar da Silva Lisboa published in *Guanabara* in 1854. It tells the story of the "brave Tamoio nation" who fight for freedom against the Portuguese aggressors, who are uncivilized adventurers. The oppositions are not limited to this pair: the whites can be divided into the brutal Portuguese colonizers, whose shame it is to have turned a free nation into slaves, and Jesuit priests, also associated with the future empire; the Native Americans are divided into the jungle dwellers, barbarian or converted, and indomitable natives as free as nature. In this battle of colors, the one that is praised always has purity on its side—the Portuguese of the future empire, representing national unity and above all the Christian faith, and the natives unsullied by civilization.

At a key moment in the plot, Tibiriçá, a converted member of the Guaianá tribe, tries to convince his rebellious nephew Jagoanharo of the advantages of the civilized world. Then Jagoanharo has a prophetic dream in which he foresees (this is in the middle of the sixteenth century) the arrival of the royal family, the independence of Brazil, the empire, the Rio da Prata wars, and the reign of the just monarch, Pedro II. Magalhães declaims:

> See, the victory belongs to the defenders
> Of this empire of the Cross, of the just cause
> That God loves and protects; and there flee,
> Stained with blood, the savage enemies
> Of Brazilian liberty, newly born.[7]

The empire as the realm of the just is thus opposed to colonized Portuguese territory, a terrain of inequality. The arrival of Dom Pedro II is the great moment everyone is waiting for: acclaimed as a "genius of tender years" who "grasps the scepter by the nation's will," Dom Pedro comes into Magalhães's book as God's messenger, a messiah of peace. In his dream the fierce Indian declares, "Indian! If you love the land where you were born / And can love its future / Accept and adore the truth of the Cross."[8]

Literature, then, gives way to official discourse, and the Native American, transformed into a model of nobility, takes part, though as a victim, in the genesis of the empire, now in the hands of Pedro II. In the words of the story's losers, the Indians who are not yet converted, destiny is inevitable:

> Araraí! You do not know how much empire can be gained
> By a great, new and holy idea
> That is penetrated by the soul and subjugates the heart.[9]

The exemplary Native American, then, is the hero and victim of a process that is destroying him. Born free and dying in freedom,

> A great future in heaven
> The Indian will pursue. The illustrious victim
> Of the love of the land where he has his home and freedom,
> He who was born leaves us the example
> Of how we should love these two gifts . . .
> Let us imitate Aimberé who died defending
> Honor, the beloved fatherland, and liberty.[10]

The first mass celebrated on Brazilian territory brings the story to a close. (This was also the theme of Vítor Meireles de Lima's painting, certainly inspired by Magalhães's work.) And the epic ends as it began: as an ode to the monarch "who justly grasps the scepter of Brazil . . . and whose support must be the altar of freedom, justice and peace."[11]

José de Alencar, soon to become Brazil's most important Romantic novelist, was indirectly linked to the group, but he directed serious criticism at Magalhães's book. Under the pseudonym Ig, he wrote that the Indians in the *Confederação* could have come out of an Arabic, Chinese, or European work. This irony displeased the emperor, who, under the pseudonym "The Poet's Other Friend," wrote in the *Jornal do Commercio* in support of Magalhães and, in a letter of 25 March 1860 to Councilor Saraiva, said, "I have already planned for the defense of the poem . . . I will not abandon my position as a defender and eulogist . . . Perhaps this is the moment for some inspired pen to write some poems accentuating the beauties of the *Confederação* . . . As for [Ig], either you're in the group, or you're outside it."

In politics, too, Alencar fell out with Dom Pedro. As deputy and later as minister of justice, he so opposed official policy that the emperor is reputed to have said of him, "That son of a priest is very stubborn," and set out to get his revenge: in 1869, when Alencar was the candidate with most votes on the triple list for a place in the Senate, Dom Pedro vetoed him. "He is an estimable man, but a very rude one," he said.

The quarrel between Dom Pedro and Alencar did not stop there. In his novel *A guerra dos mascates* (The Peddlers' War) (1873) Alencar placed hidden portraits of some of the politicians of the time among his fictional characters, even one of Dom Pedro himself. (He appears as Castro Caldas.) And in two issues of the weekly *O Protesto*, in February and March 1877, he went on attacking the emperor's intellectual qualities: "Wouldn't our people be much happier if their perpetual defender . . . were giving some thought as to how to solve our difficult financial situation and examining the ills that plague us?"

In spite of these divisions—Dom Pedro II made friends and enemies and was attacked by members of the so-called Bohemian Generation for his encouragement of an official clique of Romantic writers—he continued to act as the center of this group and to mark out those who favored and opposed him. Magalhães (later viscount of Araguaia), Porto Alegre (later baron of Santo Ângelo), and Dias were regularly favored with the emperor's attention.

Considered the greatest Brazilian Romantic poet, Antônio Gonçalves Dias brought Indianism into poetry and rose to Ferdinand Denis's challenge: in 1826 Denis had said, "America should be as free in its poetry as in its government." The government itself was not so free, and the emperor's circle was limited. Taking his cue from historical and ethnographic documents in the Historical and Geographical Institute, Gonçalves Dias created a poetic dedicated to the country's formation: a virgin land, untouched until its first contacts with civilization. In his most important collections, *Primeiros cantos* (1847), *Segundos cantos* (1848), and *Últimos cantos* (1851), many of the poems concerned this theme.

His most famous poem, "I-Juca-Pirama," brought the theme of heroic cannibalism to Brazil and gave expression to it within the precincts of the Rio Institute. (The literal translation of the Tupi title is "He who will be killed" or "He who is worthy to be killed.") Only brave men, indomitable spirits free even in death, were fit to be eaten in a ritual fashion: this was the argument of the poem, which tells the story of a brave Tupi warrior captured by the Timbira Indians, who awaits his death but fears for the fate of his father—old, weak, and blind—for whom he has been a guide. When the young Tupi weeps, the Timbiras free him: you can't kill and eat a coward. But his father is profoundly disappointed and bewails his son's weakness and curses him:

> You wept in the presence of death?
> In the sight of strangers, you wept?
> The coward is no son of the strong man;
> If you cried, then you are not my son!
> May you, the accursed descendant
> Of a tribe of noble warriors,
> Beg the help of cruel foreigners
> And be captured by the vile Aimorés [another tribal group].
>
> May you, isolated on earth,
> Without support and fatherland, wander
> Rejected by death in war,
> Rejected by men in peace,
> May you be a ghost despised by your fellows
> Finding no love with women,
> Your friends, should you have friends,
> May they all be inconstant and false![12]

It is then that, like the "incorruptible spirit" he is, the young warrior leaves his father and determines to prove his courage by facing the Timbiras alone. In turn, they recognize his courage and allow him the privilege of a public death. Father and son are reconciled: "Yes, this is my beloved son." In the end, to vouch for the "truth" of the narrative, Gonçalves Dias puts the memory of these heroic feats in the mouth of an old Timbira: "And at night in the camps, / If anyone doubted / What he recounted, / He said, wisely: 'My lads, I saw it!'"[13]

The Native American is thus an example of purity, an honorable model to be emulated. Those who suffer such irreparable loss—sacrificed twice over, for one's own nation and for the future nation—are given an idealized representation. The boundary between literature and reality, between fiction and true national reality, seems fragile. History is put to the service of a mythical literature that selects the origins of the new Brazil, the new nation.

Thus did Brazil witness in the 1850s and 1860s the consecration of Romanticism, and its most "genuinely Brazilian" manifestation, Indianism, had its moment of greatest prestige.

Paradoxically, and in spite of Dom Pedro's personal feuds, and in spite of its author's controversial position among Indianists, in 1865 a novel was published that became a kind of icon for this generation. *Iracema*, José de Alencar's best-known work, not only dealt with themes and landscapes familiar in the genre but its very title was an anagram of "America."

In the Indianist fashion, Alencar claimed that "knowledge of the language of the indigenous people is the best criterion by which to judge nationality in literature."[14] In his own work, his constant demonstration of knowledge about the natural life and native inhabitants of Brazil is very marked; indeed, the didactic and ethnographic impulses in the text and notes hinder the development of the narrative.

In *Iracema* a beautiful "honey-lipped virgin" is portrayed as living in a mythic past, the untouched natural setting of northeastern Brazil in the early seventeenth century. Once again we have a representation of the birth of Brazil—and again as a consequence of sacrifice on the part of the indigenous population. Martim and Iracema symbolize the first inhabitants of Ceará, and from their union will come a new, predestined race. Toward the end Iracema dies so that her offspring Moacir (whose name means "son of suffering") can live, and Martim leaves the shores of Ceará to found new centers of Christianity. From now on, everyone should have "one God, as they had one heart."[15]

This is very distant from the real Brazil of the nineteenth century, with its black slaves. White and indigenous heroes live together in the inhospitable terrain, and barbarous natives are limited to a few isolated groups. Like the Europeans, the Indians are noble, if not in their titles at least in their gestures and actions.

This is also true in *Ubirajara* (1874)—the name means "lord of the lance"— which Alencar in his "Preface for the Reader" insists is a "brother to *Iracema*."[16] They are "brother and sister" inasmuch as their author defines them both as "legends"; they are related, too, in their use and treatment of the historical record. In both works, the "nobility of the drama of the savages" is emphasized; and the condemnatory descriptions written by "missionaries who were thus able to exalt the importance of their catechism; and by adventurers who tried to justify the cruelty with which they treated the Indians," are criticized.[17]

Alencar's first experiments with Indianism predated *Iracema* and *Ubirajara*. *O Guarani* was first published in serialized form in the *Diário do Rio de Janeiro* between January and April 1857, and then appeared in book form in the same year. The novel—which is divided into four parts, "The Adventurers," "Peri," "The Aimorés," and "The Catastrophe"—takes place in the seventeenth century on the banks of the River Paraíba do Sul, inland from Rio de Janeiro. Its hero is Peri, romantic partner for the blond, white-skinned Ceci. From the title onward Alencar wanted to show Brazilian natives at first contact "in a moment of vigor, and not degenerate as they later became."[18]

Peri is the perfect representation of Rousseau's noble savage: strong, free as the wind, loyal, and always doing the right thing. The plot centers on two great points of tension: on the one hand, Peri protects the family of the Portuguese noble Dom Antônio de Mariz, Ceci's father, from the attacks of the "barbarous Aimorés"; on the other, he helps to uncover the wiles of the "wicked" Loredano, an "adventurer" who wants to lay hands on the family's wealth and Ceci's beauty. Again, it is a fight between virtuous, courageous, and worthy people and savages or adventurers. The theme of Peri's nobility returns constantly through the novel, in the happy encounter between a white nobility come to Brazil from Europe and the "nobles of the land." Dom Antônio says, "Believe me, Álvaro, Peri is a Portuguese knight in the body of a savage." At another moment Alencar tells us, "As the Indian spoke, a spark of savage pride coming from his strength and courage shone in his black eyes and gave a certain nobility to his gestures. Though ignorant, the son of the forests, he was a king; he had a regal strength." And he is king of the forest: "This monarch of the jungle, surrounded by all the majesty and splendor of nature" is "in the middle of the wilderness, free, great, as majestic as a king." He is very different from other Indians "in whom courage, ignorance, and bloodthirsty instincts had almost effaced the mark of the human race." The Aimorés, described as ignorant, barbarous, and instinctive cannibals, represent the savages, so "devilish" that they must be crushed by "civilization."[19]

Unable to prevent the disaster about to befall the Mariz family, Peri tries to save Ceci, whom he passionately adores. The two are separated only by their origins: "one the daughter of civilization, the other the son of uncultivated freedom."[20] They end the novel together, carried away by the waters of the river, presaging an almost platonic love between the Indian and the "blond virgin." The future is either in Rio de Janeiro or in "the heaven that unites us." Only Alencar's readers know which it is to be.

Thus did Alencar create a mythic past for the new Brazil, a past with generous, valiant lords, and loyal, honorable Indians. In Dom Pedro's tropical court, nothing could be more fitting than imagining a king of the jungle, who would live in the company of the civilized world's royalty and, centuries later, pay them homage.

In 1870 an opera named *Il Guarani*, composed by Carlos Gomes (1836–96), with a libretto inspired by Alencar's novel and produced with support from Dom Pedro, opened at La Scala, Milan.* Gomes aimed to combine European norms with original aspects of Brazilian culture—to write Romantic music that was both universal and local and that had indigenous themes. The exotic sets and costumes seem to have made a favorable impression. The indigenous people might as well have been Greeks as far as their costumes were concerned, and of course all the singers were white. What mattered was the constructed past for this empire in the Americas.

Romanticism in Brazil was thus not just a matter of aesthetics: it was a cultural and political movement with profound links to nationalism. And Brazilian nationalism, painted in local colors, originated above all with the *carioca* elite who, together with Dom Pedro, wanted to achieve cultural emancipation. Their themes were national, but with the culture based more in the court than in any popular experience, they aestheticized Brazilian nature, far removed from real life.

Openly attacked by historians like Varnhagen, who called them "*caboclo* patriots,"[21] the Indianists succeeded, however, in imposing the image of the Indian as Brazil's national symbol. Even Machado de Assis, by no means part of the group, in his article "Instinct for Nationality—A Report on Modern Brazilian Literature" (1872), recognized the "instinct" in their epic style. Ma-

*The Bragança had a respectable tradition of supporting and participating in musical performances. Dom João VI had developed the musical program in the imperial chapel and encouraged music courses in the Fazenda de Santa Cruz to be given for slaves, who sang in church choirs. Dom Pedro I was a musician and a reasonably good composer; Dom Pedro II studied piano and music theory.

Bordalo Pinheiro's homage to the opera
Il Guarani, presented at the Teatro
Lírico in 1878; a Native American offers
flowers to the composer, Carlos Gomes.
O Besouro, 19 October 1878. MMP

galhães, when accused by Varnhagen of being overimaginative and defending savages to the detriment of civilized people, replied:

> We who are Brazilians, because we were born in Brazil, whatever our
> origins might be—indigenous, Portuguese, Dutch, or German—make
> common cause with those who were born here before us, and we
> think of others as foreigners. All men think this way about their com-
> patriots . . . The fatherland is an idea, represented by the land we were
> born in. As for the origin of the human races, that is a matter for his-
> tory, and patriotism is not tied to that. Moreover the hero of a poem is
> but a pretext, a rule to create unity of action.[22]

Literature was an exercise in patriotism, then, and as such had its own
place in the state's plans. Emphasizing above all what was picturesque in the
landscape and its inhabitants, what was typical rather than generic, the Indianists made the indigenous people their movement's chief symbol. As an
ideal image, the Native American was not only authentic but also "noble."
Quite differently from the blacks, who brought slavery to mind, they allowed
one to think about a unifying, mythical origin. This is the reason for the am-

biguity of this group of writers about slavery. Antonio Candido called them the "hesitant generation"—hesitating at a time when pressure to end slavery was intensifying.

If Brazil had no medieval castles, ancient temples, or heroic battles to recall, it had the biggest river in the world and the most beautiful flora. The monarch and the nation were thus depicted among palm trees, pineapples, and other fruits: the exuberance of the peerless natural setting was underlined. Royal ritual closely followed this mixed tropical style, juxtaposing local and foreign elements. The elaboration of local rituals may have been initiated by Dom Pedro I and José Bonifácio, together with Debret and other members of the French Artistic Mission, but the originality of these ceremonies and of the Romantic project for representing the state became truly visible only over the long years of Dom Pedro II's reign. With the Order of the Southern Cross always on his chest, surrounded by a halo of stars and branches of tobacco and coffee, the classical laurel crown (or one of white acacia and yellow sassafras flowers, as in Gonçalves Dias's epic *Os Timbiras* [1857]), the feather mantelet, the medal of the battle of Paissandu—everything in Dom Pedro's presentation was made up of borrowings and adoptions.

But the cultural project of Indianism moved only slowly from the restricted circles where it had been created to reach Brazil's urban middle classes, who saw in it the answer to their desire for national affirmation. If, at the beginning, Indianism had been a means of covering up slavery's role, it now began to have a wider influence on bigger sectors of society, particularly in the court and in Rio de Janeiro. It affected political iconography, too, and the representation of imperial power. The empire was carrying out a kind of "American mimesis."[23] Side by side with classical allegorical figures appeared near-white Native Americans, idealized in a tropical environment. In one picture produced not long after Dom Pedro II's acclamation, Indians alongside the cherubim and allegorical figures seem to legitimate the monarch, standing as they do for the incarnation of a mythical, authentic past. In another, Dom Pedro, now much older, is crowned with the traditional laurel and surrounded by coffee branches, tobacco leaves, and tropical fruits; in the background are steamships, a globe, books, and a palette—symbols of progress and modernity that link the tropical monarch to the advances of civilization.

Cosmologies are even more obviously mixed in an engraving published at the end of the 1860s. The emperor in the center of the picture shares honors with a Native American—higher up, now on a pedestal—who carries the flag of the monarchy and crowns him with laurel. The elements are mixed: the

Ceremonial garments, with embroidered national symbols. The imperial cloak is adorned with stars from the Brazilian sky; other garments show coffee and tobacco. FBN

Indian carries the signs of Western royalty, while the emperor carries a coffee branch, emblem of local wealth. To the right, we see the royal escutcheon, with an eternal flame, and the crown, placed on the book of the Constitution, and to the left, a ship and workers seem to symbolize Brazilian progress. The whole thing is framed, like a gift, with a poem again exalting the Brazilian monarch, "idolized in a fortunate land." The dialogue between the writers at the Historical and Geographical Institute and other sectors of society gained new forms as the monarch's image spread through the nation.

Native Americans appear in advertisements for Rio shops. *Jornal do Commercio*, 1853. FBN

Dom Pedro paid homage by divinities and Native Americans. Lithograph, c. 1840. FBN

The Perpetual Defender of Brazil. The Native American, representing the empire, crowns the monarch with a laurel wreath: their positions are inverted. Woodcut, 1869. FBN

The Imperial Academy of Fine Arts did much to propagate the Brazilian version of Romanticism and to choose the exotic objects that would symbolize local reality. Soon these were adapted to the monarchy's plans in other areas. The Academy was responsible for the transformation in Rio de Janeiro and some of the provincial capitals in which the Baroque was superseded by neo-classicism.[24] In the rest of the country the Romantic academic style still ruled and portraits remained popular, especially in wealthy families, until the spread of photography.

The Academy was the result, and the main aim, of the French Artistic Mission that came to Brazil in 1816.* Teaching, which began ten years later, faced funding difficulties, and only in the Second Reign did it achieve stability, mostly thanks to the emperor's public and private assistance. As he did with the Historical and Geographical Institute, the emperor gave funds, prizes, medals, and scholarships to study abroad; was assiduous in helping the annual general fine arts exhibitions; and gave honorific orders, like the Order of Christ or of the Rose, to outstanding artists. In 1845 he began to fund an annual travel prize that provided a stipend to live abroad for three years.

Apart from official financial help, evidence of Dom Pedro's close ties with the Academy can be found in the number of portraits produced on order of the emperor. Félix Taunay, for example, did one for all the provinces of the empire and all the government offices in Rio de Janeiro; it was used for pupils to copy. Similarly Manuel de Araújo Porto Alegre and Pedro Américo fulfilled imperial commissions; Américo's picture of Dom Pedro at the opening of the General Assembly shows the emperor in imperial robes, with his crown, the mantle with embroidered coffee and tobacco leaves, the toucan-feather mantelet, and the scepter with the gilded serpent. Indeed, the Institute's links with the palace formed a closed circle. The monarch financed the artists who painted these more or less official portraits. The paintings, in turn, were circulated all over Brazil in the form of lithographs.

*Its members included Jean-Baptiste Debret, a painter of historical pictures; Nicolas Taunay, a landscape painter; Auguste Taunay, a sculptor; Auguste H. V. Grandjean de Montigny, an architect; and others. In 1817 the brothers Zépherin and Marc Ferrez, the former an engraver, the latter a sculptor, joined the mission, and in 1820 the mission's school was turned, by decree, into Brazil's Royal Academy of Drawing, Painting, Sculpture, and Civil Architecture. At the end of the same year it changed its name to the Academy of Arts (and was changed again in 1827 to the Imperial Academy of Fine Arts). Of the founders there remained only Debret, Grandjean de Montigny, Félix Taunay, and the Ferrez brothers.

Drawing by Dom Pedro II
in his diary: "Pretty little
house with climbing plants,
which hardly dared grow
over the veranda." MIP

Many of these artists were teachers—Simplício Rodrigues de Sá and Félix Taunay, for instance, who later became official court painters, even taught Dom Pedro and his sisters. The emperor came across Pedro Américo when he was a pupil at the Pedro II School and was secretly painting a portrait of him. This demanded a favor in return: the monarch enrolled him in the Academy and paid for his studies. Vítor Meireles also went to study in Europe, as did José Ferraz de Almeida Jr., Francisco Sá, Daniel Bérard, and Rodolfo Bernardinelli. For Dom Pedro, himself an amateur portraitist who filled his diary with little pencil illustrations, protecting this kind of artist was almost a state duty, a way of ensuring the existence of an official iconography. Not only did the Academy reward its prize-winners with scholarships and journeys abroad; Dom Pedro personally financed his protégés, who became known as the "emperor's students." (The emperor helped twenty-four Brazilian artists to work abroad, notably Américo and Almeida Junior.) The Academy was so closely linked to the monarch's fortunes that, toward the end of the empire, the school itself declined, with many posts vacant, and the funding policy ended.*

Glorification of the exotic, of nature, and of Brazil's indigenous population became a standard. In the colonial period the Baroque style had been dominant, and it was followed by artists, guilds, and even slaves. This is one reason why a prime objective of the Academy was to produce a contrast, to change styles, models, and techniques. It would bring in new methods of teaching, including anatomy courses; it demanded of its students a certain

*After the end of the empire, the republic appointed Rodolfo Bernardinelli to direct the Academy, and the reform of 1890 turned it into the National School of Fine Arts.

level of educational attainment and a minimum of experience. History paint-ing, above all of biblical inspiration, as well as genre scenes, allegories, and portraits predominated: the visual arts followed the same process of breaking with the past as poetry had experienced.

The Academy imported from France the idea that an ethical dimension should be shown in pictures, with exemplary figures as representatives of virtue and the power of the will winning out over the world of the passions. Unlike the revolutionary French model, in Brazil this academic style came under royal influence and followed the grandiloquent historical model, di-rectly linked to the imperial project.

The Academy, which from now on produced all the official images of the empire, dictated themes as well as styles: uplifting subjects, portraits, land-scapes, and history painting. These fashionable representations of the empire paralleled the literary production at the Historical and Geographical Insti-tute. Because of the funding policy they were in many cases executed abroad: these works presented an idealized version of Brazil and its people, as if cre-ated by someone looking at them from far off, without contact. Examples are Vítor Meireles's *The First Mass in Brazil* (1860) and *Moema* (1866) and José M. de Medeiros's *Iracema*, which were part of the Indianist cycle, a trend that came to painting later than to literature: only in the 1860s.

In these pictures, passive, idealized Native Americans are part of the scene's composition but do not fundamentally affect it: they are almost ap-pendages. The same is true of *The Last Tamoio* (1883) by Rodolfo Amoedo, and of the terra-cotta sculpture *Indian Symbolizing the Brazilian Nation* (1872) by Francisco Manuel Chaves Pinheiro. This last was the most em-blematic document of Chaves's generation: the Indianist intention could not be plainer. Chaves's Indian, with his body in exactly the same position as that of the emperor in the official image painted by Américo, carries the royal scepter instead of a spear, and a shield with the imperial arms on it instead of a club. He is crowned with a headdress, but the emperor's mantle covers the natural nudity of this "noble, pure symbol of our origins." Half Indian, half noble: half savage, half king, Chaves's sculpture creates a new synthesis.

Brazilian Romanticism deeply affected the public consciousness with these images of the Indian. The idealized Indians in literature and paintings had never been so white, while the Brazilian monarch and Brazilian culture itself were becoming increasingly tropical. For an elite that continually ques-tioned itself about its identity, about what really made it different, this was the answer: once the black slave and even the white colonizer had been rejected,

Indian Symbolizing the Brazilian Nation. Sculpture by
Francisco Manuel Chaves Pinheiro, 1872. MNBA

the Indian was the only worthy, legitimate symbol. "Pure, good, honest and
courageous," the Indians were kings in the exuberant setting of the Brazilian
jungle and in total harmony with it. In Brazil, a country but not yet a nation,
symbols arose with the same speed that the image of the empire was consolidated. And Indianism was a way of covering up the truths about the process
of Portuguese colonization.

Imagining things often took the backseat to conveying a message that gave
a poem, novel, or painting the necessary credibility. Travelers, chroniclers, and
historians like Gabriel dos Santos, Sebastião da Rocha Pita, and Manuel da
Nóbrega were cited in explanatory notes accompanying the texts, which in
turn were used as subjects for paintings. Once more, history and myth went
hand in hand: the Indian surely had existed in a remote, glorious past, and he,
thus mythified, inspired the Romantic dramas produced in Rio's theaters, the
grandiose tropical paintings, the operas that celebrated an exotic but noble
empire for European listeners. As the saying goes, *Se non è vero, è ben trovato,*
or in Gonçalves Dias's version, "Lads, I've seen it."

In spite of the criticisms of realists and bohemians who attacked Indianism as excessively imaginary, subjective, and dependent on the empire, these

The emperor and the Native American incarnate Brazil, the former as its leader, the latter as an often frustrated and discontented national symbol. In this satire the symbol laughs at the model personage. Ângelo Agostini, in *Revista Ilustrada*. IEB

Romantic images took root.* Their popularity was due perhaps less to their artificial aspects than to their process of invention, re-elaboration, and adaptation to the reality of the tropics. As a tropical noble savage, the mythified Indian allowed the young nation to discover an honorable past and foretell a promising future. If there were disagreements, this official project tried to expunge them.

Indianism was so completely absorbed in Brazil that by the 1880s it became a favorite target in the satirical press. Using him in a comic vein as a figure of mockery, Ângelo Agostini selected the Indian as the emblem of Brazil's delusions—something of a comedown for such a patriotic model.

But we must not jump ahead. In 1861, in a moment of relative stability, Dom Pedro summed up what he thought of Brazil's cultural situation at the time:

> I am gifted with some talent; but what I know I owe above all to applying myself, for study, reading, and the education of my daughters are my principal amusements . . . I was born to dedicate myself to letters and to the sciences, and if I am to occupy a political position, I would rather be president of the Republic than emperor . . . I confess that I could have done much more in twenty-one years; but I have had

*Silvio Romero was one of the most important opponents of Romanticism. In his view, the movement simply copied foreign models and had no connection with the mestizo reality of Brazil.

the pleasure of seeing the good results of eleven years of peace at home, thanks to the good nature of the Brazilian population.

Dom Pedro certainly applied himself to disseminating his image as patron of the arts and ruler. Political calm was of service to him: because of it, he could dedicate himself to what he thought his real task was. He was attracted by novelties, enjoyed studying sciences and foreign languages; for him the word *progress* meant science and the intellectual life. As the historian Jorge Caldeira says: "Economics was not one of the emperor's favorite subjects."[25] Dom Pedro thought it more important to change minds than to change economic structures, and he never hid his boredom with politics. He was interested not just in art: languages, astronomy, mineralogy, and geology all aroused his enthusiasm. He brought geologists like Orville Derby and Charles Hartt to direct the imperial Geological Commission—which collected more than a half million samples—and in 1864 he gave the first concession to exploit petroleum in Brazil to an Englishman, Thomas Sargent. In 1876 the Mining School in Ouro Preto, Minas Gerais, was created. Henri-Claude Gorceix, its first director, was recommended by Auguste Daubrée, a friend and colleague of Dom Pedro's in the Paris Academy of Sciences.

A polyglot, an assiduous correspondent, and member of several international institutions even before he traveled abroad, Dom Pedro had in his palace a library, a museum, a laboratory, and his famous astronomical observatory. He was often present at competitive examinations at the School of Medicine, the Polytechnic School, and the Military and Naval Academies, not to speak of the Pedro II School, his great enthusiasm.* Once a humble orphanage, the "Pedro II," as it was called, became the jewel in the crown of Brazilian education, a symbol of civilization and of the elite who sent their children there.

With its imposing uniform in the Brazilian colors—a green frock coat with yellow buttons (which from 26 December 1855 bore the symbol of the monarch, "P II," in relief), the fur top hat, neckerchief, and flat cap—the school little by little remade itself as Pedro's institution. In a letter to José Bonifácio o Moço

---

*Founded in 1733, this institution had had several names—the St. Peter's House for Orphan Boys, the Seminary of St. Joachim, the Imperial Seminary of St. Joachim. Abolished in 1818, it was restarted in 1821 by the then Prince Dom Pedro. On 2 December 1837 the school gained imperial patronage and was called the Pedro II Imperial School. Reinaugurated on 25 March 1838 by Dom Pedro, it took its first pupils on 27 April.

(nephew of José Bonifácio de Andrada), Dom Pedro proudly said, "I rule only two things in Brazil: my own house and the Pedro II School." Even if this was said for effect by a monarch who never gave up his "moderating power," at the very least it tells us something of the close relationship he had with the school, the only one in Brazil that ever partly escaped from the overly bookish, anti-scientific, limited educational standards of the time. Even though it was theoretically obligatory, primary education in Brazil was inadequate, and what few schools there were were almost all concentrated in Rio. But Dom Pedro seemed unaware of this reality. He was present at the school's exams, selected its teachers, and set its tests. In his diary, he wrote, "If I weren't emperor of Brazil, I would like to be a schoolmaster."

This is why the empire invested so much time in the reform the school went through in 1874. João Alfredo Correia de Oliveira, the minister in charge, wrote that "the cultivation of letters and science would be one of the main claims to fame of the reign of this prince whose name honored the institution, and whose generosity to it would never change."[26] Bethencourt da Silva, a disciple of the architect Grandjean de Montigny, was contracted to rebuild the old seminary; the main facade looked out on the Rua Larga de São Joaquim, and the others onto the Rua da Imperatriz and the Rua da Prainha. The famous Dom Pedro II Room, officially inaugurated on 27 February 1875, was adorned with sculptures of the great sages of humanity, and between the doors was enough room to set up the imperial throne with its Bragança dragons. Here degrees were bestowed on bachelors of letters and

The Pedro II
School, 1861.
MIP

doctors of medicine as well as graduates of the school itself, who received their much-awaited diploma, a sure passport to a promising future in Rio, from the hands of the monarch or his consort.

Dom Pedro's patronage had other facets, too. His enthusiasm for opera is famous, as is the suggestion made to Richard Wagner in 1857, when the composer was in difficulties, that a work be commissioned for staging in Rio de Janeiro. That was the year Dom Pedro created the Imperial Academy of Music and the National Opera, with the object of training Brazilian musicians and making the art of singing more popular. The suggestion was turned down, but in 1876 in Bayreuth Dom Pedro was present along with Kaiser Wilhelm at a performance of the *Ring* cycle. He thought of himself as a historic Wagnerian, not a last-minute convert. Once again "patriotic memory" selected certain moments and gave them status over others. Wagner was an icon worthy of the Brazilian Empire.

The monarch was also interested in medicine: he financed the studies of Brazilian doctors and gave support to a new asylum built in Rio in 1850 and named after him. The empire's first Scientific Commission—called the Butterfly Commission by its opponents—made collections in northern Brazil in 1859; it, too, was supported by Dom Pedro.

Whether as scientific fashion or as literary and artistic subject, the indigenous "savages" were the subject of historical, geographic, linguistic, and ethnographic studies. Dictionaries and grammars were published under the emperor's auspices, and he assembled a library of indigenous linguistics and ethnography. Though its objectives were often simplistically patriotic and eulogistic, the Institute played an important role in encouraging early research and in publishing ethnographic monographs.

A good part of the monarch's daily life was taken up by his own studies. In 1861 he wrote,

I want to divide my time in the following fashion. Get up at six and study Greek and Hebrew until seven. Lunch at ten. From nine to eleven writing this book and sleeping. On Fridays, I am present at English and German lessons given to my daughters . . . On Tuesdays the *Lusiads* from seven-thirty to eight at night. Wednesdays Latin with my daughters. Thursdays *Lusiads* . . . Sundays and holy days readings from Lucena . . . Greek verbs at night. Time not otherwise employed will be given over to reading, conversation, and receiving visits.[27]

Dedicating himself to astronomy, engineering, medicine, Hebrew, and the translation of classical texts, Dom Pedro opened up literary salons in his São Cristóvão Palace, chaired the meetings of the Historical and Geographical Institute, went to the opera, followed the examinations at the Pedro II School, and opened the annual exhibitions of the Academy of Fine Arts. These were the columns of the edifice he had built.

Outside these limits, however, Dom Pedro's patronage hardly existed. The writers and academicians who surrounded him, the "emperor's artists," collected prizes and gained important political positions during the Second Reign, while elsewhere the so-called Bohemian Generation (Paula Nei, Henrique Maximiano Coelho Neto, Artur and Aluízio Azevedo, Olavo Bilac, and others) and many other artists had to seek publishing opportunities far from the court's interference. In *A república* by Coelho Neto and *Mocidade morta* by Luís Gonzaga Duque we learn about the significant part of this generation in the 1880s who broke with the academic institutions financed by the empire and whose testimony shows that not everyone was in harmony with official culture.

Moreover, the emperor's interest in education and the sciences notwithstanding, expenditures in these areas were modest. Though the 1824 Constitution defined primary education as an obligation of the state, in most provinces little was done to promote it. The central government concerned itself only with higher education except in the capital and, as we have seen, for the institutions of secondary education that were apples of the emperor's eye: the Pedro II School, the Imperial Observatory, the National Museum, the Public Archive, the National Library, the State Laboratory, the Botanical Garden, and the Academy of Fine Arts. Illiteracy was the reality for the greater part of Brazilians; in the provinces there seemed to be no interest in increasing the number of enlightened citizens.

Again, Rio de Janeiro was an exception in this regard: at the end of the empire, it was said that half its population was literate. It was natural, then, that the capital should become a center from which culture spread to the rest of the country. New directions in politics, fashions in literature, rules for the Portuguese language—made public in politicians' speeches published in the newspapers—ways of dressing, gestures, habits of cleanliness, and new rules of etiquette were dictated from Rio and adopted by an elite who imagined it was living in Europe, even when it was in the tropics and surrounded by slaves.

Nothing was closer to court fashion than the Romantics' official projects.

The calculating, strategic side of Magalhães, the "mixed" theater and architecture of Porto Alegre, and the Indianist activities of Gonçalves Dias were all facets of a reformist Romanticism linked with the "tropical fashion" that was advanced as a project for all Brazil. The empire gave its tropical aspect an official stamp of approval and ignored the slaves.

In the 1860s Dom Pedro began to give titles to his improvised nobility and indigenous names taken from Tupi place names; these were not very popular with those who received them. Maciel Monteiro was made baron of Itamaracá; Pereira da Fonseca, marquis of Maricá; Gonçalves de Magalhães, viscount of Araguaia; Torres-Homem, viscount of Inhomirim; Cândido José Araújo Viana, marquis of Sapucaí; Cardoso Menezes, baron of Paranapiacaba. The titles and the hierarchy of dukes, marquises, counts, viscounts, and barons (with or without *grandeza*) were European but the names were local and indigenous.

Agostini satirizes Dom Pedro's relative lack of interest in politics: "It is hoped that His Majesty, who is a perfect painter when it comes to politics, will add a few touches." *Revista Ilustrada.* CEA

EIGHT

How to Be Brazilian Nobility*

Portugal's colony in the Western Hemisphere had, already in Dom João VI's time, had a "bath in civilization" and gotten its first cultural institutions: the Royal Museum, the Royal Press, the Royal Garden, and the Royal Library. As we have seen, the Portuguese monarch transplanted the entire ritual of the House of Bragança to Brazil, with its whole program of festivals, processions, uniforms, and titles.

The Brazilian system of heraldry was set up at this time; the creation, on 8 May 1810, of the Noble Corporation of the Kings at Arms was closely linked to the royal household. The process of giving titles followed the traditional Portuguese model, with some innovations resulting from the transplantation: the king at arms, who had the words "of Portugal and the Algarve," in his name, now added the words "America, Asia, and Africa." The kingdom was growing, along with the court. During the time that Dom João VI stayed in his Brazilian colony, he gave 254 titles in all—eleven dukes, thirty-eight marquises, sixty-four counts, ninety-one viscounts, and thirty-one barons†—as well as guaranteeing the continuing noble status of Portuguese aristocrats

---

*Written with Ângela Marques da Costa.
†The titles given by various rulers—Dom João VI, Dom Pedro I, Dom Pedro II, and Princess Isabel— tallied here are based, among other sources, on wide-ranging research carried out by the staff of the National Archive in Rio de Janeiro. Although this work is ongoing and has not yet been published, I had access to its results thanks to José Gabriel da Costa Pinto, to whom I am grateful.

who had come to Brazil. This was the beginning of the "émigré, recreated" court that introduced some rules from a distant Europe into Brazil. Dom João paid for favors with honors and a large-scale campaign of bestowing titles, while the *carioca* ruling elite struggled to get near the king.

After Dom João returned to Portugal and during the reign of Dom Pedro I, intense debates surrounded the Constituent Assembly of 1823 and the Constitution in 1824, but one item went through almost unseen alongside so many more polemical ones: Article 102, Clause XI of the Constitution guaranteed what until then had been merely given by custom: that one of the roles of the emperor, as chief executive, was that of "bestowing titles, honors, posts in military orders, and distinctions for services rendered to the state; gifts in money depend on the Assembly's approval, when they are not already designated and fixed by law." Also, among the attributes of the controversial moderating power, in Article 142, Clause VII, was that of "awarding remunerations, honors, and distinctions, as a recompense for services, in conformity with the law and the approval of the General Assembly." Thus was formalized the birth of a nobility directly linked to the emperor. As opposed to European nobles, who could be granted not only life peerages but also hereditary ones, Brazilian nobles were "born young and stay young": the hereditary principle applied only to royal blood, and aristocratic titles were limited to their present owner. Between 1822 and 1830 Dom Pedro I ennobled at least 119 men: two dukes, twenty-seven marquises, eight counts, thirty-eight viscounts with *grandeza* and four without, and twenty barons, ten with *grandeza* and ten without.

Under the guiding hand of the second emperor this monarchical project flowered, and the "tropical court" took root. By Dom Pedro II's side a considerable segment of society was differentiated by its noble titles and use of an escutcheon. Then, in the period 1870–88, at the end of Dom Pedro's reign, the monarch ennobled 570 new peers; these were the members of the new elite that had grown up with the young emperor. During the entire imperial period the total number of titles bestowed reached 1,439 (sometimes a single person was granted more than one in his lifetime).[1] This was a nobility based on merit. Though special events often led to the granting of titles—"His Imperial Majesty's birthday," "the day of His Imperial Majesty's consecration and coronation," "the arrival of the empress," "for marriage, christening, and official birthdays"—in many cases the actions of the person honored had led to the bestowal: "for services rendered," "proven acts of patriotism," "fidelity and loyalty to His Imperial Majesty," "services in the fight against cholera," "services in the Paraguayan war," or even "work in universal exhibitions."

Officially, these aristocrats formed the highest rung of Brazilian society, but in practice they were an elite selected on the basis of merit or public importance; they were not necessarily privileged, wealthy, or landed. Businessmen, teachers, soldiers, politicians, plantation owners, lawyers, diplomats, and civil servants could all show, with their own coats of arms, that they were the best of their profession. With no principle of heredity and no likelihood that the title would be perpetuated, one could presume the importance of one's achievement in one's own right.

Among the Brazilian nobles, other hierarchies had their importance too: grandees of the empire, which included dukes, marquises, counts, and viscounts and barons with *grandeza*, was the special small group who, according to the *Almanak Laemmert*, headed the royal processions and accompanied their imperial highnesses; they were to be addressed as "Your Excellency."

Beyond these nobles, a select entourage occupied posts and fulfilled roles in the royal palace; they shared in the emperor's formal activities and intimate life and had a certain status for this reason. Councilors of state, knights, and officers of the royal (later imperial) household formed, together with the titled nobles, the special group who during the Second Reign made up the Brazilian court. Many people lived in the palaces, side by side with the imperial family, trying to follow European etiquette, a little embarrassed still by some of the different skin colors in the court. (A few visitors from Europe were surprised by the "brownness" of the imperial pages.)

The aristocratic terms became mixed up. In theory, nobles had received their titles from the emperor, but in practice the word had a more elastic meaning. The "court" might be the group of people close to the king, or it might mean all peers. On the other hand, there was also "the court of Rio de Janeiro," meaning the city, with the São Cristóvão Palace as its key point. This was the "court" that until the 1880s was a kind of center for Brazil, from which fashion, the latest slang, politics, and culture all radiated outward.

Noble means "well-known, notable, illustrious, famous."[2] The word, then, is an index of a certain condition: nobility has gone through several stages in the history of humanity, but in modern times it has become the ornament of kings, something especially credited to the monarchy. And the history of monarchical courts, inseparably linked to that of royalty, begins with the sovereigns themselves, the premier nobility in the social hierarchy.

It is said that the people of Alba Longa and the Sabines, predecessors of the Romans, doubled the names of their most outstanding representatives. The custom came down to the Romans, and their descendants, too, used honorific names. In ancient Gaul, there was a fashion for names of distinction, and the same occurred with the Spaniards. The Portuguese, however, originally used only patronymics and later took over the habit of having names linked to a certain geographical area, and, still later, to feats of war.

Nobility, in any case, was a fundamental symbolic capital from the times of the absolute monarchies on. In France, the chief model in such matters, the various laws over the years show that it was a central issue. The feudal regime and titles were abolished on 4 August 1789, as if they were synonymous with the decadence of the *ancien régime* itself. On 21 January 1790 the end of any kind of hierarchical order was decreed. In the same year King Louis XVI abolished hereditary nobility and all titles. But in 1804, nobility was installed again, and in 1814 the old noble titles were restored. In 1848 it was the turn of the Second Republic to abolish titles, only for Napoleon III to re-establish them (without restoring the old nobility). After this point no other law suppressed noble titles officially, which meant that the situation remained unchanged, defined only by mutable laws and the force of habit.

Simultaneously, from the Renaissance onward the court grew in importance in all European countries and in the seventeenth and eighteenth centuries was the exemplary model for customs and politics. While in England Parliament decisively curbed the autonomy of the king and court, and Germany was divided into smaller principalities with many differing systems, in France the most complete expression of court society developed, with the appropriate trappings. Norbert Elias notes that at Versailles the link between the greatness of the kingdom and the greatness of the court was strongest when King Louis XIV required the nobility to revolve around himself and his court, the center of its existence. The idea of a public life developed, as opposed to the more private bourgeois world, and Versailles's constant theater reaffirmed its rigid hierarchies.

Obvious categories differentiated the nobility from the rest of the population. Not only their residences but their clothing, their expressions, garb, habits, and celebrations gave visible form to their conception of the world. What is normally thought of as luxury, Elias suggests, is in fact a necessity for a structured society. Royal courts operate in terms of external signs where every detail is converted into a status symbol, a demonstration of hierarchy, a rule for evaluating prestige. In societies given over to the "prestige-fetish,"[3] an aesthetic sensibility develops that is summed up in the concept of etiquette: a set of rules governing dress and behavior and a fundamental element in the process of exhibition, implying as it does differing degrees of privilege. Etiquette underpins the machinery of ceremonial, the strictness of ritual, and by being able to "read" it one could identify the intricate hierarchy of its world.

"Every kingdom gets the nobility it deserves" or that best suits it. In Brazil a court developed that was distant in time and space from its Portuguese model, which itself was not very strict and in which the influences of the French model could be glimpsed only fleetingly.

When in the twelfth century Afonso Henriques established his kingdom, governed from Lisbon, he molded Portugal to a new reality that differed from the old Castilian forms. Unlike the French knights, whose system kept its feudal nature and who were always linked to the possession of land, in Portugal the knights were always predominantly military. Nobility was linked to courage in warfare. A knight "of" a given entity was not "of" the territory he owned, but "of" his place of origin or "of" the site of his military victory. The first Portuguese heraldic document, dating from 1183, shows the royal arms of Afonso Henriques, with its circular symbol. At that same time, thirty descendants of knights from the kingdom of León established themselves north of Portugal. These *ricos-homens* (rich men) were powerful, since as well as their noble origin, they had the authority and prestige of holding public office.

The nobility was divided by degrees according to their importance. *Infanção*, from the Spanish *infanzón*, or *filhos de alguém* (sons of someone), were blood nobility, from which comes *fidalgo*—*filho de algo* (son of something); these *cavaleiros*, or knights, kept saddle-horses for battle and were favored by the king with gifts and privileges. Later, these *cavaleiros* were made members of chivalric orders. An *escudeiro* (from *escudo*, "shield") was the son of a nobleman who had not yet received his arms; it was his duty to help the knights don their armor and to fight in the rear guard. These primary nobles, who lived on properties gained by conquest and shared with the crown, did not have to pay the king tributes and charges: their only duty was to give military services.

Gradually, the Portuguese kings subdued these knights to their power, and in the fourteenth century they abolished the right of the *ricos-homens* to arm knights. At this time the word *fidalgo* fell into disuse and was replaced by the word *conde* (count, earl), who represented not merely himself but the *condado* (county) he owned. In the fifteenth century the nobility was finally made to submit to the king by means of *filhamentos*, a bureaucratic device that regulated the descendants of *filhos de alguém*. Aristocratic rights and privileges were limited to their third generation; the fourth generation had to go through the formality of *filhamento*, proving the services they had rendered to the throne. The nobility thus became increasingly palace-centered and subject to the king. But it was still a hereditary aristocracy, though unlike the Spanish and French models, in Portugal "presumptive" heredity was the rule: for every new title, a fresh decree was necessary. Interestingly, this small discrepancy was later reinterpreted as an opportunity to deny the right to hereditary titles.

With Afonso V, in 1466, an effort was made to legitimate certain norms, first by establishing the competence of the king at arms, who then drew up the genealogy of the nobles and guided them in devising their escutcheons. Also in the fifteenth century the nobility was organized into two orders, each comprising three degrees: first, *moço* (youth)-*fidalgo*, *fidalgo escudeiro*, and *fidalgo-cavaleiro*; second, *moço da câmara*, *escudeiro-fidalgo*, and *cavaleiro-fidalgo*.

Power struggles between the nobility and the crown over lands, jurisdiction, and privileges commonly occurred, but gradually certain palace functions came to be taken over by the nobles, as favors were exchanged for posts in the royal household. An intermediate stratum between the nobility and the people began to surround the king: by becoming a squire or a knight without rank *(cavaleiro raso)* plebeians could rise to the aristocracy.

In a series of acts in 1512, Dom Manuel I set up Portugal's official heraldic regulations, ordering and codifying the granting and use of arms and heraldic devices. In the same vein, trying to assure the crown's control, King Felipe I published a decree in 1597 that required *fidalgos* to document their titles by presenting their genealogical trees, which had to be preapproved by the king at arms and which established the coat of arms as primary evidence for knighthood.

In the eighteenth century, in the reign of Dom José, noble titles and honors were widened in scope and began to be granted to writers, artists, diplomats, merchants, industrialists, and important bankers, as well as to military officers and politicians who gave service to the crown. After 1466, those who received titles were obliged to pay for the favor. From then on titles used in Portugal followed the model and meanings usual in Europe as a whole.

These were *duke* (from the Latin *dux*), the highest rank; *marquis*, a word of German origin meaning one who governed a march, or frontier area; *count*, from the Latin *comes*, the king's companion or the man who "committed himself" to be just and look after children, orphans, and widows—and whose title implied the link to ownership of land; *viscount*, from the medieval Latin *vicecomes*, one whom the count designated to deputize for him in government; and *baron*, from the Latin *baro*, a valiant man who fights alongside the king.

As the immediate meanings of these titles were forgotten, they came merely to signify honors, or a way of participating in the court's hierarchies and disputes. Divisions characterized these titled people in spite of their apparent cohesion as a class. It was possible to rise in the hierarchy and change one's titles. This process became so complex that after the Bragança dynasty came to the throne in 1640, barons and viscounts were also divided, following the Spanish model, into those with or without *grandeza*.

Studies of coats of arms—their composition, use, and interpretation—are formalized in the specialized study called heraldry, which tells us that the origins of coats of arms go back a long way, and it was in the twelfth century, during the Crusades, that their symbols were subjected to fixed rules of composition, dictated and supervised by royal power and institutions. The emblems and colors on the shields and helmets of knights, and on the saddles of their mounts, were there to identify the combatants, but as time passed, they became symbols of the family or clan or group. (During the Third Crusade, King Philip II of France and Henry II of England decided that each group of

Baron   Viscount

Count   Marquis   Duke

knights would have its own colors, which allowed for easy recognition: the French used white, the English green, and the Flemish red.)

Gradually these purely practical or religious emblems became individual badges of courage or rewards given to vassals who distinguished themselves in the service of their lord, and became hereditary by favor and by tradition. In the thirteenth century, with the division of heraldic coats of arms, the practice became formalized and the shield became a symbol in its own right.

Although military feats justified carrying a coat of arms to start with, the motives multiplied: the escutcheon could indicate possession or sovereignty (of a sovereign prince or feudal lord, ruling over a country, province, city, or town); patronage (enjoying the protection of the king); family (heading a line, when the coat of arms could be transmitted by succession); ambition (a coat of arms inherited from an ancestor to whom the carrier believed he had a claim); community (a military, religious, or civil order, brotherhood, corporation, institution, or society). But royal control prevented the creation of new coats of arms, and the laws governing them were rigid, as were the rules for displaying them, which were always subject to prior approval.

The shield, representing the central part of the coat of arms, followed different patterns, and its shape was significant, too—the oval shield was used by women and the clergy—and the shields of different nations varied in size and format. Heraldic colors were also fixed: metals of gold and silver; enamels of red (gules), blue (azure), green (vert), black (sable), purple, and in some countries, orange; and furs—ermine and counter-ermines. Each color could be displayed graphically in black and white by means of diagonals or dots that had their conventions—essential at a time when color printing was virtually impossible. Thus, when graphic reproduction was imperfect and societies were basically illiterate, the colors and the exactness of details were key to understanding heraldry's esoteric codes.

The divisions of the escutcheon were also subject to rules. The parts and the emblems had fixed positions, as did the sections, whose positioning— vertical, horizontal, oblique, bend sinister or barred, or crossed—had different meanings. To use more than one enamel on a coat of arms, one had to divide it into parts, a partitioning that also followed laws determining how the escutcheon was read, as if it were a document. Coats of arms had to be analyzed from dexter to sinister (right to left) and from chief to base (upper to lower). There were also *differences*, personal features by which a descendant distinguished himself from his ancestor, and *breaks*, which modified the original meaning and showed the position of each family member. In this way (by bends and bends sinister) a legitimate son (with a bend) was distinguished from a bastard (who put in a bend sinister with blue, green, and red enamels).

There were also heraldic motifs, though they were often not given much importance in European coats of arms. The cross, the Christian symbol par excellence, was the most frequent motif, with the most variations. Animals were also important. The "lion rampant," meaning leadership and courage, appeared in profile, showing its tongue and with its tail raised. Leopards, wolves, foxes, dogs, deer, goats, eagles, cocks, falcons, peacocks, doves, swans, pelicans, some insects, a few fish, and some shells sometimes referred, like totems, to the animals themselves but more usually to qualities associated with them. Fabulous creatures were also invented: the griffin (a mixture of an eagle, lion, and leopard), the serpent (a stylized form of dragon, with the body of a crocodile, a bat's wings, and the head of an eagle, the symbol of the Braganças), the unicorn, the siren, the basilisk (a cock's head and a dragon's body), the hydra (a snake with seven heads), the salamander, the phoenix (an eagle in profile, always among flames), the centaur, the pegasus, and the sphinx.

Vegetables and flowers were less frequent and so stylized as to make their identification difficult. Lastly there were human beings, celestial motifs (sun, moon, and stars) and terrestrial ones (air, rivers, mountains, sea), and buildings (castles, towers, bridges). The symbolism of these motifs was varied, but some were constant. Lions, leopards, and serpents alluded to strength and victory in war; fish, waves, and ships to events at sea. Stars represented truth, light, clarity; crescent moons, victory against the Moors. Castles showed that they had been conquered or defended with one's own might. Bends, stripes, bands, bars, and saltires referred to victories, as did axes, swords, and other instruments of war. Keys referred to popes and eagles to emperors.

These symbols were found within the escutcheon, but others external to it—crowns, decorations, and mottoes—pointed to one's place in the hierarchy. The crown had already been used in antiquity, and from the time of Charlemagne all royal princes used it. Then its use was extended to feudal lords, and in the seventeenth and eighteenth centuries different forms were established for each category of crown: those of popes, emperors, kings, dukes, marquises, counts, viscounts, and barons.

There were also the various *orders*, which had their origins in political and religious events. Here it is enough to recall the oldest examples in Portugal—the Orders of Christ, of St. James of the Sword, and of Aviz. In Brazil, the orders during the colonial period simply imitated the Portuguese ones, but after the arrival of Dom João VI Brazilians prided themselves on their originality with the Order of the Tower and the Sword, the Order of Our Lady of the Conception of Vila Viçosa (used through the period of the United Kingdom of Portugal, Brazil, and the Algarve), and the Imperial Orders of the Southern Cross and of Pedro I and the Rose. As the number of persons with coats of arms grew, the special knowledge that controls, authenticates, and orders the art of escutcheons grew with it. Every detail could reveal either legitimacy or bastardy; courage or shame; marriage or descent; position or power. Nothing in this symbolism, from the colors to the divisions and motifs, was accidental; in this unlettered society, heraldry was a fundamental form of discourse.

Dom Pedro I, headstrong in both life and politics, was not one to abandon the prerogative of bestowing titles, honors, and distinctions. A sketch for the Constitution (in his assistant's handwriting, with corrections by the emperor), when it came to the subject of "the monarch" in Article 19, said: "The right of giving titles is the prerogative of the monarch, as is that of conferring honors and distinctions of any kind, excepting pecuniary ones."[4] After the word "honors," Dom Pedro added "titles."

Article 102 of the Constitution defined the emperor as the head of the executive power, and among his other attributes were: "11th—bestowing titles, honors, memberships of military orders and distinctions as a reward for services rendered to the state; rewards in money depend on the approval of the assembly, when they are not designated and fixed by law." The initiative of recommending people for titles and distinctions could come from the ministers of state or even from people close to the emperor, but he would always have the final word.

Nobility became official in Brazil, then, through the actions of a polemical monarch at a time when the regime's legitimacy could well have been thought doubtful. Nobility survived in Europe almost as a matter of custom, removed from the privileges of governmental bureaucratic order. In Brazil it gained a new originality: the decadence of the European model did not undermine the vitality of the Brazilian copy. In this newly independent country, the monarchy reinvented a nobility, filling out the transplanted forms with new content, symbols, and colors.

Before the abdication of Dom Pedro I and the acclamation of the boy Pedro II as emperor, the habit of giving honors to Brazilians who had distinguished themselves had already become routine. The *Aurora Fluminense* noted in 1829, "The Portuguese monarchy, founded 736 years ago, had, in 1803, when the system was reformed, 16 marquises, 26 counts, 8 viscounts, and 4 barons. Brazil, which has been in existence for 8 years, has 28 marquises, 8 counts, 16 viscounts, and 21 barons in its bosom." And the prerogative of granting titles and honors seems to have been one of the first powers exercised by Dom Pedro II. On his fifteenth birthday, only four months after becoming head of state, the young emperor wrote in his diary, "Soon after breakfast" he had time to "think about favors, and to decide whether or not they were deserved."[5]

Specific laws announced in 1847 only altered the judicial procedure for confirming noble status and the use of the escutcheon in hereditary coats of arms of Portuguese origin. Another decree of the same year defined the honorific posts in the imperial household, dividing them into major officials (among them chief ensign, gentleman of the chamber, chief steward, and chief porter) and minor ones (storekeeper, household clerk, stableman, chief cook, keeper of the jewels, officer of the household, and household musician, to name but a few). Titles, roles, and everything that surrounded the monarchy and the palaces were formalized.

With no important modifications, the Noble Corporation of the Kings at Arms—the registry of nobility—had been set up at the court in Rio in 1810, continuing on Brazilian soil the usual Portuguese procedures for formalizing the bestowal of titles and letters patent. Those charged with this service were a king at arms, a herald, a *passavante* (another kind of herald), and a scribe for the escutcheons of the imperial nobles.[6] The king at arms was a minor official, whose function was, as we have seen, to detail the genealogy of the nobles and give them advice as to how to set out their escutcheons. The herald and the *passavante* aided him.[7] At solemn acts, funeral rites, and levees, they had to wear, on their chest, the royal arms in silver. They also exercised functions similar to those in Portuguese rituals: when a monarch came to the throne, after the chief ensign unfurled the royal banner, the king at arms acclaimed him, saying "*Ouvide!* [Oyez!] *Ouvide! Ouvide!*" and the ensign would reply "*Real!* [Royal!] *Real! Real!* For our Lord, the King of Portugal!"

The clerk of the nobility of the empire was charged with registering grants of titles and escutcheons in the appropriate books. An imperial decree was not enough for the newly titled person to have the right to use a title: one had to pay a tax for the receipt of the new letters patent, and its registry was necessary to complete the legal process. The right to use an escutcheon also depended on payment and on registry of it. Tributes were given a great deal of attention. To acquire a letter patent, a right to another title, or a post in the imperial household, one paid a stamp tax. Over the years innumerable decrees and laws regulated the changing amounts to be paid, but it was always a significant amount of money, as was openly stated.[8] Letters patent for titles cost small fortunes, indeed: for a dukedom, 2,450 mil-réis; marquis, 2,020 mil-réis; count, viscount and baron with *grandeza* 1,575; viscount, 1025; baron, 750. The letter for the escutcheon alone cost 170 mil-réis. The title of counselor, and the right to be addressed as "Your Excellency" and "Your Lordship," also had to be paid for. There was much additional expenditure, paperwork, and red tape, as the following table from the *Armorial Brasiliense* of 2 April 1860, by Aleixo Boulanger, shows:

Petition to His Majesty the emperor and related procedures	30 mil-réis
Parchment for album, four sheets	32 mil-réis
Letters of nobility in gilded gothic lettering	130 mil-réis
Copy of the arms, for the secretary of the empire	25 mil-réis
The same, for the archive of the king at arms	25 mil-réis
Composition of the new arms according to precepts of heraldic science	40 mil-réis
Velvet binding	50 mil-réis
For the scribe of the letter of nobility	40 mil-réis
Dispatch to secretary of the empire	10 mil-réis
Emoluments for the clerk of nobility	50 mil-réis
The same, for the king at arms	50 mil-réis
New rights, in the treasury	20 mil-réis
Seal of the letter of nobility	70 mil-réis
Total expenses	572 mil-réis

After so much outlay, titled persons deserved a certain amount of protection. The unauthorized use of a title, decoration, or escutcheon was a matter for the police: it led to imprisonment and a fine. In 1871 it was defined as fraud and punished as such.[9]

During the Second Reign, honorific favors were classified:

1. Titles of duke, marquis, count, viscount, and baron
2. Titles of counselor* and the right to be addressed as "Excellency" and "Lordship," when these were not part of the job or associated with a rank
3. Posts in the imperial household, major and minor
4. Decorations of the various orders of the empire
5. Honorary military ranks

It was the monarch's place to choose those who would have one of the distinctions in the first group, which permitted the symbolic use of a crown, with different designs corresponding to the different titles, inspired like most European ones by French designs.

The vague notion of "services rendered to the state," and the absence of set rules for the granting of titles, made the decision very subjective. Whom was the emperor to choose? In great part, Brazil's nobility were people linked to productive agriculture (plantation owners), legislators, soldiers, and members of the liberal professions. Then came people in public posts, including those of the imperial household; merchants and businessmen; teachers, intellectuals, and so-called capitalists (the term meant they were living off capital); doctors, diplomats, bankers, and priests. Classifying these people was not so simple, for many fell in several categories: there were plantation owners who were also soldiers, or had government positions, or were in the legislature.† And in some cases, the biographies are unknown, and we do not know why they were honored. (Sometimes the reason was detailed in the *Register*, as in the case of the viscount of Baependi, of whom it was noted, "for services rendered during the cholera epidemic.")

Titles were given to people from all over the Brazilian Empire, but the province and city of Rio de Janeiro were most often honored‡:

---

*Counselors were considered to be a kind of intellectual aristocracy: ex-ministers of state and presidents of provinces, ministers of the Supreme Court, heads of large government departments, career diplomats, and university professors.
†Of the nobles in São Paulo and Rio de Janeiro provinces, 24 percent were both plantation owners and soldiers; 20 percent were plantation owners and legislators; and 9 percent were plantation owners, legislators, and soldiers.[10]
‡From *Almanak Laemmert*, 1860.

Place	Number of entitled people in 1869
City of Rio de Janeiro	55
Province of Rio de Janeiro	39
Bahia	24
Pernambuco	22
Minas Gerais	19
São Paulo	17
Rio Grande do Sul	10
Paraíba	7
Mato Grosso	4
Sergipe	4
Alagoas	3
Maranhão	3
Ceará	2
Pará	2
Espírito Santo	1
Paraná	1
Piaui	1
Amazonas	—
Rio Grande do Norte	—
Outside Brazil	11
Uncertain	13
Total	238

During the years of the United Kingdom of Portugal and Brazil, and the First and Second Reigns, more than fourteen hundred titles were bestowed, of which, as we have seen, Dom João VI gave 254. In the nine years of Dom Pedro I's reign, about 150 were granted, more than fifteen a year, and the regents, during the period 1831–40, were prohibited from giving titles and honors. Therefore, in the forty-eight years of his reign, Dom Pedro II chose about a thousand new people to be honored, about twenty a year. Also, while his grandfather and father insisted on higher titles, Dom Pedro created the "hegemony of the baron without *grandeza*": the lowest title of the hierarchy, generously distributed to the coffee-plantation owners of the province of Rio de Janeiro.

A good proportion of these new barons were old acquaintances, companions who had played important roles in the politics and culture of the empire

Dom Pedro had helped to create. And in ennobling them he altered the profile of Brazil's recent aristocracy. According to Sérgio Buarque de Holanda, the old nobility of agrarian landowners gave way to another, urban one favoring men of letters.[11] The emperor, as well as trying to create a tradition, was surrounding himself with a court of specially selected people.

By the end of the empire, 387 people had noble titles, which does not mean to say that the number of bestowals diminished with time: indeed, in 1889, the last year of the empire, 107 new titles were distributed and eleven promoted. Even on 15 November 1889, the day the empire fell, Elias Dias de Novais received the title of baron of Novais. (Curiously, in the period of the emperor's greatest popularity, the distribution of titles had been lower, and it grew during his gradual decadence; this seems to prove that they were not only used for private purposes but were subject to political manipulation. At a moment of crisis, giving a new title could quiet discontent and help state revenues.)

Those honored always seem to have coveted their titles and decorations and appreciated receiving them. Very rarely, they were refused: Prisciano de Barros Acióli Lins, lieutenant-colonel of the National Guard and owner of the Tinoco plantation, rejected the title of baron of Rio Formoso when it was offered in January 1882, saying that he was a republican. In a different case, Francisco Baltasar da Silveira, when he retired from the magistracy in 1886, was offered a title but said he didn't possess the means to correspond to such a glorious position and accepted the Grand Cross of the Order of Christ. The great majority, however, received these "passports to court" with pleasure.*

New Titles	1869	1879	1889
Duke	1	1	—
Marquis	11	7	7
Count	11	8	10
Viscount	36	55	54
Baron	180	249	316
Total	239	320	387

This included women, though the number of them receiving titles was derisively small. During the entire period, only about thirty women (about 2.5 percent) were considered worthy of the distinction, either because of their

*Again, the source is *Almanak Laemmert*, 1869.

charitable acts, or because they were near to the royal household. Thus, Mariana de Werna, who had been Dom Pedro II's governess Dadama and became chief lady-in-waiting, was made countess of Belmonte in 1844 and appointed lady-in-waiting to the empress. Josefina de Fonseca Costa, governess and companion to the empress, was made baroness and viscountess of Fonseca Costa and even had her own coats of arms. She had been appointed lady-in-waiting to the empress when the latter came to Brazil in 1846 and was her companion for forty-three years until her death in exile in 1889; these titles were decreed in 1877 and 1888 by Princess Isabel, as regent, in the emperor's name. A well-known case is that of Luísa Margarida Borges de Barros, lady-in-waiting to the empress, governess to the two princesses, friend and, it is said, lover of the emperor: she was countess of Pedra Branca, though she was better known by her French husband's title as countess of Barral. The Pedra Branca title belonged to her family, but she was allowed to keep it because of the position she occupied.

When the emperor gave honors to the widows of noblemen, they were always given higher titles than those of their deceased husbands. This is the case, for example, with the countess of Andaraí, Maria Cândida Rooke, widow of the husband of the same name, and of Maria Romana Bernardes da Rocha, of Rio de Janeiro, who after the death of her husband, the count of Itamarati, was made a marchioness. The widow Raquel Francisca Ribeiro de Castro (from Campos, in the province of Rio), many years after the death of the baron, became viscountess of Muriaé, and the same happened to Querubina Rosa Marcondes de Sá (from Paraná), who became viscountess of Tibaji.

There are cases of women whose husbands were commoners, but who as widows got their own titles: the Bahian Francisca de Assis Viana Moniz Bandeira, baroness of Alenquer (the title given in 1872 "in recognition of the distinguished services she rendered, donating a large sum for the continuance of the works of the Pedro II Asylum"); Carlota Leopoldina Moreira de Castro Lima (from Lorena, São Paulo), viscountess of Castro Lima; and Engrácia Maria da Costa Ribeiro (Rio de Janeiro), countess of Piedade ("In memory of the services rendered to humanity by her late husband," Senator José Clemente Pereira, she received the title on 13 March 1854, three days after her husband's death). The same happened to the *mineira* plantation owner Inês de Castro Monteiro da Silva, baroness of São José do Rio Preto; Francisca Maria do Vale de Abreu e Melo, baroness of São Mateus; and Maria Teresa de Sousa Fortes, baroness and viscountess of Monte Verde.

Ana Rufina de Sousa Franco Correa just missed being a baroness. Three years after the death of her husband, the emperor decided to honor her for the services rendered the state by her husband and, by decree on 2 December 1858, made her baroness of Cametá. She, however, had married again and didn't get the title.[12] The first baroness of Santana got a title because her son, Mariano Procópio Ferreira Laje, when consulted about a title, refused the distinction for himself and suggested his mother get it instead.[13]

Of course, the wives of titled men, even when the title had been conferred exclusively on the husband and was not hereditary, were also considered noble and were called by the title corresponding to their husband's rank. There is a good example of this in the novel *Esau and Jacob* (1904) by Machado de Assis. Natividade, on her birthday, thinks it odd not to find greetings or a jewel such as Santos, her husband, has usually given her every year:

> Nothing. Then she sat down and, opening the paper, kept saying to herself, "Can it be possible he doesn't remember what day it is? Can it be possible?" Her eyes began reading at random, skipping items, going back . . .
>
> Opposite, her husband was surreptitiously looking at his wife; nothing of what he was reading had the least interest for him. Several minutes went by. Suddenly Santos saw a new expression come over Natividade's face: her eyes seemed to grow, her lips parted, her head came up, his too, both left their chairs, took two steps, and fell into each other's arms, like two sweethearts mad with love. One, two, three, many kisses. Pedro and Paulo, amazed, were at one side, on their feet. Their father, when he could speak, said to them:
>
> "Come and kiss the hand of the lady baroness of Santos."
>
> They didn't understand right away. Natividade didn't know what to do; she gave her hand to her sons, to her husband, and then kept on going back to the paper to read and reread that in the imperial dispatch of the previous day Sr. Agostinho José dos Santos had been granted the title baron of Santos. She understood it all. This was her birthday present; this time, the goldsmith had been the emperor.[14]

Presents like this were not frequent. However, marriages between titled families were common enough, with the usual motive being to preserve their wealth and prestige, as well as to guarantee continuity in the already familiar arrangements. These had to have the emperor's license and approval, granted by writ on application from the parents of the couple.

Bujuru, Sirinhaém, Batovi, Coruripe, Ingaí, Subaé, Itaipé, Juruá, Parangaba, Piçiabucu, Saramenha, Sincorá, Uruçuí, Itapororoca, Aratanha, Tacaruna, Aramaré, Icó, Poconé, Quissimã, Saicã, Sinimbu, Toropi, Tracunhaém, Solimões, Jurumirim, Uraraí—these were the names of Brazil's new aristocrats, giving an indigenous tropical ring to old medieval titles. They were real Brazilian names for people of Portuguese descent, dressed in velvet and wool, who took tea at five o'clock and read in French, fanned by black slaves who had been bought in the market down at the harbor. They were following the trends of the time, adopting the exotic tropical veneer celebrated in José de Alencar's novels and Gonçalves Dias's poetry. The fashion had appeared early on: in Bahia, for example, in 1823, "patriotic fervor" had led to altering names in favor of these Brazilian ones. But by mid-century the fashion seemed to have taken root. The Indianist vogue, propagated in the Academy's pictures and in the novels of the group around the Historical and Geographical Institute, had reached the upper classes. The elite of young Brazil decided to represent itself through models based on savages and nature.

The names cited above, many of them of Guarani origin, in general were assigned to persons by reason of their place of birth, or where their political activities were concentrated, or where they owned property or had won a battle. Sometimes the means of victory in battle was referred to: this was the case with the baron of the Amazonas, the title given to Almirante Barroso da Silva, whose victory at Riachuelo in the Paraguayan war, on the frigate of that name, was considered one of the great feats of Brazilian naval history. Choosing these names was a prerogative of the emperor, who not only gave them out but sometimes created them against the will of the person honored; they did not always enjoy having names that were not easy to understand, at least in refined European circles, like "Quixeramobim" and "Batovi."

Green and yellow, coffee and tobacco, the representative colors and symbols of Brazil's new national state, appeared soon after independence. To replace the simple armillary sphere in gold on a blue field that had been instituted by law in 1816, a decree of 18 September 1822 laid down: "From now henceforth, the coat of arms of this Kingdom of Brazil will be a gold armillary sphere in a green field, traversed by a cross of the Order of Christ; this same sphere will be encircled by nineteen silver stars in a blue surround; the royal crown of diamonds will be placed on the shield, whose sides will be clasped by two branches of the coffee and tobacco plants, as emblems of its commercial wealth, shown in their own colors, and tied at the bottom with the ribbon of the Nation." On 1 December of the same year, the crown was decreed to be imperial. Beneath the royal green and yellow, and tied to it, a mass of symbols of varying designs and colors represented the nobility of a national state still being formed and still far from conscious, autonomous liberation.

The nation proudly showed off its colors in homage to the emperor: at a dance in his honor in 1848, "more than sixty ladies appeared exhibiting the national colors in their dresses, with a sprig of the coffee bush in their hair."[15]

Every new nobleman could, if he wished, use his right to an iconographic symbol, created to link a specific image to the distinction conferred. Four kinds of requests could be lodged: requests for "clean arms" (armas limpas), characterizing the recipient as the head of a line, were the most common; requests for "hereditary arms" were for use of an escutcheon that had already been used by one's ancestor, usually one's father; requests for "arms of descent" were made by titled people with coats of arms who wanted their children also to have the right to the escutcheon; finally, requests for "ancient arms" sought to use an escutcheon of Portuguese origin.[16]

With Dom Pedro's approval, the process followed the usual bureaucratic path: authorization was expedited by the secretary of state for imperial affairs, to the king at arms, who in turn prepared a letter of arms. At this point the scribe registered the arms in the Registration Book of the Escutcheons and Arms of the Nobility of the Empire—once the fees and taxes had been paid.

Letters signed by the emperor once more recognized and confirmed the distinctions of the nobleman in question, detailing his titles and honors. They also made clear that the distinction was not hereditary, though the possibility of his descendant using the coat of arms existed. A typical and interesting case is that of the marquis of Paraná:

> By the Grace of God and the Universal Acclamation of the People, the Constitutional Emperor and Perpetual Defender of Brazil. I hereby make it known to any who see this Letter of Arms, that, heeding the request of Honório Hermeto Carneiro Leão, Marquis of Paraná, Counselor of State, Senator of the empire, President of the Counsel of Ministers, Minister and Secretary of State of the Exchequer, President of the Tribunal of the National Treasury, Grand Cross of the Order of Christ and Officer of the Imperial Order of the Southern Cross, Stew-

ard of the Santa Casa da Misericórdia [a hospital], who, having been decorated by Me with several honorable Titles came to ask Me that, to preserve the memory of such a high distinction, I should grant him the use of a Coat of Arms, of which he showed me a model, decorated with colors and gold and silver. Accepting this Petition, I am pleased to grant the use of these Arms, and order my Principal King at Arms that, using the appropriate Scribe, the escutcheon and a Coat of Arms should be drawn up, according to the above-mentioned model, and should be laid down in the Registration Book, to be transmitted to his descendants, should they wish it and should I grant it to them again. They are as follows: A shield quartered above and below, with a gold border with four blue fleur-de-lis, and four fig-leaves with their own color; above is to be gules and below azure and on them a golden Lion [Leão] rampant, armed with silver. Third and fourth should be a field of gules, a blue bend striped with gold with three fleur-de-lis of the same metal, between two silver Lambs [Carneiros], armed with a golden Marquis's Coronet. The Crest is the Lion of the escutcheon, with a fig-leaf on its head. Motto: Por unum sea una. The Order of Christ and the Imperial Order of the Southern Cross. Which shield and Arms he may use and bear in all places, for any reason, in time of peace as of war; moreover, he may use them on seals, rings, signet rings and mottoes, put them on his houses, chapels and other buildings, and finally place them on his tomb; and so I am pleased that he, and all his descendants may have all the honors, privileges, exemptions, liberty, favors, mercies and freedoms, which Knights and Nobles have; his successors may not use this Coat of Arms without Me confirming their right to use it. I thus order all My Ministers, Appeal Judges [Desembargadores], Magistrates, Public Prosecutors, Civil and Criminal Court Judges and all the other Legal Authorities of the empire, and especially My Kings at Arms and Heralds, and any other officials and persons, to whom this My Letter may be shown and may know of it, that they may accomplish and keep to what is ordered in it, without doubt or exception being placed upon it, since this is My Will. He has paid ten mil-réis for the rights of Chancellery, as has been taken cognizance of by the Tax Office of the Municipality of Rio de Janeiro, on the eighth of the present month of November [1855], under number . . . countersigned by the Scribe and the Treasurer of the Same, and is now recorded and placed on file.

The wish to display a coat of arms was, however, only moderately evident: of the fourteen hundred people given titles in the two reigns, about 166, or 15 percent, had a coat of arms. (Luiz Smith de Vasconcellos's study, more detailed in its cataloging of the escutcheons of the Brazilian nobility, gives a total of 295: about 25 percent.)[17] It seems that displaying one's title in public places or having it printed in some local newspaper was glory enough, the more so when one faced the great expense of drawing up a coat of arms. The person honored could create his own coat of arms, which had to be approved beforehand; heraldic designers did in fact exist in Brazil, but their services were one more cost, and the expenses were already steep.[18] After so many difficulties, those who opted to use their own coats of arms took full advantage of them. They displayed these marks of distinction all over the place: on the railings at the entrance to their houses, on building facades, on carriage doors, in decorative paintings and in private chapels, on furniture, tapestries, silverware, glass, crockery and household utensils, letter paper and seals, jewels, and so on.

Brazilian heraldry adopted the characteristic national forms of Romanticism: it used local color, though not always with the required tact or observation of the conventional order. In 1846 Counselor José Antônio da Silva Maia passed a harsh judgment, saying that the officials who drew up arms did their jobs "without having the instruction that King Manuel [I of Portugal] wished them to have." Many elements were interpreted in a manner unique to Brazilians. Green and purple were often used though rarely seen in Europe: the Bragança family color appeared in varied shades in both the motifs and fields. A much smaller proportion of figurative motifs were used than in European heraldry, and local animals were introduced, imaginary animals much less often; Brazilian escutcheons had a more pragmatic, realistic tone. The fleur-de-lis, symbol of France, shared honors with roses, olive trees, palms, vines, pine trees, wheat, clover, and chestnut trees—not to mention sugarcane, coffee bushes, and mango trees.

The appurtenances of war, so popular in European heraldry—crowns, caravels, towers, and castles—were displayed all over the symbolic universe of Brazilian escutcheons, but they shared space with agricultural tools—hammers, wheels, hoes, and horseshoes. There were also human beings, usually saints or patrons; parts of the body—heads, hands, hearts, and arms—which were not so frequent in their European models entered into Brazilian heraldry, as if to demonstrate the private, personal side of human relationships. Me-

Coat of arms of the baron of Passagem, Delfim Carlos de Carvalho, who was among those allowed by decree to use a count's coronet.

Coat of arms of the baron of Santo André, José de Amorim Salgado.

Coat of arms of the baron of Gravataí.

Coat of arms of the viscount of Bahia, José Lopes·Pereira.

Coat of arms of the baron, viscount with *grandeza*, and marquis of Quixeramobim, Pedro Dias Paes Leme.

Coat of arms of the baron of Mauá, with his motto "Honorable work always conquers."

Coat of arms of the baron and viscount of Maranguape.

Coat of arms of Francisco Martins de Almeida.

dieval figures crossed the Atlantic and, out of historical context, were adapted or replaced by new creations, inspired by symbols that represented what the Brazilian nobility thought of itself or what it would like others to think.[19]

In addition, a good number of Brazilian noblemen tried to perpetuate their own names or those of their ancestors on their escutcheons. There were talking symbols, plays on the names of their owners: olive trees for Oliveira, pine trees for Pinheiro, sheep for Carneiro, lions for Leão, peacocks for Pavão, cauldrons for Caldeira, straps for Correia, towers for Torre, and so on. Many of these motifs were placed on quartered escutcheons: in each quarter appeared a symbol of a different side of the family, in most cases, a motif associated with the family name, not the title. The aim was to allow a more pragmatic, at times explicit and direct, reading of the shields.

For example, in the viscount of Rio Branco's escutcheon, the motif of a silver river appeared. And for Delfim Carlos de Carvalho, who was given the title of baron of Passagem for having forced the "passage" through enemy forces at Humaitá, his escutcheon showed not only a dolphin (delfim), a coin signifying Carlos, and an acorn (Carvalho means "oak tree"), but beneath, a large armored ship sailing on a blue river with silver waves, with the motto Avante! completing the picture. If there were any doubts about the baron's role in the Paraguayan war, this escutcheon would resolve them.

The escutcheon of the baron of Oliveira Roxo displayed an olive tree, as many others did, but on an enameled purple (roxo) background. José de Amorim Salgado, baron of Santo André, had engraved on one quarter of his escutcheon the arms of the Salgado family: a golden saltcellar between two towers, under the open legs of an eagle. Pushing things a bit, the baron of Gravataí did not hesitate to put a gravatá (a kind of tropical plant) on his shield, and José Lopes Pereira, viscount of Bahia, highlighted the flies that plagued his plantations.

Escutcheons linked to the source of the person's wealth were often quite original: Boaventura José Gomes, a plantation owner and baron of Itaquatiá, had, on one side of his shield, which was divided bend sinister, an ax, a hoe, a spade, and a rake, and on the other a landscape with cattle grazing. Francisco Pinto Duarte, baron of Tinguá, a plantation owner from Iguaçu, had a very similar escutcheon. And the baron of Mauá, although an important advocate of modernization in Brazil, was still fascinated by the illogical symbolism of nobility: on his arms figured a black locomotive with smoke and rails, a steamship, and four gas lamps, unusual symbols in Brazilian heraldry but revealing of the entrepreneurial man who designed his own shield. A ribbon with the motto completed it: *Labor improbus omnia vincit*—"Hard work always conquers."

In the empire of "bachelors of law" (*bacharéis*), so valued by Dom Pedro II, marks of learning could be worth as much as those of property. And homage was paid to learning on the escutcheons: books, pens, globes, and compasses. The scales of justice appeared on lawyers' coats of arms. On that of the baron of Vila do Conde, a doctor of law and plantation owner from Bahia, there were two pens, a magistrate's skullcap, two sugarcane plants, and a ruby ring.

There were truly Brazilian symbols: sugarcane and coffee quite often, of course, but also a golden puma on a green background and two silver spoonbills on a blue background, which were the two sides of the escutcheon of the baron of Catu. Leopards, which sometimes looked like jaguars, also made frequent appearances. Palm trees appeared in the arms of the Lopes family and on the escutcheon of the baron of Maranguape, where on the top of the palm sat a crow. Lastly, the "most typical of all national attributes"—the Native American—was used by the barons of Japaratuba, Rio Negro, Antonina, Barra Mansa, and Vila Maria: Indian heads (arranged like Moors' heads, often used in Europe), a native holding a coffee branch and a bow and arrow, a native cutting cane, and an Indian being instructed in the catechism.

Looking for the vestiges of nineteenth-century Brazilian history in these escutcheons means, however, coming right up against the self-image that this nobility wanted to perpetuate: European but "Romantically Brazilian," traditional but slightly modern, rich, learned, Christian, eager to catechize, victorious, and all-conquering. Slave-owning? Don't even think about it . . . Only one escutcheon shows a motif of blacks, and even then it copies the European style: in the first quarter of Francisco Martins de Almeida's coat of arms three black men's heads appear on a silver field, with rings in their ears and noses, and collars, all in gold.

So if we think of a coat of arms as a mirror in which the nobleman *reflects* the image that he wants to see (and others to see) and *produces* another, and if we look at the repertoire of the escutcheons compiled by Smith de Vasconcellos, we find a number of possible groups. One is made up of images of the nobleman himself and his self-explanatory name, suitable for display in its own right: *I am.* The second is that of the nobleman proud of his learning. These are the graduates, proud of their judgment, their laws, their knowledge: *I know.* Next, the plantation owners who transform sugarcane or coffee beans, the ones who own land, money, and power: *I own.* Then the image of those who make war, defend their country, and construct the future nation: *I act*. Next, the image of those who are rich because they believe in hard work: *I own because I act*. Finally, those who display the exotic, romantic, Christian country they live in: *I am a patriot*.

In the new heraldry of Brazil, however, the mystical side of the imagery was lost, and one can see only the direct evocation of material conquests. Far away from Europe's imaginary animals and the symbolic references of a distant past, Brazilian nobles designed and invented their own past, their paradoxical youth. Particularities emerged in small details: in a profusion of motifs, in the fluid rules and divisions of the shields, in unorthodox colors and combinations. It could also be found in the lax rules, the ease with which coats of arms were granted, or the emperor's personal criteria in setting up court.

In Dom Pedro II's hands, in part because of the sheer length of his reign, nobility took on a color all its own, not only from the indigenous names but from the startling makeup of its component parts. Nouveaux riches among landowners, men of the liberal professions, a few blacks (like the baron of Tijuca), even fewer indigenous people (like the baron of Guapi), artists, and literary men from Dom Pedro's circle: this was a group of valued friends—and a new image of civilization.

But it was the nonhereditary nature of Brazilian nobility that gave it its most special character. In the old colony, the court had changed with each viceroy. But in independent Brazil, people were not noble forever, and one's deeds had to be praised in one's lifetime. A whole new logic evolved. Already in Dom João's time the giving and receiving of titles was not just an honor but a real case of "you scratch my back, I'll scratch yours." Elias Antônio Lopes—a businessman who lived in the São Cristóvão Palace, a building that became the regent's official residence—was made Commander of the Order of Christ, and Knight of the Royal House. Dom Pedro II, too, chose his moments and often, as in the last year of his reign, used his privileges in strategic ways. It was common, for one thing, to give titles to old men so that their use would be short. Often a title was a political reward. At the end of the Paraguayan war, Dom Pedro ennobled a good number of men, as he did in 1888 after the liberation of the slaves (when several resentful landowners were made barons without *grandeza*). Moreover, titles meant expense for the person honored and revenue for the state: this was a strange nobility of people who wanted titles but paid for the results of their considerable efforts and their flattery of the emperor.

Perhaps what lies behind this is a kind of affirmation of the individual rather than of ancestry. In a context of *embourgeoisement*, potential and personal advancement was the fundamental quality, and the nobility, too, asserted itself by its deeds and affirmed them by means of the escutcheons, titles, and honors. In Brazil, to be a nobleman was a passing status, confirmed by a privileged intellectual, economic, or political situation. It was not a question of the prerogative of one's birth but the result of an effort, a personal achievement, and it was nontransferable: a meritocracy, not an aristocracy. While Europe saw the *embourgeoisement* of the nobility, in Brazil the opposite happened: the bourgeoisie took on noble titles. What the Brazilian system had in common with the seventeenth-century European model was the central figure of the king, who by bestowing titles, or refusing to, encouraged alliances and disputes and kept himself center stage.

As Sérgio Buarque de Holanda has written, "In a land where everyone is a baron, no durable collective agreement is possible, unless it be from a respected and feared external force."[20] So along with the young Brazilian monarchy arose a nobility cast in its image, while heredity was a principle affirmed only in the imperial family.

As we have seen, Dom Pedro II used the power to give titles frequently, and we can also see that he used it to manage his relationship with the landowners. The title of baron without *grandeza* was, basically, assigned to wealthy landowners; politicians were given higher honors. "Although the barons were 77 percent of the titles given by Dom Pedro II," observes Carvalho, "they were only 14 percent of the ennobled ministers of the Second Reign." Baronetcies became the distinctive mark of the major coffee growers of Rio de Janeiro, São Paulo, and Minas Gerais: thus did Dom Pedro co-opt the plantation owners and compensate them after the laws of 1871, 1885, and 1888 had abolished slavery. "While 51 titles were distributed in the five years of 1860–64, between 1870 and 1874 the number went up to 120. In the last five years of the empire, 238 titles of baron were bestowed, 173 of them in 1888 and 1889. The crown was trying to pay with a status symbol what it had taken away in material terms."[21]

These statistics point to the tension that grew between the emperor and his barons. Brazil's was not a mercantile economy like Portugal's, but one of agriculturalists relying on slave labor. In this "empire of bachelors of law," political power slipped from the landowners' hands, and what was left were the trophies the crown could give. As Buarque de Holanda says, "the empire of the plantation owners . . . began only with the fall of the empire."[22]

I AM

I KNOW

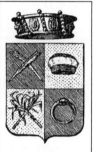

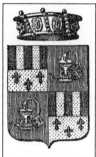

The baron, viscount, and count of Itaguaí (with *grandeza*) Antônio Dias Pavão.

The viscount of Rio Branco (with *grandeza*) José Maria da Silva Paranhos.

The baron of Vila do Conde, Dr. João Gomes Ferreira Veloso.

The baron of São Félix, Dr. Antônio Félix Martins.

I OWN

The baron of Maranguape (with *grandeza*), Flávio Clementino.

The baron of São Fidelis, Antônio Joaquim da Silva Pinto.

The baron of São João da Barra (first baron with *grandeza* and viscount), José Alves Rangel.

I ACT

I OWN BECAUSE I ACT

The baron of
Melgaço (with
grandeza), Augusto
Levergen.

The baron
of Itaquatiá,
Boaventura José
Gomes.

The second baron
of Tinguá,
Francisco Pinto
Duarte.

I AM A PATRIOT

The baron of
Antonina (with
grandeza), João da
Silva Machado.

The baron of Vila
Maria, Joaquim
José Gomes da
Silva.

The economic influence of these barons during the Second Reign, far from the splendor of the court, can hardly be denied, but the same cannot be said of their political or social hegemony. Eduardo Silva has commented that "contrary to the myth of the brilliant, aristocratic rural past, what we have is a nobility not always accustomed to using shoes or forks, who slept in hammocks, who didn't live in castles and mansions exactly but in hovels." Quoting Gilberto Freyre, Silva wrote of "barons in clogs" who mixed up their *rr*s and *ff*s, were barely literate, and boasted of the titles they had got for four *contos* apiece.[23] So there was the court, there were the noblemen who met in the Rua do Ouvidor, and then there were the titled plantation owners in the provinces, the rural reality of the empire.

One of the first acts of the republic, on 24 February 1891, was to abolish the empire's honorific titles. With the nobility so near to and so dependent on the emperor (at least for getting their titles), their continuation might have symbolized the survival of the monarchy itself. So titles were abolished, but in the process curiously symptomatic mistakes were made. It became habitual in Brazil for a noble family to keep not its title but the name accompanying the title, incorporating it into the family name. The former baron of Rio Branco now called himself José Maria da Silva Paranhos do Rio Branco; many others, too, tried to lay claim to a noble origin in the dim, distant past. The noninheritability of titles was forgotten, and titles remained as a kind of symbolic tradition brought into play when one wanted to claim prestige and authority. In a country with a short history and a flimsy memory, to claim nobility was to vouch for one's antiquity.

How did Brazil's nobility behave? In the mid-eighteenth century, just before the revolution that turned the Western world upside down, the French aristocracy had laid down rules and standards of conduct, of behaving in public, and in many ways these rules of etiquette were eventually followed in Brazil.

The napkin replaced the handkerchief during meals; forks were no longer used only to eat stews and thick soup; and eating with one's fingers was strictly limited. Clean dishes were introduced with greater regularity (preferably at each meal), and the table knife began to be used to cut meat that had already been carved, as servings became smaller; the old habit of bringing large pieces of meat to the table was discouraged—it looked like cannibalism, or caveman behavior—the diametrical opposite of civilization. The proper way of using a knife was insisted on, because of its association with death and danger when used impolitely or in an uncontrolled way. People who insisted on cleaning their teeth with this same implement could be reprimanded: all in the name of civilization.

Knowing how and when to use these table tools not only showed a repugnance for anything that might remind one of animal nature but pointed to a new view of social life. Knowing how to use and handle knives and forks was a clear indication that one belonged to a separate elite.

Not only table manners were transformed—the speech of the court was gradually shaped and regulated, for there was no room for the free expression of feelings and intentions. Everyday expressions were subject to a process of revision, and rules were fixed for the art of greeting others, thanking them, showing appreciation or regret, congratulating or commiserating.

In the name of "courtesy," other rules of social behavior became important. Instructions not to speak too loudly, not to interrupt, not to dominate the conversation were more than well-meant pieces of advice: heeding them showed whether one was well or badly behaved. Habits that today might be explained as a matter of reasonable conduct, or dictated by hygiene, were justified merely by "etiquette," because to ignore them caused "embarrassment." It was not polite to spit at the table, and it was not thought nice to pick one's teeth in front of others. In dress, expressions, and gestures, social differences were created and visibly defined; these differences were easily perceived in societies where illiteracy was still common. Etiquette was not a social adornment but a fundamental tool, as Norbert Elias has put it. In rigidly structured societies where external signs became status symbols, proof of hierarchy and prestige, a certain sensibility to ritual developed, a "ceremonial machinery" that ended by controlling and containing any manifestation of feelings and sensations, as well as by regulating influences and positions. The fact that "civilization" led to a growing division between the public and private spheres, between secret and social behavior, has often been commented on. But it is important also to see that this break between containing and demonstrating one's feelings was absorbed, becoming compulsory and internalized.

At the end of the eighteenth century, a new literary genre rose dedicated to teaching good manners and behavior. As literacy became more widespread and the publishing industry grew throughout the next century, guides to the rules and models of social interaction became popular.

Written in a clear, didactic manner, they were dedicated to the "science of civilization" and introduced their readers to the signs marking the modern ideas about social life. They also show us the limits on contemporary ideas of hygiene and polite behavior. Directly, almost sharply, the manuals gave clear warnings, not just instructions on how to set out the knives and forks. Advice was given on the daily evacuation of the bowels, personal cleanliness (to avoid clouds of insects), bathing every fortnight or at least once a month, and changing one's underclothes as soon as they were dirty, sweaty, or damp. *The Imperial Cook or The New Art of the Cook and Butler in all its Aspects*, written and published in Brazil for the first time in 1852, remarked:

> It is at table that one sees the clumsiness and faulty education of a man who is not a gastronome . . . he helps himself to various dishes with the same spoon he has already put into his mouth twenty times, knocks his teeth with his fork, picks at them with it or his fingers or knife, which disgusts those seated next to him. When he drinks, he never wipes his mouth . . . he gulps, and coughs as a result, spitting half of what he has drunk into the glass and spattering his neighbors, making disgusting grimaces. If he tries to pick up a piece of meat, he cannot find the joint, and after vainly trying to cut it, he breaks the bones and splashes those sitting next to him with the gravy, staining himself with the grease and bits that fall into his napkin, whose corner he has stuck in his buttonhole as he sat down. Sometimes, too, he spills coffee from his cup or saucer onto his coat. True, these accidents are not criminal acts, but they are ridiculous and annoying to decent people.

Conversation, and speaking in public, was another topic of special interest. Napoleon Raisson Horace in Paris wrote a *Code of Conversation: The Complete Manual of Elegant and Polite Language*, which circulated widely in France and in other countries in the 1830s. And in the *Code of Good Manners or Rules of Civilized Behavior and Good Living*, first published in Portugal in 1845, a member of the Church, J. I. Roquete, instructed his readers on the secrets of the social world. This guide had faithful readers among the newly titled Brazilian nobility, with whom the author had frequent contact. Having lived in Paris and London and knowing the Portuguese court well, Roquete intended to educate his countrymen in polite manners. As he said, one of the difficulties of civilization was learning how to copy while at the same time adapting to local conditions: "For you must know that every nation is jealous of its customs and usages, and those who change for capricious rea-

sons, merely to imitate foreigners, have already lost the sense of their own independence and are on the way to decadence." However, the *Code* leaves no
room for doubt about where fashion originated: the instruction is to read
"with your heart in Portugal, your eyes on yourself and your intelligence in
France."

From the France of the *ancien régime* came the principle of hierarchy
that guides the whole book; social inequality is to be hidden under the cover
of an almost biological naturalness: "Don't ask me why, in this society, which
sprang from the loins of one man, some seem to be happy, others miserable;
some give orders and others obey . . . Only see that nature made aristocrats,
that is, privileged beings, stronger, more beautiful, more intelligent, more
courageous than others, and do not be astonished that men have imitated nature; equality has never existed on earth; but woe to those who forget that it
exists in the eyes of God."[24]

The solution in a country like Brazil is to attribute social differences to nature and habit, to understand that "society has its grammar," which has to be
studied just as laws and rules must. In church, at christenings and weddings,
at parties and funerals, at the palace and among friends, in everyday existence
and when traveling—there is an etiquette for every place. One should control
one's conversations and fix the times when one weeps and when one doesn't.
Sneezing should be domesticated and limited to private moments, as should
conversation itself. One should know when to speak and when to keep quiet,
and one should watch to make sure one is heard.

Everything has its logic and order, just like a well-served meal, which begins with the napkin, placed on one's lap, to be followed by the soup (to be
eaten with a spoon, not a fork), eggs (the shells should be left on the plate),
poultry (whose precise name—chicken, capon, or turkey—should not be
mentioned); bread should be torn with the hands and not with the teeth or a
knife. When the coffee is hot, it should not be poured into the saucer but
drunk gradually; bread should never be soaked in wine or gravy; nor should
one use it to clean one's plate. One should not swallow hurriedly; put soup in
one's mouth when it's hot; or eat large mouthfuls. Don't chew so loudly you
can be heard at the other end of the table, don't serve others with the same
spoon you're using, don't nudge your neighbor with your foot or put your elbows in other people's plates. As for toothpicks, the advice is even stricter:
don't keep them in your mouth, in your hair, in your jacket, or behind your
ear—and don't talk with one in your teeth.

The number of don'ts in this kind of book is very great, yet for all that etiquette is a "science of artificiality," the good student makes everything appear "natural, with no hurry involved," learns the details of polite behavior by heart, and uses them as though they were expressions of his individuality.

There is no social activity that cannot be regulated, no attitude that cannot be controlled. When it comes to written communications, for instance, the best thing is to reproduce previously composed models, so as not to put one's foot in it. Model letters of all kinds are proposed, from the most formal to the most intimate, from business letters to personal notes, letters of condolence or congratulation, letters to distant friends, regretting or accepting an invitation, moralizing letters, letters of advice. Anyone who thinks good style displays originality is naïve; the only way to be correct is to know the rules.

In this world, which was trying to adjust to the rules of civility, the art of writing had to be controlled when possible. Grammatical errors are not allowed, of course, nor is leaving a letter without a prompt reply. A letter should always begin with a general, pleasant topic, and the right mode of address should not be forgotten: *Alteza* (Highness) for a prince of the imperial house; *Parente* (Relation) for a relative of the royal house; *Excelência* (Excellency) for a court grandee, minister, senator, or counselor. It was important not only to use the right title, but to use it at the right moment. In *La science du monde* (1877) — often advertised in the Rio newspapers — explicit warnings are given about the use of titles: "We should . . . only mention the title without emphasizing it, as if it were something natural, which is, moreover, what it is." The secret, as always, is to make what is artificial look natural, and vice versa.[25]

A good number of the rules highlight particularities in the behavior of the two sexes. Men require politeness and urbanity; women should be soft-spoken, with a reserved look. Men should speak intelligently and correctly; women should be modest and quiet. "If they are quiet, you must be quiet too. If you enjoy yourself, show only a moderate happiness; if you are bored, hide it and don't let people know about it. Never prolong the conversation on your own account. Accept and eat what you are offered, and if you want something else, do not say so. Don't show off your gifts in public."[26] While men are recommended to drink three glasses of wine at the outside (and never more than two kinds), it is suggested that women not drink wine at all until they are at least forty. Conversation between men and women must be controlled: "always speak to ladies in a softer voice than to men, do not address them as *tu*, do not recount any disagreeable events, or anything vulgar, much less cruel and bloodthirsty: recount nothing that might not be pleasing to a woman's characteristic sensibility. On journeys, a man will not forget to take a good book, paper, and an inkwell for writing; a woman will be happy enough with some embroidery or perhaps a book about botany."[27]

The maxims in these guidebooks always ask for dissimulation in place of sincerity. Never say what you like and don't like, and avoid creating problems. Never be vehement on any question. Always abandon your position, and never get into an argument, even if you are sure you are right. "What is the advantage of politeness? By showing oneself to be generous, disinterested, and capable of denying oneself, one inspires these qualities in others; it is not falsity that makes us avoid showing our defects, but the desire to hide them."[28]

In an isolated South American monarchy surrounded by republics, in a slave-owning empire that did not want people's attention drawn to this aspect of its life, among recently created noblemen, these etiquette guides were received with enthusiasm by those who wanted to cover the tracks of the nation's recent, improvised character. Brazil's cities were taking on new life, and the rural elites were beginning to have a more active social life. With the coffee boom and with plantation owners leaving their plantation houses for the cities, communal and social life gathered strength; balls, theaters, dinners, and concerts were welcome novelties in the capital. Far from the isolated world of the countryside, in the Rio de Janeiro of the 1860s calendars were marked with parties, rituals, and trips. Suitable clothing was needed for each occasion—trips to the Rua do Ouvidor, meeting in a patisserie, promenading at the theater, attending a dinner: the guides were essential.

One had to know how to behave in these new situations. Even walking down a street was subject to rules: one must "(1) keep one's body perpendicular to the ground, or almost; (2) not swing one's arms like pendulums; (3) walk in a straight line without deviating; (4) not run or walk too slowly or affectedly; (5) walk with one's toes pointing slightly outward, and look at the ground often, so as not to trip up."[29] "Social education" was the name of the science of good relations among people. One is to be contained or, rather, to reveal things to the right degree, without exaggeration or omission. Greetings, for example, "take place (1) to show interest (a) when someone is ill or (b) after a long absence; (2) every time we meet someone we are intimate with."[30] More formal salutations, "actions by which we show our human feelings to others," have to be accompanied by appropriate gestures: "(a) taking one's hat off; (b) taking one's gloves off; (c) turning to the front." And visiting had to wait for the right motive: "(1) to see the person visited and find out how he is; (2) to congratulate someone or present one's condolences; (3) on birthdays and holidays; (4) when someone is departing or saying good-bye."[31]

The new elite around Dom Pedro II were especially avid readers of this kind of reading-matter, which reinforced social distance and distinguished among different kinds of behavior. Treatises were printed over and over again; *The New Manual of Good Form* had had six editions by 1900. It and other etiquette books were sold by the thousands in the streets of the capital and heavily advertised in newspapers. The historian Gilberto Freyre, alert as always to cultural habits, emphasized that parents encouraged young men and women to read such works, which were very fashionable among barons and viscounts.

To serve dinner to guests, one had to follow the recipe of R.C.M., the anonymous author of *The Imperial Cook*. The secret was to introduce European, mostly French and Italian, dishes but give them Brazilian seasonings. (Not only foodstuffs were "tropicalized": utensils also varied. Pans and drinking cups made from gourds were used in Brazilian kitchens as were wooden flour dishes and mortars for pounding corn, and paper decorations like those on the trays of Bahian sweet-sellers. Earthenware pots stood side by side with porcelain from the Portuguese East India Company or the imperial family's silverware.) The local nobility had to follow a European system with Brazilian flavors added. In the kitchens of the capital, earthenware vessels and wooden troughs, with wooden spoons used for serving, gave dishes that *je ne sais quoi*, and seasonings (pepper, cinnamon, and coriander) gave them a local flavor. Finally, exotic meat and game were witness to a cuisine made up from many borrowings and innovations. And the absence of certain ingredients would lead to innovation. In their new social life and customs, the Brazilian nobility showed the consequences of their more or less pragmatic reinterpretation of rules from abroad.

Observing such formalized behavior, it is difficult to see where artifice ends and history itself begins. But what interests us here is how important details of the Brazilians' memory were being constructed.

NINE

*Dom Pedro's Residences**

The City Palace, sketched at three different moments in its history. From *Guia do Paço Imperial*, 1995.

In the symbolic construction of the emperor Dom Pedro II's public image, his sumptuous palaces are a constant theme. Beside pictures of the monarch and his family, drawings and, later, photographs of his residences frequently appear. This is not a coincidence. If a noble's house distinguished him as an aristocrat and its external aspect symbolized his important position in a hierarchy, an emperor's palace had to be better still. In the France of Louis XIV, the word *palais* could be used only to refer to the king's dwelling; the nobles had *hôtels*.[1] And Brazil's nineteenth-century empire also kept a distinction: the word *palácio* belonged to the emperor or to members of the imperial family, while the urban dwellings of noblemen and courtiers were *palacetes*. In his palaces the monarch was considered in an ideal setting, surrounded by his courtiers and servants (described as "cashew-colored").

The imperial household, which administered the emperor's palaces, was carefully structured, its several departments all subordinate to the chief stewardship. The chief steward, appointed by the emperor along with the other staff, was responsible for the monarch's finances; this powerful figure had close contact with the emperor and his ministers, to whom he was accountable.

Funds from the public treasury for the upkeep of the palaces and the imperial family were entrusted to the steward, and called the "endowment."

---

*Written with Ângela Marques da Costa.

Through him the treasury dealt with "active and passive affairs concerning the imperial household," as the Constitution had it. In addition, the Constitution stipulated that the palaces and lands owned by Dom Pedro I would belong to his successors, and the nation would care for any acquisitions and buildings thought appropriate for the enjoyment of the emperor and his family.[2]

As we have seen, when Dom João, the Portuguese regent, arrived, bag and baggage, in Brazil in 1808, there was great excitement in Rio de Janeiro. After all, it was the king himself in person—a figure who had hitherto only floated in the local imagination—who was disembarking. Dom João did not have to go far to find lodgings. Right opposite the quay was what was then called the Palace of the Viceroys.[3] As well as sheltering the royal family, this building now became the administrative center of the United Kingdom of Brazil, Portugal, and the Algarve and was renamed the Royal Palace, reserved by law to be the residence of the monarchs.[4]

Some reforms and modifications were made. In the part of the palace facing the sea and the square—Palace Square, or Largo do Paço—were the audience room, throne room, and the royal family's quarters. The floor above was for gentlemen of the court. The Carmo monastery, at the back of the palace, was requisitioned as accommodation for Queen Maria I and her ladies: a raised passageway was built to connect the two buildings.* Another passageway also put the palace in direct communication with what had been the town hall and jail, where escorts and court servants were installed. But this could not accommodate all the new Portuguese arrivals, and many people failed to find lodgings. Rio had no infrastructure for absorbing such a sudden change. A Royal Lodgings Decree became the means by which a gentleman, by the sovereign's favor, could requisition any house he pleased: when the decree was invoked the letters PR (Prince Regent) were written in chalk on the door of the chosen house, which Rio people translated as *Ponha-se na Rua* (Into the street with you).

In Dom Pedro II's reign a third passageway linked the palace to the royal pews in the imperial chapel, passing through the Carmo monastery. In this

*Queen Maria I was Dom João VI's mother; prevented from governing because she was mentally disturbed, she was known as "the madwoman" (*louca*); she died in Rio in 1817, and the prince regent was then acclaimed king. The expression *Maria vai com as outras* (Maria follows the lead) originates in this period, when the queen was seen in the streets of the city with her ladies, who took her out for walks.

manner, the imperial family was spared the necessity of going down to the street and walking up the length of the church. In 1817 a third floor was added to the palace on the side facing the sea, designed as the king's apartment. Here Dom João lived and carried out his public duties. Nearby, his court was installed in Rio's best houses. Within the palace, the frontier between public and private life was drawn by a staircase, a solid door, or heavy velvet curtains.

In 1817, some years after his arrival in Brazil, Dom João changed his lodgings. In search of privacy, perhaps, or of a more comfortable, healthy spot, he moved to the distant neighborhood of São Cristóvão, the Quinta da Boa Vista (literally "the country villa with the good view"), a property given him by a rich Portuguese merchant. But he continued to carry out his public functions as a monarch in what was now called the City Palace, where he kept his apartment and occasionally stayed. (His wife, the princess Carlota Joaquina, with her daughters, went on living in the City Palace, as well as in a house in Botafogo and a small country house in Mata-Porcos, now Estácio, where they spent the summers.) Ceremonies requiring pomp and circumstance, the kissing of his hand, and great festivals still took place there in full public view, as the acclamation of Dom João VI as king did; so also the christening of Princess Maria da Glória, and the arrival of Dona Leopoldina to be married to Dom Pedro I. The people of Rio who did not participate directly in these rituals showed their loyalty in other ways, decorating their houses, covering their windows with quilts or tapestries, and waving handkerchiefs—in this way preserving old Portuguese habits in new Brazil.

With the departure of the Portuguese king and the declaration of independence in 1822, the City Palace continued to represent the nucleus of politi-

The City
Palace. IHGB

cal power for the emerging Brazilian state. And right there on the square in front of it, and in the old jail building where Dom João's functionaries had been put up, Brazil's first legislative building was set up. Dom Pedro I lived, like his father, in the Quinta da Boa Vista, also called the São Cristóvão Palace, but the City Palace was still an administrative center and the setting for the spectacles that the monarchy needed to stage for itself. A German officer wrote:

> The City Palace is not very different from the other buildings in the city. Its interior is hardly dazzling, and hundreds of private houses are better decorated, but its setting turns it into a fairy palace. Refreshing sea breezes come into the high-ceilinged upper rooms. The view over the harbor and bay is stunningly beautiful. Around it is a square, at whose edge is a solidly built quay where one can watch the colorful, milling crowds. Splendid churches and good houses surround it.[5]

Under Dom Pedro II the City Palace continued to be the official seat of the court: the place where documents were drawn up, where official receptions and solemn events were held, and whence the sovereign left for public functions elsewhere: the inauguration of the legislature, reviews of troops, formal openings. So the moments when the monarchy displayed its symbols of power and prestige had the City Palace as their inevitable backdrop: the "Fico" day celebrating Dom Pedro's decision to stay in Brazil; the consecrations of the two emperors; the signing of the "Golden Law" in 1888 abolishing slavery; processions for christenings, masses, and Te Deums; birthdays, marriages, and funerals of the members of the imperial family—all the moments appropriate for pomp and circumstance, moments showing off a monarchy that was creating its own history and that, because it was hereditary, thought of itself as eternal. Thus it gave itself an aura of permanence, perceived by the spectators crowding into the streets to watch the magical display, and thus it gained additional power. The luxury within the palace was quite limited, but the pomp shone out all the more against these relatively modest surroundings.

The calendar of festivities, published every year, was quite clear: in 1843 Dom Pedro II decided to establish, as well as the national feast days set down by law, the court's gala days. On all these days except 6 January there would be a procession at the City Palace at around midday for their majesties and their imperial highnesses.

The Portuguese custom of the kissing of the hand: a ritual display of servility. Anonymous, 1826. CGJM

1 January: New Year

6 January: Epiphany (The Day of the Three Kings)

11 March: Birthday of the Most Serene Imperial Princess

14 March: Birthday of Her Majesty the Empress

18 July: Anniversary of the Consecration and Coronation of His Majesty the Emperor

23 July: Anniversary of the Acclamation of the Majority of His Majesty the Emperor

4 September: Anniversary of the Marriage of Their Imperial Majesties

15 October: The Day of the August Name of Her Majesty the Empress

19 October: The Day of the August Name of His Majesty the Emperor

26 December: Festive Season[6]

In 1846 Dom Pedro ordered that his public audiences should be transferred to São Cristóvão, where they took place on Saturdays from then on.[7] On 1 January 1857 a printed sheet announced the list of the gala days when the emperor would receive for the presentation of compliments at the Quinta da Boa Vista. People had to dress according to the norms established in 1840 and appear between five and seven in the afternoon.[8] By 1864 twenty-four of

the monarchy's thirty-five ceremonies were to take place at the Boa Vista,
nine in the City Palace, and two at the Ajuda monastery.

Access to the emperor thus became more difficult, given the distance
from the city to the far-off neighborhood, though the trip between the two
palaces was eased in 1847 by Rio's police chief, who tried to set up one-way
streets in the growing city:

> Chaises, carriages, tilburies, and carts should go in only one direction,
> and for this purpose I will lay down some streets they should go up,
> and others they should come down . . . I would not dare put such a
> measure into practice without asking if Your Excellency would first do
> me the honor of laying it before the August Presence of his Majesty
> the Emperor . . . so that he may choose the streets by which he would
> come into the city, and those by which he would leave for the Imper-
> ial [City] Palace and give the orders for the execution of these mea-
> sures . . . My aim is above all to facilitate His August Majesty's
> journey.[9]

In any case, by the mid-1870s access to São Cristóvão was easy. Rio's first
horse-drawn streetcar was inaugurated in 1868, and this form of transport
quickly spread through the city. (There were four streetcar companies: Botanical Garden, São Cristóvão, Vila Isabel, and Carris Urbanos, whose routes
were identified by written signs and a differently colored lantern for each

This daguerreotype, dated
1840, is generally considered
Brazil's first and is attributed
to Louis Compte. But it
must actually have been
taken in the 1850s, since the
City Palace has a flower
border that did not exist in
the previous decade. From
Vasquez, *Dom Pedro II e a
fotografia.*

line. The streetcars or *bonds* [modern Brazilian Portuguese *bondes*, from the bonds issued by the companies when they started] were popularly known as milk cows [*vacas de leite*], because like cows they had bells, and tortoises [*jabutis*], because of their shape.)

Programs were printed and distributed in profusion for all the major celebrations, which were always connected to the imperial family, epitome of the forces of civilization in Brazil. A great deal of money was spent on these occasions. Platforms, temporary walkways, and pavilions were lavishly decorated with works of art. At Princess Isabel's christening, more than eight contos were spent just on the construction and decoration of a walkway in Palace Square to the imperial chapel.[10] The funeral expenses for Prince Afonso reached almost thirteen contos.[11] And after the ceremonies objects that were no longer of any use were sent to the palace storehouses. Bought with public money, they now belonged to the imperial household. It was difficult to keep complete control over this new patrimony. In 1846, after the celebrations for the christening of Prince Afonso, several carpets and globes that had decorated the palanquin erected in Constitution Square "walked." When the steward's department had to explain this to the treasury, the only solution was to say that the objects had simply been damaged beyond repair.[12]

The City Palace and the imperial chapel continued as ceremonial backdrops until the end of the empire. But none of the imperial routines were completely cut and dried. The City Palace was also a stage for imperial amusements: sometimes the emperor let guests and artists lodge on the ground floor; some—the Austrian sculptor Pettich, the French painter Biard, and the Neapolitan Cicarelli are usually mentioned—even set up their workshops there. (It was said that when the palace was being repaired, a walled-up skeleton once appeared in one of the rooms, creating a buzz, but it turned out that a painter who had had his studio there had used the skeleton for anatomical study.) And as we have seen, Dom Pedro II authorized sessions of the Historical and Geographical Institute to take place there for a while, as well as the School of Medicine. In addition, some of the officials appointed to functions in the imperial household lived in the palace by grace and favor of the monarch. In 1878 the scribe of the nobility, Aleixo Boulanger, who also had the post of king at arms, requested that the emperor permit him to lodge in the palace, as he was in financial difficulty.[13]

It is not easy to give a reliable account of the appearance, internal divisions, functions, and material wealth of Brazil's imperial palaces, for the opinions and descriptions of travelers, diplomats, and contemporaries, as of later visitors and researchers, are contradictory. It was common—especially among foreign visitors—to find the palaces lacking in any charm, yet other witnesses praised their solidity and refinement. An inventory of the City Palace in 1859 describes everything in each area of the palace and gives the sequence of rooms: "The throne room, the anteroom for the canopy, the canopy room, the anteroom for the candle, the candle room (where one was always kept alight), the red room, the big yellow room, the blue room for foreigners"—all faced the square on the northern side. Then the new rooms: "dining room number 1, room 2, 3, 4, 5, 6, 7, and 8; the grandees' room, the chamberlains' room, the ladies' room, the room for official business," and others.[14]

But for all the doubts about its appearance, the City Palace was the backdrop preferred by the monarchy. Its imposing structure symbolized the power of royalty, and its central position in the city was synonymous with the monarchy's radiating power.

It was a wonderful present. Dom João "willingly" accepted the *palacete* in the far-off neighborhood of São Cristóvão* that had been built in a huge park there by the merchant Elias Antônio Lopes. In 1817 it became the property of the state and the residence of the royal family. Considered at the time as the "best and most spacious of all existing constructions," as one priest called it, it was ample enough to lodge, without undue constriction, Dom João himself, his widowed daughter Dona Maria Teresa, his grandson Dom Sebastião, and his sons Dom Pedro and Dom Miguel as well as many officials of the royal household and courtiers. (Carlota Joaquina, his queen, preferred to go on living in a big house in Botafogo.) The palace was far from the center of Rio, but on the other hand, its situation was cool and airy, and the prince, later emperor, enjoyed a more countrified and private life there; he appeared at the City Palace only for commemorative events and ceremonies. From the Quinta da Boa Vista, looking over toward Caju, one could see the sea, and in another direction the forest of Tijuca and the Corcovado. The family's affection for the place became a tradition. Dom Pedro I always lived there, and Dom Pedro II was born there: it continued as the official residence of the monarchs until the end of the empire.

*The area gets its name from a chapel, dedicated to Saint Christopher, built in the early seventeenth century.

The palace was impressive from the outside. Travelers of this period described it as an enclosed square, with an inner courtyard, a veranda on three sides, and glazed windows protecting the inhabitants from the excessive heat. It underwent various alterations and was extended when Dom Pedro I bought—with money from the public purse—further lands belonging to the donor's heirs. The facade was yellow, with white moldings.

At the very start Dom João—recently accustomed to "British protection"—acquired sumptuous iron gates made in England. The architect John Johnston who came to install them was also charged with enlarging the palace; he planned neo-Gothic towers at each corner, but he managed to build only one, on the north side, with three bedrooms and two living rooms. A large square was also laid out in front of the palace.

When the empire was established, the famed architect and decorator Manuel da Cunha made extensive changes to make the building look more like a palace.[15] In 1827 Dom Pedro I decided to proceed with Johnston's project, and under the direction of a Frenchman, Pierre Joseph (usually known as Pedro José) Pezerat, a tower was built on the south side. The style changed, however: this tower was neoclassical; several of its five living rooms and waiting room, like the Chinese room and the boudoir, were used by the empress Amélia. In 1845, while Dom Pedro II was in the southern provinces, other changes, overseen by Manuel de Araújo Porto Alegre, enlarged the building and made its style more uniform. (Porto Alegre, who had become an official of the imperial household, also painted, and many of his works decorated the palace walls.) More important alterations came in 1857–61; Mário Bragaldi sumptuously painted and decorated the imperial family's rooms in the south tower as well as the throne rooms, the counsel rooms, and the room used for the diplomatic corps (the foreigners' or ambassadors' room), for many aspects of Brazil's politics and high society were now centered here. And Dom Pedro still received his subjects on the veranda in weekly public audiences.[16]

Accounts of the palace's interior decorations, as with the building itself, vary in their opinions about its luxury or decorum, its refinement or simplicity. One can see, though, that there was a certain insistence on keeping the image modest, showing an emperor removed from comforts and material wealth and fond of more intimate rooms where he could be among his beloved hobbies: the library; the upper glass-roofed terraces where G. Dolond's telescope was set up; the so-called Emperor's Museum, where he kept a collection started by his mother, Leopoldina, of numismatic, mineralogical, archaeological, and anthropological objects old and new from all corners of the globe; and a handsome modern study. Dom Pedro also had an herbarium with specimens of wood types, plants, flowers, and fruit, known as his "botany study."

In the vast properties around the palace, roads were built—numbered ones, as well as the Alley Road, the Emperor's Road, the Crown Gate, Sant'Ana's Road, Custódio Road, the Park Road, Joana's Stream. The kitchen, linen room, infirmary, and pharmacy were behind the palace, where the slaves who worked in them were kept at arm's length. Houses large and small

The Sâo Cristóvão Palace (Quinta da Boa Vista) at the time of Dom Pedro II's childhood. MMP

The São Cristóvão Palace in the 1880s. Drawing by Lavasseur, based on a photograph by Marc Ferrez, 1889.

were built, a hospital, a school, all directly linked to the emperor. Palace servants and their families lived there, greater or lesser officials, court members, and people with no fixed role who were simply the emperor's protégés.

On Sundays, access to this so-called noble area was open and free: anyone could walk on the palace grounds even if they had no connection with the royal family or its entourage.[17] There were plenty of attractions. Dom Pedro II invested in projects to improve and beautify the landscape as soon as he came back from his first journey abroad, in 1871. He paid a great deal of money to the French landscape gardener Auguste Glaziou so that he could enjoy his garden and give Rio its own Bois de Boulogne, and a handsome park took over from the tangled jungle vegetation. Where an irregular, narrow road had once led to the palace, now an imposing avenue of strictly aligned sapucaia trees took the visitor to the emperor's presence. Princess Isabel herself, remembering the gardens of the Quinta with their mango trees and tamarinds, described another "superb avenue of bamboos, whose tops met so high up they looked like a cathedral roof."[18] But this chic did not last forever: although Glaziou stayed on with a fat salary as director of parks and gardens until the end of the empire, in the 1880s the garden was reported as poorly maintained—like everything else surrounding the emperor at that time.

The comfort of the palace notwithstanding, the emperor was often away from it. In the 1860s he had a full calendar.[19] After lunch—always eaten in a hurry—he usually went to an educational or research establishment or to the Academy of Fine Arts for its lessons and exams; he visited barracks, warships, and hospitals; he appeared at concerts, at the theater, and at dances and dinners, often accompanied by the empress; every Thursday they dined at Princess Isabel's home.

On ordinary days the emperor was escorted by horse guards provided by the First Cavalry Regiment. This detachment, lodged in the Quinta and always on call, was commanded by a captain, with a lieutenant, a sublieutenant, two cadets (outriders), twenty-four privates, and a bugler. When the empress departed with her husband, they went in two coaches; in the first the royal couple, with a chamberlain and the courtier on duty, and in the second the ladies-in-waiting. The outriders went first, clearing the way; other officials followed, with the privates and the bugler, continuously playing a march. When the emperor went out on his own, there were only half a dozen privates. It was impossible not to see this procession as it passed through the streets.

The imperial couple's bathing trips were more discreet. In the early morning and without the company of the duty courtier, they went to Caju point, where they had a small house backing onto the beach. There the cadets and the six privates—the small detachment, even though the empress was there—stayed at the entrance, and the captain accompanied the pair to the sea.

The opulent furnishings of the palace were carefully listed in the inventories of the imperial household and in the lists of auctions of the São Cristóvão Palace that took place after the family was banished at the end of the empire. By then the air of negligence, of a certain abandonment, and of melancholy was clear: the imperial family was no longer the only center of attention. But the building itself was indestructible. For seven decades and through three generations, the monarchy turned its private living quarters into a visible symbol that became more and more imposing, solid, and grandiose.

When Dom João arrived in Rio in 1808, he was installed in the City Palace and later moved to the Quinta da Boa Vista. But there was also another property put at his disposal for his private use: the Fazenda de Santa Cruz. This plantation, about forty miles southwest of the city, had been founded by the Jesuits, then confiscated and incorporated into the goods of the Portuguese crown in 1759, when the Order was banned by the marquis of Pombal and its priests were expelled from Brazil. It was not exactly a palace, but it was enormous. The property occupied an immense area, from the islands of Guaraqueçaba and Itinguçu to the Mata-Cães range in Vassouras, where one could see endless country bathed by the River Guandu and its tributaries; it also bordered on Guaratiba, Marapicu, and Mangaratiba.[20]

Sea, beaches, jungle, plains, hills, mountains—the Jesuits' work came on top of nature's wealth: they made the plantation into a model of rationality, social harmony, and profitability. Hydraulic engineering transformed marshy fields into fertile pasture. More than eleven thousand head of cattle were distributed among twenty-two centers; there were thoroughbred horses, goats, sheep for wool, birds, and other domestic animals, rich in variety as well as numbers. It had fish farms and several kinds of workshops—a flour mill, a brickyard, a lime kiln, a locksmith, a carpentry shop, a spinning mill, a goldsmith. Something of everything happened here. The land was shared with twenty-six tenants who had small properties on the plantation, and there was a village of Carijó Indians, administered by the priests.

There were also many, many slaves (sixteen hundred at the time when the Jesuits were expelled), who were treated rather unusually, according to ac-

The Fazenda de Santa Cruz. Watercolor by Jean-Baptiste Debret, 1818.
CGJM

counts of the place. They worked three days for the priests and another three on their own plots and animals; Sunday was a day of rest and, of course, Mass. The slaves were responsible for their own sustenance; each family head could pasture up to ten head of cattle. They lived in houses built in groups on either side of the monastery; these became two villages with streets, alleys, and passageways that converged on the square in front of the monastery itself. Punishments were fixed by established norms, and priests who broke the rules were not exempt from them;[21] good conduct was rewarded. (Many slaves fled, however, and formed runaway communities, called *quilombos*, in the immense jungle lands of the plantation.) They had well-equipped hospital facilities and a pharmacy. Their own culture could find expression only in the diminished space permitted by the insistent, disciplined, rigid teachings and Catholic practices administered daily by the priests.

The house the Jesuits built for their own living quarters was a solid, simply proportioned monastery, but they lavished care and expense on the chapel: on the altar, a mechanism in the shape of a shell that could be opened and shut during the ceremonies caused a sensation.

> They ordered a large hollow sphere of light wood to be constructed that opens and shuts in two halves held together by a cord at the back, their surfaces painted green and decorated with gold stars, the edges adorned with golden rays. The moment the priests arrived at the altar,

this magnificent shell would open, and the Holy Sacrament would be revealed, splendidly housed in a rich monstrance illuminated by seventy-two wax candles spread all around the steps of the throne![22]

A large wooden cross placed on the square in front of the monastery gave its name to the plantation and the region. Around it, the Day of the Holy Cross was celebrated annually in May.

> For this festival, the perimeter of this eloquent monument was lit from above by hundreds of lanterns and torches; there were most lively popular dances, profane and religious songs. This took place in the church and, at night, in front of the imposing symbol of redemption. Time has not expunged this custom; the feast day of the Holy Cross is still celebrated nowadays on the appropriate date in May.[23]

The most curious thing about the Fazenda de Santa Cruz was that the Jesuits there trained adolescent slaves, both boys and girls, in sacred music: they sang in choirs, played instruments, and became music teachers themselves. Because of the high quality of their performances, these musicians and the Conservatory of Santa Cruz became famous.

For fifty years—from the expulsion of the Jesuits to the royal family's arrival in Brazil—the plantation had been decaying and stagnating. An initiative to transform Santa Cruz into a model tea plantation, using Chinese laborers brought from Macao, did not succeed.[24] It never regained the smooth efficiency and profitability of its earlier years. There was a drastic reduction in the number of cattle compared with the time of the Jesuits, only

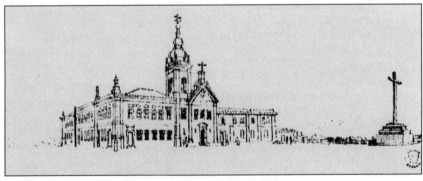

The Cross at the Fazenda. Drawing by Maria Graham, 1823. MB

four thousand head during the imperial period. The plantation never achieved its immense potential because of insoluble administrative inefficiencies. But the music teachers carried on as best they could, continuing their traditions; this was "the first establishment in which music was seriously cultivated, so much so that notable virtuosos were educated there: not only instrumentalists but singers suitable for all religious ceremonies and for singing in opera."[25]

The Conservatory was given further encouragement by Dom João VI— Portuguese kings had a musical tradition—and the whole plantation took on a new momentum. In 1817 the building was renovated and given bigger rooms and valuable paintings; the chapel was redecorated for orchestral and choral concerts, all according to the taste and habits of Portuguese royal palaces. Then Santa Cruz became the summer residence of the royal, eventually imperial family. The festivities and ceremonies encouraged and mounted by Dom João became famous for their pomp and for their profusion of allegorical figures—processions and services in the refurbished chapel with rich tapestries in the palace windows, lights, fireworks, salvos, rockets, and of course a great deal of music. The traditional May festival and that of Our Lady of the Conception in November stood out. Particularly memorable events included the day in 1818 when Dom João heard that the Pernambucan revolution of that year had been suppressed, the Corpus Christi procession in 1819, and Holy Week in 1820.

In 1822, Maria Graham, an English traveler, was astonished by the magnificent view of the wide plains with their cattle, grazing between clumps of virgin jungle; the horizon extended on one side to the sea, on the other to the hills and mountains. "The palace itself is on the site of the old Jesuits' School. Three modern wings: the fourth contains the beautiful chapel of the reverend fathers, and a few adequate rooms. The new part was built by King João VI, but the work was interrupted when he left. The rooms are beautiful and comfortably furnished. In this climate, the tapestries and wallpapers, whether made of silk or paper, are liable to rapid decay because of the damp and insects."[26] She was also impressed by the plaster decorations on the walls, with cornices and decorative bands, by the friezes painted with beautiful designs and arabesques, by the paintings of local fruits, flowers, birds, and insects: "all done by mulatto and black artists."

Dom João VI, who loved Gregorian chant and was not so fond of the Baroque tradition followed by the Jesuits, was delighted by the orchestra and the slave singers: he was "amazed and indescribably happy when he found, in the famous Conservatory of the Jesuits, a chapel with a choir such as there had never been in Brazil; the same was true of the gentlemen, nobles and distinguished musicians who accompanied him." (He made Gregorian chant a subject of study in the São Joaquim Seminary, too. This was abolished later by Dom Pedro I, who replaced it with lessons in geography, French, and elocution, more useful, in his opinion, than the "royal singing classes.")[27]

The slave musicians spent a great deal of time on theoretical study and practice under the guidance of teachers like the musician, composer, and conductor José Maurício—a mulatto priest known as the "Brazilian Mozart"—who inspired the envy and respect of Marcos Portugal, Dom João's honored music teacher from his time in Lisbon. The first music teachers in Rio de Janeiro also came from the Conservatory, like Salvador José (José Maurício's teacher); and black singers like Joaquim Manuel, known for his performances of the famous songs called *modinhas*, became famous.

As soon as he heard the Santa Cruz orchestra and choir, Dom João requisitioned the first violinist, the clarinetist, and the bassoonist, and the singers Maria da Exaltação, Sebastiana, and Matildes, to join the orchestra at the royal chapel of the São Cristóvão Palace. The plantation thus gained a new vocation: it began to train slave musicians for the imperial palaces. The emperors followed this custom, and musicians from Santa Cruz were regularly transferred to the orchestra, choir, or band at the São Cristóvão Palace and the imperial chapel.

With the departures of Dom João VI and later Dom Pedro I, and with the disappearance of the famous teachers who had given it such brilliance during the first two decades of the century, the Conservatory lost some of its luster. But the reorganization of one band, originally created in 1818 and later called the Imperial Plantation Music Band, brought some popularity back to the musicians of Santa Cruz.[28]

When the emperors stayed at the plantation, the band played for them every day, and the musicians also played at São Cristóvão for solemn occasions and receptions. When they were asked, and when they got the requisite authorization from the plantation's administrator, the group went around to every corner of the province playing at ceremonies, parties, and dances. In 1856, they took part in the Festival of the Divine Holy Spirit in Itaguaí, playing for ten days. They went to Valença, Campo Grande, Marapicu, Realengo, São Pedro e São Paulo, Maxambomba, and elsewhere, too.

The band also looked good. When it was reorganized, the players exchanged the jacket and trousers of their old uniform for shiny new attire:

blue, with a kepi of the same color, red trimmings, and gold stripes and buttons. The polished black belt had gold buckles (changed to silver in 1888). In 1841 the band played at a dance given by Dom Pedro II in the City Palace, and according to the description of an American naval officer, the musicians' uniforms were "very dashing": "Finally, the court chamberlain, with his little gold-tipped stick, gave the sign, and at the end of the room a band of thirteen or fourteen black musicians, in red velvet clothes adorned and striped with gold lace, began to play a lively waltz."[29]

They played everything: fiddles, violas, cellos, clarinets, flutes, bassoons, trombones, trumpets, cornets, recorders, bass drums, ophicleides, fifes, and baritone and bass horns. They played military and patriotic marches, waltzes, *modinhas*, and quadrilles, operas, too, the favorites of Pedro II and Teresa Cristina. The imperial household paid the bills: teaching manuals, scores, instruments, and accessories like strings, skins, reeds, keys, bows, and batons were ordered from the Casa Arthur Napoleão.

In the 1830s the band had thirty-six musicians: thirty instrumentalists and six female singers. In 1856 there was a master of music, four female singers, and twenty-two instrumentalists. The slave Antônio José, first flute, stood out at this time, and in 1860 Dom Pedro granted him his freedom "for his exquisite performances, which gave so much fame to the Plantation Band."[30] The emperor noted in his diary: "At the music lesson I heard an excellent flautist, a good cornet player, and a clarinetist who was not so good but passable. A female slave sang a rather shrill version of Elvira's beautiful aria from Act I of Verdi's *Ernani*. Sometimes the orchestral ensemble jars on the ears; but even then they are well advanced, and the master of music Joaquim de Araújo Cintra seems zealous." In 1867 Cintra gave the emperor a list "of the thirty-four slave musicians" on the plantation, noting what instruments they played and what their conduct had been like: "good, fair, rebellious," or even "drunken."

In 1887, according to the *Almanak Laemmert* of 1888, the thirty-one black musicians in the band regularly played at private balls in Rio, which were also enlivened by other groups of slave singers and instrumentalists. José de Alencar described a party in 1871 in the house of a rich plantation owner, in which nothing was missing, not even "the sound of the music of the blacks from the plantation, who played quadrilles and waltzes."[31]

Music was not the only activity at the Fazenda de Santa Cruz, however. Slave carpenters, masons, smiths, tanners, brick-makers, woodsmen, coopers, cowherds, cobblers, field-workers, foremen, nurses, weavers, basket-makers,

The black band made
up of slaves of Antônio
Luís de Almeida, 1870.
From Schnoor and
Castro, *Resgate.*

and midwives were divided into work "squads"—the system and the name went back to the Jesuits' time—and they made everything the plantation produced. During the imperial period—when the number of slaves increased notably, from 2,065 in 1834 to 2,128 in 1849 and 2,235 in 1855[32]—the slaves were no longer sharecroppers, as they had been in the Jesuits' time. They were now "dressed and fed at their own expense, and for this purpose have Saturdays, Sundays, and holy days free,"[33] but the children, who once had been maintained by the priests, were now the responsibility of their own families. In 1860 the emperor noted in his diary that the slaves were complaining of hunger: their free Saturdays and Sundays had been taken away in exchange for rations so that they could work for the plantation all week; the families of the runaways did not even get these rations.

The plantation had three "settlements" (*feitorias*), large areas of land rented out to third parties—Peri-Peri, Bom Jardim, and da Serra, or Santarém—which gave it a good income, and it had other rents and tributes, too. In 1875 more than seven hundred tenants were spread around Santa Cruz.

Always known as a cattle farm with good grazing, Santa Cruz never again had flocks or herds as large as it had had in the eighteenth century, but it rented out pasture and provided the animals for the imperial household; later a slaughterhouse produced more income. Money also came in from the planting of rice, coffee, and a little tea and from the brickyard, the storehouse, and the making of cane alcohol (*aguardente*), so even though inefficient and badly administered, the plantation made a profit.

The slaves themselves, as merchandise, were quite profitable, and they, too, were rented out, generally for three- or six-month periods, the price varying according to the specialty. In the 1860s, wood-turners produced most money, followed by brick-makers, plumbers, barbers, masons, carpenters, and kitchen help; the ones who brought in the least money were the street salesmen and the women.[34] And of course the Fazenda charged for the presence of their trained musicians at festivals and ceremonies, though when they played in the gardens, palaces, and other departments of the imperial household they were not paid. The emperor had the use of his slaves—they were part of his property—and while he could not sell them, he had the power to free them.

At Santa Cruz Dom Pedro II enjoyed the healthy air, but his visits to the plantation became less frequent after a new summer palace was built closer to Rio and in an even more pleasant climate, at the top of the Serra dos Órgãos—not only a new summer palace but a whole town. Then the heir to the throne, Dom Pedro Afonso, born in 1848, died at the Fazenda de Santa Cruz on 10 January 1850, when the family was in residence for the summer. After that, the emperor and empress were perhaps even less keen to frequent the place. Yet the religious rituals continued with or without the emperor. Parties and dances for the court were put on, too, more to the taste of Princess Isabel and the count d'Eu, whose palace was nearby.

Even after the emperor no longer spent the summer in Santa Cruz, he went there occasionally for short inspection trips, looking over the garden, the fields, the corrals, and the improvements, chatting with the tenants. He went to the "little field"—a kind of garden—tested the schoolchildren, listened to student musicians, looked at their instruments, drank milk, meandered through the rooms and salons of the main palace, and went to look at the sunset from the belvedere, where he could see the entire Marambaia beach on one side and, on the other, the vast plain. At night, he recorded in his diary, after listening to the drum that signaled curfew for the slaves, he drank some of the locally grown tea—"as good as the real Chinese article"—and lay down to read until he went to sleep.

"What a harebrained scheme! True, Brazil is about the only place it could be justified, since there's nothing more pleasant to do there than keep cool! That arid, mountainous place could never produce anything, even if they were to spend as much as Louis XIV did on Versailles!"[35] This was what the French diplomat Jules Itier thought of the imperial household's plan to build a palace in the "alpine" region of the province of Rio de Janeiro. Itier knew the place because in 1844, when he passed through Brazil, he went to the Serra da Estrela to a place called Córrego Seco (dry stream). His impressions were understandable, for at the Córrego Seco plantation in the hills, there was nothing more than the typical natural setting of a tropical mountain range, with a few light touches of a temperate climate. Nonetheless, a lot of money was spent and a great deal of mental energy expended on populating this region and making a palace for the emperor, his family, and friends.

The district was famous for a few extensive, isolated plantations, like Padre Correa's, where Dom Pedro I had stayed from time to time—he had wanted to buy it, but its heir had been unwilling to sell. It was also where a mule road (later the Union and Industry Road) passed to Minas Gerais.

In 1830 the emperor bought the Córrego Seco plantation for about 20,000 mil-réis (twenty contos) with the object of building a summer palace there: the cool mountain air would be a change from the sultry humidity of Rio in the hot season. But after his abdication in 1831 and his death in 1834, when people to whom Dom Pedro I owed money had to go to court in both Europe and Brazil to get their money back, the plantation, now valued at 13,974 mil-réis, was assigned to the late monarch's creditors to cover the debts recognized in his will. In 1840, when Dom Pedro II achieved his majority, questions about the inventory there and the division of the spoils were still dragging through the courts. Eventually the Brazilian government paid over the value of the plantation, incorporated it into the national patrimony, and declared it the property of Dom Pedro II and his successors. "The Legislative Assembly authorizes the use of up to 14,000 mil-réis to redeem the plantation of Córrego Seco, at the top of the road to the Serra da Estrela, which in the inventory of the late emperor was to be given to creditors. The said plantation will belong to His Majesty the Emperor and his successors, and incorporated into the National Property." Public and private spheres thus provided mutual assistance: the true mark of a monarchical regime.

In 1843 the steward's office of the imperial household began to administer Córrego Seco. In the intervening time the land had been rented out to third parties. It may be that the chief steward, Paulo Barbosa, who had been in his post since 1833, had already been planning for the plantation, because he presented an entire plan of action already approved by the young emperor on 16 March. Barbosa himself later explained that the need was for a palace where their majesties could flee from invasions of either diseases or enemies. Despite the resistance of conservatives who did not want to break with the tradition of imperial summers at the Fazenda de Santa Cruz—so much closer to

"The court has moved to Petrópolis; our imperial lord and master has gone to get some fresh air." Ângelo Agostini, in *Revista Ilustrada*, 1881. IEB

Rio de Janeiro—Dom Pedro II plunged enthusiastically into this daring, seductive enterprise. The dream of the father became reality in the hands of the son.

The place was called, at Barbosa's suggestion, Petrópolis: "I remembered Petersburg, Peter's city, went to the Greek language, found a city with this name in the archipelago, and since the emperor was Dom Pedro, I thought the name would be well suited."[36] (He might also have remembered José Bonifácio's proposal in 1823 for a new capital for the empire in the Brazilian interior, which would be called Brasilea or Petropole.)[37]

The plan was for the plantation to be leased to the engineer Major Frederico Koeler for 1,000 mil-réis a year (a very generous price, for the previous tenant had paid 1,800 mil-réis); he would separate off one area for building a palace for the emperor with annexes and gardens; another area for a town, whose properties would be rented to private individuals; and a third area for a church dedicated to Saint Pedro de Alcântara—of whom the monarch was a devotee—and a cemetery.

As well as being the tenant, Major Koeler became the plantation's superintendent, subject to orders of the chief steward. As it happened, Major Koeler and Paulo Barbosa were fellow members of the imperial engineers' corps and good friends. Koeler was also charged with the public works of the provincial government. To populate this empty area, an agricultural colony of the province of Rio de Janeiro had been proposed, and Koeler was also made its director. The provincial president of Rio was then Aureliano Coutinho, who also facilitated the arrival of the German settlers and the maintenance of the colony. Together with Barbosa, Aureliano exercised an enormous influence on Dom Pedro II and the political development of

Brazil, for they were the so-called palace faction, forcing the majority in 1840. It seems Petrópolis was created at the behest of these two men, who relied on Koeler to carry out their project. Koeler was also charged with building the road going to the mountains. Within this powerful triangle, then—the imperial household, the provincial government, and the administration of the plantation and colony—the major-engineer had the means to develop the project.

As Petrópolis began to take shape, everything happened in a hurry. Where there had been nothing, suddenly a town had appeared, and an 1844 decree of the government of the province of Rio created the district of Petrópolis in the parish of São José do Rio Preto and the area of Paraíba do Sul. The first land allocations were demarcated in 1844, and some time limits for rentals were set. Dom Pedro II assigned lots to "certain men made notable by services rendered the state," making sure he got the neighbors he wanted.[38]

The first settlers were all German immigrants who had come to Brazil originally to work on the road. They built their houses, planted their gardens, and gave a real identity to Petrópolis. Their duties and rights were quite clear: they had use of the land, but it remained state-owned. Their travel expenses had been advanced by the province but had to be repaid. "They received land by the system of lease, in which they were to pay a perpetual *emphyteusis* [an inheritable rent] of 5 mil-réis annually, every January forever (this payment was to begin some time—up to nine years—after the contract came into effect); they could sell the property, paying 2.5 percent of its value to the imperial household; the new owner would then, in his turn, pay perpetual *emphyteusis*. If they failed to respect the contract, tenants could be ejected and their lands returned to the emperor." (Right up to the present day, the inhabitants of the central area of Petrópolis and of the neighborhoods of Quitandinha, Mosela, and Itamarati pay to the Companhia Imobiliária de Petrópolis, which belongs to the Orléans e Bragança family, a perpetual rent equivalent to 2.5 percent of the value of the property. In 1975 the company had 26,385 leaseholds, and there was an annual average of 1,000–1,500 property sales.)[39]

Those who lived on the plantation were also extended credit to buy cattle, goats, chickens, and pigs; they had to pay off debts within three years. Ships continued to arrive from Europe, the families went on growing, and in 1859 the German population was 3,300. The imperial property also grew with the purchase of neighboring plantations, like Quitandinha, Itamarati, and Morro Queimado. In 1853 the plantation had 1,218 leaseholds.

The Germans were not the only ones working on the roads, heaving stones and planks, and putting up the walls of Dom Pedro II's palace: slaves from the Fazenda de Santa Cruz, from the house of correction, and from the naval arsenal were also there from the beginning, though they were not counted among the personnel since they were the property of the site itself. A report from Koeler in 1845 attests that "His Majesty's slaves who came from Santa Cruz, 16 women, 17 men, and 6 children, arrived here completely without clothes."[40] In 1853 there were forty, and the eldest got a weekly gratuity of 320 réis. Free Africans in Petrópolis, at the same time, numbered more than twenty, and they were included in the aforementioned personnel, together with the Germans, making an overall total of ninety-six.[41]

Among the commercial establishments that soon began to be set up on the Rua do Imperador, there stood out a slave market to supply local needs. As inevitable as the slaves were the runaways and their settlements (*quilombos*), one of which became famous: the Quilombo da Vargem Grande. Another, farther inland in the area of São José do Rio Preto, left its name—Quilombo—behind.

Three years after the blueprint for the construction of the emperor's city was drawn up, a major scandal erupted. José Maria Velho da Silva succeeded Paulo Barbosa, who was removed and sent to Europe, while Major Koeler, accused of fraud, was dismissed from his post as director of the colony by the provincial government. (Not long afterward he died in an accident.) Up to 1847, the year of his death, he had spent two hundred contos on the construction of a quarter of the palace, an amount considered excessive. Koeler was followed by Ribeiro Cirne (1847–53); an engineer, José Maria Rabelo; and finally Vicente Marques Lisboa. And the project went full steam ahead.

In the summer of 1849–50 the family went back to Santa Cruz, but after the death of Dom Pedro's son there in January 1850 they spent their summers in the mountains. It was also in 1850 that yellow fever seriously attacked the capital, and those who had the means fled into the hills, as the emperor did. Apart from offering the pleasures of living near the royal family, Petrópolis became a place to escape the annual epidemics.

In 1846 Petrópolis became a parish in its own right, under the name of Saint Pedro de Alcântara, attached to the town of Estrela and municipality of Magé. Then, skipping a rung in the promotion ladder, for it was never made a town, it was made a municipality in 1857, with its own council. However, in the centralized state that was Brazil, it was like any other town, a cog in the monarchical machine, and had no juridical autonomy. It could make decisions only with the approval of the provincial government, which was tied in its turn to the central government that appointed the provincial president.

Ground plans of Petrópolis,
1846 and 1854. MIP

"With no financial resources, and rigorously supervised, municipal autonomy was merely decorative, the only exception being the direct election of
councilors . . . but since the emperor was always concerned about this 'apple
of his eye,' which he never abandoned, he always found provincial funds so
that the town never went short."[42] (It is worth remembering that voting was a
jealously guarded privilege: when Petrópolis became a city, it had six voters!)

Going up into the mountains from Rio gradually became less of a struggle, and traffic there increased: people and animals carried seeds, building
materials, and furniture. On foot, or on the backs of donkeys or slaves, on
horseback or in carts, everything went up to this new city specially built for the
emperor's delight and protection. At first it took more than four hours to get
there. But slowly the situation improved, especially after the arrival of rail-
roads. The first line was laid across the low-lying areas and then, in 1884, another one going up the mountains to Petrópolis. One took a boat across the
bay from Prainha—at the Pharoux Quay, right opposite the City Palace—and

in little more than an hour reached the harbor later called Porto Mauá; the eleven miles from there to the foot of the mountains was a journey that took about an hour by train. The third, two-hour stage, uphill, was done by stage-coach or carriage, with a stop to change animals in the middle of the journey, until the train came, when the trip became much quicker. The Union and In-dustry Line, which went to Juiz de Fora, eased transportation throughout the whole area.

The large and imposing palace grew, wing by wing, and was almost fin-ished in 1856, when Paulo Barbosa had returned to the stewardship. The ex-ternal architecture, planned by Koeler and Bonini, and the interior, by Porto Alegre, Guilhobel, and Rabelo, delighted Brazilians as well as foreign visi-tors, who felt less out of place in such surroundings.

In general, according to Norbert Elias, the most visible result of the inter-action between a kingdom's greatness and a court's splendor is the monarch's home.[43] And in Brazil, the new palace was no different. It was solidly con-structed, with hardwood supports; the entrance hall impressed visitors with its black and white floor of Belgian and Carrara marble and its two Greek columns at the back. The best Brazilian woods were used for the other deco-rative floors, doors, door frames, and windows: cedar, jacaranda, *peroba*, sat-inwood, and rosewood. The metalwork was of the highest quality. The molded stucco ceilings displayed a profusion of symbols and motifs. In this department, Porto Alegre—known for introducing Brazilian motifs into painting and architecture—went to town: amid the European classical mod-els and the symbols of the imperial family (the crown, the emperor's initials, the Bragança dragons) there appear pineapples, cashew-fruit, *araçás*, Brazil cherries (*pitangas*), and guavas. In the imperial couple's bedroom, painted poppies helped to lull their majesties to sleep.

The park and the gardens were laid out by the Frenchman Jean-Baptiste Binot, who decided to introduce, as well as Brazilian varieties, Australian palms, Indian cedars, *incensos*, and Madagascan trees. There was an aviary with rare foreign birds, and it was one of the emperor's hobbies to look after them. And the buildings for the gentlemen-in-waiting, other officials, and ser-vants, for the kitchen, stables, and lodgings, for all the infrastructure to main-tain and run the palace were in back, out of sight of anyone coming in the front door.

The building works, finished around 1850, added one more facet to Dom Pedro II's public image. Pedro's town, which one could see from afar as one approached, thanks to the neo-Gothic cathedral rising out of the tropical jun-

The Rua do
Imperador at
Petrópolis; a slave is
in the foreground.
H. Klumb, 1862. MIP

gle, was a palace in the woods; it became the emperor's favorite place, and he
missed no opportunity to escape to it: "Tomorrow we are going to Petrópolis
to open a new hospital and lay a stone in the new church. I will take advantage of the journey and stay a few days in my beloved city. I will be back on
Monday, between 9 and 10. The afternoon is free. At 3 p.m. I will go and see
the works for the Dom Pedro II railway. At 10 p.m. I want to go back to
Petrópolis, and only come back the next day for the reception at the palace."[44]
The emperor spent a total of forty summers at Petrópolis, during the vaca-
tions of the Chamber and Senate.

The Fazenda de Santa Cruz, the emperor's favorite property in his youth,
lost its position. Dom Pedro's principal residence continued to be the São
Cristóvão Palace, but he paid little attention to that great building, which remained unchanged. Its gloomy aspect had links with Dom Pedro's childhood
and his father's brief reign. The City Palace, too, became increasingly a place
for official engagements only, for audiences on Wednesdays and Fridays, while
Petrópolis had more and more attention paid to it. In the list of expenses for
1858, prepared by Paulo Barbosa, we can see its importance:

Imperial wardrobe	9,467 mil-réis
Their Majesties the Emperor and Empress	8,459 mil-réis
Her Highness the Princess Leopoldina	8,100 mil-réis
Expenses and food, City Palace	4,932 mil-réis
São Cristóvão Palace	92,849 mil-réis
Works and repairs	58,445 mil-réis
Imperial coaches	100,894 mil-réis

Books, printed matter, gold, diamonds, theaters	36,335 mil-réis
Fazenda de Santa Cruz	26,426 mil-réis
Petrópolis	199,002 mil-réis[45]

To offset the large amount of money that had been spent on the construction of the palace and the imperial family's annual stays there, there was the rental income—in 1849 7,699 mil-réis, in 1851 9,134 mil-réis, and in 1853 11,766—and money made in the workshops, selling excess material (roof tiles, zinc, and the like). It is interesting that in some of the balance sheets, like that for the period from January 1845 to June 1848 and again in 1882, expenses and income were recorded as being exactly the same. But expenses to maintain these symbols of monarchy were, in the logic of court society, inherent in its very existence; in this sense, there was no such thing as luxury or waste. This is how Ernesto de V. Magalhães, in a letter to his friend Paulo Barbosa in 1851, described the town:

> I don't want to finish this letter without speaking a little about your Petrópolis, which for me is also Paulópolis . . . Where you once saw puddles, now there are only beautiful streets, with shops, butchers, magnificent hotels, the palace on the hill, which makes a lovely sight, principally when the emperor is there, because the court always comes to welcome him. Groups of ladies, fireworks, a festival atmosphere that does the heart good. At the Bragança Hotel or the Swiss Hotel were several people who had come from Rio de Janeiro and wanted to be presented to the emperor. All this together gives a European impression . . . In the summer, if you're not quick off the mark, you won't find houses to rent. The whole court is here . . . the imperial family has nowadays exchanged Santa Cruz for Petrópolis.[46]

With the distribution of plots of land around the palace, diplomats and Brazilian politicians began to build their own *palacetes* in Petrópolis, tired as they were of the hotels. In the 1860s a few score mansions for *carioca* nobility had already been built for the barons, marquises, and viscounts who "in the season" chose the town as the proper place for political meetings and social dances. It became a kind of European town, where people thought they lived as if they were "in the civilized world." During the season it was soirées and boring politics in Rio de Janeiro; during the holidays there were the fresh breezes and mountain air of Petrópolis. If it hadn't been for the black servants and slaves and the German immigrants, one might have thought one was in a new Europe. The French diplomat Arthur de Gobineau, on his first visit, was surprised by the dark hue of the empress's ladies-in-waiting. Yet the slaves stayed in the background in Petrópolis — naturally enough in a court that kept looking at itself in a European mirror.

Gradually, the emperor's time in Petrópolis with his family extended beyond the height of summer; they spent more than five months a year in the mountains. In the 1880s, when he was ill, he hardly left it. And every time the imperial family returned, the people of Petrópolis awaited their arrival in a festive mood. The town council organized a welcome, beginning with a commission appointed to collect a sum by subscription to take care of the expenses. Bands played, houses were decorated, and there were fireworks. Before the railway, people went to greet the imperial carriages at the top of the road, and when he came into Petrópolis, the emperor was given the keys of the city. There were processions, cheering crowds, damask quilts hung out the windows, carpets of flowers, a Te Deum in the cathedral.[47] More elements were added later: arches made of green branches over the streets, rustic musical instruments, serenades.[48]

In Petrópolis as in São Cristóvão, only a thin line marked the boundary between the emperor's private and public lives. In the architecture of the palace itself, public life had a prominent place, with the fine salons on the ground floor to receive diplomats and senators in elaborate ceremonies. New rituals were introduced: the emperor, always with frock coat and the insignia of the Orders of the Southern Cross and the Golden Fleece, accompanied by the chamberlain or a liveried servant, appeared in town on daily walks, trips to the station, and visits to schools and baths. Public acts took on an air of being the personal decisions of the emperor, and the town responded. As the symbolic center of society, Dom Pedro II made his own habits those of the court, and his influence spread out to affect all those who came to him in search of prestige and political support.

Petrópolis soon had good hotels, theaters, restaurants, beer halls, pastry shops, billiard halls, hairdressers and barbers, a hospital, musical societies, a church and smaller chapels, chic shops, baths, good schools, and fine houses. Breweries and textile factories flourished. In February 1859 the newspaper O Paraíba commented:

Petrópolis is becoming a livelier place. Emigration from the capital is growing day by day; houses are rented, the hotels are full, and amuse-

The Petrópolis Palace. IHGB

An air view of Petrópolis. MIP

ments follow one on the next, hot on each other's heels like peals of thunder, and carriages pass one another like flashes of lightning. There are popular dances, middle-class soirées, aristocratic soirées, carousels, and games of quoits; there are dinners; there's mass every Sunday and holy day; there are plays, songs, and dances at the theater, people visit each other's houses, and there are newspapers for reading and laughing, and shocking cartoons.

The *Mercantil*, in a more analytic mood, showed that there was more than one swallow in this summer:

In the middle of summer, in January or February, Petrópolis shows all its splendor: but what marks the change of season is not the calendar, nor the heat, nor the gyrations of the sun and the earth: it is the coming of the imperial family. For the courtiers, the leisured classes, and for what is called polite society, the emperor is the thermometer. While he is in São Cristóvão, none of these people wants to emigrate: but as soon as his imperial majesty comes up, "the heat down there gets unbearable," and the swallows get restless.[49]

Petrópolis wanted to be elegant and civilized in all things. For the cream of Brazilian society, sharing in the emperor's parties and soirées, nothing was missing. Balls, French theater companies, Brazilian plays, concerts and recitals, lectures, variety shows: Dom Pedro II was assiduously present at all these events, though he did not stay for long. There were even race courses; no one had to go without this chic, thrilling pastime. The Petrópolis Jockey Club began operating in 1857 on a flat area near the bottom of the mountain road; the Petrópolis Hippodrome was in Itaipava, the Vila Teresa Fields on a small flat area near the top of the road, and the Derby Club in Correas.

No modern town could do without water, gas, and sewage installations, and a contract for these works was signed in 1888. Hence the proud refrain:

> There are racehorses,
> And so we have a race course;
> We'll get gas, we'll get sewers
> And lots of water, of course.[50]

Weekly receptions given by the "fun-loving" princess Isabel and her husband the count d'Eu were an extension of, an "extra arm" for, the emperor in his activities as monarch and in his relationship with the court. The princess, always very attentive to her palace duties, followed fashion to the letter. She had a glass pavilion imported from France to be used for horticultural displays, the first of which took place in 1875. But the idea was not to everyone's liking, for the conservatory was set up where a splendid garden had been. But it seemed an essential image of modern imperialism. After all, Brazil's Crystal Palace, named after its English original, was an obvious image of the empire's aspirations.

The daily "meetings" (as they were called, in English) at the station to await the train, walks around the streets among the country houses, exhibitions and balls in the Crystal Palace, and visits to the Orleans Hotel—these were the moments when the emperor and his family encountered the *carioca* elite. In addition, the morning round of the royal family could be easily witnessed: the princess and her cab, the count d'Eu on his thoroughbred horse,

The Crystal Palace in Petrópolis, in a recent photo. The building's frame was imported from France. MIP

or the imperial carriage with a few attendants and one of the empress's ladies-in-waiting.[51]

Brazil was no different from the European models that Dom Pedro emulated in respect to how he imposed himself by means of symbols. His palaces were developed according to Portuguese models, though there was more luxury outside than in: a characteristic that reminds us how little private space was allocated to monarchs. Yet Brazil was not France—however much it might have liked to be—and Dom Pedro's court was not Versailles. A quick look at the African Brazilian domestic servants of the royal family was enough to show any visitor that it was the slaves who did the manual labor in Brazil.

The Empire of Festivals and the Festivals of the Empire*

Popular festivals.
Carlos Julião, 1795.
FBN

From 1808 until 1889 Brazilians grew accustomed to having a king presiding over the political scene, and they developed an intense relationship with the monarchy. But the monarchs themselves—Dom João VI, Dom Pedro I, Dom Pedro II, and Princess Isabel (when her father was absent)—on a day-to-day level interacted principally with other kings and queens. These royal creatures from distant kingdoms—present in the memory both of African slaves and of Portuguese settlers nostalgic for their homeland—dominated Brazil's popular celebrations and peopled an overcrowded calendar of festivals. A jigsaw puzzle of ritual from various traditions and different cosmologies made Brazil the country of festivals, a repository of a wealth of symbols, customs, and values. These were not simply repeated and reproduced mechanically but, like a kaleidoscope, ended up creating new celebrations or making new and original interpretations of the earlier material. In these ritual stagings of a great symbolic game, royalty was a frequent participant, if not the main one. Accounts by travelers, folklorists, and other curious observers, who for one reason or another were present at and described these nineteenth-century festivals, reveal a wealth of royal images that were by no means limited to the events that Dom João or his son and grandson decreed.

*Written with Valéria Mendonça de Macedo.

What these festivals created was a kind of "mystical royalty." When the monarchs were not themselves present, their portraits or some other images were carried in procession. This was royalty retranslated in the popular imagination, something quite distant and separate from the image of the king as head of a system of government and its constant reproduction by the *carioca* elites. Another logic took over, whose structure went back to colonial times.

Alongside the calendar of civic celebrations, a program of popular festivals developed, out of habit, as it were, and these were of course celebrated by the monarchs and the "grandees of the empire." In civic festivals and on official anniversaries, the Portuguese kings, and then the first monarch born in Brazil, guided the harmony of the ritual; in other street processions, however, the Emperor of the Divine Holy Spirit ruled, and other figures of the popular imagination took the stage even if only fleetingly.

Indignant, sometimes far from impartial European and North American travelers, whether Catholic or (more often) Protestant, criticized these "mixed rituals," and some of the folklorists thought the real monarch in them was made prisoner by the celebrants. At the coronation and at commemorations of Independence Day and of the emperor's majority, birthday, and death, the population could watch the parades, approach the emperor, and wave at him as he waved back.

But in other festivals and processions—like the Festival of the Three Kings or of the Divine Holy Spirit, in cavalcades, *congadas*, and drum sessions (*batuques*), *entrudo*, or Carnival—other kings and queens told different stories about Brazil, its people, and its destiny. At the coronations of these black kings, elected by the slaves, we see monarchs coexisting, as if the festival suspended conflict for a few hours and joined together different kinds of authority: Catholic priests and *candomblé* priestesses, masters and slaves. This "sugared Catholicism," as Gilberto Freyre called it, reinvented relationships in an atmosphere characterized by violence and a striking difference from normal life. These festivals blurred the relationships among the distant African continent, the local kings, and the Portuguese crown.

In addition, there was evidence of Sebastianist cults transplanted to Brazil. This was a Portuguese tradition, oral and written, going back to the sixteenth century, which had its origins in the dramatic career of King Sebastian, "the desired one" (*o desejado*), and the tragic end of his reign fighting the Moors at the battle of Alcácer Quibir in 1578. King Sebastian was supposed to have disappeared without a trace, and there grew up around his memory a movement with clearly messianic characteristics. The figure of King Sebastian incarnated and appropriated the myth of "the hidden one" (o encoberto), the belief in the return of the savior king who would restore Portugal to its previous eminence in the world. In later versions by the cobbler Gonçalo Annes Bandarra and by the seventeenth-century Portuguese missionary Father Antônio Vieira (who predicted the coming of the Fifth Empire), or in claims of false pretenders to the throne, there was always a return to the "kingdom of the desejado." Dom Pedro II was not only a Brazilian monarch of Portuguese origin but also, in a way, Emperor of the Divine Holy Spirit and, perhaps, the hope of the consecration of the Third Millennium, as predicted by Vieira in his History of the Future, published posthumously in 1718.

Dom Pedro II was surrounded, then, by many kinds of royalty. In a country of festivals and myths it is hard to work out which version of the truth predominates: whether it can be found in the processions and merrymaking associated with the imperial palace or, like King Sebastian, at the bottom of the sea.

The travelers who came to Brazil are a fundamental source of information about the festivals of the empire, partly because of the lack of written evidence from a population that was mostly illiterate. Many of them were more interested in understanding Brazil's flora and fauna, but Brazilians themselves came to intrigue them.

At first it was the indigenous people who caught their attention because of their alleged cannibalism and polygamy, but by the nineteenth century the mixed, mestizo character of Brazil's entire population awakened their curiosity. It was mixed not just biologically but in customs and religion as well. Where did Christian rituals end and popular festivals begin? A good proportion of these travelers came from Protestant and/or Anglo-Saxon and Germanic cultures, far removed from this hybrid universe. The interaction between the Iberian inheritance and the African and indigenous cultures had produced a different shape of things, very distant from the restrained, ascetic, and rationalist models that motivated these foreign scientists.

If, as Clifford Geertz says, to understand a culture we have to enter the web of its meanings until we can distinguish between a mischievous wink and the simple shutting of an eyelid, perhaps we ought to be wary of the distorted evidence that these travelers may have left behind. They analyzed what they saw according to their own scheme of values, and they did not even try to understand the particular meaning of popular manifestations within the

Brazilian cultural universe. Yet this same alienation helped them to highlight certain elements that were so familiar to Brazilians as to have seemed natural.

On 7 December 1809 the Englishman Henry Koster arrived in Recife.[1] At that time Brazil was undergoing rapid, deep transformations because of the coming of Dom João and the Portuguese court. Koster followed these changes closely, and he ridiculed the way European customs unsuitable to Brazil were nevertheless adopted. He was also a ferocious critic of slavery, though this did not prevent him from admiring the physical beauty of Brazilians and especially those of mixed blood: "it is among the women of colour that the finest persons are to be found—more life and spirit, more activity of mind and body; they are better fitted to the climate, and the mixed race seems to be its proper inhabitant. Their features too are often good, and even the colour, which in European climates is disagreeable, appears to appertain to that in which it more naturally exists; but this bar to European ideas of beauty set aside, finer specimens of the human form cannot be found than among the mulatto females I have seen."

Johann von Spix and Carl von Martius had a quite different point of view. These two German naturalists came to Brazil along with other scientists, contracted by the emperor Francis I, father of the archduchess Dona Leopoldina, at the time when she was preparing herself for her marriage to Dom Pedro de Alcântara, later Dom Pedro I. Spix and Martius stayed in the country from 1817 to 1820, during which time they traveled to many of the provinces: Rio de Janeiro, São Paulo, Minas Gerais, Bahia, Pernambuco, Maranhão, Pará, and Amazonas. Most of their observations concerned the vegetation, but the customs of the local people did not escape their attention: black African dances, inhabitants, religious festivals, processions, and Sebastianist rites.[2] At several points Brazil seems to them like a new country that in a short span has incorporated elements of several cultures, coexisting strangely: "What will its fourth century bring to this country, which in three has already been able to assimilate all the tendencies and degrees of civilization through which the genius of humanity has led the Old World over thousands of years?"[3] Mostly, the German naturalists were optimistic about the future of Brazil, or so they said when they stayed in Minas Gerais at the home of a convinced Sebastianist: "Sr. Inocêncio looks to a more fortunate future in Brazil: we assured him that, even though we did not expect the coming of King Sebastian, we shared the same hope that Brazil was still on its way to a flourishing future."[4]

If some travelers came with their objectives already defined, others looked for one as soon as they disembarked. This was the case with Carl Seidler, who came to Brazil in 1825 with no scientific or intellectual pretensions, ended up by staying in the country for ten years, and became an officer in the imperial army. His views about Brazilian society and Dom Pedro I were quite negative. He had no liking for the first emperor, whom he nicknamed "Pedro Napoleon" or the "imperial Tom Thumb" because of his despotic character,[5] and he also criticized Brazilian women's lack of virtue (calling them "easy") and the people's religious character, which filled ceremonies with "vices" like drink and sensual pleasures. He thought mulattos were a "patched-up version of nature" and was made uncomfortable by their presence in the cultural life of the Brazilian elite.

Religious motives could also be the justification for making the journey. This was the case with Daniel Parish Kidder, a North American Methodist pastor who stayed in Brazil from 1836 until 1842 (the troubled times of the Regency) and who is considered the pioneer of Protestantism in Brazil. Like other travelers, the Reverend Kidder was shocked most of all by slavery and by the lack of decorum in religious ceremonies. And a little later, the Reverend James Cooley Fletcher came to Brazil on an evangelical mission in 1851 and stayed until 1865. As a member of the Brazilian Historical and Geographical Institute, he got to know Dom Pedro II. In writing *Brazil and the Brazilians* (1857), he incorporated part of Kidder's book (*Sketches of Travels and Residence in Brazil*, 1845), but the lack of correct references to his source makes it difficult to distinguish where the descriptions of one end and the commentaries of the other begin. Fletcher was in Rio during what we might call the golden age of the empire, when Brazil was politically and economically stable and the regime was quite popular, so it is not surprising that he does not stint in his praise of the Brazilian monarch, revering his "religious tolerance and his goodness to the population." (What pleased Fletcher most was that Dom Pedro, although he had adopted Catholicism as the official religion of the empire, did not prevent Protestant sects from operating in the country.)

The hardships of this "savage country" could also be faced for reasons of professional curiosity. This was the case with the German doctor Robert Avé-Lallemant, who traveled in the northeast in 1859. He was in Brazil, then, at the same time as Fletcher, but the latter stayed in the capital. In *Journeys Round the Provinces of Bahia, Alagoas, and Pernambuco and Sergipe* (1859), we see what the beauty and sensuality of black and mulatta women could provoke in this professional man, who at times, it seems, forgot his scientific preoccupations.

During the same period Prince Ferdinand Maximilian of Habsburg, a cousin of Dom Pedro II, visited Bahia. He had little liking for Brazilians, and his commentaries, in *Bahia 1860: Sketches from a Journey* (1861), although witty in themselves, cannot hide a certain aversion to local customs.

Finally, there was no lack of journalists, like Carl von Koseritz, a German who lived for thirty-two years in southern Brazil. In his book *Images of Brazil*, Koseritz published some of the material he had written for the Brazilian press in 1883, when he stayed in Rio de Janeiro and met Dom Pedro II several times. It is interesting to compare his commentaries with Fletcher's, for while the latter never tires of praising the pomp and magnificence of the palace and the royal processions, Koseritz paints a caricatured picture of a decadent court and monarch. He describes Dom Pedro II as a humble, kind man who has lost his majesty by failing to care for his palaces, his dress, or his carriages. A lack of etiquette has made him almost indifferent to his people, who in turn miss the court's former brilliance. The gap of thirty years between the two texts reveals the effects of time on the monarchy. Quite apart from their own personal sympathies, these travelers were tracking the decadence of an empire and the end of its rituals, which no longer enchanted the eye.

Though these travelers had different aims, interpretations, and views of Brazil's future, they were in agreement about its fascinating nature, their aversion to slavery, and their indignation about its religious rituals. As well as being very different from the "purer" European religious celebrations, these rituals promoted, as they saw it, an extreme degree of mixture among groups and "races"—to use a word common to them all—that was totally unacceptable. And what were they to say of the participation of the emperor and the court in these colorful festivities? Their condemnation was severe; it seemed impossible to conceive of mixing the old traditions of the Habsburgs with the "superstitions" of Africans and mulattos.

The State drew its strength, which was considerable, from its powers of imagination, its semiotic ability to make inequality attractive. —*Clifford Geertz*

Geertz's work on the "theatre state" of Bali in the nineteenth century helps us think about the Brazilian monarchy of the same period. With a similar "semiotic ability" to make "inequality attractive" by means of public ceremonies—corteges and processions, wearing the rich apparel used for gala occasions—the Brazilian monarchy at least until the 1870s transformed its ap-

pearances into spectacles. There were several occasions for these spectacles — birthdays, historic events, and official religious holidays — but in all of
them the same machinery was put in motion in order to transform reality into
its representation.

This was not exactly a local invention. Both Portuguese and Africans, in
their countries of origin, were in the habit of watching royal corteges and
processions. In some African nations coronations of local kings were common after the eighteenth century, not to mention the kings and queens of
congadas, cheganças, and *maracatu.* And the Portuguese and their descendants were familiar with "cavalcades," a fairly widespread festivity in which
horsemen dressed as medieval knights (divided into Christians, under the
command of the "Emperor Charlemagne," and Moors) participated in shows
of equestrian feats and simulated jousting.

With so many of these legacies and with real monarchs living in Brazil,
these royal processions were very popular. Several social groups could share
the streets and give living form to different kinds of cultural inheritance, all
with a single aim: to pay homage to the emperor. Because he stayed in power
longest, Dom Pedro II was the Brazilian monarch who joined most often in
these events. From his childhood, with the abdication of his father, Pedro II
became the image of a mixture of a young King Sebastian and the Emperor
of the Divine Holy Spirit: a divine but Brazilian monarch incarnating the
hopes of the people. Seidler was in Rio de Janeiro for Dom Pedro I's abdication and the acclamation of Dom Pedro II:

> Fireworks, illuminations, in fact celebrations of all kinds suddenly
> transformed the political sky — which until then had been heavy and
> dark with the menace of storm — into a pure, ethereal blue. The
> Brazilians were dreaming of a happy future, which they thought was
> close at hand, though it was in fact far off . . . Drunk with triumph,
> dizzy with happiness, indeed almost mad with it and with alcoholic
> beverages, they told one another stories of Brazilian heroism, of love
> of freedom, and of the "spirit of the nation reaching to the stars."
> There was no stronger, grander people on earth; every ragged mulatto
> thought himself a prince, because he thought his "I'm a real Brazil-
> ian," uttered with pride, was a kind of nobility in itself . . . Parades, in
> which the recently created National Guard took part, processions,
> dances, performances, and celebrations of all kinds took place, and on
> these occasions, too, the little emperor was displayed like an interest-

ing doll. The imperial tutor on these occasions was on his left, the regent on the right, and these two sworn enemies had between them the little boy weighed down with little stars and diamonds . . . Every time thousands of blacks and mulattos gathered and shouted an inharmonious chorus of "Long Live Dom Pedro II."[6]

These parades and processions seemed to unite different logics and ideas. On the one hand, the elite, represented by the tutor and the regent, surround the little emperor and make him into a kind of glittering puppet. On the other, the people in the streets, captivated by the spectacle, see in the young king a mystical subject of processions that have been going on for four centuries, "the little boy weighed down with little stars and diamonds," and they are proud of him.

During the Regency Kidder was present for Dom Pedro II's birthday in Bahia:

The Bahians were preparing to celebrate the birthday of their youthful Emperor, the 2d of December. This anniversary is, throughout the nation, a favorite one among the several *dias de grande gala*, or political holidays. Of these the Brazilians celebrate six. The 1st of January heads the list with New Year's compliments to his Majesty. The 25th of March commemorates the adoption of the constitution. The 7th of April is the anniversary of the Emperor's accession to the throne. The 3d of May is the day for opening the sessions of the national Assembly. The 7th of September is the anniversary of the declaration of the national independence; while the last in the catalogue is the 2d of December, the Emperor's birthday. On all these days, except the 3d of May, his Majesty holds court in the palace at Rio. Presidents of provinces, as the special representatives of the crown, follow the example of their sovereign, by holding levee in the several provincial capitals; but they do not presume to receive imperial honors in their own person. The place of honor in their *sala de cortejo* is always allotted to the portrait of his Majesty . . .

In addition to the usual *cortejo*, there were to be ceremonies for three successive days and illuminations for as many nights. On the first day, there was to be a grand *Te Deum*, with a sermon; on the second, a military ball at the palace; and on the third, an unrivaled exhibition of fire-works, on Victoria hill, at the Campo de S. Pedro . . .

In another quarter, upon a high parapet overlooking the sea and the bay, had been constructed a fancy pavilion, in the style of an Athenian temple. In front of this, supported by the central columns, had been placed a full-length portrait of his Majesty, that day fourteen years old. In the saloons of this palace were stationed bands of music, surrounded by ladies and dignitaries of the province. The portrait of the Emperor was concealed by a curtain until a given hour of the evening, when the president made his appearance, and suddenly drawing it up, gave successive vivas to his Majesty, the Brazilian nation, and the people of Bahia; all of which were responded to with deafening acclamations from the multitude around, while the heavens above were emblazoned with the discharge of a thousand rockets.[7]

Every 2 December, then, the emperor's presence in the minds of his people was underlined all over the country. Since the monarch cannot divide up his own presence, in the capital he was complimented in person, and in the provinces the presidents, as representatives of the crown, took his place without of course taking his full part. In these cases his portrait stood in for him in public rooms and in processions and was reproduced on large banners. Along with it went a kind of symbolism that linked his figure to a religious and sacred context.

As well as personifying the hope of resuscitating in Brazil the great empire that Portugal had lost, Dom Pedro had in common with King Sebastian the fact that both of them had been anointed and consecrated in a coronation ceremony. These ceremonies had lapsed in Portugal after King Sebastian's death: the Bragança kings, for example, were only acclaimed. But with Brazilian independence the former colony dusted off this old custom and made it a public ceremony, to everyone's delight:

Dom Pedro I, laying the foundations of a new empire, thought it was a good policy to surround his investiture with religious ceremonies that proclaimed divine right and restored the medieval tradition of consecration. This was carried out in the cathedral on 1 December 1822, in a long ceremony full of pomp, too long to be described here. The crown was placed on his head by the bishop of Rio de Janeiro, Dom José Caetano da Silva Coutinho. Invested with the imperial insignia, mantle, crown, sword, and scepter, Dom Pedro heard mass, gave the oath, and took communion: a Te Deum was then sung. Dom

Pedro, accompanied by Dona Leopoldina and the courtiers, came from São Cristóvão in a carriage, to the Campo de Sant'Ana. We should note that the guards who accompanied the carriage had been chosen in a symbolic statement: a white man, an Indian, a mulatto [*pardo*], and a black man, in showy uniforms . . . The same ceremony, though with greater pomp and luxury, was repeated on 18 July 1841, for the anointing, consecration, and coronation of Dom Pedro II . . . These ceremonies always occurred with a huge number of people present. They could hardly get into the cathedral, which was filled to bursting with the imperial family, authorities, persons of noble rank, diplomatic representatives, parliamentarians, and notables. The dense mass of the people spread out through the square and the areas close by in the spaces left free by the marshaled troops. After the official ceremonies, there were popular celebrations throughout the city, decorated for the occasion: these culminated with fireworks displays in the public squares at night. The sumptuousness of these festivals was deeply etched on the memories of those present.[8]

It is worth emphasizing that all the "races" were present in Dom Pedro I's cortege: a white man, an Indian, a mulatto, and a black man: four, and not, as one might think, three.

Kidder was in Rio de Janeiro on the occasion of Dom Pedro II's coronation and tells us how the whole city was mobilized for this imposing ceremony:

Thus, for two months longer, the anticipated coronation continued to be the all-engrossing topic of conversation and of preparation in every circle, from the Emperor and the princesses, down to the shoeless slaves. That anxiously looked-for event transpired at length, on the 18th of July, 1841. It was magnificent beyond the expectations of the most sanguine. The splendor of the day itself—the unnumbered thousands of citizens and strangers that thronged the streets—the tasteful and costly decorations displayed in the public squares, and in front of private houses—the triumphal arches—the pealing salutes of music and of cannon—the perfect order and tranquillity that prevailed in the public processions and ceremonies of the day, together with nearly every thing else that could be imagined or wished, seemed to combine and make the occasion one of the most imposing that ever transpired in the new world . . . The illuminations at evening were of the most brilliant kind, and the festivities of the occasion were prolonged nine successive days.

So far as pomp and parade could promote the stability of a government, and secure a lasting respect for a crown, every thing was done in Brazil on that day, that possibly could be done without greater means at command . . . It was thought to be an object of the first importance to surround the throne with such a degree of splendor as would for ever hallow it in the eyes of the people. It may be questioned, however, whether this very policy, instead of consolidating public sentiment, did not beget a morbid fondness for scenes of extraordinary ceremonies, which would only be satisfied with their frequent repetition.[9]

Although he criticizes the structure of the ritual, Kidder is the first to underline—not without a certain irony—the effect that "pomp and parade" had for the stability of the power of the throne. The criticism he makes of what he calls the "morbid fondness for scenes of extraordinary ceremonies" is repeated in his account of the anniversary of Brazil's independence: "I was present in that city on the 7th of September, at the celebration of the anniversary of Brazilian independence . . . There was, at the same time, a fair display of the military. On this occasion I was impressed more forcibly than ever with the fact that none of the public ceremonies of the country seem at all calculated to improve the public mind or morals. The only ambition manifest, runs in the line of seeing and being seen."[10]

The great days of the civic calendar were adapted to fit the pattern of popular processions and were given new features and new interpretations; following the theatrical logic of "seeing and being seen," they reconstruct a mythic king close to local mythologies. The German Koseritz was present at a celebration of Independence Day many years later:

Yesterday [7 September 1883] was the great national day, the anniversary of independence from the Portuguese yoke . . . we got into a tram at night and went to the popular neighborhoods, to see the people celebrating in Rossio Square and enjoy the sight of the city lit up . . . We were welcomed by a sea of lights, for all the houses in the square were lit up, and the garden around the statue of Pedro I was shining in the glow of thousands of gaslights. A huge mass of people filled the square, and I really didn't understand what they were all doing there, because apart from the lights and music being played in the two bandstands, nothing was happening . . . But from up there in the darkness the founder of the empire was looking down at the sea of lights and the shifting multitude.[11]

The festival was not, then, homage to the emperor Dom Pedro I, who had been deposed many years before and whose statue, after all, was in darkness. The date was almost a pretext for a party, and the foundation of the empire simply provided a lofty rationale for the commemoration.

Fletcher, who lived in Rio de Janeiro during the emperor's maturity, witnessed several civic and religious festivals at which Dom Pedro was present. The principal attraction of the Festival of the Glória, as he described it, was the imperial procession:

> Salvoes of artillery announce the approach of the Imperial party, who, when the weather permits, leave their carriages at the foot of the hill, and slowly ascend the steep path that leads to the church. This has been previously strewed with flowers and wild-cinnamon-leaves.
>
> On some occasions, troops of young girls in white, from the different boarding-schools, are in waiting at the top, to kiss the hands of their Majesties. This is the prettiest part of the exhibition,—the Emperor, with his stately form, and the Empress, with her good-humoured smile, passing slowly through the lines of bright-eyed girls who are not without a slight idea of their own prominent part in the graceful group.[12]

The Festival of the Glória was a model in this respect—an official part of the palace's calendar in which the people "touched the king," as if different universes did really touch one another for this brief moment: the dynastic monarch and the king of the imagination. Surrounded by the population as if by another kind of ornament, the emperor and empress were an integral part of the cortege. The imperial family had a fixed part in many features of the crowded calendar of official celebrations. In January there was New Year and the Day of the "Fico"; in February, the anniversary of the death of Dona Maria Amélia (the emperor's sister); in March, that of the swearing of the Constitution. May was the month of the empress's brother's birthday; July, of Dona Leopoldina's birthday, Princess Isabel's birthday, and the anniversary of the emperor's consecration; August, the princess of Joinville's birthday; September, the marriage of their imperial majesties and the independence of Brazil; October, Saint Teresa's day; November, the birthday of Dona Maria II (Pedro II's sister and queen of Portugal); and December, the emperor's birthday.

> "Holidays," in the understanding of many of the country's inhabitants, are the days to which all other days are subordinate. It is at festival time that nature produces its tastiest fruits and most beautiful flowers. Old and young look forward to these festivals with great eagerness. The poor and the wealthy spend freely at this time. The rich display their wealth and the poor will sometimes sell their last slave — thought of as being the most essential of all possessions — to buy new clothes, ornaments and sweetmeats for the celebrations.[13]

In this slave-owning country with its fixed hierarchy, the "white people's" festivals mostly took place inside palaces and theaters, as did balls and soirées, while the "black people's" festivals happened in the city streets and the plantations' slave quarters. At the balls the courtiers dressed in European clothes, and the slaves became part of an almost transparent backdrop; in the popular festivals the colors and props were different. At religious festivals several social groups converged in the same space and enjoyed a kind of communion that was more than purely religious.

Civic celebrations also produced excitement in the streets, but the people were spectators rather than participants. This passive role changed on procession days, when they became part of the procession itself: courtiers of their favorite saint, as it were. The mixture of individuals, groups, and "races" usually shocked foreigners — Spix and Martius, for example, when they watched a procession in honor of Nosso Senhor do Bonfim (literally, Our Lord of the Good End) in Bahia:

> The sumptuous procession of numerous brotherhoods of people of every color, who try to outdo each other with the wealth of their apparel, their flags and insignia, with alternate groups of Benedictines, Franciscans, Augustinians, Carmelites, both shod and barefoot, Jerusalem mendicants, Capuchins, nuns and penitents, the latter hidden under their hoods; in addition, Portuguese regular troops and municipal militia; the gravity and unction of the European priests and all the

glitter of the old Roman Catholic cult in the midst of the savage noise of the enthusiastic—we were almost tempted to say half-pagan— blacks, and surrounded by the tumult of agile mulattos: all this is one of the most striking pictures of life that any traveler might encounter. As in a magic mirror, the wondering spectator sees representatives of every period, every continent, every kind of temperament, the whole history of human evolution, with their highest ideals, their struggles, their achievements, the obstacles in their way; and this unique specta- cle, which neither London nor Paris could possibly provide, is still more interesting.[14]

Bringing their tradition of processions with them, these Africans and Por- tuguese and mulattos re-created their "ancient kingdoms" in the streets. What struck observers was not only the mixture of social strata but the osten- tation of the clothes and gestures, the sensuality and happiness. We can take it that religious or civic feelings were bypassed at such events; the commem- orations became a pretext for communal celebration.

[A]ll the religious celebrations are deemed interesting and important in proportion to the pomp and splendor which they display. The de- sireableness of having all possible show and parade is generally the crowning argument urged in all applications for government patron- age, and in all appeals designed to secure the attendance and liberal- ity of the people.

Few seem to look on with any very elevated emotions. All could see the same or kindred images in the churches when they please; and, if the design is to edify the people, a less troublesome and at the same time more effectual mode might easily be adopted. There ap- pears but little solemnity connected with the scene, and most of that is shared by the poor brethren who tug and sweat under the plat- forms . . . No class enter into the spirit of these holiday parades with more zeal than the people of color. They are, moreover, frequently complimented from time to time by the appearance of a colored saint, or of Nossa Senhora under an ebony skin.[15]

Kidder is also indignant about certain festivals called "religious" that, in his opinion, border on the ridiculous:

I was informed that the present was the greatest season of religious feasting which occurs at Parahiba during the whole year, the 5th of August being the day of *Nossa Senhora das Neves*, the protectress of the town . . . Large fires were blazing in different parts of the area. Around them were groups of blacks, eager to fire off volleys of rockets at appropriate parts of the service that was going on within the church. After the novena was finished, all the people sallied out into the campo to witness the fire-works. These commenced about nine o'clock, and continued, I was told, till after midnight. What I saw of them was exceedingly ill-contrived, and bunglingly executed; nevertheless all seemed to pass off to the admiration of the crowd, and certainly with its thundering applause.

Had this been a scene of professed diversion for a company of rude and ignorant Africans, it would have been more sufferable. But professing to be part of a religious service (honra á Nossa Senhora Padroeira), performed on God's holy day, and joined in with enthusiasm by priests, monks, and people, I confess it shocked my feelings in the extreme, and I wished myself almost any where rather than witnessing it.

One of the most painful impressions of the scene arose from seeing whole families, including mothers and their daughters, out in the damp night air to gaze upon spectacles not only partaking of the most low and vulgar species of the ludicrous, but having a decidedly immoral tendency—and all this under the name of religion![16]

Fletcher and Kidder, even as they reject what they see, give us interesting evidence about the importance of festivals in Brazil. Black converts to Catholicism used religious festivals and processions and found elements they could identify with, adhering to Catholic rites, but creating new versions for themselves. The practices of painting the images of saints black and conducting the processions in a relaxed atmosphere are clues allowing us to enter their world of reinterpreted cultural practices.

Religious themes were always present, motivating the slaves, their masters, and the monarch himself. Even if the ritual was not explicitly Catholic, as was the case with the *batuques* and dances of African origin, their occurrence came to coincide with Catholic festivals: this was the case with the festivals of the Three Kings, of the Empire of the Divine Holy Spirit, of Our Lady of the Rosary, and many others. It was difficult to keep worlds separate:

the Catholicism of the Portuguese kings was openly mixed with the religion of the African slaves. And civic celebrations, coronations, and imperial processions were welcomed with *batuques* and *congadas,* hardly the usual court etiquette. Several travelers commented on this:

> The unbaptized negro feels that he is considered as an inferior being, and although he may not be aware of the value which the whites place upon baptism, still he knows that the stigma for which he is upbraided will be removed by it; and therefore he is desirous of being made equal to his companions. The Africans who have long been imported, imbibe a Catholic feeling, and appear to forget that they were once in the same situation themselves. The slaves are not asked whether they will be baptized or not; their entrance into the Catholic church is treated as a thing of course; and indeed they are not considered as members of society, but rather as brute animals, until they can lawfully go to mass, confess their sins, and receive the sacrament.
>
> The slaves have their religious brotherhoods as well as the free persons; and the ambition of a slave very generally aims at being admitted into one of these, and at being made one of the officers and directors of the concerns of the brotherhood; even some of the money which the industrious slave is collecting for the purpose of purchasing his freedom will oftentimes be brought out of its concealment for the decoration of a saint, that the donor may become of importance in the society to which he belongs. The negroes have one invocation of the Virgin (or I might almost say one virgin) which is peculiarly their own. Our Lady of the Rosary is even sometimes painted with a black face and hands . . . Their ideas are removed from any thought of the customs of their own country, and are guided into a channel of a totally different nature, and completely unconnected with what is practised there.[17]

The travelers who deprecated this "Catholicism of the blacks" tended to caricature it. Kidder saw this kind of veneration during his visit to Maceió:

> Near this locality a chair had been placed in the street, and spread over with a cloth. In it stood a small image case . . . An old colored man sat close by, with a scarf over his shoulders and a plate in his hand. I inquired of him, "What have you got in that case?" "Our Lady

of the Rosary," he replied. "What is she doing?" "Collecting alms to build a church." Our conversation continued some minutes, during which I listened to a profound eulogy upon the religious virtues of the image, which, had I trusted my eyes rather than my ears, I could hardly have distinguished from a child's doll.[18]

In Paraíba, during a festival in honor of Our Lady of the Snows, the patron saint of the city, Kidder discovered how many names the Virgin Mary had in Brazil: "I inquired who Nossa Senhora das Neves was, but no one could tell me anything more than that she was Nossa Senhora, the same with Nossa Senhora da Conceição, Nossa Senhora do Rosário, and a score of other names for the Virgin Mary! I doubt whether the mythology of Greece or Rome ever became more absurdly confused."[19]

It is said that the appellation of the Rosary was popular because the slaves were illiterate and, unable to read the Bible, clung to the rosary beads. Whether this is true or not, the fact is not only that the blacks' Brotherhood of Our Lady of the Rosary is very old (our first record of it dates back to 1711, coinciding with the first official information of the designation of a king of the Congo in Brazil),[20] but that its acceptance by a part of the black population is clear. On the other hand, the great "white" brotherhoods were also very active in Brazil. Koster was shocked by how many of their shrines there were: "The number of churches, chapels, and niches in the streets for saints is quite preposterous; to these are attached a multitude of religious lay brotherhoods, of which the members are merchants, and other persons in trade, and even some are composed of mulatto and black free people. Some of these continually beg for a supply of wax, and other articles to be consumed in honour of their patron."[21]

Fletcher and Kidder describe these brotherhoods as follows:

These fraternities . . . are generally composed of laymen, and are de-nominated Third Orders, — as, for example, Ordem Terceira do Carmo, Da Boa Morte, Do Bom Jesus do Calvario, &c. They have a style of dress approaching the clerical in appearance, which is worn on holi-days, with some distinguishing mark by which each association is known. A liberal entrance-fee and an annual subscription is required of all the members, each of whom is entitled to support from the general fund in sickness and in poverty, and also to a funeral of ceremony when dead. The brotherhoods contribute to the erection and support of churches, provide for the sick, bury the dead, and support masses

for souls. In short, next after the State, they are the most efficient aux-
iliaries for the support of the religious establishment of the country.[22]

In Pernambuco, Henry Koster had to negotiate the rent of a piece of land
with a black brotherhood:

> I gained my object of renting the lands through the interest of some
> persons who were intimately acquainted with the principal officers of
> the brotherhood. I attended at the council table of these black direc-
> tors, and heard the arguments for and against the policy of placing the
> whole of the property in the hands of one person; however the matter
> was decided as soon as one of them rose up, and reminded the rest that
> the community was in debt, and that the new tenant was prepared
> with one year's rent in advance . . . the health of our Lady of the
> Rosary was drank first; then that of the chief of the brotherhood and of
> the new tenant. These fellows amused us much; for their politeness to
> each other, and to the white persons who were present sat awkwardly
> upon them; but which was displayed to shew the importance they
> imagined themselves to possess.[23]

Although he makes fun of the "importance they imagined themselves to possess," the traveler himself notes the advantages of belonging to a brotherhood.
As he says, many slaves donated to the brotherhoods some of the money they
collected to buy their freedom, and they joined them in order to obtain more
prestige.

Spix and Martius were present at a festival in honor of Our Lady of the
Rosary in Rio de Janeiro, and in spite of their joking tone, they too saw its
importance:

> Some days after our arrival, we were invited by some of our compatri-
> ots to be present at a church festivity, which the blacks celebrated on
> the day of their patroness, Our Lady of the Rosary. A chapel on a point
> jutting into the bay, not far from the royal gardens of São Cristóvão,
> where we went, was filled in the afternoon with an enormous number
> of colored people, and the black orchestra of São Cristóvão played
> jolly, almost comic music, which was followed by a moving sermon;
> rockets and explosions in front of the church and the quiet sea height-
> ened the solemnity of the occasion.[24]

The "black orchestra of São Cristóvão" was only one of many examples of black participation in bands organized for the pleasure of the white masters. Koster commented in astonishment on the way things went on the plantation of Colonel Simplício Dias da Silva, vice-governor of Paraíba: "[H]e has there a most noble establishment, part of which consists of a band of musicians, who are his own slaves; some of them have been instructed at Lisbon and at Rio de Janeiro."[25] And this was not an isolated example:

> Here we were entertained with such music as has yet found its way into these parts of the country. Three negroes with bagpipes attempted to play a few tunes whilst we were at dinner, but they seemed to play in different keys from each other, and sometimes each appeared to have struck up a tune of his own composing. I think I never heard so bad an attempt at producing harmonious sounds as the *charameleiros*

"After the show there was a lively dance, for which all the music was played by the twenty-member band, slaves of the viscount. There was great variety, and the music was excellently played, showing the musicians' skill and training and the taste of the conductor." *O Cruzeiro*, 24 April 1879.

[wind players] made. The possession of a band of these bespeaks a certain degree of superiority, consequently the planters pride themselves upon their musicians.[26]

Seidler noted that blacks and mulattos played in orchestras and acted in theatrical spectacles, which made him very indignant, for, he said, "they went to most disreputable stores and picked up drunken mulattos to participate in the imperial band."[27]

On the provincial plantations festivals for Our Lady of the Rosary were organized by the blacks themselves, but the whites also participated, as Koster saw in Pernambuco:

> The festival, at which I intended to be present, was for Our Lady of the Rosary, the patroness of negroes. The expense which was to be incurred was subscribed for by the slaves of the estate, and the festival was entirely managed by them. Three friars attended to officiate at the altar; but the lights, the fireworks, and all the other necessary articles were provided for by a committee of the slaves . . . Before the commencement of the prayers and the singing in the chapel, the black people extended several mats upon the ground in the open air; and our party sat down upon them to converse and to eat cakes and sweetmeats, of which many kinds were exposed for sale in great abundance.[28]

So black bands were a kind of local fashion. It was no accident that the imperial household maintained a group of slave singers at the Fazenda de Santa Cruz. The model might be European, but the interpretation and the art were local.

The world of Dom Pedro II was, then, much more complex than a mere logic of conversion might imply. In Brazil rituals were interpreted by means of many codes. In the case of the black population, while their participation in religious festivals was already great, they were even more enthusiastic when it was in honor of their patroness: then the Christian king became the king of the Congo, and the Virgin Mary was recognized as Our Lady of the Rosary.

Alexandre José de Mello Moraes describes the clowns who dressed as the Three Wise Men during Christmas celebrations in Bahia in the early 1890s:

The slave band of the Vale do Paraíba, with a medieval castle as the setting.

Then these characters, dressed as the Three Kings, strumming on their instruments, danced and sang . . . The slaves of good masters have a specific position in the noisy drum ensembles . . . Pastoral dances, more revealing of the specific individuality of Christmas night in Bahia, are performed in the houses of both the poor and the moderately well off, and in the golden palaces of the rich . . . The silvery strings of the guitars, contrasting with the black fingers of those playing them; the shepherdesses, tanned and ebony-colored, dancing, singing, and talking in front of a crib made of *pitanga* branches; the women in their showy turbans, adorned with collars, bracelets, and jewels, delight the eye and ear and take our imagination to the realms of the Orient, to the land of sunshine.

You might think these torsos of darkness and shadowy twilight had been part of the retinue of the kings of Sheba, Persia, and Babylon on their journey to Bethlehem; that this clamor, raised by a crowd of different races, was nothing other than the distant echo, two thousand years old, of the caravans of the Three Kings with their entourage of conquered kings, odalisques, and captives, with their camels weighed down with the frankincense and gold, amulets and diadems of a hundred dynasties—offerings for the newborn God.[29]

This famous Festival of the Three Kings, on 6 January, may have had European origins, but it took on Brazilian features. Many Africans in Brazil embraced Catholicism and its saints but changed their names, their features, and their content. And they added a new pantheon: they paid discreet homage to their own African kings and saints in celebrations venerating the kings of Portugal and, later, the Brazilian emperors.

Fletcher was present on the Day of the Three Kings in Rio de Janeiro in the 1850s: "The passing of this holy day is marked in such a way as not to escape the memory of the most indifferent of us, for, early in the morning, the butcher kindly sends us meat for free. The festival takes place in the Imperial Chapel, in the presence of the Emperor and his Court, who give it a truly majestic character."[30] Here it was the emperor of Brazil who went to pay homage to the Three Kings of the Orient.

Processions had been common in Brazil since colonial times and were present throughout the empire. Seidler gives us an account of one in which Dom Pedro I took part:

> [The Imperial] chapel is just one humble instrument in the imperial theater and looks it when one considers it in the wider context. Dom Pedro used to appear at religious services there, even accompanying the procession as it departed on festive occasions like a faithful page, carrying the bishop's canopy. Often it was extremely comic to see how the monarch of one of the largest and richest countries on earth stooped to accompanying pieces of gilded wood and saints' images . . . These festive processions are very popular at the moment and can be seen almost daily, winding with their variety of colors through the main streets of Rio. They are preceded by the music of military bands, and in the most important festivals, like that of the Sacred Heart or

Our Lady of the Conception, the chief functionaries of the state take part, with heavy, life-size statues of the Madonna, and crucifixes—the heavier and more brightly painted, the better. The other saints follow them, in hierarchical order, which varies with tradition and the season of the year, all laden down, more than decency should allow, with clothes, wings, and real jewelry, and all followed by richly dressed pages, and lit candles, their flickering flame spreading a dim light . . . Finally comes the interminable procession of the members of the cathedral chapter and monks of the most varied orders, each in their own form of baroque apparel. There is a lot of kissing, drinking, and snuff-taking . . . and they cover their eyes, as if there was anything to be seen other than human foolishness.[31]

Prince Ferdinand Maximilian was horrified by this "mulatto religiosity," which he witnessed at the festival for the Senhor do Bonfim in Bahia:

In the church square, was the confused atmosphere of a fair. Blacks in colorful, gaudy festive clothes were pushing and running, with a great deal of noise and shouting. Carriages with ladies on pilgrimage or with curious observers from the city tried to get through the human tide to the terrace in front of the church, like boats in rushing waves. Little groups of people providing *cachaça* [a strong local rum] formed islands in this sea of people. A platform in the Plaza of the Theater, like that raised for the emperor, advertised marvels for the oncoming evening . . . Next to one of the walls, happy black girls were seated in a long line—their bronzed charms were not hidden but enveloped in transparent gauze and gaudily colored kerchiefs—in the midst of many loud voices, selling in a very relaxed, sensual and slovenly fashion all kinds of religious trinkets, amulets, candles, and food, some of them out of baskets, others from glass boxes. *For a respectable Catholic, all this noise must seem like blasphemy, for remains of paganism were mixed in this popular black festival, more than should be allowed, in a so-called pilgrimage* . . . The whole thing had a kind of Oriental, savage touch, in a civilized frame . . . Suddenly, everything became clear, and I shuddered with indignation: our sallow-complexioned priest was quietly carrying on the ritual of the mass, for himself alone. The Brazilian priests say that the blacks have to be led to fear God in this way: they would not understand anything more sublime, and only by this kind of merry-making, mixed with *cachaça*, can they be more or less brought to church. For the slave masters, this is no doubt a very comfortable belief, because it confirms that the blacks are half-animals and so in a way disguises slavery.[32] (my italics)

The two descriptions have a common element: the profound rejection of the mixture of realms considered separate—the profane and the sacred, sensuality and strong drink in close coexistence with the saints. Ferdinand Maximilian also expressed his aversion to the idea of a white priest celebrating the blacks' mass, even in the face of the argument about the Church's control. In spite of his disgust, perhaps Ferdinand Maximilian was right: the priests were far from being in charge of the situation.

Years earlier Spix and Martius, who also observed a procession in homage to the Senhor do Bonfim, agreed:

For the lower classes, trips out on feast days are the favorite amusement, and they take advantage of the saints' days of their various patrons to celebrate in the Recôncavo [the area inland of the city of Salvador, Bahia] with fairs, which are visited by a large multitude. The festival of Nosso Senhor do Bonfim . . . attracts innumerable crowds of people, and they last some days and nights: the church and the nearby buildings are illuminated. The hubbub and the extraordinary amusements of the large number of blacks who congregate there give this popular festival a strange, eccentric aspect that only someone who has seen the races mixing in this promiscuous fashion can imagine.[33]

Koseritz, writing in 1883, tells us of a strange spectacle in Rio. Far away from court dances and soirées, from his meetings with ministers and counselors, Dom Pedro II was a participant in a Corpus Christi procession:

Near the imperial chapel we found such a crowd (many more than ten thousand people) . . . It should not be thought that it was there to greet the ministry; no, they wanted to be present at the classic Corpus Christi procession . . . at which even today the emperor, his ministers, et cetera appear and carry the canopy over the holy sacrament. On this occasion the emperor wears the semimonastic clothes of the Order of Christ, and the courtiers are dressed in gala costume—and this is a sufficient reason for the people to gather.[34]

This same procession had been witnessed by Fletcher decades earlier. With his head bare, like the other faithful, Dom Pedro II followed the ritual:

> The procession of *Corpus Cristi* is different from most of the others. The only image exposed is that of St. George, who is set down in the calendar as the "defender of the Empire." How this "godly gentleman of Cappadocia" became the defender of Brazil I have not been able to ascertain; but his festival—falling as it does on *Corpus Cristi* day—is celebrated with great pomp. It is a daylight affair, and occurs in the pleasantest season of the year. St. George is always carried around the city on horseback . . .
>
> The Emperor walks bareheaded, and carrying a candle, in this procession, in imitation of the piety of his ancestors, and is attended by the Court, the cavaleiros, or knights of the military orders, and the municipal chamber in full dress, with their insignia and badges of office. Whenever the Emperor goes out on these occasions, the inhabitants of the streets through which he is to pass rival each other in the display of rich silk and damask hangings from the windows and balustrades of their houses.[35]

The case of Saint Benedict, to whom blacks all over Brazil were devoted, is especially interesting. Consider, for example, this procession in Sergipe in honor of the saint, who was believed to be black and (though born in Italy) of Ethiopian descent: "In Sergipe Saint Benedict's festival is celebrated in the elegant cathedral church of Our Lady of Mercy on 6 January . . . It ended the cycle of the January festivals, such is the pomp and splendor of Christmas and the Festival of the Three Kings . . . This celebration and the preliminary revelry belong exclusively to the blacks: dressed as usual, proud of their patron . . . in procession, dancing and singing, in the area of the church and all around the streets."[36]

The folklorist Luís de Câmara Cascudo comments on the origins and importance of the Festival of the Divine Holy Spirit* in Brazil:

---

*In Portuguese, this name is commonly shortened to *Império do Divino*, literally "Empire of the Divine."

In Portugal they say that the festival of the Divine Holy Spirit was instituted by Dom Diniz and Queen Isabel, in Alenquer, in the thirteenth century . . . In Brazil it was a much-loved festival, especially in the south—Minas Gerais, São Paulo, Rio de Janeiro, et cetera. It was also celebrated in Bahia. The Emperor of the Divine Holy Spirit may be a child or an adult, and in the latter case, it is one of the wealthier persons in the place, who is as prodigal as possible so as to try to outshine his predecessor. As witness to the popularity of the Divine Holy Spirit, we have only to remind ourselves that José Bonifácio preferred the title *emperor* to that of *king* because the former was better known and loved among the people in the guise of the Emperor of the Divine Holy Spirit. This is the reason why Dom Pedro I became emperor and not king of Brazil.[37]

When the monarchy arrived in Brazil, the Emperor of the Divine Holy Spirit was already a popular and recognized figure. The little "divine king" served as a model for the "real king" who was to take his title and inspiration from him. This was a festival of the greatest importance in the popular calendar, and when Dom João arrived from Portugal, it was already giving delight:

Next to the Church of Sant'Ana was the Empire of the Holy Spirit. The Festivals of the Divine Holy Spirit are a tradition even today in the countryside, among the most popular and best attended. They are put on at Pentecost by the appropriate brotherhoods . . . soliciting for funds, with the brothers in their short surplices carrying the flag of the Divine Holy Spirit and the "emperor" at the head, going around to ask for help in making the celebrations as brilliant as possible. The band is received by every family and the flag is carried around all the rooms in the house to bless them; special properties are attributed to the multicolored ribbons hanging in profusion from the banner pole . . . The masses and solemn processions, with all the liturgical props and tradition; and the celebrations, which lasted a week or more, around the "empire" itself—with a mixture of secular amusements in the traditional stalls and ritual ceremonies celebrated in the small chapel—these are old customs and practices that the Portuguese brought with them, that put down roots and flourished. With small local variations, the Festivals of the Divine Holy Spirit have a uniform, traditional pattern throughout Brazil.[38]

Fletcher and Kidder also noted the popularity of the Festival of the Divine Holy Spirit:

> On Whitsunday the great feast of the Holy Spirit is celebrated. In preparation for this, begging processions go through the streets, a long while in advance, in order to secure funds. In these expeditions, the collectors wear a red scarf (*capa*) over their shoulders; they make quite a display of flags, on which forms of a dove are embroidered, surrounded by a halo or gloria. These are handed in at windows and doors, and waved to individuals to kiss: they are followed by the silver plate or silk bag, which receives the donation expected from all those, at least, who kiss the emblem. The public are duly notified of the approach of these august personages by the music of a band of tatterdemalion negroes, or by the songs and tambourine accompaniments of sprightly boys who sometimes carry the banner.[39]

Mello Moraes tells how lively these festivals were in the towns near Rio de Janeiro:

> Through vales and mountains, along roads and through villages, months before the Festival of the Holy Spirit, joyful merrymakers wandered in bands through the interior of the province of Rio de Janeiro, collecting alms for the festivals in the main towns . . . Three, four, or five groups, depending on the size of the parishes or districts, set out on their journey . . . The flag of the Divine Holy Spirit, on which a painted dove on a background of sunbeams stood out on the red silk field, fringed with gold, silver, or wool, depending on how rich the brotherhoods were, and on top a wooden dove, silvered or gilt, with myriad colored ribbons flying from it . . . When the news came that the flags were in the neighborhood, there was no house that wasn't honored to receive a visit from them; even the poor man, in his humble dwelling, prepared himself to give the merrymakers an appropriate welcome . . . Hardly had the novenas begun than the oxcarts bringing families, pilgrims on horseback, and freedmen and slaves on foot made their way to the main church of the town . . . And the festi-

val—opulent, magnificent, full of pomp—culminated at the church . . .
At the same time, standing in the middle of four red-painted posts, was
the emperor: a child ten to twelve years old, dressed in a frock coat of
green velvet and a scarlet cloak, breeches, silk stockings, shoes with
buckles, with a crown and a scepter, and the gleaming emblems of
the Holy Spirit on his chest. Two stewards, with frock coats, wide-
brimmed straw hats, short swords, and breeches, held his train . . . On
this occasion there were cavalcades, and the traditional tournament
between Christians and Moors took place.[40]

Not only in the interior were these celebrations popular. In Rio de Janeiro
they were just as grand:

Until 1855 no popular festival in Rio de Janeiro was more attractive,
more infused with popular enthusiasm . . . At the time when we saw
this festival [1853–55] "empires" and bandstands were erected in three
of the capital's parishes . . . Barbershop bands of black slaves re-
hearsed marches, quadrilles, and fandangos when they were invited to
the celebrations . . . Forty days before the Sunday dedicated to the Divine Holy Spirit, the black boys' band, heading up a noisy crowd of
people, stopped in the Largo da Lapa, in front of an "empire" of white-
washed stone . . . As the music delighted the bystanders and brought
everyone together, two strong black men made holes in the ground
with heavy, pointed crowbars. When this was finished, the classic mast
was set up, with a newly silvered wooden dove, hovering a little below
the flag of the Divine Holy Spirit, with its gilt shining and its bright
colors . . . One [of the merrymakers] took the emperor by the hand;
he was a child of eight to ten, dressed in a red frock coat, breeches, and
cocked hat . . . On the "empire" the emperor, with his green mantle
and golden crown, stood out in the middle of his court.[41]

In Diamantina, Minas Gerais, Spix and Martius witnessed a triple celebration: homage to the coronation of Dom João VI as king of Portugal and
Brazil, the coronation of a king of the Congo, and a cavalcade:

Horsemen dressed in red and blue richly embroidered in gold, armed
with lances, acted out fights between Moors and Christians; these

jousts reminded one of the glorious chivalric period in Europe. Before this simulated combat, Christians and Moors mingled with each other; then they separated into two lines and ran at each other, attacking with lances or with swords and pistols. In the next show, running at rings, they managed with great agility, one after the other, to carry the ring speedily from the governor's seat to the opposite end of the track, where they hung it up again . . . A[nother] wonderful entertainment that reminded one of the gallant days of chivalry consisted of horsemen carrying beautiful wax pomegranates full of flowers, which they kissed, as a present to their ladies, and then threw them at one another as they ran, filling the field of battle with flowers. These amusing spectacles finished with single-file gallops in meanders, turns, and circles, in which the actors showed themselves to be very skilled horsemen, and so passed symbolically from warfare to friendship and Christian love.[42]

How strange that in the Brazilian interior, from the seventeenth century and continuing into the nineteenth, rituals were performed which included mulattos acting out armed conflict between Christians and Moors. The festival had a medieval atmosphere, with its heavy fabrics and velvet—all in the heat and color of the tropics. This strange scene was popular even though little was known in Brazil of European history; by such means, however, other conflicts found expression.

In Bahia, too, Spix and Martius were surprised by a spectacle of chivalric, medieval pomp:

Young men dressed as Moors and Christian knights, accompanied by loud music, went through the streets to a wide square where a tree was planted, decorated with the Portuguese coat of arms, like a German maypole. There was then violent fighting between the two hosts, which gave a special opportunity to the knight representing Saint George to show off his skills as a servant of the patron saint of Ilhéus. Both parties, however, following truly picture-book customs, soon forgot their enmity in a noisy banquet, followed by the sensual *lundu* [a popular dance, predecessor of the samba] and an almost immoral *batuque*.[43]

Such cavalcades were a constant in most major Brazilian civic and religious celebrations. Even when there was no explicit representation of a king, the knights were often called "peers of Gaul of the Emperor Charlemagne."

In 1859, Robert Avé-Lallemant saw a masked procession on New Year's Eve in Canavieiras, in which Christians and Moors did mock battle:

> Then came the masks: they abruptly divided up into two kinds. The first were those on horseback. One was made up like a Botocudo Indian, painted in bright red with all the jungle attributes and a Brazilian flag. The other was a blue horseman, another was a harlequin, and the others were divided up according to whether they had a piece of red or blue cloth in their hands. By their side there was a little army of the time of the Crusades, Christian and infidel infantry, who then fought around a fort improvised in front of the church, a new Jerusalem. All this was done with great dignity and devotional seriousness. These people spent some time going back and forth and did the most absurd things in the town but were always quite conscious of their dignity.[44]

Putting Botocudos together with medieval knights and harlequins, this festivity was plainly a translation itself, and its logic was greater than the object celebrated: nothing could be stranger than portraying the Crusades in a South American context.

Like cavalcades, *congadas* imitated combats between Christians and Moors. Their participants were not landowners, however, but slaves and freedmen, and they were perhaps more popular than cavalcades. The plot of a *congada* was fairly uniform: the king of the Congo, king of the Christians, receives a deputation from the king of the Moors (in some variants, Queen Ginga). He demands the infidels' conversion, they refuse, and immediately a battle begins. The struggles, transformed into dances, continue until the Moors are defeated and converted to Christianity. Henry Koster witnessed a *congada* in Pernambuco in 1814:

> We then adjourned to the sea-shore, for the purpose of witnessing the christening of the king of the Moors . . . Upon the sea-shore were two high thrones . . . The Christian king sat upon one of them, and the Moorish king upon the other, both of them being habited in fine flowing robes. The affair began by the former dispatching one of his officers on horseback to the other, requiring him to undergo the ceremony of baptism, which he refused to do . . . War being declared the nu-

merous sailing rafts and canoes of each party were soon in motion, making towards the fortress in the water; some were going to assist in protecting it, and others to obtain possession of it . . . There was much firing, and at last, after many struggles on both sides, it was taken by the Christians . . . The armies met on shore and fought hand to hand for a considerable time, but in the end the Moorish king was taken prisoner, hurled from his throne, and forcibly baptised.[45]

According to the folklorist Alfredo João Rabaçal, the first record of these dances dates to 6 June 1760, when in Santo Amaro, a town in Bahia, the marriage of Dona Maria I of Portugal to Prince Dom Pedro was celebrated. The second document is from 1793, when there was a *congada* for the birth of the princess of Beira. And in Tijuco (present-day Diamantina, Minas Gerais) another *congada* was enacted as part of the festivities surrounding the coronation of Dom João VI. So these first references to *congadas* coincide with commemorations of events linked to Portuguese royalty. The dialogue is between the kings of the Congo and "Dom Joãos" and "Dom Pedros," or between the Queen Gingas and "Dona Marias" and "princesses of Beira." Together these symbolic and real kings and queens constructed what we might call a system of royal imagery in Brazil.

Rabaçal found historical records of *congadas* in every Brazilian state. One, taken from the work of Silvio Romero, tells of a *congada* in 1883 in the town of Lagarto (Sergipe), on the Day of the Three Kings, when the Festival of Saint Benedict was also celebrated:

> The Congos are black men, dressed as kings and princes, armed with swords, who make up a kind of guard of honor for three black queens. The queens go in the middle, accompanying the procession of Saint Benedict and Our Lady of the Rosary, and are protected by this guard of honor from two or three of the group who try to take their crowns from them. The one who succeeds in getting a crown gets a prize, and this is shameful for the queen.[46]

The *congada* as rite tells us a great deal about nineteenth-century Brazil: two peoples and two nations are in conflict or engaged in some kind of negotiation. There is a dialogue between African and Portuguese "embassies," who struggle for political or at least cultural hegemony. In the end, conversion to

Christianity is inevitable, just as European political domination is unquestionable. But the cultural logic is different and develops differently: everyone is converted to Christianity, but the agent of this conversion is the king of the Congo. In some way this ensures that Africa wins and its memory persists.

Among the nonreligious festivities, *batuque* was one of the most widespread, a dance that took place on special occasions, like marriages, but also on ordinary nights. Luís de Câmara Cascudo comments on the African origin of the rite:

> Once the circle has been formed, two or three pairs of men and women jump into the middle of it, and the fun begins. The dance consists of a calm swaying of the body, marked by a slight movement of the feet, head, and arms. These movements speed up as the music gets livelier and more ecstatic, and soon we are witnessing an amazing shaking of the hips, which almost seems impossible to do without the dancers' dislocating their joints . . . The songs that accompany these lascivious dances are always immoral and even obscene, usually imitating love stories described with the most repellent, indecent nudity.[47]

And Seidler described a *batuque* during a black wedding ceremony in Rio Grande do Sul with the same critical eye:

> Hardly had midday come when the expected guests arrived, mostly blacks and mulattos, generally decorated with multicolored rags and all kinds of trinkets, and carrying black paper masks which they put over their faces, with openings only for the eyes and nose . . . An enormous, enthusiastic din accompanied the music, much worse than the noise made by a thousand parrots in the virgin Brazilian jungle, which threatened to burst our eardrums, already hardened to loud noise. Then the dance in the open air began, taking its rhythm from the music and the singing. Imagine the most unpleasant contractions of the muscles, with no cadence, the most innocent movements of half-naked arms and legs, the most daring leaps, flying skirts, the most disgusting imitations of gestures in which the crudest carnal desire was evidenced—this was the dance, in which these graceful people right from the beginning turned into bacchants and furies.[48]

Batuque. Rugendas, 1835. CGJM

What astonished Spix and Martius, however, was that "groups thought to be inferior"—the blacks—showed so much organization and enthusiasm in their festivals and dances:

> Whoever has had the opportunity to be present at these happy songs and dances, often carried to extremes of unbridled enthusiasm, which happen at sunset in the streets of Bahia and involve numerous groups of slaves, can hardly believe that these are the same slaves who, from the exaggerated description of philanthropic writers, one would imagine have been brought down to the condition of animals, to the crude level of instruments of the vilest form of egotism and of all the shameful passions.[49]

To the travelers *batuque* was like a shared ritual in which the slaves compensated for the rigors of everyday life and were freed from the harshness of slavery. This awareness is surprising: the travelers thought of European cultures as more or less advanced along the stages of civilization, but they saw these black rituals as spaces of liberty. "On feast days," wrote Seidler, "they [the slaves] are also allowed to indulge fully in their amusements. They then get together in places intended for such things, near the towns, to forget the pains and sorrows of the week in music and dance . . . One cannot expect much harmony from instruments like these, but the blacks feel very happy, for during these times they have the illusion of being independent and free."[50]

Not a few travelers commented on the blacks' liveliness in their conversation and songs even on ordinary days. Fletcher says of the black porters who worked in the narrow streets of Rio, "As one hand is sufficient to steady the load, they frequently carry musical instruments resembling children's rattle-boxes in the other: these they shake to the double-quick time of some wild Ethiopian ditty, which they all join in singing as they run."[51]

Both black festivals and religious rituals in the European tradition were altered in the Brazilian context. As Spix and Martius wrote, "The formalities of religious practice are observed with such fervor [by the blacks] that they take over leadership from the whites, and these latter, in many contexts, in some sense let them take precedence."[52]

Carnival in Brazil today is thought of as mongrelized, as mixed with black music and dance. When it first came to Brazil, however, it was imported from Portugal as a festival for the elites, who danced to the music of marches and fandangos. In the nineteenth century, celebrants enjoyed public dances and masked balls in halls and theaters, which, according to Vivaldo Coaracy, had been taking place since 1835.[53] It was not until 1855 that Carnival went into the streets with its allegorical floats. *Entrudo*, which predated Carnival and was much more popular, also came from Portugal. "The Monday and Tuesday before Ash Wednesday," Koster observed, "are properly the days of the *intrudo*, but the sport . . . often commences a week before the appointed time. Water and hair powder are the ingredients meant to be hurled, but frequently no medium is preserved, and every thing is taken up heedlessly and thrown about by all parties, whether it may do mischief or is harmless."[54] In spite of this critical tone, Koster seems to have enjoyed himself at the *entrudo*:

> Even the blackened pots and pans from the kitchen were introduced to besmear each other's faces. We obtained here a view of the females belonging to the house; but everywhere else, they had been rigorously guarded or were naturally too reserved to enable us to see them. Some excuse was made by the young men who were acquainted with the family to draw them into the sport; and the ladies and the slaves were nothing loath to see and participate in what was going forwards. A cir-

Carnival Scene. Jean-Baptiste Debret, 1835. FMCM

cumstance occurred which created much laughter and which is but
too characteristic. One man whom we had met at this place had all
along begged of those were engaged in the sport, that they would not
wet him, because he was unwell; however, it was seen that he did not
observe towards others that forbearance which he entreated from
them towards himself. One of our party, seeing this, attacked him with
a large silver ladle filled with water . . . the women made a general attack upon him; he went to the stable, mounted his horse, and set
forth; but his misfortunes had not yet ended, for the path by which he
must retreat lay under two of the windows of the house, two large tubs
of water drenched him and his steed, which immediately quickened
its pace, amidst the hooting of everyone present.[55]

Fletcher has given us his account of the festival:

The Intrudo . . . extends through the three days preceding Lent, and
is generally entered upon by the people with an apparent determination to redeem time for amusement in advance of the long restraint
anticipated . . . Before it was suppressed by the police it was a marked
event. It is not with showers of sugar-plums that persons were saluted
on the days of the Intrudo, but with showers of oranges and eggs, or

rather of waxen balls made in the shape of oranges and eggs, but filled with water. These articles were made in immense quantities beforehand, and exposed for sale in the shops and streets. The shell was of sufficient strength to admit of being hurled a considerable distance, but at the moment of collision it broke to pieces, bespattering whatever it hit. Unlike the somewhat similar sport of snowballing in cold countries, this *jogo* [game] was not confined to boys or to the streets, but was played in high life as well as in low, indoors and out. Common consent seemed to have given the licence of pelting anyone and everyone at pleasure, whether entering a house to visit or walking in the streets.

In fact, whoever went out at all on these days expected a ducking and found it well to carry an umbrella; for in the enthusiasm of the game the waxen balls were frequently soon consumed: then came into play syringes, basins, bowls, and sometimes pails of water, which were plied without mercy until the parties were thoroughly drenched . . .

The magistrates of the different districts formally declared against the Intrudo from year to year, but with little effect until 1854, when a new *chef de police* with great energy put a stop to the violent Intrudo and its peltings and duckings. It is now conducted in a dry but humorous manner, more in the style of Paris and Rome.[56]

Entrudo engaged large sections of the population, who gave themselves over to the "game," temporarily forgetting differences of age, rank, and sex. Even after it was prohibited in 1854, *entrudo* went on, though on a lesser scale, for some time. With its transgressive nature, *entrudo* was a kind of elder brother to Carnival, which brought together members of the elite and the imperial family. Carnival's zenith, according to Mello Moraes, was between 1854 and 1871, which is when the merrymakers went into the streets and made it a national festival.

Mello Moraes describes the first allegorical parade in Rio de Janeiro in 1855, when the Congress of Carnival Highnesses (Congresso das Sumidades Carnavalescas) held its procession. A commission went to the São Cristóvão Palace to ask Dom Pedro II and the princesses to be at the City Palace when the Congress passed. The request was acceded to, and the emperor watched the parade, in which several "men of letters" also took part, like José de Alencar, Manuel Antônio de Almeida, Pinheiro Guimarães, Augusto de Castro, and Laurindo Rabelo:

The people formed themselves into ranks in front of the palace; in the crowd the "old bigheads," with a stick and a pair of eyeglasses, held up huge papier-mâché heads in the air, shaking them back and forth; the bearded "little devils" twirled their masks and rolled their red tails round their waists . . . The sense of expectation was amazing! The imperial family came to the balconies, and the hurrahs and cries of *viva*, like a pyramid of sound rising from the multitude, had, at its undulating base, the awe of all those people . . . And the sounds could be heard coming closer and closer . . . Soon the brass band of the Congress of Carnival Highnesses crossed the square dressed in the picturesque uniform of Ukrainian Cossacks . . . It is impossible to describe the crowd's enthusiasm![57]

We cannot fail to see the social gap between *entrudo* and Carnival: the first more individualist and anarchic, "the second a more organized game, intellectualized and seen from above, from up on the floats or from high society ballrooms."[58] Until 1870, in fact, there were constant complaints about the people who came to the central part of Rio to see the *entrudo* processions. The "new Carnival" was in fact part of a wider "civilizing project," an attempt to change the character of the Brazilian ritual and copy the Venetian model. It was characterized from the start by the higher social standing of its participants, differentiated from mere rabble amusing themselves in the streets. Students, artists, journalists, and literary men were among the members of the Grandes Sociedades created in the 1860s and 1870s.

To the distress of the *carioca* elite, however, Carnival went on sharing the streets with *entrudo* into the 1880s. In a letter dated 22 February 1887, mailed in Petrópolis, the emperor wrote to the countess of Barral: "Nothing new. It has rained quite a lot; but it is still hot. *Entrudo*, thank heavens, has been very quiet in Rio, and here, it hardly took place at all."[59]

Carnival highlighted Dom Pedro's palace-bound, elitist side; it was also an ideal locale for political criticism of him. In the 1880s, the emperor was a frequent character on the allegorical floats, either as Pedro Banana or Pedro Cashew, and his lack of public participation in the last years of the empire was often noted. Still, it was only after the real monarchy fell that a king of Carnival was elected. In the nineteenth century Momus was not a king but a mocking Greek god, a lover of laughter and revelry. In 1933 he became King Momus and a common citizen. Habits changed with the times.

It is unusual for nineteenth-century travelers who visited the provinces of northeastern Brazil not to comment on the ceremonies of the coronation of the "king of the Congo":

> In March took place the yearly festival of Our Lady of the Rosary, which was directed by negroes; and at this period is chosen the king of the Congo nation, if the person who holds this situation has died in the course of the year, has from any cause resigned, or has been displaced by his subjects. The Congo negroes are permitted to elect a king and queen from among the individuals of their own nation; the personages who are fixed upon may either actually be slaves, or they may be manumitted negroes. These sovereigns exercise a species of mock jurisdiction over their subjects which is much laughed at by the whites; but their chief power and superiority over their countrymen is shown on the day of the festival.[60]

These popular black rituals, with their luxury and pomp, their group dances and songs, dated from seventeenth-century Portugal. Sometimes they recalled episodes from African wars, but they were enacted on Catholic saints' days.[61] In Minas Gerais, as we have already mentioned, along with festivities surrounding Dom João VI's coronation, Spix and Martius observed the coronation of an African king:

> From the moment of our arrival in Tijuco, measures had been taken to celebrate the king's coronation with patriotic festivities, organized simultaneously throughout Brazil . . . Heralds opened the procession, followed by a chorus of singers and four more figures representing the vast dominions of the Portuguese monarchy, who had a globe, decorated with emblems of the European, the Indian, the Oriental, the black, and the American, on which appeared the image of Dom João VI . . . The blacks also tried to participate in this extraordinary patriotic celebration in their own way; choosing a king gave them the best opportunity to do so. It is the custom among the blacks of Brazil, each year, to appoint a king and his court. This king has no civic or political prestige over his fellow blacks but simply enjoys an empty dignity,

like that of the King of Beans on the day of the Three Kings in Europe: for this reason the Luso-Brazilian government does not impede this meaningless formality. The king of the Congo and Queen Ginga were chosen by general vote, and several princes and princesses, with six *mafucas* (servants, male and female), and they went, in solemn procession, to the blacks' church . . . The newly elected king, a freed black and a cobbler by trade, became so shy when he saw the local governor that he dropped his scepter when he was asked to sit on the couch. Ferreira da Câmara affably picked it up and gave it back to the king, already tired of governing, with the words: "Your majesty has dropped his scepter!" . . . The festivities finally ended with a shout from the king of the blacks, which all his people repeated: "Long live El-rei Dom João VI!" There is plenty of opportunity for interesting reflections on the past, and on the vision of the future, at the sight of this strange festival![62]

The heralds' emblems, in their turn, were decorated with models that spoke of different universes: "the European, the Indian, the Oriental, the black, and the American."

The festival affirmed Portuguese sovereignty in this tropical colony, which although it was respected did not fill the space of kingship for the blacks, for whom the coronation of Dom João VI became almost a pretext for choosing a new king of the Congo.

Mello Moraes described an earlier coronation of a black king in the Chapel of Our Lady of Lampadosa on 3 December 1748, when the black Brotherhood of the Saint and King Balthasar received authorization to crown one of its members:

And along the streets, through the city, going into the plantations of Engenho Velho, Engenho Novo, Santa Cruz, as far as they were permitted to go, there were groups of blacks, dancing and singing . . . Men, women, and children, fully rejoicing in their one day of freedom, for a while forgot the palm trees of their country, the idols of their homeland, and awaited the ceremony of the coronation of their sovereign, and adored the Saint and King Balthasar, who reminded them, by his skin color, of the color of their skin and of their destiny . . . From the little chapel with its closed doors, the chaplain enjoyed the savage spectacle, and the African blacks, on the Day of the [Three] Kings, thought themselves lucky, forgetting the deserts of their homeland and the crossing of the ocean.[63]

After so many kings, we must not forget to mention an African queen who lived on as a character on Brazilian soil. Queen Ginga and her court were regular features in the processions of Our Lady of the Rosary and Saint Benedict and sometimes in the *congadas*, when they occasionally took the place of the king of the Moors. Avé-Lallemant was present at a festival in which this queen figured:

Black men and women were swarming in front of the church and in the adjacent streets. All the old court of Queen Ana Chinga seemed to be gathered: an original, genuine picture of Africa. I really could not fail to watch the many black women, and many were as perfect as the beauties of the Costa da Mina. Some of them were fine sculptures in basalt, *en negligée*, with one breast bared, splendidly erect, with strong, flexible, rounded forms of shining black, many with their shoulders bare quite far down, their backs decorated with hieroglyphs tattooed on their skin, symbols, perhaps, of a certain noble origin. These are hieroglyphs that Europeans cannot decipher and cannot even tell apart, but that have a meaning for Africans.[64]

This pride of the "court of Chinga" (or Ginga) corresponds to the historical figure of an African queen who, legend says, had an ambiguous relationship with the Portuguese. Although she converted to Catholicism and exercised a great fascination for Europeans, she also quarreled with and made war on the colonizers.* This same complexity in the cultural sphere—dialogue and rejection, alliance and warfare—was present in the daily lives of

*In 1558 nomadic people had occupied lands to the south of the kingdom of the Congo and founded the dynasty of the Gingas, which was finally established in Angola. Some generations later, in the seventeenth century, the sister of the king of the Gingas, Queen Ginga, took power and ferociously resisted Portuguese rule. In 1621 the queen led a delegation whose object was to establish a dialogue with the governor, João Correia de Sousa, in Luanda, and he, impressed by Ginga's vivacity and imposing figure, took her under his protection and baptized her with the name of Dona Ana de Sousa. In 1623, when her brother murdered her son, she abandoned Catholicism and took up her campaign against the Portuguese again. But in 1656, when Portugal reconquered Angola, Ginga returned to Christianity and was married in the Catholic Church in the next year.[65]

the slaves and their masters in Brazil. Parallel desires for resistance or acceptance expressed their duality in rituals like the *congada*. Perhaps that is why
this queen crossed the ocean and became a symbol, and why, in the *congadas*, Queen Ginga took the role of the adversary of the Christians.

Opinions of the significance of the black kings differ, however. Mário de
Andrade, for example, notes that on the plantations the king was an interme-
diary between the master and the other slaves:

> Nor is it surprising that the cunning white man, whether religious or
> secular, encouraged the blacks to have these delusory kingdoms. One
> of the pieces from the *congadas* that I collected goes like this: "Our
> king is the only one that / Tells us all to work." A text like this proves
> the real function of these colonial Congo kingdoms: at a time when
> slaves were in the majority, these black kings and queens, whom the
> priests and masters respected and whom the secular leaders of the
> colony even honored and paid homage to, as if they were legitimate
> kings—these delusory kings were useful instruments in the hands of
> the masters . . . [They] had a very useful function for the whites.[66]

It is difficult to disagree with this assessment, for the black kings and
queens often muffled latent conflicts between masters and slaves. But culture
is not merely the reflection of political structure, and as we have seen, if it is
manipulated, it also "manipulates," and it gives evidence of imaginative
structures that transcend the immediate context. At the same time as the
black kings functioned as an instrument of domination, they also opened a
space to new interpretations, and became a way to incorporate Portuguese
domination into certain African cosmological worlds and value systems.

The election of kings of the Congo, the creation of black brotherhoods,
the festivals and processions with their own patron saints—these were means
to create loyalties and see oneself as a member of a group and thus as less "foreign." The veneration of particular kings and saints represents in some way
the construction of a nation, of a "familiar Brazil" within "foreign Brazil."
True, it did nothing to change the slave's condition and even added to the
means of domination. But by these cultural means the different worlds entered into dialogue, and groups excluded from higher social and political
echelons found ways to give specific, parallel meanings to official rituals. All
these processes dwindled away, so to speak, as Brazil began to urbanize, and

in this respect they accompanied the fate of the monarchy itself. These festivals are no longer part of Brazil's official calendar, but they survive as an ethos, as it were, in a country still strongly marked by "festival time," where official rulers often give way to the ones celebrated in the imagination.

In Rio de Janeiro, very close to the São Cristóvão Palace, was a district known as Little Africa. Commentators on life in Rio like the novelist Afonso Henriques de Lima Barreto spoke of the "African fortress" when they saw, over by Prainha, Conceição, and Santa Rita, the mass of miracle workers and herbalists, of little stalls and chicken coops. In this district lived a royal African distinguished by being a "friend" of the emperor Dom Pedro II:

> An outstanding figure at the receptions at São Cristóvão [is] Sublieutenant Galvão, a deceptive title beneath which is hidden an illustrious personage, no more no less than King Obá II, of Africa, a pretender to the throne who, stripped of his right of inheritance, has now set his sights on sovereignty over the whole of Africa. Galvão is a black man born in Bahia, and his father, Obá I, was in fact a king in Africa;* he was, however, defeated in war and sold as a slave in Brazil, where he later bought his freedom—far too late to return to Africa and reclaim his throne. His son, who is called Galvão in Brazil, fought in the war against Paraguay and was so distinguished by his bravery that he was made an honorary sublieutenant in the army. It seems that the honor went to his head, because as soon as his father died, he put out a manifesto in all the papers here, to all the people of Africa, in which he made it known that he was ascending the throne as Obá II, and since then he has from time to time offered public manifestos in the press, less correct grammatically than they are interesting, in which he discusses Brazilian questions as Obá II. He is naturally a monarchist and a conservative, for he is a prince . . . Obá II is a big, strong black man, with a Henry IV–style beard; he has smart black clothes and a gold pince-nez with blue lenses. He treats everyone with condescension, as befits a prince; he comes forward to the front line without looking around him . . . with his superior smile he then looks at the others,

*Obá means "king" in Yoruba.

loftily greets the servants, and, dignified, awaits the arrival of the emperor. Then, however, his pride melts like butter in the sun. He does not shake his hand as prince to prince. No; His Majesty Obá II bends his knees like a humble vassal and, still on his knees, kisses the emperor's hand . . . This scene is repeated more or less every Saturday.[67]

Prince Obá, or Dom Obá II, reigned in Little Africa and presided over its rituals and festivals. He moved through the streets as if they were rooms in his palace and, correctly attired, was greeted appropriately: "Obá! Prince Obá!" Regularly received by Dom Pedro, Obá dressed on these occasions in his military uniform. Sometimes the palace guards saluted his arrival, calling him king, at which Obá was moved and answered with tips and thanks. Mello Moraes reports on interesting details about his political life:

It is said that on 2 December [Dom Pedro's birthday], following the proclamation of the republic [in 1889], Prince Obá went to the palace as usual to present his compliments to the emperor; that, finding the doors shut, or being ordered to go away, he became furious and burst out with "hurrahs" and other nonsense. We are not sure how much truth there is in this; what is true, however, is that the provisional government of the republic removed his sublieutenant's commission and that he survived this painful event by only a few months.[68]

The day after his death, Rio's main newspapers dedicated obituaries to Obá, according to which he was a favorite figure in the endless gallery of types who inhabited the streets of the city.[69]

It is interesting to ponder the relations between these two "royalties," so different but in some sense drawing together toward the end of the empire. Dom Pedro II received a self-styled monarch who mixed African titles with medals from the Paraguayan war and treated him as a real king. He, in turn, recognized the hierarchy, like a vassal to the king. Monarchical loyalty was stronger than the "storms of politics." Dom Pedro did not survive into the new times any more than Obá, who died almost at the same time as the Brazilian monarchy.

Obá is not an isolated case. Mello Moraes highlights the fact that figures like King Neuvangue, Queen Nembanda, the princes Menafundo, the wizard Endoque, and the Uatafanos—slaves who were vassals of the emperor—were traditionally present at African festivals celebrated in Rio de Janeiro. Apart from these individuals, another popular character in the capital was Prince Dom Miguer

Manuer Pereira da Natureza, Sová, Gorá, Vange.* Better known as Prince Nature, this Miguel—a former slave and an employee of the navy—used to say that he was a member of His Majesty's Council and a "most faithful subject of Lord Dom Pedro II of Brazir, decorated by Lord Dom Miguer I of Portugar, and grand cross of the Princes of Marta of the times of Afonso Henriques."[70]

So there were tropical quasi-European emperors living in palaces beside enslaved African kings who reigned among their fellow slaves. Fletcher tells the story of an African king who came to Brazil and was sold into slavery:

> There is now a Mina black in Rio remarkable for his height, who is called "the Prince," being, in fact, of the *blood royal* of his native country. He was a prisoner of war, and sold to Brazil. It is said that his *subjects* in Rio once freed him by their toil: he returned, engaged in war, and was a second time made prisoner and brought back. Whether he will again regain his throne I know not; but the loss of it does not seem to weigh heavily on his mind. He is an excellent carrier; and when a friend of mine embarked, the "Prince" and his troop were engaged to transport the baggage to the ship.[71]

Once a king always a king: so it was that, without the throne but with the "poise," many African kings continued to be respected as such. It was a paradoxical situation. When the slaves came to Brazil, they were no longer identified by the kingdoms they had belonged to, nor by their old positions in the African hierarchies. For this reason they developed structures that no longer corresponded to African reality and elected kings of the Congo who did not necessarily come from the Congo.

> The election of the King of Congo . . . by the individuals who come from that part of Africa, seems indeed as if it would give them a bias towards the customs of their native soil; but the Brazilian Kings of Congo worship Our Lady of the Rosary and are dressed in the dress of white men; they and their subjects dance, it is true, after the manner of their country; but to these festivals are admitted African negroes of other nations, creole blacks, and mulattos, all of whom dance after the same manner; and these dances are now as much the national dances of Brazil as they are of Africa.[72]

*The name is comic: Miguer and Manuer imitate the black pronunciation of Miguel and Manuel, themselves "ordinary" names like "John Doe," as is the surname Pereira.

At Carnival in 1996 a famous Rio samba school presented the following *samba-enredo*:

> At the bottom of the sea
> There's a castle belonging to King Sebastian
> There's witchcraft, there are secrets
> My love, I'm frightened of dreaming of ghosts.

The Sebastianist cults in nineteenth-century Brazil involved manifestations of fanaticism and apocalyptic notions about the end of the world and the birth of a new era:

> The distinguishing tenet of this [Sebastianist] sect is the belief that Don Sebastian, king of Portugal, who, in 1578, undertook an expedition against the Moors in Africa, and who, having been defeated, never returned, is still alive, and destined yet to make his re-appearance on earth . . . The Portuguese look for his appearance in Lisbon, but the Brazilians generally think it most likely that he will first revisit his own city, St. Sebastian.*
>
> It appears, however, that a reckless villain named João Antonio fixed upon a remote part of the province of Pernambuco, near Piancó, in the Comarca de Flores, for the appearance of the said Don Sebastian. The place designated was a dense forest, near which were known to be two acroceraunian [*sic*] caverns. This spot, the impostor said, was an enchanted kingdom, which was about to be disenchanted, whereupon Don Sebastian would immediately appear at the head of a great army, with glory, and with power to confer wealth and happiness upon all who should anticipate his coming by associating themselves with the said João Antonio.
>
> As might be expected, he found followers, who, after a while, learned that the imaginary kingdom was to be disenchanted by having its soil sprinkled with the blood of one hundred innocent children! In default of a sufficient number of children, men and women were to be immolated, but in a few days they would all rise and become possessed of the riches of the world. The prophet appears to have lacked the

---

*By a strange coincidence, in March 1565, *before* the death of King Sebastian, Estácio de Sá founded the city of St. Sebastian of Rio de Janeiro, as a homage to the young prince. But from then on, and because of Sebastian's sad destiny, different places claimed to be the place to which he would return.[73]

courage necessary to carry out his bloody scheme, but he delegated power to an accomplice, named João Ferreira, who assumed the title of "His Holiness," put a wreath of rushes on his head, and required the proselytes to kiss his toe, on pain of instant death. After other deeds too horrible to describe, he commenced the slaughter of human beings . . . In the course of two days he had thus, in cold blood, slain twenty-one adults and twenty children, when a brother of the prophet, becoming jealous of "His Holiness," thrust him through and assumed his power.[74]

Even as Kidder displays horror and skepticism, his story shows how this sect developed in Brazil. Nor was it only impoverished and despairing Brazilians who adhered to Sebastianism. In the Caraça mountains, near Vila Rica de Ouro Preto, Spix and Martius were guests in the house of a Sebastianist who seemed to enjoy a good social position: "The demeanor of our distinguished host, with his gray hair, was a little solemn, and he reminded us unintentionally of the Quakers. In fact, he was one of the adepts of Sebastianism, who are always waiting for the king to return. These Sebastianists, distinguished by their diligence, thriftiness, and charity, are more common in Brazil, and especially in Minas Gerais, than in the mother country itself."[75]

At the time of the foundation of the Brazilian monarchy, José Bonifácio underlined the correlation between royalty in the Western Hemisphere and the emergence of millenarianism of the Fifth Empire—"the empire of the earth on the earth"—as Vieira had prophesied in his *History of the Future* (1718). When Dom Pedro II was born, he was acclaimed not only as the first "genuinely Brazilian" king but as a little King Sebastian, who summed up the hopes of the young nation. As cosmologies mixed with one another, Portuguese mysticism became a Brazilian affair.

Looking at these festivals, we get a closer view of Brazil's popular imagination, which kept its distance from the official world of politics. Here participation was above all religious and social and, as José Murilo de Carvalho says, "It could be found in the great popular festivals, like those of the Penha, the Glória, or at *entrudo*: it was found in small ethnic communities, limited to one place or even to one house."[76] Whether or not the festivals were linked to the elite's project of giving prominence to the empire, their representations of royalty gave the monarchy greater visibility, even if in unusual forms. Surrounded by so much hope, Dom Pedro became a king with many crowns; he reigned

The emperor and empress, with their daughters and sons-in-law.
Insley Pacheco, 1865. MMP

like a king among kings. In 1864 Dom Pedro's daughters, Dona Isabel and
Dona Leopoldina, were married, the first on 15 October, the second on 15 December. It is said that when the two suitors arrived—Gaston, the count d'Eu
(son of the duc de Nemours, married to Victoria of Saxe-Coburg), and his
cousin Luís Augusto, duke of Saxe—everything had been fixed. It was to be
Augusto for Isabel, Gaston for Leopoldina. But when they got to know them
the sisters exchanged suitors. Again, the court experienced the opulent pomp
and circumstance of royal marriages. The first one was the more important,
since Isabel was crown princess of the empire, but the second repeated the
ceremonial pomp at full volume.* Still, the atmosphere was already beginning to change. The ill winds of war were blowing over the Brazilian Empire,
and they would alter the mystique of a monarchy made sacred by the Catholic
Church and given new dimensions in the eyes of the people.

*The marriage of Princess Isabel and the count d'Eu was a long one. She died in France in 1921, and
he in 1922 on board the *Massilia*, which was bringing him back to Brazil for the first time since the
proclamation of the republic. Leopoldina died in Vienna in 1870, leaving four children; her widower
did not marry again and died in 1907.

The count d'Eu. Margeon and Van Nagel, Princess Isabel. Insley Pacheco, 1869. MMP
c. 1870. MMP

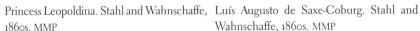

Princess Leopoldina. Stahl and Wahnschaffe, Luís Augusto de Saxe-Coburg. Stahl and
1860s. MMP Wahnschaffe, 1860s. MMP

ELEVEN

The Paraguayan War

VOLUNTEER NUMBER ONE

Dom Pedro II. CPCL

Festivals were not everything in Brazil. The decade of the 1860s was a turning point in the placid world of imperial politics: Dom Pedro took an active part in Brazil's conflict with Paraguay in 1864, and assumed the central role in Brazil's politics that he already had in its cultural life. The Paraguayan war was a high point in the history of Dom Pedro's reign, the moment of its greatest maturity, but we can also see, even if only in hindsight, that paradoxically it was also the beginning of its fall. In its first year the conflict brought many benefits to the monarch, who as warrior-king became even more popular in the national imagination.[1] But the war was not as short as Dom Pedro, his ministers, generals, and allies, Argentina and Uruguay, had hoped. And as it went on, the Brazilian government was so exclusively dedicated to pursuing it that it left little time for internal reforms. Also, the expenses entailed by the war were immense—614,000 contos, eleven times the annual budget for 1864—which created a deficit that persisted until 1889.[2] And in the last two years of the war, when the conflict was virtually over, the emperor took on as his personal mission to hunt down Paraguay's leader, the *caudillo* López, an enterprise that ended up costing him dear. In the end, the army that the imperial state had developed during the war along more modern, organized lines helped, together with the Paulista Republican Party, to overthrow Brazil's monarchy.

Let us first take a brief look at the setting. Even before the war broke out in 1865, the storm was approaching. In 1862, when Brazil was proudly preparing to take part in the London Universal Exhibition, the so-called Christie Question arose. William Dougall Christie, the British representative in the Brazilian capital since 1860, had created several diplomatic deadlocks during his time there. First he clashed with the Caxias cabinet, when it objected to his removing some crewmen from a British frigate at anchor in Rio; the Brazilians believed they should have been brought to justice in Rio. Later in 1861 he protested about another incident, the pillaging of the wreck of the *Prince of Wales* off the coast of Rio Grande do Sul. Things got worse in the following year, when three British officers wandering around drunk in Rio were arrested for insulting policemen, which Christie took as an affront to the United Kingdom. In reprisal, he ordered the commander of the British fleet in Rio to blockade the port, which nearly led to a serious diplomatic crisis.

Brazilian politicians took Christie's attitudes with a grain of salt. "He learned diplomacy in mosquito land," said the baron of Penedo; Zacarias said that these incidents were "Mr. Christie's lunacies."[3] But his worst was not to appear at the celebrations for Dom Pedro II's birthday, on 2 December 1862, to which the entire diplomatic corps had been invited. For the first time since the construction of his summer palace in Petrópolis, the emperor did not go there, as he usually did every year after Christmas, so as to be able to deal with this crisis in Rio. Given the emperor's determined intransigence, Christie gave way, but relations between Brazil and Britain were sundered for two years. Only in 1865 did a special British envoy acknowledge that the British were to blame in the incident.

In 1865, Dom Pedro's cousin, the archduke Maximilian, who had reigned as emperor in Mexico City for two years, with the support of Napoleon III and French troops, was executed. With the end of its own Civil War, the United States had turned its attention to the Mexican situation and forced France to retreat from Mexico in 1866. Former president Benito Juárez returned to power and ended this short, fragile experiment in having a puppet emperor. Even though he knew that Maximilian was doomed, Dom Pedro had hardly intervened in Mexico. Maybe his cousin's ironic comments about Brazil stayed in his memory. In his *Bahia 1860: Sketch from a Journey* (1861), the archduke had painted a pitiless portrait of the Brazilian court, which was far too provincial in his view.

The 1860s also saw the campaign for the abolition of slavery intensify. With the end of the transatlantic slave trade in 1850 and the Civil War in the United States, the question became one of major importance for Brazil.

But the new crisis in the Rio da Prata region slowed down the vital process of adjustment on the slave issue and itself became a national issue, above party politics. Though Brazil was the victor, the disastrous Paraguayan war (also known as the War of the Triple Alliance and, in Paraguay, as the Great War) had many more negative than positive consequences for the Brazilian imperial government.

Tensions on Brazil's southern frontiers had momentarily relaxed in the early 1860s, though the unsolved riddle was clearly dangerous: four nations— Argentina, Brazil, Uruguay, and Paraguay—all had borders along three great rivers, the Paraná, the Paraguay, and the Uruguay, and were competing not merely for land and for access to navigable channels, but for hegemony in the region. Long before the war, there had been a ministerial crisis in 1849, caused by a deadlock over Brazil's policy in the Rio da Prata region, and on how to deal with the threat posed by the Argentine dictator, Juan Manuel de Rosas, who wanted to realize an old dream of bringing Uruguay and Paraguay into a confederation like the old Vice-Royalty of the Rio da Prata. He had already secured allies in Uruguay, and now threatened Brazil's frontier along the Rio Grande do Sul.

In Rio, Foreign Minister Olinda knew of these intentions but, perhaps remembering the disastrous policy of Pedro I that had led to war with Argentina, insisted on continuing with negotiations. He was then removed as president of the council, and Minister of Justice Eusébio de Queirós replaced him. The emperor's participation in these events was decisive. He was by this time a father and was breaking free of his old tutors; he was beginning to intervene more directly in national policy.

From then until the end of the Paraguayan war, Rio da Prata affairs became the principal subject of Brazilian foreign policy. As the historian Heitor Lyra says, for a large part of the elite they were an education in diplomacy. Paranhos (future viscount of Rio Branco), Sinimbu, Pimenta da Veiga (later marquis of São Vicente), among many others, played important parts. The emperor made the vital decisions, but these men did the hard work. The first war was at least short: with Paulino José Soares de Sousa as foreign minister, Brazil began hostilities in 1851, Rosas was surrounded, and he capitulated in February 1852.

It was a precarious equilibrium. In 1863, civil war had broken out in Uruguay between the Colorados, led by General Venancio Flores, and the Blancos, led by Atanasio Aguirre, president of the divided country. Brazil and Argentina both supported Flores, since they feared the more nationalist attitude of the Blancos, who were opposed to the treaties that had been signed with Brazil, which they considered humiliating. When negotiations broke down on 21 July 1864, the Brazilian government sent an ultimatum to Aguirre, and eventually the crisis subsided; on 15 February 1865 Aguirre handed over power to a Colorado government. Tomás Villalba, elected president, soon signed a peace treaty with Brazil.

But war started up again, with new issues at stake and with a new enemy, Paraguay. There, President Carlos Antonio López had died in 1862, and his son, Francisco Solano López, continued his father's policy of importing foreign technology to develop the country. He soon came into conflict with Brazil, where the Liberals came to power after two decades of Conservative rule. For one thing, Dom Pedro did not welcome his failed attempt to mediate between Brazil and Uruguay, and for another, Paraguay competed with Brazil for the position of chief supplier of yerba maté in the Latin American market. Lastly, in Argentina, the Federalist Party, although recently defeated by Bartolomé Mitre, who began a process of centralizing the state, was still active and, like Paraguay, saw the port of Montevideo as an alternative outlet for exports. There were thus two opposing informal alliances: on the one side were the Argentine Federalists, the Uruguayan Blancos, and Paraguay; on the other, the Argentine government, the Uruguayan Colorados, and Brazil.

The kindling had been laid, and all that was needed was a spark. It happened on Uruguayan territory in 1864, when the Brazilian government sent a fleet led by Admiral Tamandaré to investigate accusations of violence perpetrated against Brazilian citizens there, demanding that measures be taken within six days, and that those responsible be punished. These Brazilian demands were not acceded to, and the reply was immediate: a brief invasion of Uruguay. On 10 November the Paraguayan authorities, without having broken diplomatic ties with Brazil, captured the Brazilian ship *Marquês de Olinda* as it went upriver toward the Brazilian province of Mato Grosso, and in December López's troops successfully invaded Mato Grosso. Four months later, in April 1865, López invaded Argentina, attacking Corrientes. Then, in June, he entered the province of Rio Grande do Sul.

Rather unexpectedly, the emperor decided to go to the frontier as soon as he heard what had happened. This reaction was unusual for Dom Pedro II: military men were, "for this insatiable student of the sciences, . . . if not people who would in the future become useless, [were] at least a necessity for which he could find better roles—not as soldiers but as mathematicians, astronomers, or engineers."[4] Nobody expected so much daring from a monarch whose peaceable nature, removed from the slightest experience of war, might lead him unwittingly into danger. The emperor was very far from being a wartime leader and was not interested in military affairs. Some accounts even exaggerated his "civilian" nature, claiming, for example, that he had once, while watching a military parade, said, "They are all legalized assassins."[5] So this news of his departure for the front was badly received and misunderstood by the cabinet, who argued against his going.

Paying no heed, on 7 July Dom Pedro II, or "Volunteer Number One," as they said at the time, set out for the south, accompanied by the minister of war, Ângelo Ferraz (later baron of Uruguaiana). (The sailing of his boat the *Santa Maria* caused a certain commotion, because the duke of Saxe, Dom Pedro's son-in-law, his younger daughter's husband, went with him.) The count d'Eu met them in Caçapava, and after their long trip they set up a large square tent for the emperor, the princes, and the principal officers. The official images were those of a monarch getting ready for combat.

The march ended at Uruguaiana, where the emperor met his military commanders—Manuel Marques de Souza Porto Alegre, Caldwell, and Tamandaré—and prepared to meet his allies.

The emperor ready to leave for Uruguaiana and the war, shown in the background, S. A. Sisson. MIP

Who benefited from this war? What caused the unexpected determination of the Brazilian monarch, who until then had emphasized his moderate, noninterventionist intentions? There are various interpretations. According to one school of thought, the origins of the war lie in López's overweening ambition and his dictatorial, authoritarian aims, his truculence and his treachery, and in Dom Pedro's supposed aversion for a man whom he saw as a typical *caudillo*. But this explanation overemphasizes personality and omits the strategic questions in play at the time.

More recently, a so-called revisionist analysis has found the explanation of the conflict in British imperialism: eager to maintain its own economic influence in the area, Britain interfered in the conflict, creating enmities and friendships. If this is true, the common enemy shared by Britain and Brazil was Paraguay, a challenge to Britain because of the more autonomous economic model it was creating, so different from the slave-owning Brazilian Empire and from Argentina, two nations dominated by an oligarchy of landowners and merchants, and inimical to Brazil because it posed a threat to the region's stability. In this perspective, López is an anti-imperialist hero and the victim of an international conspiracy.[6] These studies grasp the larger conceptual context, but they fail to be convincing for lack of supporting facts and empirical evidence.

A third interpretation concentrates more on the different processes of national development that each country was passing through and on the geopolitical and economic interests at stake in the Rio da Prata region.[7] Brazil, for instance, wanted to guarantee navigation rights along the rivers Paraná and Paraguay, since only in this way could the province of Mato Grosso maintain contact with the rest of the country. In addition, trade there was extremely dynamic.

Argentina's expansionist aims had been suppressed, but the country still had a latent desire to annex neighboring territory, which must be remembered as one of the reasons for Brazil's immediate support for the independence of Paraguay and Uruguay. As for Paraguay, once its independence had been recognized and Argentine impulses were under control, it then came under pressure over disagreements about borders and navigation rights. Brazil wanted these rights guaranteed, while the Paraguayans made it conditional on the formalization of the borders at the River Branco. (Brazil wanted the Apa to be the border.) We should not forget its mistrust of Brazil, a gigantic slave-owning empire that was doubtless a real threat to the small South American republics, which were frightened by imperialism within the continent itself.

The meeting of the allies in Uruguaiana was unprecedented, for Dom Pedro had never before had personal contact with any Latin American leaders.[8] The Argentine Bartolomé Mitre was forty-five, tall, and elegant. The Uruguayan Venancio Flores, who was much older, was dressed like a man of the pampas. The surprise of these two leaders when they met the emperor—in his military uniform in front of his "royal tent" with his steward—can be imagined: the publication in Brazil of these pictures presaging war was equally a surprise.

On 1 May, in Buenos Aires, the secret Treaty of the Triple Alliance was signed. It was agreed that peace would be negotiated only on condition that the Uruguayan dictator Francisco Solano López was deposed. New borders were also established for the contending countries at the end of the conflict, and it was decided that Paraguay, as the aggressor nation, would pay for the costs and damages of the war.

The arrogance of these treaty terms was obvious: the allies seemed encouraged by Paraguay's surrender at Uruguaiana and wrongly thought that it would be a quick war, considering their clear military advantage. In demographic terms, the allies had a total of 11 million people (of whom 9.1 million were Brazilian), while Paraguay had only a little over 300,000. On the economic side, the allies had external trade valued at about 36 million pounds, while Paraguay's trade was no more than half a million.[9]

The leaders of the Triple Alliance are shown as the "three Swiss heroes." Drawing by H. Fleiuss, in *A Semana Ilustrada*, 1865. MMP

Argentina had a small but well-trained army of 6,000 men in 1865, and Uruguay 4,000, which soon went down to 1,000. The Paraguayan army was estimated at 55,000, which was drastically reduced as the war continued. But the growth in numbers of the Brazilian army is very clear: there were 18,000 recruits in 1865; 67,365 in 1866; 71,039 in 1867; and 82,271 in 1869. The imperial navy was also growing, from 45 warships in 1865 to 94 in 1870. The army rapidly gathered strength after a few compulsory call-ups and with voluntary enlistment, which was most evident in the first year of the war, when participation was thought of as a real "patriotic crusade."[10] The great Brazilian novelist Machado de Assis, in *Iaiá Garcia* (1878), for example, tells the story of Jorge, a perfect "dandy from the Rua do Ouvidor, who might have been born there and might even have died there" and who worked only so that his name would be printed in the *Almanak Laemmert*.[11] Madly but unrequitedly in love with Estela, he offers to fight in Paraguay to atone for trying to force her to kiss him. With little thought of the war, and far away from any act of patriotism, he sees the combat in a romantic light, as a desperate way of declaring his love. When he goes, Jorge is more interested in the creases in his uniform and the shine on his boots; he is remote from the real theater of war. This is also the case with Mr. X, who in Machado's story "A Volunteer Captain" (1906), having discovered that his wife has betrayed him with a good friend, enlists as a captain in the volunteers (even though he says he opposes the war) and dies in battle.[12]

"Whoever is not for Brazil is against it." Drawing by H. Fleiuss, in *A Semana Ilustrada*, 1865. MMP

In the early years of the war, every act was a symbol of heroism and patriotic fervor, and Dom Pedro was the first hero of all. Drawing by H. Fleiuss, in *A Semana Ilustrada*, 1865. MMP

A jingoistic atmosphere predominated in Rio, where each victory was celebrated enthusiastically. Fulano Beltrão, in Machado's story "Fulano" (1884), decides to celebrate the victory of Riachuelo with a ball in which he places "an ornamental trophy with naval arms and flags in the main salon, opposite a portrait of the emperor," as well as "proposing some patriotic toasts at dinner, as the newspapers reported in 1865."[13]

At the beginning of the war, there was a euphoric, general optimism, especially on the emperor's part, as he took up his position as commander in chief. "The war is going well," he wrote to the countess of Barral in 1865, "and I hope it will not last long. I hope it will be finished by March, which would be best for Brazil."[14] Nobody was more identified with the war than the emperor, and his popularity soared. But Paraguay's surrender at Uruguaiana did not mean the end of the conflict. A five-year war was beginning, even though López was no longer on the offensive, having been defeated in Rio Grande do Sul. But he kept up his resistance, and Brazil gradually lost its allies and had to fight on alone. By then the war no longer enjoyed unanimous popular support, and disagreements in the Brazilian army began to make themselves felt. The commander Tamandaré was old and tired, but General Caxias had great prestige and was also a Conservative senator (this when the Liberals were in power). Caxias's appointment as commander began a new phase in the war and the reorganization of the army.

Caxias arrived in Paraguay in November 1866 and found an army that was reduced in size and low in morale. The environs were unhealthy, and the

troops had been inadequately prepared. In addition, the number of volunteers presenting themselves was going down, which forced the government to
intensify conscription. The early praise gradually turned into fierce criticism,
like that in the *Correio Mercantil* on 9 November 1866, which called the war
the "Paraguayan butcher's shop."

As the conflict intensified, blacks were increasingly used to make up the
Brazilian army. Slaves were freed on condition they entered the army, which
also meant good business for the slave owners, who were compensated when
they provided this kind of "volunteer." There is no reliable estimate of the
number of slaves who enlisted, and historians differ on the subject: historian
Robert Conrad estimates that 20,000 slaves achieved their freedom through
the war, while Ricardo Salles believes slaves were never more than 10 percent
of the army. In any event, as the war went on, the black participation became
increasingly important.

The emperor himself encouraged the army's buying of slaves: "More and
more strength should be given to Caxias," he wrote in December 1866;
"speed up the process of buying slaves and increase the numbers of our army
by any means possible."[15] The imperial household not only freed some of its
own slaves but also helped in the purchase of others and compensation of
their owners. The "change of color" of the Brazilian army did not pass unnoticed in the Paraguayan press, who began to call the Brazilian soldiers "the
little monkeys [*los macaquitos*]." The *Cabichuí*, an organ directly linked to
López, published a series of cartoons portraying not just Brazil's soldiers but
also its generals, emperor, and empress as monkeys. This kind of mockery
seemed only to increase Dom Pedro's obstinacy: he became even more inflexible in his persecution of the "*caudillo* López." López in turn created a
personality cult around himself, through a manipulated and censored press;
he also executed traitors and those he believed responsible for defeat in battle.

Meanwhile in Rio efforts were made to play down the increasing bitter-
ness of the war. In its protected environment life went on, and after his return, Dom Pedro II continued his old routine: he visited schools, supervised
exams, and toured hospitals. He was meant to be linked to the image of
Christ or to that of his patron saint, Pedro de Alcântara, known for his care of
the sick. In 1867, a cholera outbreak in Brazil was frightening the population,
while combat at the border was not yet at its bloodiest. Yet images of Dom Pedro II stressed his continuation of regular daily activities along with the old
symbols of the country—coffee, tobacco, cotton, and sugar—though his dress
was now military.

As 1868 began, matters got worse. Dom Pedro was now sometimes even accused of being responsible for the continuation of the war, because of his obsession that it would be finished only when López was deposed. Even General Caxias argued that the war should end that year (when his party returned to power). But 1868 is also remembered for its extensive military campaign, with many battles — Humaitá, Itororó, Avaí, Lomas Valentinas. In early 1869, after Asunción, the capital of Paraguay, was captured by Brazilian troops without resistance, Caxias regarded the war as over. Claiming that he was ill, the general abandoned the conflict, despite the emperor's objections. When he returned to Rio, there were no celebrations, no fireworks, and no emperor to greet him at the wharf, but paradoxically he was awarded the Grand Collar of the Order of Dom Pedro I (which no other Brazilian had been granted since the beginning of the empire) and the title of duke, which made him one of only two dukes in the empire. In spite of disagreements between himself and the emperor, then, this was a way of highlighting the importance of a man who had pursued the war in the face of much public opposition.

Even without Caxias the hunt for López continued, now with a new protagonist: the count d'Eu, who took over the army leadership on 22 March 1869. Only twenty-seven years old, the count had at that time no problems with either political party, but his departure for the front was also not as glorious as it

Dom Pedro Visits a Cholera Victim. Oil by François-René Moreaux, 1867. FBN

The count d'Eu and some of the officers of the general staff, in Vila do
Rosário. A mestizo army. 13 January 1870. MMP

was made to appear in later descriptions. Although in 1865 the count had several times vainly asked the emperor to send him to war, the situation was now
different, and the count now hesitated. Even his wife sent a letter to her father,
on 22 February. Isabel did not mince words as she expressed her personal view:
"I remember, Daddy, that by the Tijuca waterfall three years ago, you told me
that passion is blind. I hope that your passion for the affairs of war has not
blinded you! It seems that you want to kill my Gaston: Feijó [his doctor] was
very insistent that he should not catch the sun, or be exposed to the rain or
humidity; and how can these things be avoided when one is at war?"[16] However, not even the most emotional of arguments could move the emperor,
who wrote to the count on 6 April: "Caxias has resigned from the command
of the army . . . In this situation, I have proposed you, because I trust in your
patriotism and sense of initiative. The government thinks as I do . . . that we
must free Paraguay of López's presence as soon as possible . . . and has decided
that we must accept Caxias's resignation and appoint You."[17]

Thus on 16 April, the count d'Eu found himself at the head of an army of
26,000 men, who were tired and wanting to desert. This was not a glorious
task: the prince consort was turned into a kind of headhunter in the search
for López.

On 12 August, in the first confrontation, 700 Paraguayans were killed and
1,100 taken prisoner. On 16 August, in a further battle (called Campo Grande
by the Brazilians, Acosta-Nu by the Paraguayans), 2,000 Paraguayans were

killed and 2,300 captured. This time López had sent adolescents and children into the fight, and even though Brazil was victorious, when the details were known, the outcome seemed shameful. And as the war went on, things deteriorated still further. The persecution of the Paraguayan leader ended only on 1 March 1870, when Brazilian troops trapped López at Cerro-Corá and killed him, along with his teenage son, who had been made a colonel.

The result for Paraguay was not only that it lost its leader, but that the state was destroyed. The losses for Paraguay were very high—some of the estimated figures go as high as 800,000 to 1.3 million people, which is certainly an exaggeration. As for Brazil, the discrepancies begin with estimates of the number of men sent to war, which vary between 100,000 and 140,000; in 1870 the total number of losses accounted by the imperial government was 23,917: 4,332 dead, 18,597 wounded, and 988 unaccounted for.[18]

Whatever the precise truth, the war ended with a very costly victory. The image of the emperor was also affected; after all, what had been the point of persecuting López when it ended by making him posthumously into a hero and a patriot? Some biographers suggest that the Paraguayan leader had asked for the hand of one of the Brazilian princesses, which the emperor considered an affront. Others say that Dom Pedro could not abide the republican rulers of Span-

A battlefield massacre. In the painting *Gift to Contributors to the War Effort in Paraguay* by F. Fortury, n.d. In Marques, *A Guerra do Paraguai.*

ish America and wanted to give the *caudillos* a lesson. But in any case this peace-loving monarch, this "Maecenas of the arts" averse to politics, had turned into a bellicose leader and an inflexible ruler. This new image of him gained currency even in Europe and in the United States, which had favored Paraguay.

Another argument can be put forward: Dom Pedro may have been profoundly irritated by the depiction of his empire as a kingdom of monkeys. In the Paraguayan press, in the government paper *El Semanario*, for instance, Brazilians were called *los macacos, los negros*. In *Cabichuí* the caricatures showed a bloodthirsty army of soldiers with tails and monkeys' ears. Nothing could have been more insulting to a monarch who wanted to make his court "a Paris in the sun" or to the public image of an empire on the European model, tropical only in the romantic sense of having lush vegetation and indigenous peoples.

The "triple infamy"—the mocking name given to the three-nation alliance—had completely miscalculated. In Buenos Aires, on 16 April 1865, General Mitre had announced to the crowds, "In twenty-four hours we'll be in barracks, in three weeks in Corrientes, in three months in Asunción."[19] But the war lasted for five years and reached terrible proportions. In a letter of 23 October 1869, the baron of Penedo revealed his fears concerning the future of the empire: "Paraguay has been reduced to its female population, and we have been reduced to beggars. Other questions will arise later, and who knows what an army made up of conceited, undisciplined volunteers will do? The slavery question is knocking at the door and will create chaos among the workforce. All of this affects me greatly, and makes me despondent."[20]

In 1865, before the signing of the Treaty of the Triple Alliance, the Brazilian army had had 18,000 men; a year later, the estimates vary between 38,000 and 78,000. Before the war began the army was in fact of little significance, for the important armed force was the National Guard, directly formed by landowners, businessmen, and politicians. The actual army "barracks were a refuge for the idle, for dropouts and criminals . . . There was no economic or social attraction in the military profession. The army had no importance whatsoever."[21] This all changed with the war, when new units were constituted, separate from the "elite force" of the National Guard. Now the military profession became a way of climbing the social ladder, and it achieved a new kind of recognition. At the same time, the soldiers, now accustomed to living with freed black men, systematically refused to perform an old task: capture runaway slaves. Many slaves had gone to war as freedmen, only to be taken back into captivity at the end of the war. This also caused a public and press outcry. All this meant that the army became increasingly unhappy with the imperial government and began to harbor desires to destroy it. Many soldiers favored the abolition of slavery and a republic.

After the end of the Paraguayan war, campaigns to achieve both these ends began to take shape. In the early 1870s the Republican Party, the Society for the Emancipation of Slaves (in Rio de Janeiro), and the Emancipation Society for the Slave Population were founded. Also, on 28 September 1871, the Rio Branco Law was passed, which, although a conservative maneuver to calm the abolitionist opposition, was an important step toward ending slavery in Brazil. The Rio Branco Law, better known as the Law of the Free Womb, freed all slaves born after the publication of the law—known as *ingênuos*, or "innocents"—but not their mothers. These minors stayed with their mothers until they were eight, when their masters chose between getting compensation from the state or using the minor's services until he or she was twenty-one. The law gave obvious advantages to the slave owners, who apart from everything else had the habit of changing the ages of their slaves when they registered them.

The emperor, who had several times shown his intention to take the leadership in the process of abolition, and indeed was expected to do so, was slow in coming to grips with the political obstacles. After the victory of the Union in the American Civil War in 1865, Brazil had become, together with Cuba, one of only two countries in the world that legally allowed slavery in their territories. At the same time that it promoted a public image as a civilized nation, it was taking part in a bloody war in Paraguay and putting off final abolition. In the middle of the war, in 1866, the emperor received a message from the French Committee for the Abolition of Slavery, signed among others by prominent abolitionists like François Guizot, Jacques de Broglie, Edouard Laboulaye, and Charles Montalembert. They called on Dom Pedro II to take some practical measure in the right direction. He quickly replied: "The emancipation of the slaves, a consequence of the abolition of the [transatlantic] trade, is merely a matter of form and of finding the opportune moment. When the painful circumstances the country finds itself in [i.e., the war] allow it, the Brazilian government will consider it an object of the first importance to carry out what the spirit of Christianity has long demanded of the civilized world."[22]

The truth is, however, that since the end of the international trade in slaves—twenty years before—no effective measures toward emancipation had been implemented in Brazil. In fact, the emperor's position, made public in 1866, was thought to be a form of "national suicide," and so was postponed. The slaves accounted for a quarter of the population and could be considered Brazil's only agricultural workers. Politicians did not dare face the problem that, they thought, would destroy the nation's foundations. Only with the end of the war and the viscount of Rio Branco's appointment as president of the council did the first law (which followed the ancient principle of Roman law, *partus ventre sequitur,* the child follows the condition of the mother) take shape, and it divided the legislature.

The Law of the Free Womb was signed by the princess Isabel, acting as imperial regent, and she gained immensely in prestige by this act. At this time, her father was on his way to Europe. For some historians, he was deserting the country at a fundamental moment in its national destiny; for others, he was merely trying to guarantee the future of the dynasty. If the measure had political costs, it also brought glory, which would benefit the heir apparent.

In any case, while the new law and the final victory in war made Dom Pedro once again popular, the five years of combat had been painful for him. According to the viscount of Taunay, Dom Pedro had become an old man, with his forehead deeply lined, his hair completely white, "his beard without a single golden hair." André Rebouças, who saw him at the Casa Grande camp in Rio Grande do Sul, said, "The emperor is aging in front of our eyes."[23] His personal management of the war had cost him dear. Ample coverage was given to his heroism in battle. The pictures at the Academy of Fine

The Conservative cabinet of 1871 and a homage to the Law of the Free Womb. The politicians and the emperor (above) share the space with the law, represented by the central female figure, and with "grateful and humble" slaves (below). Lithograph. FBN

Arts and in the illustrated reviews featured heroes like Caxias and the count d'Eu, but the photographs and drawings also reveal the tension in the emperor's face and the first signs of his beard going white.[24]

At the beginning of the war, when he was forty, with his sturdy demeanor and uniform, Dom Pedro II presented the picture of a serene and confident ruler; during and after the war, the picture was different. At the time of the great battles, Dom Pedro II was portrayed as a soldier in trying circumstances: after all, Brazil had spent 600,000 contos and worsened its financial dependence on Great Britain. Its leader, on horseback, with a hat, or carrying a small eyeglass with a battle scene behind him, or with a cap and military boots, or with a big coat over a jacket embroidered with coffee branches, or surrounded by children, was a monarch symbolizing the nation at war. Yet the calm and tranquillity with which the photos try to impress us cannot hide the real anxiety. Dom Pedro's famous beard, a real object of the "political culture" of the time, was whitening in front of everyone's eyes, and the now well-known image of the old man, by which he is still recognized in Brazil even today, was emerging.[25] In this "battle of images," the "friendly, relaxed air" of the official photographs hides the unease of a king who has gone to war for the first time and seen the less brilliant side of his empire.

Dom Pedro with Princess Isabel.
1870. MMP

TWELVE

A Citizen-Monarch

Dom Pedro in his library.
S. A. Sisson, 1858. FBN

The experiences of the Paraguayan War left deep marks on the image of Dom Pedro II, since he had been thought responsible to a great degree for the grueling prolongation of the conflict. And when the war ended and efforts to end slavery in Brazil intensified, these, too, increased the pressures on the monarchy.

The idea of the Law of the Free Womb in 1871 originated in the Council of Ministers, and of course slave owners opposed it. Once it passed, they began to turn against Dom Pedro. In Carvalho's opinion, most of the councilors favored the law, so long as it was not passed before the end of the war,[1] while many, Rio Branco among them, feared that disturbances might result from its implementation but believed it was better to risk them now than wait for even worse problems to arise later. The idea was to anticipate developments the better to control them: to avoid a civil war, as had happened in the United States, or a general slave rebellion as had happened in some of the European colonies in the Caribbean. This was why the passing of the law was delayed to the end of the Paraguayan war, when the troops were back in Brazil. The intention was to effect the abolition but at the same time to calm feelings by means of a controlled reform in which the people were removed from the decision-making process.

The time for consensus was past. New sectors of opposition were forming, and some of the plantation owners in the Paraíba Valley, then Brazil's major coffee-growing area, thought the crown, which until then had defended the use of slave labor, had betrayed them. The political reality was very distant from the image of fraternization that the Council of Ministers' medal pretended to celebrate. In the northern provinces popular opinion favored the measure more than in the south, a symptom of fundamentally opposing interests. The 1872 census gives us the explanation: the north only had 33.7 percent of Brazil's slaves, as against 59 percent in the four coffee-growing provinces (including the city of Rio de Janeiro), with the remainder in the south and center-west.[2]

Other centers of opposition to the monarchy now took shape, in the army (strengthened by the war) and among new political groups. On 3 December 1870 the first Brazilian republican manifesto was published in A *República*, which was the basis for the foundation of the Republican Party on 17 January 1872, at first composed mostly of members of the liberal professions in the cities. The Republican Party organized its first congress in July 1873 and in 1888 was reinforced by new converts: plantation owners in the province of Rio de Janeiro who, unhappy about the abolition of slaves without compensation, swelled the ranks of opposition to the monarchy.

Nonetheless the moment was largely favorable for the empire, since Dom Pedro had recovered his image as peacemaker, taken up his usual commitments again, and begun others. Increasingly aloof from official gatherings, from the balls attended by the *carioca* elite, and even from popular festivals, he began to act and dress like a citizen-monarch. The images reproduce, as in fact they produce, a similar spectacle. His new style of dress was not new at

A coin commemorating the 1871 Law of the Free Womb. Native Americans, blacks, and whites are shown "in harmony." FMLOA

that time, but only then did it become his official uniform. With a top hat and frock coat, the monarch came to look like his subjects and the politicians surrounding him. It was as if he had been inspired by his distant relative Louis Philippe, though the French king had been deposed in 1848.

Always in civilian dress and wearing a double-breasted coat, the emperor went around Rio, visited schools and colleges, presided over exams, chatted amiably with foreign visitors, studied astronomy and dead languages, and thought about traveling abroad for the first time. One person he saw often was France's ambassador in Brazil, Count Arthur de Gobineau, who took up his post at the beginning of 1869. When he first met the emperor, Gobineau brought a letter of recommendation from their mutual friend the countess of Barral; the message was unnecessary, for Dom Pedro II already knew Gobineau's work, above all his notorious *Essay on the Inequality of the Human Races*, whose first volume had been published in 1862. The two men became close friends, and Gobineau became a faithful companion to Dom Pedro in his journeys abroad.

Little by little the ostentatious drama of the emperor's golden years was replaced by a different set, in which actors dressed in everyday clothes made one think more of a "crowned democracy" than of a monarchy. Behaving like his subjects, Dom Pedro II distanced himself from the image of the "strong king" and introduced a new version of himself. The newspapers remarked on the novelty of this self-presentation: "A foreigner walking along Copacabana beach the day before yesterday to look at the whales expressed his surprise at seeing the royal family walking through the streets, surrounded by the people and chatting most affably with people of all classes . . . Their majesties were not accompanied by any guards, only by ordinary people."[3]

In his visits to the provinces, Dom Pedro became irritated by grand rituals and openly disapproved of them: "We have heard that His Majesty ordered that the presidents should be sent all the money for his reception, since this avoided all official pomp and private expenses . . . The population was eager to see their monarch and his august consort and awaited them with pleasure. Never were so many people seen in the streets of Bahia."[4]

The similarity between King Louis Philippe and Dom Pedro II did not go much beyond clothing. "A traditional formula qualified the July Monarchy as 'bourgeois,'" observes one historian, "but even the most optimistic of Brazilian liberals could not describe the only empire in the tropics thus."[5] The emperor still wielded his moderating power, and manual labor was still carried out by slaves.

An allegorical image of a Native American is in the center, surrounded by symbols of progress and civilization—globes, palettes, and books. Their imperial majesties are arrayed above with their daughters and sons-in-law, all in civilian clothes. Early 1870s. MMP

As Sérgio Buarque de Holanda says, "The formulae and the words are the same, but the content and the meaning they took on here were different."[6]*

In fact, the monarch was trying to disguise the power he actually wielded. Called at the time the *emperrador,* meaning "stick-in-the-mud," a pun on *imperador,* or emperor, he did not hesitate to use the moderating power, which belonged to him alone, with great frequency, dismissing cabinet ministers and dissolving the legislature. Unlike the French politician Adolphe Thiers's maxim, "The king reigns and does not govern," in Brazil, as the Conservative leader Count Itaboraí said, "The king reigns, governs, and administers."[7] The head of state was declared to be "Emperor by the Grace of God and the unanimous acclamation of the people," but gradually, people stopped believing in the supernatural powers of this monarch who increasingly behaved like a somewhat obstinate citizen.

The regime's contradictions were becoming ever more visible; the princi-

---

*One could not compare the two monarchies in political terms, but the ties between the two families were strong: Dona Francisca, Dom Pedro's sister, had married Louis Philippe's son, the prince of Joinville, and after 1864, with the marriage of the two imperial princesses to two grandsons of Louis Philippe, the links became even closer.

ple of the sovereignty of the people existed cheek by jowl with the king's divine right; there was a nominally representative system but no real representation; the regime was aristocratic but had no traditional aristocrats; the written constitution was of a monarchist stamp, but the unwritten one leaned to legislative rule.[8]

Dom Pedro's own politics were also characterized by ambiguities: he toned down the rituals of his regime only in the 1870s. He renounced the title of *sovereign* (since sovereignty belonged to the people); after his first journey to Europe in 1871, he discarded the Portuguese custom of allowing subjects to kiss his hand; he upheld the freedom of the press and rejected titles and statues. (At the end of the Paraguayan war, the town council of Rio de Janeiro approved a project for an equestrian statue of Dom Pedro II, but he asked for the project to be filed away and the money used for buildings and schools.[9]) On the other hand he resisted political debate, colluded with a fraudulent legislative system, and only timidly used his power to speed up abolition, even though he publicly said he opposed slavery. His policy was to "let well enough alone" and to concentrate on maintaining the European facade of his empire. The country's structure remained unchanged: neither agriculture nor slavery, the two great foundations of Brazilian life, were touched. What was modified were the habits and images of the monarchy.

Herman Melville tells of Pedro II's visit to the warship *Neversink* during its stay in Rio de Janeiro. On this occasion, the emperor and his entourage engaged in the following conversation:

> "Que gosto!" cried a Marquis, with several dry goods samples of ribbon, tallied with bright buttons, hanging from his breast.
>
> "Que glória!" cried a crooked, coffee-colored Viscount, spreading both palms.
>
> "Que alegria!" cried a little Count, mincingly circumnavigating a shot-box.
>
> "Que contentamento é o meu!" cried the Emperor himself, complacently folding his royal arms, and serenely gazing along our ranks.
>
> Pleasure, Glory, and Joy—this was the burden of the three noble courtiers. And very pleasing indeed—was the simple rendering of Don Pedro's imperial remark.

The author of *Moby-Dick* helpfully translates the Portuguese expressions for his public and comments on the "coffee color" of the Brazilian nobility.

Together with his mixed-race court, the emperor gradually acquired new habits and determinedly altered his image.

So many of the images of Dom Pedro from the 1870s show a new tone that it cannot be mere coincidence. Now Dom Pedro appears more and more often as a "modern monarch," in formal dress, surrounded by symbols of erudition, among books, globes, pens, and columns (on which he leans so as to stay still during the long exposure time for the photograph), and looking like a thinker, the wise Maecenas.

Even in portraits with his family—the empress, Princess Isabel, and Princess Leopoldina—Dom Pedro did not abandon the symbols of erudition. A new version of the Brazilian monarch is being set out: the sober and serious man who ties his government to culture. A photo of the palace interior shows the emperor's study where, apart from the emblems of the imperial household on the furniture, we see only piles and piles of books. Nothing could suit this monarch better: in his official images, he is no longer associated with war, but with the science and learning of his time. His deportment stands out the more when contrasted with that of European monarchs of the time, who did not forgo their imperial robes. In an Italian periodical, for instance, Dom Pedro, wearing a discreet suit and white gloves, is the only figure not royally attired.

Even when he is older, now with his son-in-law the count d'Eu, he has the same severe expression and double-breasted jacket. The book in the count's hand completes the scene.

The photographs and drawings are so numerous and the depiction of elements linking the emperor to culture are so common that they indicate a deliberate policy. In the portraits circulating inside and outside Brazil, the new settings omit the features of the old tropical monarchy. Now Dom Pedro is linked to a Western modernity idealized by symbols of progress.

Even the recourse to photography was original. Unlike most of European royalty, who preferred portraits in oils to the "bourgeois" images of photography, Dom Pedro II associated himself with the modernity of technology. As well as practicing the art himself, the emperor encouraged professional photographers to come to Brazil, and began to make and distribute the royal photographs. The new technology allowed the emperor's image to be multiplied and spread all over Brazil quite inexpensively. And photography enabled the production of lithographs, pencil sketches, and even sculptures. In all of them, Dom Pedro is a citizen, and he always wears his jacket. Framed with allegorical figures, serpents, books, and royal shields, Dom Pedro is the very image of certainty and serenity, a constitutional emperor who sides with the advances of his time.

Dom Pedro represented as one civilian among many, with politicians of the time. FBN

During this same period when, as Freyre says, the emperor exchanged his "crown for a top hat,"[10] Dom Pedro II began to appear in a new posture: with one hand inside his jacket, a pose made famous by Napoleon. Whether seated or standing, alone or accompanied by his family, the American monarch reinterpreted the French general's celebrated pose. This is yet another effort to make a direct link with European culture and Western progress. Dom Pedro is surrounded by locomotives and steamships, palettes and parchments, the goddesses of culture and art, science, and industry.

The representation of the monarchy was broadcast in unusual ways. In objects of personal or household use, the presence of the imperial couple became constant. On handkerchiefs, fans, decks of cards, brooches, silverware, and crockery, the image of royalty proliferated, entering everyday life and penetrating the most intimate spheres of existence. Some objects were manufactured for general use and reproduced outside the strict control of the imperial family, but others were part of the emperor's private collection or presents from the emperor to his court. A pair of Sèvres porcelain vases was made for the imperial wedding, but copies of them were made, too, for gifts on special occasions. Dr. Inocêncio M. de Araújo, for example, in recognition of his services in the northeast during the great drought of 1877, received a pair of vases of this kind.[11] The emperor also distributed photographs of himself, with dedications on the back, brooches, and trinkets, which the recipients regarded as talismans.

Beyond the borders of Brazil, the image of the monarch, somewhat tar-

Images of the citizen-monarch published in the 1870s and early 1880s. His "uniform" is now a double-breasted coat. FBN, MMP, and MIP

nished during the Paraguayan war, gradually regained its prestige. The representation of the civilized citizen-king won out over the wartime tyrant. But it is not easy to know what impact this image had on the popular imagination, for Brazilians were attached to the pomp and circumstance that linked their emperor to the mystical, sacred kingship of parades and processions.

Kerchief stamped with the emperor's portrait. FBN

Sèvres porcelain with the imperial portraits, distributed as gifts to nobles of the court. MIP

Lockets with images of the imperial family. MIP

A plate with the image of Dom Pedro II. CEA

A clock with the emperor's bust in marble. MMP

A riding pouch. MMP

Glasses with the emperor and imperial motifs. MMP and FMLOA

A spade and wheelbarrow used for railway opening ceremonies. MIP

Porcelain with the royal arms. MMP

A bottle with the emperor's bust. CEA

A door handle with the coat of arms. FMLOA

Gobelins tapestry with a medallion of Dom Pedro II in the center. MMP

Playing cards with the imperial family. MIP

THIRTEEN

The Daguerreotype Revolution in Brazil

Dom Pedro II having his photo taken. Behind him is a stand to keep his head still. From Vasquez, *Dom Pedro II e a fotografia.*

Most images of the Brazilian Empire before the early 1860s were lithographs, oil paintings, watercolors, and sculptures, but thereafter photographs increasingly dominated. Dom Pedro II was himself an early photographer: the first Brazilian photographer, and the first photographer-king in the world. He bestowed his imperial patronage on a photographer as early as 8 March 1851, when he gave the title of photographers to the imperial household to Buvelot and Prat (two years before Queen Victoria did the same).

The first advertisement announcing the invention of the daguerreotype reached the court on 19 August 1839 through an item in the *Jornal do Commercio* in May of that year. In August, in a joint session of the Academy of Fine Arts and the Academy of Sciences, the official announcement about the invention was made in Paris, and by December a Frenchman named Hercule Florence, who lived in São Paulo, published the results of his experiments with the new machine.

The emperor acquired daguerreotype equipment in March 1840, eight months before it was publicly marketed in Brazil; he did so at the suggestion of the French abbé Louis Compte, who had also brought photography to Brazil in January of that year. Dom Pedro II was already practicing the new art when photography was introduced to the world.[1]

On 17 January 1840 the *Jornal do Commercio* spoke of the daguerreotype technique in euphoric tones:

Finally, daguerreotype has come to this side of the ocean: up to now it has only been known about in the abstract . . . This morning in the Pharoux Hotel there took place a photographic experiment, all the more interesting in that it is the first time that this new marvel has appeared in front of Brazilian eyes . . . the thing has to be seen with one's own eyes to get an idea of the speed of the operation and its results. In less than nine minutes, the fountain of the Largo do Paço, the Praça do Peixe and the Monastery of São Bento . . . were reproduced so faithfully, with such precision and detail, that it could be seen that this had been done by nature itself, almost without the intervention of the artist.

The daguerreotype's speed attracted a society in which that quality was becoming a synonym for progress — and a virtue that also marked the later inventions of the telegraph, telephone, and internal-combustion engine. In the same year Edgar Allan Poe defined photography "as an invention which represents the miracle and the magic of modern times . . . it is the most extraordinary triumph of modern science."[2] Pride at his invention is plain in these words of Mandé Daguerre:

> The discovery I am announcing to the public is one of a small number of inventions that, because of their principles and effects, and because of their beneficial influence on the arts, are among the most useful and extraordinary of all. It consists in the spontaneous reproduction of images from nature, received in a camera obscura, without their colors, but with a very delicate range of tones . . . Anyone, with the help of the daguerreotype, can obtain a view of his country house, or his livestock: people will make collections of all kinds . . . Even portraits will be made, though the model's lack of complete steadiness does, it is true, present some impediments — they will have to be overcome — in the way of perfect success.[3]

The myth of fidelity to nature and the fascination of the "real," which photography seems to reveal, covered up the other truth, always present in photography, which is that reality is arranged and framed according to the photographer's eye. In this age of certainties and positive knowledge, however, photography was believed to achieve perfect representation, and its potential in a largely illiterate society was quickly realized. Those in search of easy profits soon went beyond Rio de Janeiro. Between 1840 and 1855 several Brazilian cities were visited by traveling daguerreotypists, who went all over the interior, too, in search of clients among the rural aristocracy.

The photograph became not only the symbol of modernity but a mark of status and civilization, a distinction few possessed. The new technique was also useful to show off personal wealth. Because of the long time needed for portraits in oils and their expense, people in the expanding city of Rio de Janeiro flocked to have photographs taken by the dozen, to give or exchange as presents. Visiting cards became very popular in the second half of the century. With conventional poses and a few selected objects, to show varied themes and motifs—columns, balustrades, palm trees, and so on—the studio became a stage on which people performed.

In spite of the marvels of the new technique, which some attributed to mysterious magical arts, the daguerreotype needed a very long exposure time and could not capture moving objects. Photographs showed instead ghost cities, empty of passersby, whom the lenses of the machines could not fix. (Daguerre had taken the first portrait of a human being in 1839 by accident, when he wanted to take a picture of a boulevard in Paris.)

With the vogue for portraits in the 1850s, clients opted either for pictures done with a physionometer or physionotype,* or for torture sessions with a photographer in which they held still with the help of special instruments, hoping to avoid even the slightest movement during the exposure time. The photo thus became a real achievement in its own right.[4] We have pictures of Dom Pedro II himself, immobilized from behind so that a daguerreotype can be properly made of him, and cartoons that mock these new techniques of painting and portraits.

Fashion led traveling photographers to stay at elegant hotels and compete for business. In the 1870s the competition became fiercer and prices lower. The Casa Modelo Carneiro, in an advertisement in the *Gazeta de Notícias* of 2 February 1878, lists its new prices as follows:

> The proprietors of this establishment, always eager to learn every step of progress that takes place in their art, and having made frequent journeys to Europe . . . inform their clients that their associate, Sr.

---

*The *physionotype* was a hollow wooden box placed on a tripod and protected by a pane of glass into which was fitted a vertical pantograph. In the *physionometer* technique, a plaster mold was included in the procedure.

Dom Pedro with his sister
Maria da Glória, with painted
roses in the scenic tropical
background. FMLOA

Dona Leopoldina of Habsburg and her
children, with Pedro de Alcântara on her
lap. Domenico Failluti. MP

Dom Pedro as a boy, in the palace, surrounded by royal emblems and symbols. Armand Julien Pallière, c. 1830. MIP

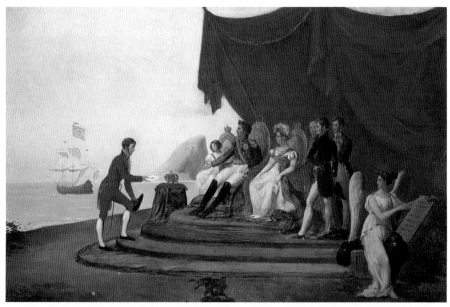

The Recognition of the Independent Brazilian Empire, by Leon Tirode. Charles Stuart, the British ambassador and mediator, presents his credentials. In the background, a British ship flies the Portuguese and Brazilian flags. On the right, a winged figure representing history engraves the "great event" on a stone slab. In the center are Dom Pedro I, the empress Leopoldina, and the princess Dona Maria da Glória (future queen of Portugal). According to Portuguese custom, the crown is placed at one side, on a cushion. MI

The second empress of Brazil, Dona Amélia, duchess of Bragança, whose beauty was always commented on. She accompanied Dom Pedro I when he returned to Portugal. She lived first in France, then in Portugal, where she died in 1867. Oil on canvas by Friedrich Durck. MIP

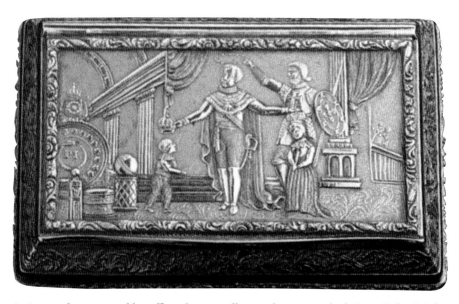

A nineteenth-century gold snuffbox shows an allegorical scene in which Dom Pedro II (who has stayed in Brazil) on one side and Dona Maria da Glória (who has gone to Portugal) on the other are both being crowned—two kingdoms in a single gesture. MIP

A rare picture of the future emperor in private. While Dom Pedro sketches a bust, his two sisters interrupt their embroidery to observe him. On the wall above them is a painting of their grandfather, Dom João VI. FMLOA

Dom Pedro at the age of twelve is shown in military uniform, as a future emperor and commander in chief of the armed forces. On his chest are the badges of the Order of the Southern Cross and the Order of the Golden Fleece. The throne bears Pedro II's monogram and the serpe, the insignia of the Bragança dynasty. Félix Émile Taunay, 1837. MIP

The Coronation of Emperor Dom Pedro II, 18 July 1841, by François René Moreaux, 1842. The emperor, at the age of fifteen, receives the imperial crown from the hands of the archbishop of Brazil, Dom Romualdo Antônio de Seixas. The artist presents the event with great pomp and circumstance, highlighting some of the important figures at court. In the background, the emperor's sisters witness the ceremony. Oil on canvas. MIP

Dom Pedro I's crown (left) was dismantled to create his son's (right). MIP

Commemorative fans celebrating the marriage of Dom Pedro II and Dona Teresa Cristina (above), and the occasion of the majority and the coronation (below). The fans usually came from China and were ordered in the so-called Casas da Índia, numerous shops in the Rua do Ouvidor that forwarded orders to Canton. MIP

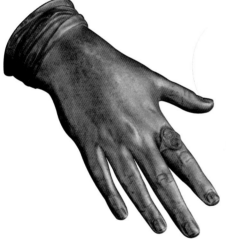

The Hand of Justice. The Hand of Emperor Dom Pedro II, by Marc Ferrez, 1841. Made at the time of the majority, the plaster-of-Paris original was used to make many copies in bronze and gilt bronze at the Royal Mint. CPCL

The top of the scepter carried by Dom Pedro II for the coronation. It was pure gold set with diamonds. Overall the scepter was six feet long—rather large for the still-youthful monarch. MIP

Dom Pedro's throne, with the image of the serpe in the middle. MIP

Dona Teresa Cristina, by José Correia de Lima, c. 1843. This portrait must have been painted after her engagement to the Brazilian emperor had been negotiated. She is wearing a miniature on her chest depicting Dom Pedro. In the background is Naples, and Vesuvius in eruption. This is said to be the portrait Dom Pedro received before his betrothed came to Brazil. MIP

The Marriage by Proxy of the Empress Dona Teresa Cristina, by Alessandro Cicarelli, 1846. The wedding took place in the royal chapel of the palace at Naples, 30 May 1843. Oil on canvas. MIP

Dom Pedro in the 1850s, attired for the *grande gala* with the famous mantelet of toucan breast-feathers and surrounded by the insignia of the empire. FMLOA

Princess Leopoldina in a Tropical Setting, by F. Krumholz, 1851. Dom Pedro II's second daughter died when she was twenty-four. FMLOA

Long before the fashion for Indianism in the arts was fully developed, Brazil was already being represented by the costumes of its "exotic" peoples, as in this allegorical image of America, mother and son. Oil by Niccolò Frangipane, 1590. CEA

Two panels: above, "civilized Europe," with its paintings, subtle tones, and temperate landscapes; below, "barbarous America," with Indians, animals, and bright colors. Oil on copper by Jan van Kessel, 1666. Bayerische Staatsgemäldessammlungen, Munich

The First Mass in Brazil, by Victor Meireles de Lima, 1860. The painter was one of Dom Pedro II's protégés, and the work was inspired by Gonçalves de Magalhães's poem *The Confederation of the Tamoios*. This was a closed circle; in Rio de Janeiro the emperor surrounded himself with his own writers, historians, and painters. Oil on canvas. MNBA

The Legend of Moema, by Victor Meireles de Lima, 1866. In this example of Brazilian Romantic academicism, the Native American represents the country. Oil on canvas. MASP

Iracema. The eponymous heroine of the novel by José de Alencar is depicted here by José Maria de Medeiros, 1881. Oil on canvas. MNBA

The Last Tamoio, by Rodolfo Amoedo, 1833. Again, the Native American is both model and victim, symbolizing the new empire. Oil on canvas. MNBA

Dom Pedro at the Opening of the General Assembly, by Pedro Américo de Figueiredo e Melo, 1872. This famous painting shows the emperor on 3 May 1872 and is also known as *The Speech from the Throne*, for thereafter the emperor wore his robes only when he spoke at the opening and closing of the Assembly. Several important politicians appear in the background. Empress Teresa Cristina, Princess Isabel, and the count d'Eu are seated in the imperial box. Oil on canvas. MIP

The Festival of the Divine Holy Spirit. It is said that the title of emperor was selected in part because of this ceremony, in which, each year, a new "Emperor of the Divine Holy Spirit" was chosen. Watercolor on paper, nineteenth century. Private collection

The Execution of Maximilian. This Manet painting shows Dom Pedro II's cousin the Austrian archduke Maximilian being executed in Mexico by local troops led by the former president, Benito Juárez. It was cut up by enemies of Maximilian. Oil on canvas. National Portrait Gallery, London

Dom Pedro II in military uniform. In the background are the usual symbols of erudition—a globe, books, and paintings. 1860s. MMP

Princess Isabel Takes the Oath, 20 May 1871, by Victor Meireles de Lima, 1875. This painting in the grand manner was executed by an artist of the Imperial Academy of Fine Arts, part of the inner court circle. Oil on canvas. MIP

In his *Album das glórias*, the cartoonist Rafael Bordalo Pinheiro depicted Dom Pedro II as described by the Portuguese writer Eça de Queirós, with the familiar double-breasted cutaway, valise in hand (the toucan-feather cape falling out of it), and crown and scepter at one side. In Araújo, 1996.

The Carioca, by Pedro Américo de Figueiredo e Melo. The first version of this painting was offered to Dom Pedro II in 1864, but he rejected it as too "licentious." It was then bought by the king of Prussia and exhibited on the Brazilian stand in the Philadelphia Exhibition in 1876, together with a poem by Sousândrade underlining the importance of "thighs" for Brazilian industry. Another version was completed in Italy in 1882 and donated, years later, to the National Museum of Fine Arts in Rio de Janeiro. Oil on canvas. MNBA

The Brazilian pavilions at the
Vienna and London Exhibitions,
1873 and 1862. The empire displayed
its tropical products: hammocks,
skins, boots, coffee, arrows, and
ceramics. IHGB

Allegory of the Republic, anonymous, 1889. The royal family's departure in November 1889 is imagined like a festival. (In reality, Dom Pedro left at dawn, quietly.) In the background the royal family gets into a small boat (with Dom Pedro waving); in the foreground republican leaders face the allegorical female figure symbolizing Brazil. The black population is depicted as cooperative and peaceful. Oil on canvas. FMLOA

Peace and Concord, by Pedro Américo de Figueiredo e Melo, 1902. Again, the Republic is depicted as a female figure. Oil on canvas. MI

Watercolors by Henrique Bernardelli,
including female representations of the
Republic. MMP

An advertisement for Bordallo shoes, "2,500 pairs produced daily." Together with the new flag of the republic, the woman carries branches and "trumpets for success," in a design with many modernist elements. MMP

The Conteville factory for making scales, founded in 1854, remakes its image by reproducing two official symbols of the young republic, the flag and the woman, and even puts its name on the scales of justice. MMP

The national lotteries had agencies in every province and boasted of distributing large prizes. Here a naked woman makes money shower over Guanabara Bay. MMP

The Guarany Drugstore joins two icons of Brazil: at the back, a Native American is portrayed in an idyllic setting; in the foreground, a female figure tries out a product. MMP

The Souto shoe factory, in Rio de Janeiro, became famous for the medals it won at exhibitions in 1915 (in San Francisco and Rome) and 1921 (in London). MMP

"New Portrait Techniques." Indigenous images appear on the wall, the client has donkey's ears, and a portrait of the donkey stands against the wall. Rafael Mendes de Carvalho, 1840. From Cunha, "Fisionotipo e fisionotraço."

Tavares, has just arrived from Paris bringing novelties with him! Every system! Every improvement! . . . It has always been the custom of this firm to provide the best and cheapest portraits.

* price reduction: A dozen portraits on visiting cards—5 mil-réis
                    A dozen of the same, enameled—12 mil-réis
                    A dozen of the same, imperial—15 mil-réis[5]

Meanwhile, the imperial family amassed their private collection of the new images. Because of very inadequate conservation techniques and the hasty banishment of Dom Pedro in 1889, many of the daguerreotypes in it have been lost, and there are very few that can be proved to have been taken by the emperor. But we know that he assiduously experimented and dedicatedly took photographs from the late 1850s onward, when true photographs took over from daguerreotypes. He sent hundreds to friends of both sexes, acquaintances, nobles, and relatives throughout the world.[6]

The royal family also joined in the fashion for visiting cards. It was said that Dom Pedro loved getting photos as presents as well as giving them out. Photography made for an enormous growth in the monarchy's visibility and in the number of situations in which the emperor could be portrayed. In a tropical monarchy like his, even slavery was portrayed on visiting cards, which attracted curiosity in Europe. He now appeared as a "real" presence, however much the landscape, props, expression, and clothes were imaginative inventions.

Most of the imperial images have a stiff, official character, and there are very few intimate pictures, which perhaps were not thought appropriate for an emperor. In only two examples do we see the figures of the emperor and empress playing with the possibilities of the technique or with its theatrical element.

A quite different image from 1855 is attributed to Dom Pedro. In the self-portrait he seems eager to impress his audience with a new, more positive vision of himself, arranged in his increasingly habitual Napoleonic pose.

Great photographers made their reputations in Brazil, like Hercule Florence, Victor Frond, and, later, Marc Ferrez, as well as firms that set up in Rio, promising wonders. Many people had themselves photographed, but no family spent as much as the imperial one. It was even common to find advertisements in the newspapers in which professionals advertised themselves as "photographers to the imperial family," to attract other clients.

Princess Isabel herself was a pupil of Revert Henrique Klumb, who was paid 400 mil-réis a year for private photography lessons. The expenses were certainly not limited to the lessons. According to the receipts and expenses book of the imperial household, Dom Pedro, in the period between 1848 and 1867, spent 730 mil-réis on photographs by Buvelot; by Victor Frond 9,127; by Joaquim Insley 243; by Stahl 730; by Klumb 2,815; by Carneiro and Gaspar

Two photographic experiments. Carneiro and Gaspar, albumin print, c. 1867. FBN

Dom Pedro II, possibly a self-portrait made at the São Cristóvão Palace, c. 1860. CDPOB

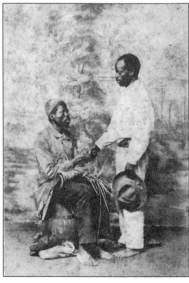

Exotic African slaves in the Americas, identifiable as such by their bare feet, photographed by José Cristiano Junior. In newspapers of the 1860s, such photos were recommended as souvenirs: "Types of black men . . . a very appropriate souvenir for anyone going back to Europe."

1,600; by Carneiro and Smith 1,045; and by the Casa Leuzinger 237. Also, albums were bought from Victor Frond and other photographers, bringing the total sum to more than thirty times the total received for all the emperor's expenses in 1846.[7]

For royalty, always associated with the idea of immortality, photography allowed the illusion of a stable and lasting presence, and Dom Pedro became an icon of the period. His photographs represented modernity and allowed the scientific emperor to continue with his experiments, though the marks of his quasi-African kingdom could not be erased. In the journeys he undertook, photography was a close companion.

FOURTEEN

A Monarch on His Travels

Dom Pedro's carriage and caravan, crossing a bridge. The emperor's entourage seems to have stopped to pose for the photographer. 1868. MIS

The Brazilian historian Heitor Lyra says in his book on Dom Pedro II that "kings are great travelers." Dom Pedro was no exception, and his journeys were strategic: even if only symbolically, they helped to mark out the borders of Brazil's great empire and to broadcast his image both inside and outside the country. He took possession of his country on his journeys, and this unified its representation, or image.

Until the 1870s Dom Pedro, however well versed he was in foreign languages and cultures, never left Brazil. He saw a significant proportion of his own empire, though: in 1845 he was away from the capital for six months on a trip to the provinces of Santa Catarina, Rio Grande do Sul, and São Paulo, and in 1847 he went into the interior of Rio de Janeiro province and stayed at the big plantation houses there. Rio was not the whole of Brazil, and he thought it necessary to confer his prestige on distant parts of the country, which would help to strengthen the monarchy and preserve national unity. In 1859 and 1860 he visited the northeast and was enthusiastically received in Paraíba, Espírito Santo, Bahia, Pernambuco, and Sergipe.

Along with Dom Pedro went his rituals and some of his ceremonies: the preparations for the departure of the emperor and his retinue; programs in the towns and provinces on his arrival; grandiloquent speeches on his return to the capital, when Rio's residents were instructed to light up the fronts of their houses and decorate them with carpets and tapestries; the streets along which the imperial cortege passed had to be strewn with sand and covered with leaves and flowers.[1] The setting might vary, but the script was the same: meticulous preparation and pomp.

In Recife, no trouble was spared in the preparations when the emperor and empress came: a commission was appointed, streets illuminated, houses decorated; there were flags, masses, and Te Deums, bands, bell-ringing, and the waving of cambric handkerchiefs. For the houses where the court was lodged, the richest families in Pernambuco lent special furniture made of the finest woods, along with silver, tapestries, silks and velvets, fine crystal, and a fine gold knife case. In Bahia the celebrations were repeated, and similarly when Dom Pedro went to the curative spa at Poços de Caldas in 1861, and in 1865 to Juiz de Fora. Platforms were constructed, whole cities were decorated, and people were told in advance of the appropriate dress for the receptions.

The imperial family's journeys made such a stir that often towns would get

"Recife Receives Dom Pedro II." Lithograph, *Monitor das Famílias*, 1859. MIP

Dom Pedro and his entourage by the River Paraibuna. R. H. Klumb, 1861. MMP

themselves ready even before a proposed visit was formalized. This was the case in Alcântara, in Maranhão, which got itself ready for a reception but then was left out of the royal itinerary, and there were several other cancellations. In these cases, the monarch's representation preceded the man himself.

In 1871 Pedro II decided to go on his first trip abroad, to visit the world he knew only from books, but the journey took place in a troubled atmosphere. In France, the Third Republic had just been proclaimed, which suggested the fragility of monarchies, while in Brazil the issue of slavery was increasingly linked to the monarchical system, and abolitionist newspapers were gaining ground and popularity.

The journey itself became a matter of controversy, opposed by people like the viscount of Rio Branco and José de Alencar. Alencar, piqued because the emperor had removed him from the list of candidates for the Senate and because he thought the country was going through a serious crisis that the inexperienced princess Isabel would be unable to deal with, proclaimed that the emperor's journey was ill timed.

In spite of his polemic, the problem was solved because of practical, nonpolitical factors. Dom Pedro's younger daughter, Princess Leopoldina of Saxe-Coburg, died, leaving young children that the emperor had to look after. Having decreed official mourning for six months, the monarch left on 25 May 1871 for Europe and the Middle East. The Chamber of Deputies had to approve the journey, and Isabel, at the age of twenty-four, became provisional regent.

The trip began with an unexpected prelude in Lisbon that paradoxically helped to define the emperor's image. Required to stay in quarantine for ten days because of epidemics, Dom Pedro refused any kind of special attention, saying that he was on an unofficial visit to Portugal as a mere citizen. This did not stop him, however, from receiving the king and queen as well as many civic and military authorities, thus highlighting the large difference between a simple citizen and a citizen-monarch. He also met with his stepmother, Dona Amélia, and brother-in-law, the widower of his sister Dona Maria da Glória.

Dom Pedro then undertook a long trip around the provinces of Portugal. He must have had a curious picture in his mind of the country: the place where his father had died, where his sister, now also dead, had reigned. But he was concerned not just with the past, for he wanted to be connected to the "modernity and science" of his time as he thought of it. He went on a real cultural pilgrimage, meeting Portuguese intellectuals like António Feliciano de Castilho and Alexandre Herculano and visiting a number of universities.

"A telegram from Lisbon announces that Dom Pedro is fine; the crew's not so good . . ." Ângelo Agostini. MMP

Dom Pedro caused a sensation: the Portuguese could not understand a monarch who did away with royal rituals. The writer José Maria Eça de Queirós found him amazing: "In the Praça da Figueira [in central Lisbon] he mixed with the people and the stall-holders and bought three enormous apples from one of the women, which he took with him to his carriage and paid for generously, with half a *libra*. He spoke in friendly fashion with the country folk from around the city and argued over prices. One of the men exclaimed: 'So that's the emperor? He doesn't look at all like a king.'"

Eça called him "Pedro with the luggage," because of the dark little leather case he always took with him, and commented ironically on the emperor's denying his royalty at one moment only to assert it the next:

> Your attention for a moment please! The Brazilian emperor, when he was among us (and even when he wasn't), was alternately, contradictorily, Pedro de Alcântara and Dom Pedro II. As soon as receptions, anthems, and banquets took place to glorify Dom Pedro II, he hastened to declare that he was merely Pedro de Alcântara. When the train times, library opening hours or overly familiar citizens wanted to treat him as Pedro de Alcântara, he soon showed that he was Dom Pedro II.[2]

And Rafael Bordalo Pinheiro, a famous Portuguese cartoonist, issued a pamphlet entitled *Notes on the Picaresque Journey Around Europe of the Emperor of Razilb*, which shows a parody version of Dom Pedro, with thin legs, his shortage of cash, his jacket, his valise in hand, wandering around various places and scientific institutions unloading his "parroted" erudition on the curious people with him. Hurried visits, eager attempts to show "a democracy among the savants," and an excessive lack of formality are Bordalo's themes.

In France Dom Pedro II met the countess of Barral, of whom we shall hear more shortly, as well as Count Arthur de Gobineau, and before he left for Belgium for an official meeting with King Leopold II undertook the usual program of visits to distinguished people and institutions.

In Germany the emperor avoided meeting the chancellor, Otto von Bismarck, but did not miss the opportunity of getting to know Richard Wagner, one of his favorite composers. Then, after visiting Italy, the emperor left for Palestine and Asia Minor; he had his photograph taken in Egypt, completely

Satirical images from Notes on the Picaresque Journey Around Europe of the Emperor of Razilb, by Rafael Bordalo Pinheiro, 1872. CGJM
"Razilb is a flourishing nation that governs itself but has the generosity to pay an emperor, so that he, for the good of the country's public administration, finances, and development, may study Hebrew and other dead languages. One day His Majesty the emperor of Razilb has an inkling that his people are beginning to be bored with him and he with them. So he decides to travel. He decides to search throughout the world for (1) people who think well of him, and (2) wise men who will tell him things. And he departs, disguised as a democratic emperor . . . leaving as regent the princess Zuzu-Bibi-Toto Fredegundes-Curegundes (see Almanach de Gotha) and in a prudent law on slavery proclaims that: Article 1: All those not yet born in the empire of Razilb are free. This gives a middling sort of pleasure to the future parents."

"He swears never to be parted from his valise, where he keeps his booze and his democratic coats."

"In Fine Arts he discovered the parrot Melo, and very amiable he was, too."

dressed in black, in sharp contrast with the stones and sand, hat on head, with a serious, somewhat smug look. The monarch is the only one looking directly at the camera, taking an interest in how the picture will turn out.

The emperor returned to Europe laden with images of the ancient Near East, which he had so assiduously studied in books. From Italy he went to France. He was cautiously received in France, but as he went slowly through the streets, dressed always in black and without his medals, Dom Pedro began to win over Paris. Every day he went to see the countess of Barral and her son Dominique, and Gobineau little by little became a part of his official entourage.[3]

After an absence of ten months, in March 1872, Dom Pedro returned to Brazil with the duke of Saxe and two of the royal grandchildren, Pedro Augusto and Augusto Leopoldo, who accompanied their father and grandfather. At home there was still tension in his relations with many figures in the ruling elite, who disapproved of his prolonged journey. Yet in many eulogistic illustrations the emperor is shown like a conquering hero coming back to his homeland, like Caesar or Napoleon. Here is part of a poem of welcome by Machado de Assis written in 1860 and reprinted for the return of their imperial majesties:

> Caesar! More light shines out in the cries of the people,
> There is more national soul in the singing of the crowd
> When virtue and knowledge raise up the hand of the Lord
> From a new seed on the imperial forehead . . .
>
> You who return from the sea with Songs of the North,
> You who are lulled to sleep by the country's hymns,
> Can and must believe in the public enthusiasm
> As a bright saying that is the people's prediction.
>
> Welcome! say the people, and the powerful phrase
> Is like an echoing, threefold prayer.
> Hear it, you who have an angel for a wife
> Freedom for a mother, and the people for a brother.

What the poem could not show was the growing mistrust of the emperor, as he withdrew from his "civilizing project" and his efforts to enter into dialogue with his surroundings. Almost always dressed in black, with white or black

trousers, a dark tie, giving his hand to no one in public, as protocol demanded (having eliminated the kissing of hands because he thought it obso-
lete), the emperor was beginning to be misunderstood. The images revealed
a separation that could also be seen in daily life. The monarch was delighted
with the Old World, but he was removed from his own empire, at just the
time when the contradictions in its social and political order were becoming
ever more obvious. The monarch had never been at the same time so popular and so distant.

Dom Pedro showed signs of fatigue and boredom. "The needs of government are consuming all my strength," he confessed to his friend Gobineau.[4]

Gobineau, the famous author of *Essay on the Inequality of the Human
Races* (1853), during the time he spent in Brazil from April 1869 to May 1870
as ambassador of France, developed a fairly close relationship with Dom Pedro II. In letters he sent to his mother, Count Gobineau showed clear ill will
toward Brazil and Brazilians, and seemed to have respect only for the emperor, whom he went to see every Sunday. Everyone else, he wrote, "looked
like monkeys," physically and morally speaking.[5] But though he gave an inscribed copy of his polemical essay to Dom Pedro, the emperor never commented on it but simply thanked him when he acknowledged receipt of the
book. He seemed to enjoy conversing in French with Gobineau and getting
his impressions, but he did not share the count's pessimistic views, and did
not agree that Brazil's miscegenation was a sign of degeneracy and had no future. He was not much interested in this kind of discussion, which contra-
dicted the official policy favoring Brazil's indigenous people, yet for a short
time the emperor made Gobineau his confidant.

Dom Pedro frequently confessed that he would rather be a teacher than
occupy such an obviously powerful political position, but this did not make
him release his grip on power. Imagination and reality became confused at
this time, especially after the publication of *Les Pléiades*, a novel by Gobineau, in 1875. Dedicated to the countess de La Tour (who is supposed to
have been Gobineau's muse, but also Dom Pedro's mistress), this roman à
clef is clearly inspired by the figure of Dom Pedro, who is indirectly portrayed
in it, alongside the count d'Eu, Princess Isabel, and Gobineau himself.

The Dom Pedro figure is Jean-Théodore, son of Dom Pierre, a king who
has an adventurous career in Portugal. Théodore is an isolated character, frustrated by the rigidity of official life, which prevents him from fulfilling his true
vocation: "For what is a prince, when faced by the problems of existence? The
most unprotected of beings." Gobineau, who as Dom Pedro's traveling com-

panion knew of his marital unhappiness, also sets this lament in Théodore's perspective: "His wife weighed on him. This was a great unhappiness for him, since in making his mistakes and, generally, in moments of disillusionment he would have been ready to return to her, and been happy with small mercies, not asking for more than a kind, silent form of friendship."[6]

"An orphan in childhood," "an orphan on the throne," Dom Pedro had his myth rewritten in the page of *Les Pléiades*, and to these images was now added the image of a "martyr to politics," of a man who "suffers silently for the good of his country." The fictional representation of a monarch who distances himself from his own interests in order to represent the nation took on political reality.

It is interesting to think that, at the same time that Gobineau was writing his novel and trying to redeem his friend, José de Alencar was writing his well-known ridicule of the emperor *A guerra dos mascates* (The Street-Sellers' War) (written under the pseudonym Carlos Eneide). Nothing escaped Alencar: Dom Pedro's squeaky voice, his capacity for dissimulation, his changeability, his doodles, his famous, often-mocked complaint: "I know, I know." The two books present the same personality with opposing characteristics. Each writer in his own way shows us the curious traveler, the irritable ruler, the defender of press freedom, the humanist thinker, the man who wielded the moderating power . . .

By 1876 a bored emperor, no longer hiding his irritation with the narrow confines of Brazilian reality, planned a second journey abroad. He left in May, and after an official visit to the Universal Exhibition in Philadelphia, he and the empress took the waters at the German spa of Bad Gastein. Then he went on to Jerusalem. Planned with the same care as the previous journey, this trip included, in balanced measures, time in the United States, Canada, part of Africa, Europe (Denmark, Sweden, Norway, Greece, Austria, Belgium, Holland, Switzerland, and Portugal), Russia, Turkey, and above all, six weeks in Paris. The emperor as traveler had been slow to take the plunge; now he seemed to be in a hurry.

The official reasons for the journey were the empress Teresa Cristina's bad health and the opportunity to visit the Philadelphia Exhibition and "see for himself the progress of the great American nation." As before, Dom Pedro presented himself as a citizen-monarch, insisting on removing the "Dom" and signing himself simply "Pedro de Alcântara." He wore his black overcoat and liked to say: "The emperor is in Brazil. I am only a Brazilian citizen."[7] In spite of the usual opposition from some quarters, and from people who said that Isabel was too inexperienced to be regent, there was no way to stop the emperor from traveling.

His arrival in New York in April 1876 was the focus of a great deal of attention. It was the first time a monarch had come to U.S. territory, and after all, he was the only *American* monarch. It was also the centenary of United States independence and natural, therefore, that the imperial couple should arouse interest.

Dom Pedro was astonished by everything he saw and had himself photographed whenever he could, but it was the Philadelphia Exhibition that interested him most. The exhibition began on 10 May at ten in the morning, and the emperor, it seems, was one of the first people to enter its grounds. His visit was paradoxical to say the least: the show celebrated a hundred years of independence, a hundred years of the republic, but there was Dom Pedro, opening the show along with President Grant and behaving like an "interested scientist," looking at all the exhibits with the curiosity for which he was famous. Among the people he met were Thomas Edison and, later, Alexander Graham Bell, who showed him his most recent invention. Asked to say something into the telephone, the emperor, showing his wide reading, said, "To be or not to be . . ." The device "did in fact speak," he marveled, and added, "Congratulations, Mr. Bell. When your invention is put on the market, Brazil will be your first customer." Fact or folklore, the story is typical of a king who was filling his journey with images and events ready for reproduction. As he is supposed to have said to his entourage: "This time, we have put on a good show."[8] As for the Brazilian pavilion at the fair, it displayed everything that related civilization to the tropics: coffee-grinding machines, indigenous artifacts, and products of Brazilian forests.

Dom Pedro had commissioned from the then-famous general Couto Magalhães a scientific treatise conforming to the tenets of Brazilian Romantic literature. The first edition of *O selvagem* (The Savage), according to its author, was "a little carelessly printed because it had been hurriedly proofread so as to be ready to take its place in the American library of the universal exhibition."[9] The book was a survey of the languages and legends of the Tupi, and it described the origins, customs, and places where the "savages" lived as "a means of domesticating them." In this patronizing official work, says one

Dom Pedro and his consort shown as urban figures in a slave-owning empire, above a view of Rio de Janeiro. *Harper's Weekly*, 1876. FBN

Dom Pedro meets American citizens, 1876. IHGB

Dom Pedro II and President Ulysses S. Grant open the Philadelphia Universal Exhibition, 1876. From Hardman, *Trem fantasma.*

commentator, "the myth of the Tupi, as a Brazilian race with superior qualities capable of developing toward perfection and a positive basis for mixing races" was fully revealed.[10]

Somewhat stranger, in this context, was Pedro Américo's painting shown at the Brazilian pavilion. In *A carioca* a naked figure of a sensual mulatta appears in a manner that clashed with the official version of indigenous life in Brazil. And if the work was not out of place, the symbolist poet Joaquim Sousândrade's verse about it certainly was, with its highfalutin neologisms: "Antediluvian paleosaurus, our Industry at the Exhibition. What thighs! What idiots! Of blue glass is the patriogonic sun!"

In the United States Dom Pedro carried out the ritual he had monotonously adhered to in his other travels: endless visits to schools, institutions, museums, and distinguished intellectuals. He met Louis Agassiz and Henry Wadsworth Longfellow, opened factories and roads, and went, inevitably, to Niagara Falls. Tourism suited him. The viscount of Bom Retiro, who accompanied the party, couldn't resist making fun of his energy: "The emperor is increasingly active, sometimes taking things to real excess, and causing

constant astonishment to the Americans, who thought they were the most active people on earth."[11]

In July, Dom Pedro and his party left the United States and went to London; then in Brussels he met the famous French doctor Jean-Martin Charcot.
Leaving the empress in Bad Gastein, his party continued on to the Baltic
countries, Gobineau still in tow. In September 1876 the emperor reached
Greece, where he was hailed as "king of unknown peoples, the Tupinambás,
the Guarani, the Botocudos, the Manaus."[12] Received as a monarch from the
tropics, Dom Pedro astonished everyone by behaving like a civilized king. In
November 1876 the party reached the Middle East, where they rejoined the
empress and her party, which included the countess of Barral.

Back in Europe, the emperor passed through Rome and Vienna and
stopped in Paris, where he was received like the king of a remote country, a
relative of the Orléans family, who no longer had any hope of restoration to
the throne. Again he made his presence felt by his "democratic attitude" (it
was said that he took buses and trains like any normal person and shook the
hands of passersby), by memorable phrases, and by his meetings with intellectuals: Ernest Renan, Louis Pasteur, and above all Victor Hugo. Like his
meeting with Bell, Dom Pedro's encounter with the great poet and novelist is
mentioned more than once in the accounts of this journey. When he was introduced by Hugo's daughter as "His Majesty of Brazil," he is said to have responded: "My girl, there is only one majesty here: Victor Hugo." Afterward
Dom Pedro took the initiative of asking Hugo for a photo and in return offered him one of his. Scenes like this show us a monarch who lived more for
his public image than for himself. The meeting was a hard blow for Brazilian
republicans, who thought of Victor Hugo as a hero of their own school.

Rumors about the relationship between the emperor and the countess of
Barral date from this period and this trip. She had been tutor to the emperor's
daughters, but after they married, her role at court diminished, until she began to travel abroad as the empress's lady-in-waiting and became Dom Pedro's traveling companion. She went with him to England, Scotland, Holland,
Scandinavia, Germany, Greece, and Turkey.

Born in Bahia, the daughter of diplomats, Barral had been educated in
France during the reign of Charles X and was a close friend of the emperor's
sister Francisca (Chica), which is how her name came to the emperor's ears
when he was looking for a tutor or governess for his daughters. Dona Francisca, married to the prince of Joinville, lived in Paris, where the viscountess
(later countess) of Barral had been a companion. Barral was forced to flee

from France after the fall of Louis Philippe in 1848, and after a short stay in London, she finally came to Brazil.

The princesses each had a lady-in-waiting, but although they were suitable court ladies, they did not have the requisite level of education.[13] Finding an experienced person of refinement was no easy task in the provincial *carioca* milieu. Dom Pedro first used the widowed empress Dona Amélia, duchess of Bragança, who lived in Munich at the time, and had good contacts in European courts. But on 31 December 1856, he invited Barral to be the empress's lady-in-waiting and governess for their daughters, and the countess accepted. She was forty at the time and had a fragile, premature son, three servants, and fourteen slaves: she thought it would be good to "return to court," even such an unusual one.

It was also very convenient for the imperial household to be able to count on Barral: "she spoke the principal living languages fluently, had a delightful conversational manner, wrote charming letters, with the natural style and confidence of the letters of Madame de Sévigné."[14] This cultivated and talented woman had, according to contemporary witnesses, the habits of a French noblewoman, thanks to her years in Louis Philippe's court, but she also had the advantage of being Brazilian.

The emperor, writing in pencil, explained the roles and responsibilities of the new governess when the countess inquired about them. She would be included in the category of servants of the greatest distinction and could live in

The countess of Barral. Franz Xavier Winterhalter, 1870. FMLOA

São Cristóvão or in town, "in the apartments which had belonged to the countess of Belmonte, with a separate entrance." Her remuneration would be twelve thousand francs a year, and she would have the right to a lifelong pension of half this sum as soon as the education of the princesses had been completed, "and a carriage to ride in."[15]

Thus began a friendship that lasted until her death—in France, on 14 January 1891, eleven months before the death of Dom Pedro II—and whose great intimacy became a matter of general suspicion at court. But Dom Pedro's behavior, unlike his father's, was marked by the utmost discretion. Having mistresses was no problem. Especially in a country like Brazil, any general comment on the emperor's insufficient virility would have been a bad sign. (It was said that Dom Pedro distributed to all his natural children the name Alcântara Brasileiro, in recognition of his paternity and as a homage to his patron saint.) There are many stories and rumors about Dom Pedro's mistresses—Guedes Pinho, countess of Villeneuve, Maria Francisca, countess of Goiás, the countess of La Tour—but it is the silence that is most impressive. The emperor himself, in his 1861 diary, which is the only one with any reflections of a slightly personal nature, spoke with moderation about his relationship with his wife: "I sincerely respect and esteem my wife, the basic qualities of whose character are excellent," for over time he had become used to her. But he found her overly religious and seems to have been delighted by the company of a lady like Barral, well educated and full of personality.

After the countess had left the court in the 1880s, both of them fondly remembered their earlier moments of intimacy. In innumerable letters, the affectionate tone stands out. Dom Pedro wrote his letters by hand, and Barral often replied on the same letter. In one, of 3 December 1884, Dom Pedro wrote of their rare occasions of greater privacy: "Do you remember the Hotel Orléans?" Barral replied, "Of course!" Dom Pedro then asked, "Do you remember the name of our porter?" Barral responded, "Of course I remember Senhor Rozano. I can still hear the bell!!"[16]

Born a public person, Dom Pedro had little chance to speak to anyone of his private life, if indeed he had one. The letters refer often to the weather, good or bad, but there are few signs of human intimacy: "Today it rained heavily all day, and there have been bursts of thunder. When the rain comes down it seems to me that the glass door of the courtyard opens and you appear in front of me, and I hear the rustling of your dress before I see you."[17] Barral, for her part, did not shrink from writing to him about political matters, complaining about difficulties, and calling on him to act firmly. She remembered

In Egypt, Dom Pedro, the empress, the countess of Barral, the viscountess of Fonseca Costa, the viscount of Bom Conselho, the baron of Itaúna, and the archaeologist Auguste Marrich. O. Schoeff, 1872. FBN

their shared moments with affection and made humorous comments on the monarch's scrawl: "Go then, letter, and take to my royal friend my fond remembrance and my thanks for his letter of 19 and 24 September. Let him be careful in what he writes, for soon not even I will be able to read his writing."[18]

It was during Dom Pedro's second trip abroad that Barral's position at court changed, and it did so very quickly. From being tutor to Dom Pedro's daughters, she became the empress's lady-in-waiting virtually overnight: "Have a decree appointing the countess of Barral lady-in-waiting to the empress published tomorrow, for Barral has just arrived." But the monarch and his lady friend then separated, in Switzerland, and the emperor went back to Brazil on 26 September 1877, while Barral stayed in Europe with her son.

Only in his letters to the countess of Barral did the emperor's anguish at his lack of privacy appear with any clarity, for his life was swamped by his role as monarch: "In the end, it's this that particularly distresses me, the man cannot but be confused with the emperor, and I will be accused of egotism, when to live happily I need only to enjoy my freedom, which I will sacrifice so long as I am useful."[19] Dom Pedro II, the public person, had no space in which to be an "individual," however much he may have wanted to in this era so affected by the idea of romantic love. As Norbert Elias observes, even the most personal actions of a king can take on the character of acts of state, in much the same way that acts of state are often characterized as the personal actions of a king.[20]

In the case of the emperor of Brazil, the public image was always above reality itself. Although he had quite an active love life, the press and contemporary accounts never exploited or pursued it, insisting, on the contrary, on portraying him as serene, morally superior, above worldly matters—in other words, the antithesis of his father. We do not know if the image of a "newly bored king, citizen of the world," reached the people of Rio, but they would have been surprised by it. For the rest of the country this image became increasingly strong. Theater imposed itself on the life of the sovereign, and, as often happens with political symbolism, reality became myth.

Dom Pedro II in his bourgeois uniform, book in hand. CPCL

FIFTEEN

Universal Exhibitions

CELEBRATIONS OF LABOR AND PROGRESS

The electricity fairy.
Postcard made for
the 1900 Universal
Exhibition in Paris.
Private collection.

In the 1880s, Dom Pedro II laid more and more emphasis on giving Brazil a progressive image abroad. The image of the inventor-monarch who was enthusiastic about new scientific developments suited the world citizen who went about like a tourist and wanted to be "just like anyone else." In his diary toward the end of the decade, he wrote: "On my journeys all I have had time for was to make Brazil better known and to make personal contacts, which have already been useful. If I tried to show off my knowledge, it was so that people would know that in Brazil there are people more studious than I, for they have more opportunity than I."

This civilized image that the emperor was so keen to impress upon people abroad was also much appreciated in Brazil's capital, itself enthusiastic about foreign fashions. In July 1883, for example, the ballet *Excelsior*, staged by the Italian Opera Company from Milan, created a stir in Rio de Janeiro. The six thousand seats in the Dom Pedro II Imperial Theater were in hot demand during the run, and the emperor himself was present at seven out of the eight performances. The gist of the ballet was described as follows:

The impression made by *Excelsior* was brilliant. The huge ballet fills the evening, and even though not a single word is uttered all evening, the spectator is never bored. Almost two hundred women (mostly pretty), among them dancers of the first rank, beautiful costumes, magnificent decor, wonderful lighting effects, and graceful movement mean that there is no chance of tiring of it. The subject of the ballet is the struggle between light and darkness. Darkness (Obscurantism) is represented by a medieval knight, and light by the Genius of Progress. At the beginning the Genius lies in chains at the feet of Obscurantism; the Inquisition flourishes, and poverty and decadence rule the world.

Then the struggle begins; the Genius frees herself from her chains and rises in all her loveliness, crowned by electric lights. She gives a signal, and at the back of the stage appears the Temple of Science; Light and Civilization take hands, and several Genii surround them, dancing.

The second act opens in a country village near Bremen, on the banks of the Weser: [French physicist Denis] Papin appears, with the first steamship he built; they want to drown him, but the Genius of Progress appears and saves him; again she gives a sign, and then the port of New York appears at the back of the stage, locomotives run along tracks linking two rocks, and a modern ship passes by in front. Obscurantism flees and Genius triumphs.

The next act shows us [Italian physicist Count Alessandro] Volta's laboratory in Como; he is working on his battery and finally produces the electric spark. Obscurantism appears and wants to destroy the battery, but gets an electric shock that knocks him over. Genius appears, the back of the stage opens up, and we see a telegraph exchange, where hundreds of Genii send and receive telegrams in a truly enchanting ballet. Obscurantism flees and again Light triumphs.

Next is a brilliant scene representing the Sahara Desert with a caravan of live camels crossing the stage; the simoom begins to blow, and the Bedouins take advantage of momentary disorder in the caravan to attack and despoil it, then flee on horseback. The desert wind blows stronger and stronger, a fine dust covers the caravan, and the whole stage is filled with whirling dust. Obscurantism remains on stage alone, happy with what has happened. Now it is the turn of Progress to improve the paths of the desert . . . The Genius of Light appears, the horizon opens up, and we see the Suez Canal, navigated by proud ships.

The next part shows the Mont Cenis tunnel; the French are excavating it from their side. Obscurantism laughs, but the Genius of Light appears, the last layers of rock are broken through, the French and Italians meet and exchange fraternal embraces.

The Genius of Glory now comes to the front, carrying a bust of [Suez Canal promoter Ferdinand] de Lesseps. Obscurantism is defeated and tries to flee, but the Genius of Light does not allow him to. At a sign from the Genius, the back opens, and we see an allegorical representation of the fraternization of all nations; the earth opens up and swallows Obscurantism.

Now the clouds vanish; on stage appears a large temple in which all the nations embrace; the Genii of Progress, Civilization, and Concord give their blessings. The final scene shows the apotheosis of peace and science, in a wonderful *mise en scène*. All the action is portrayed in dance, and hundreds of dancers appear together on stage. The costumes are wonderful, the sets of astonishing beauty; all in all, it couldn't be better, and nowhere in the world could one see anything more delightful.[1]

The plot of this ballet is more than an illustration of the times: it is a virtual summary of its themes. An industrial middle class, self-satisfied and proud of its advances, thought of science as the expression of its greatest needs and desires. Each new discovery led to new novelties, which in turn opened up new perspectives and plans for the future. Dom Pedro was not alien to this new world. On the contrary, he enjoyed adjudicating requests for "industrial privileges" and patents. From the most important inventions to the most unusual, like floating bathing costumes and portable showers with hosepipe and bucket, from large constructions to the smallest details, a whole universe of novelties bedazzled the Brazilians.

Nothing suited the emperor more than the universal exhibitions, at which he delighted to appear as a "modern, cosmopolitan citizen."[2] These fairs began in the middle of the nineteenth century, as industrial capitalism developed, and they were the ultimate expression of modern energy and optimism.

Organized on a national basis starting in 1844 in Belgium, Prussia, Austria, and Spain, after the Great Exhibition of 1851 in London they became international shows in which European, American, Asian, and African representatives took part. The Great Exhibition, which lasted for 141 days, laid down the template for others to imitate. Thirty-four countries accepted the invitation to participate, and their products—shown in four categories of manufactures, machinery, raw materials, and fine arts—were seen by the more than 6 million people who visited it.[3]

The exhibitions were conceived by intellectuals, politicians, and entrepreneurs as a place to show off products and new scientific techniques, but they gradually became places where the bourgeoisie could proclaim its pride in recent advances. With an evolutionist ideology guiding them, the planners organized giant exercises in classifying and cataloging humankind: the Western world was the acme of civilization, and indigenous cultures "humanity's past." The spectacles of human evolution had something for everyone: from flesh-and-blood Africans to French art, from natives with their artifacts to the most recent inventions. The introduction to the 1889 Paris fair gives a notion of the intention of all these exhibitions:

> Why should we see the exhibition? We should see it in the same spirit in which it was organized: to be instructed and entertained . . . The industrialist will find models he can learn from. The peasant will get a general idea, sufficient for his purposes, of the marvels of the modern world. Others may find the road to fortune, thanks to seeing the manufacturing processes on display here; yet others will find useful objects. Artists will find new sources of inspiration . . . Amateurs will be able to satisfy their curiosity . . . In these pavilions one can find every country, with all its architectural styles, reproductions of its famous monuments, and the streets of its towns: the whole world is concentrated in this exhibition. It is a world tour not in 24 days but in a few hours.[4]

Competition among the participating nations and especially among the host nations was rekindled with each new fair. The size and architectural style of the buildings, the variety of the pavilions and the products: everything was done with an eye to showing off to other nations. A whole new architecture, and a new way of presenting products and objects, was invented. Characterized by modern speed as well, these fairs were "orgies of modernity,"[5] as one commentator has written: monumental cities built only to be destroyed, a grand spectacle that lasted only for a few months.

The first international exhibition, in London in 1851, created a symbol that left its mark on our idea of the whole epoch: the Crystal Palace, designed and built by the architect Joseph Paxton, became a "cathedral of progress," a monument to the British industrial revolution. In the six months of the exhibition, it is said that a fifth of the English population visited this monument to modernity. The palace with its huge iron beams produced an impression of immensity, but it could be dismantled with the same quick ease that it had been put up. In Foot Hardman's words, a new monumentality had been invented, prosaic and magical at the same time.

Year	Place	Number of Exhibitors	Profit/ Loss	Number of Visitors (in millions)	Acreage	Duration (in months)
1851	London	13,937	+	6.0	26	4.8
1855	Paris	20,839	-	5.2	34	6.7
1862	London	28,653	-	6.2	25	5.7
1867	Paris	43,217	+	6.8	215	7.2
1873	Vienna	25,760	-	7.3	42	6.2
1876	Philadelphia	60,000	-	9.9	285	5.3
1878	Paris	52,835	-	16.0	192	6.5
1883	Amsterdam					
1885	Antwerp					
1889	Paris	61,722	+	32.3	237	5.7
1893	Chicago		+	27.5	685	6.1
1900	Paris	83,000		48.1		
1904	St. Louis			19.7		
1915	San Francisco	30,000		18.7		

Sources: Hardman, *Trem fantasma*, and Benedict, *The Anthropology of World's Fairs*

Other obvious aspects of these events were their enormous size and the losses they incurred, compensated for only by their propaganda value for the host countries. But it is important to see these fairs not only in terms of their commercial returns (the exhibitions encouraged economic development and expanding markets) but also as crucial symbolic capital. Each fair was a kind of trophy, its success synonymous with prestige in the eyes of other nations. This is why, in spite of their obvious commercial purpose, the exhibitions always boasted of their importance in bringing nations together: "Universal exhibitions are for the human race what the Olympic Games were for the Greeks, a family reunion in which, for a while anyway, mindless rivalries and trivial hatreds are renounced and the mind feels new affinities with others."[6] This was the reason for the innovation introduced by France in 1867, when each country was allowed to build its own pavilion in its own image and likeness: an English cottage, a Mexican temple, an Egyptian palace.

As one exhibition succeeded another, the attractions multiplied. It was not only the fantastic architectural achievements—the Crystal Palace (1851) and the Eiffel Tower (1889)—that delighted visitors' eyes; reproductions of typical houses, local food, and costumes allowed the public to "travel," as it were, without leaving their own country. Souvenirs, postcards, and photographs were sold: it is no accident that the first automatic camera was set up at the 1889 exhibition. For the great majority of the public, these fairs were for amusement, not for buying products or inventions.

Conceived in an imperialist context, the displays tried to underline unity in a divided world, despite the competition among exhibits. So while it is true that they were not limited to "civilized countries" or what we would call today the First World nations, the status of each nation's participation was obvious enough. Only British colonies took part in the 1851 exhibition in London; in the 1855 Paris exhibition, other colonies, and countries farther from Europe, began to be present. Brazil was always recognized by its "jungle." But for Brazil itself, participation in these exhibitions was a strategic necessity: the country wanted to display not only its national specialties, its indigenous peoples, its jungle, and its agricultural products, but also its more civilized aspect.

From the third universal exhibition in London in 1862 onward, Brazil was a constant presence. The intention was clear:

> To make the empire known and appreciated through specimens and products, and to give an idea, however feeble, of our enterprise and civilization, destroying prejudices that operate in our disfavor. The exhibitions are the congresses of the people, and they lay the basis for peace in the world. These festivals of intelligence and industriousness, as Your Majesty says, always give reason for justified celebration . . . a motive for glorifying our nation . . . The advantages of this exhibition [London 1862], with its wide scope and range, will not have escaped Your Majesty's superior intelligence. This is the first time we have participated, and the monarchy's voice produces sympathetic echoes.[7]

The emperor's participation could not have been more direct: Pedro invested in the Brazilian pavilion on his own initiative, helped to select the products to be displayed, and personally handed out the prizes.

There was a systematic plan to ensure the quality of Brazil's pavilion: each province held a preliminary fair, and the products chosen from them were sent to a nationwide show, where the best were selected for the universal exhibition. The emperor organized and sponsored the national exhibits and gave prizes in four categories: a silver medal, a copper medal, "honorable mention," and "exceptional." The shows were not small: in 1861, five thousand people visited the national exhibition in Rio de Janeiro, where seventy-six exhibitors displayed 750 objects divided into different sections. The government financed these events even though it knew that expenses would outrun receipts. (In 1861 the fair cost 66,164 mil-réis and in the forty-two days it was open made only 15,367; the figures were comparable for the shows in 1868 and 1873.) It was clear that the link with the emperor was close—not accidentally, the 1861 show opened on Dom Pedro II's birthday.

Brazil brought its best products to its first international show, in 1862: coffee, tea, maté, *guaraná*, rice, rubber, tobacco, wood, vegetable fibers, bees,

Statue of Dom Pedro II cast for the opening of Brazil's first national exhibition. Instituto Artístico, 1861. MIP

and cotton. Some industrial products were shown—machines, materials for railways and construction, telegraphs, arms—but they attracted no attention. The prizes went to coffee and to *marajoara* ceramics made on Marajó, a large island at the mouth of the Amazon. As always, it was the exotic aspects of Brazil that interested people most.

In 1867, when Brazil prepared for the Paris exhibition that year, the situation was not good, for the country was at war. But to miss a fair would be to show weakness:

> The unfavorable conditions in which we are organizing the second Brazilian exhibition, now that the empire is involved in an unexpected war, have absorbed our energies . . . and have not allowed Brazil to take due part in the universal exhibition in Paris or to give an idea of its immense natural wealth and productive power. For Brazil to be one of the greatest countries on earth, all that is needed is communications. With this in mind, it seems necessary to us to accompany the catalog with information about the empire, even though this will of necessity be incomplete.[8]

But there was no money for a costly venture, so Brazil's presence in 1867 and 1873 was still on a small scale. Only in 1876, in Philadelphia, was there a real change. As we have seen, the emperor thought it vital, in his own words, to "put on a good show." "If the exhibitions cannot yet, for Brazil, signify competition in industry," the brochure acknowledged, "they have given an opportunity for Brazil to be better known and appreciated as a region with very fertile soil, whose people are peaceful, intelligent, and hard-working." No mistaking, Brazil in these competitions was an agricultural nation, but it needed to emphasize its exceptional temperament. It was distant from the anarchy of the Latin American republics, and though it had just emerged from a violent war, it wanted to present itself as a harmonious country where natives and whites (whose products were both displayed) lived in harmony.

Brazil's constant presence—at the exhibitions of 1862 (London), 1867 (Paris), 1873 (Vienna), 1876 (Philadelphia), and 1889 (Paris), when other Latin American countries were not present at all (except Argentina, after 1889)—says a great deal about the effort on the part of the emperor and the elites of court and capital to put forward an image of Brazil not as far away, agricultural, monarchical, and slave-owning but as modern and cosmopolitan, led by a king who was a "pioneer," open to new technologies. The early

introductions of the telephone and camera are important examples of this attitude. Yet in the end the effect was to stress that Brazil was above all a country of "noble savages" where nature was found at its most imposing.

At a time when the triumphant bourgeoisie aimed to conquer the whole
world—perhaps, as Cecil Rhodes said, the planets too—and when positivist
and determinist science thought it had accounted for every theme and every
possible space, the world fairs displayed for all to see, in didactic form, the
progress of some and backwardness of others, technology in the hands of
some, exoticism the privilege of others. They were a perfect corollary of the
imperialist policies of the time. For Brazil, with its "citizen-monarch, bored
with power," it was a good time to project its new image abroad, saving the
country from being known only for slavery and monarchy. This was emancipation by culture; it was also an idealized way to redeem Brazil from its old
colonial status.

Although Brazil brought materials in all four categories (manufactures,
machinery, raw materials, and fine arts), the proportion of items in each category varied. Coffee, wood, sugar, and tobacco won the most medals and
honorable mentions, industry relatively little. The pavilions themselves highlighted agriculture and indigenous products, such as hammocks, oars, arrows, and plumage.

Brazil at the International Exhibition
of Hygiene and Education in
London; a romantic portrayal of a
Native American empire, 1884. FBN

Still, Brazil made an effort to seem like more than an aggregation of local products. Informative books about Brazilian geography and economy were produced and distributed in French, German, English, and Portuguese. Transportation was organized for these exhibits, and to crown the undertaking, the monarch himself often sat in front of the pavilion, as if to complete the display. "A king in spite of himself," "a civilized man in a slave-owning country," "a citizen in a country with no notion of citizenship," Dom Pedro II had an ideal set for his theater, even as the drama became more hollow. The greatest of all universal exhibitions, planned for 1889 in Paris, was to commemorate the centenary of the French Revolution and show off the modernity and democracy of the fin de siècle. Thirty million tickets were anticipated, and the participation of 38,000 exhibitors, who were spread over the Grand Palais, the Trocadero Gardens, the Champ de Mars, the Quai d'Orsay, the Avenue de Suffren, the Foreign Ministry, and the Esplanade of the Invalides. A monument was constructed especially for the occasion—no more, no less than the Eiffel Tower. Works of art, education and pedagogy, furniture and accessories, textiles, clothes, extractive industries, mechanical industries, electricity, food products, agriculture, viticulture, horticulture, and fisheries would all be represented.

The exhibition was soon seen as a glorification of the French republic and as such was boycotted by the European monarchies. Dom Pedro, however, heeding the advice of the viscount of Cavalcanti and Eduardo da Silva Prado, decided to have Brazil participate and thus show his progressiveness. In the copy of the *Guide Bleu* to the 1889 exhibition that is said to have belonged to Dom Pedro II, the organizer's remark, "He is the only sovereign to have done this!" is underlined in blue pencil with Dom Pedro's comment: "That is true."[9] As *Revista Ilustrada* of 1889 put it:

> In truth, the 1889 exhibition symbolizes the apotheosis of the modern world. Only a confident people, aware of their own strength and believing in civilization, could have produced the magnificent things there . . . The soldiers of democracy had enough power to impress us with their own picture . . . As an exception, and one that does us honor, our country figures officially as the only monarchy that, overcoming prejudices, joined in this great celebration of the rights of man.[10]

Eduardo da Silva Prado, F. J. Santa Anna Nery, and the viscount of Cavalcanti were entrusted with the work of preparing the Brazilian pavilion on

14 March 1888. The commission received 800,000 francs from Rio de Janeiro, 50,000 from Bahia, 100,000 from Minas Gerais, and other smaller donations to construct the pavilion. The products were submitted for approval at an exhibit in Rio de Janeiro, opened by the emperor. The work went well, but in June Cavalcanti regretted the pavilion's central placement: it was right on the Champ de Mars and immediately to the right of the Eiffel Tower. That was what Dom Pedro had asked for, but the results were disappointing: the Brazilian pavilion looked tiny beside the monumental tower.

Even so, it was no disgrace to the country, with its three floors, galleries and atrium occupying an area of more than fourteen hundred square yards. The floor was made of Brazilian woods, cut to size in Rio de Janeiro. The decoration was special, too: six statues represented Brazil's principal rivers (the Amazon, Tocantins, Madeira, São Francisco, Parnaíba, and Paraná), with plants, shrubs, and large set-piece arrangements. Fountains decorated the other spaces, along with the Brazilian flag, showing off its green and yellow. The frame was of open ironwork, with the cupola and friezes decorated with garlands and cameos. One gallery displayed faience and elegant ceramics. Another had a collection of Brazilian flowers and plants. The external structure was also covered with Brazilian plants, especially palm trees and orchids. A little pond, its 86°F temperature kept constant by a special heating system, had the very large water lilies from the Amazon known as Victoria Regias: this was the pavilion's big attraction.

In addition, the pavilion offered a *gracieux pavillon de dégustation* for the consumption of coffee, maté, and fruit liqueurs, and a Palace of the Amazon, dedicated to the history of the indigenous people of Marajó, with funerary urns, vases, statues, arrows, lip plugs, bows, masks, baskets, objects made from feathers, weapons of war, and portraits of Botocudos (Native Americans from the Rio Negro) and mestizos from the Amazon. The French newspapers were delighted and enthusiastically described the wonderful "art of the savages," so well organized by the director of the National Museum of Rio de Janeiro, Dr. Ladislau Netto.[11] What really delighted the public were the exotic objects and the jungle. "Would you like to be surrounded by incredible vegetation? Come along to the Brazilian Palace": this was how the Brazilian pavilion was advertised in the *Guide Bleu*, efforts to publicize Brazil's industry and civilization notwithstanding.

In the 1889 *Journal Exposition de Paris* the reaction was no less enthusiastic: "Don't miss the great attractions that await you. Walk through a tunnel of foliage, alongside trees, those terrible trees, so near the walkways, hanging with mangoes, about which they tell you to be careful." The French public enjoyed discovering "the natural products of a Latin and American empire, particularly rich in mineral and vegetable raw materials . . . the Victoria Regia, that giant aquatic plant now about to flower in Europe."[12]

Once again the Brazilian monarchy itself did not go unnoticed, but only for its exoticism. Dom Pedro had made an effort to show the progressive side of his empire in international events, but the magic worked only in part. It was not the image of civilization that characterized the Brazilian Empire, but its eccentricities.

Even within Brazil the glamour of the monarchy was becoming tarnished. The tropical monarch participating in festivals and rituals had been much more popular than the citizen with his double-breasted black coat, looking more, in the words of Gilberto Freyre's book title, like "a gray emperor in a land of tropical sunshine." The support the emperor gave to France's universal exposition was not enough to strengthen the modern image of the Brazilian monarchy. Four months after the pavilion had been set up, it was the monarchy's turn to say good-bye to Brazil.

SIXTEEN

The Monarchy Will Fall

"Speeches from the Throne concocted by our governments seem to have the single object of undermining the throne itself, putting the monarchy in a parlous situation." Behind Dom Pedro can be seen Counselor Rodolfo Dantas. CEA

In his story "The Mirror," Joaquim Maria Machado de Assis recounts a strange episode in the life of Jacobina, a young man who, when he reaches his twenty-fifth birthday, is made a sublieutenant in the National Guard, much to his family's delight. He accepts an invitation to spend some time on his aunt's farm; she is as thrilled as everyone else. "I asked her to call me Joãozinho as before," he says, "but she shook her head and loudly insisted that no, it had to be 'Mr. Sublieutenant.'" As a sign of her affection, she orders a large mirror to be put in his room. From then on, "the sublieutenant eliminated the man. For some days, these two natures were in equilibrium; but it wasn't long before the original state gave way to the other; a minimal part of humanity was left over . . . The only portion of the citizen that remained was the part that had to do with my rank; the rest vanished into the air, or into the past." Later on, when he looks at the mirror again, Jacobina cannot see himself: he is not "clear and entire but vague, fuzzy, the faint shadow of a shade." Then he decides to put the sublieutenant's uniform on: "the glass reproduced the entire figure; not a line was missing, not a contour out of place."[1]

In this little story we can see the impasse faced by our citizen-monarch. When he took off his robes of majesty, Dom Pedro II was naked, as in Andersen's fairy tale, or he lost his own image, as in Machado's mirror. All that faced the emperor was his own reflection; Dom Pedro no longer held the Brazilians' imagination in thrall.

When he came back from his second journey abroad in 1876, a Te Deum welcomed his return, but the emperor seemed like a foreigner in his own land. Almost like a spectator, he watched his country's new political movements—especially the new Republican Party and the new movement for the abolition of slavery. The Society for Liberation as well as the Society for the Emancipation of the Slaves had been founded in Rio in 1870, and in that same year the newspaper A *República* published the Republican Manifesto. The Republican Party followed in 1871, and the Convention of Itu, held in 1873 in a small town in the vitally important province of São Paulo, was the first Republican meeting in Brazil. As if from a box in a theater, Dom Pedro witnessed the removal of the Conservative cabinet and the return of the Liberals who had been out of power for ten years. Serious problems affecting the whole country, such as the rebellion in Paraíba and Pernambuco in 1874 set off by the modernizing plan to impose metrification—the so-called Quebra-Quilos, or "smash-kilos"—or the terrible drought of 1877 seemed not to affect him. And he also abandoned some of his old rituals. The symbol he chose for himself—a capital P in blue, tied with a ribbon—all but made explicit his distance from the people; the ceremony of kissing his hand had been abolished, and for some time now he used his gala robes only on the most solemn occasions, like the obligatory Speech from the Throne that began and ended each legislative session.

Carl von Koseritz, with his predictable criticism of the court's lack of luxury and etiquette, gives us a different view of the situation in 1883. In contrast to his accounts from several decades before, which had extolled the imperial pomp and richness, now he could not but deplore the poverty of the imperial dress, the decadence of the palaces, and the dilapidated condition of the royal carriages. Neither the emperor's charitable donations nor his support of students and scientists brought him respect or thanks. Worse, the imperial processions no longer delighted the people in the street.

> In the company of my friends . . . I manage to get a place to see the court pass by, and the procession soon begins. What a strange sight! First comes a cavalry unit galloping by on panting horses and brandishing virgin, unsheathed sabers; soon after them come four court carriages with the noblemen and chamberlains in attendance, and the ladies-in-waiting. Court carriages I say, but what a sight . . . They all date from the last century . . . The gilt has long since darkened, the upholstery has worn away, and everything is in a very sad state. The

old liveries worn by the coachmen, most of them black, are in equally
sad condition, and as a result they look like circus monkeys . . . One
after the other, the old carriages empty themselves of their contents: a
lady-in-waiting (the baroness of Suruí), old and very ugly but with a
very low-cut neckline, and five or six nobles of the court—decked out
in uniforms that were once brilliant, embroidered with gold, with tri-
corn hats under their arms, swords by their sides, and their thin legs in
silk stockings. They get out of their carriages and put one in mind of a
Carnival procession . . . From no less ancient and ruinous a carriage
comes the count d'Eu with the heir to the throne. In his gala field
marshal's uniform, he makes a very favorable impression. One can see
the soldier in him, and his pride in a princely lineage (which, however, does not shield him from a painful concern with money matters)
is written on his forehead. The princess has aged rapidly, and her features have taken on a kind of hardness, but her blond hair still goes
well with her healthy complexion and her full, rounded form. She is
quite simply dressed, wearing only a few diamonds. The people let her
go on her way, and only here and there a few sarcastic remarks can be
heard about the count, who is not held in great esteem. Now comes
the worthy empress. Her carriage is a little better, but still worn and
battered . . . She is wearing a heavy low-cut dress, ceremonially sprinkled with diamonds, and a diamond tiara in her hair, which is completely white, while around her neck she has the famous diamond
necklace, her greatest treasure . . . Finally the emperor appears: four
outriders in new livery, four horses richly harnessed, and a carriage
that, if not new, has at least been completely restored, decorated, and
adorned with silver, with the imperial crown over the door, announce
his arrival. No applause greets him, not even a simple "hurrah." He
himself seems to be disappointed at this, for as he gets out of his carriage, he stands up to his full height and gives a lingering, penetrating
look at the people around him. I can see no majesty in him, with his
buckled shoes, his silk stockings, breeches, feather collar, and green
velvet mantle, under which shine his gold medals. The curious
feather ornament (of toucan breast-feathers) reminds one almost of
Carnival. The emperor walks with something of a stoop and has aged
a great deal lately. He is also getting visibly bald, and his worries, as
well perhaps as his physical suffering, show in the deep furrows in his
cheeks. He is preceded by servants carrying the crown and the scepter,

while the sword hangs by his side . . . The overall impression of the
ceremony is calculated to produce more laughter than respect. When
monarchy shows off its magnificence, it must be in an imposing,
grandiose form, and here this does not happen. I know the emperor
cannot have a brilliant court because he spends his civil list on works
of charity, but however noble this may be, it does not justify his tact-
lessness in showing off old junk as the splendor of the empire.[2]

As Koseritz observes, at this spectacle there are no cheers from the people,
who are no longer entranced by the impoverished, mundane show. The same
is true in the once magnificent palaces:

> [The emperor's] old palace in the city is a shack . . . Old, rotten, ru-
> ined, ill treated, never repainted, there it is, opposite the Pharoux
> Quay, like an old shed. It is true that the emperor and his family only
> very rarely use this so-called City Palace, because he lives at São
> Cristóvão, but even the latter palace . . . cannot be that much better.
> There is something strange about the emperor's position: he has no
> personal fortune, and his civil list, which is not sufficient, goes mostly
> to charitable works, so that he can no longer maintain any pomp or
> ceremony and can do nothing to give splendor to his residences . . .
> Doubtless this is very laudable as far as the man is concerned, but it
> contributes little to the necessary imperial prestige . . . Still more
> comic (and inconceivable, for a European) is that the whole ground
> floor of the part of the palace facing the courtyard is rented out to
> shopkeepers, barbers, and so on! This would not happen in the case of
> even the most modest German prince, but here it is inevitable, for the
> emperor's income is insufficient for his charitable works. In political
> matters I have often found myself having to censure the emperor and
> criticize his actions, sometimes quite harshly; but I still respect the
> man, as any honorable citizen should, because he has a big heart, is a
> friend and benefactor to his fellow men, and abstains from luxury so
> as to improve the plight of others.[3]

It was said that the decaying City Palace had been abandoned, with its
old, worthless furniture, since the emperor only slept there during Holy
Week. In the 1880s there was only one person in charge of maintaining it and
two servants. To get to the bedrooms on the upper floor, one had to go along

dark corridors lit by candles or kerosene lamps. Even the São Cristóvão Palace had problems, notably termites. In a letter of 9 July 1886 it was observed, "There is no palace in the city fit to receive imperial visits. The termites have even eaten clothes that nowadays are only used in processions. We'd better stick to Petrópolis."

Over time, the royal processions lost their fascination. Until the 1870s all cultural life in Rio revolved around the court, but now other groups formed that were alien to the previous splendor of the imperial family. The famous Bohemian Group, which met in Rio's cafés, was acutely critical of Dom Pedro II and the group of writers surrounding him.

From London, on 22 March 1887, the baron of Penedo, Brazil's ambassador to the Court of St. James, sent a letter reporting on the celebration of Queen Victoria's Golden Jubilee. It is worth noting the advice he gave his own sovereign:

> As I am a sincere monarchist and [the emperor's] representative here, I would be very disappointed if the American monarch were not eager to congratulate the queen, for he is, after Queen Victoria, the monarch who has reigned longest . . . I am quite aware of the emperor's state of mind, but it does seem to me that the count d'Eu could be sent, with a signed letter, to present at the jubilee. He is the queen's second cousin, the emperor's son-in-law, and it would have a good effect. Prince Pedro Augusto would also be a suitable person to undertake this work: he too is a cousin of the queen and grandson of the emperor . . . Without wishing to go into too much detail, it remains to be said that Prince Dom Pedro Augusto cannot be presented at court without some kind of uniform (I assume he does not have one): this would be a great cross to bear, for he would stick out like a black swan.[4]

We are clearly no longer in the era of Louis Philippe — the great model of monarchy is now British. And the strength of the British monarchy was not just a matter of its immense territorial possessions. Queen Victoria's family personified changes in patterns of morality, behavior, and conduct, and its image as model family became inseparable from the monarchy itself, which did not forgo the etiquette, pomp, and ritual that have always been the essence of royalty.

But things were different in Brazil, where the lack of royal elegance and pomp was so obvious that sometimes others in the party stood out favorably in comparison to the "poor emperor." Even in the 1860s the "intolerant" Maxi-milian von Habsburg had commented that the blacks, in processions of brotherhoods, seemed more distinguished than Dom Pedro II himself:

> Waiting for us in front of the entrance to the arsenal was a so-called fashionable carriage to take us to the religious festival that the blacks were to celebrate, at the pilgrim shrine of Our Lady of Bomfim, as they do every year on this day . . . It was a light carriage, very richly adorned. Four white horses harnessed to it were prancing in the or-nate trappings, like horses for a coronation carriage. In the box were two individuals as black as boot polish, but their exotic skin was ac-coutered with beautiful green frock coats with silver braid and tassels, and velvet breeches, leggings, ties, and pure white gloves. Big collars with long points, framing the faces with their grinning teeth, reached up to the curly hair. Then below the collar was a tie decorated with a long silvery tassel, which swung around, either hitting the shoulders or dancing to and fro in front of their face.[5]

Ina von Binzer was present at Dom Pedro's arrival in São João del Rei, Mi-nas Gerais, in 1881: "Finally the train arrived; the locomotive had broken down on the way, and the emperor had to wait two hours at the station, which was still being adorned with carpets and flowers. But nothing affected his good humor . . . They also arranged a concert and a dance. When are we to hear it? he inquired."[6] Out-of-place etiquette can certainly produce laughter.

Though Dom Pedro was a monarch in a society that cherished its rituals and festivals, he had abandoned not only the many values dear to royalty as a system but elements important in a context that was itself defined by its festi-vals. If, by the 1880s, he gave up on the "ethics of ostentation" and took on the image of an aged gentleman, fed up with power, and could scarcely endure civic, official ceremonies, what could be expected where popular festivals were concerned? Political forces were distancing him further and further from matters of state. Yet in the "land of Carnival," festivals cannot simply be abandoned. One cannot neglect the symbolic importance of the mainte-nance of political power. Clifford Geertz has written, "When kings journey through the interior of their realms, showing themselves in public, conferring honors, exchanging presents, or challenging rivals, they mark their territories out, just as the wolf or the tiger does when it spreads its scent, as if it were a physical part of it."[7] His words are relevant in the Brazilian monarchy. Dom

Pedro's public appearances in corteges and processions were like territorial demarcations, linking his image to that of the empire itself. Joaquim Nabuco, the father of Brazilian abolitionism who always affirmed his links with the monarchy, defined the exceptional character of royalty: "Pomp, majesty, the whole apparatus of royalty was, for me, a necessary artifice for governing and satisfying the imagination of the masses; whatever the culture of the society in question, royalty naturally belonged to the class of institutions that (philosopher Herbert) Spencer called ceremonials, like prizes, gifts, bowing and curtseying, titles, et cetera."[8]

By giving no attention to his image, Dom Pedro exposed the real fragility of the monarchy, whereas once it had been linked to the stability of the state itself. Not only was the "theater of politics" weakened, but the timing was unpropitious, as the contradictions of the empire became more and more visible. For example, the relationship between the empire and the export of Brazilian agriculture had never been questioned; the latter produced (through import and export duties) 70 percent of the state's income.[9] But hesitant policies concerning the abolition of slavery caused tension in the agricultural sector. The Law of the Free Womb gave an excellent example: the government's coalition with plantation owners in the northeast irritated the coffee planters in the south and undermined the regime's legitimacy. The paradox well illustrates what Guerreiro Ramos has called the "dialectic of ambiguity": at the same time as the state was the foundation of slavery, it was also the only thing that could destroy it. As Joaquim Nabuco put it, "This is the power capable of destroying slavery, of which it is also the product, and they may both die together."[10]

In José Murilo de Carvalho's opinion, the rural elite demanded decentralization of the state as well as reduced federal control over the economy and abolition of the moderating power, yet they wanted federal power on their side whenever there was a need to resolve impasses in immigration policy, problems with slavery, agricultural credit, and so on.[11] This is a long way from having total dominion over the rural landowners; but after the Law of the Free Womb in 1871, the empire's alliance with this group was broken, and the monarchy began to weaken. As the pressure for abolition of slavery mounted there was widespread fear that disorder would prevail. Dom Pedro's public image became a target of criticism and sarcastic comment: broken down and faded, like his clothes and his carriages, his empire was seen to be naked.

From the 1850s the Brazilian press had a great deal of freedom, and the emperor was a constant target of attacks and satirical drawings. Noting his indifference to matters of state and the hesitancy that he was displaying in public, caricaturists of the emperor began to portray him as Pedro Banana or Pedro Cashew. This kind of coverage expanded, so that by 1876 Rio de Janeiro had half a dozen satirical magazines with circulations up to ten thousand—*A Semana Ilustrada* and *O Mosquito* were two of the oldest, and others appeared later, like *O Mequetrefe, O Fígaro,* and *Revista Ilustrada*. Three cartoonists were especially popular: Ângelo Agostini and Luigi Borgomainerio—both Italians, whose work appeared in *Revista Ilustrada* and *O Fígaro,* respectively—and Rafael Bordalo Pinheiro, a friend of the Portuguese writers Ramalho Ortigão and Eça de Queirós, who had recently come from Lisbon and who wrote for *O Mosquito*. Then there were more than twenty magazines and almanacs that carried cartoons, often political. The most famous was the *Revista Ilustrada,* founded in 1876 and owned by Ângelo Agostini. By the end of the empire, this magazine was so popular that subscriptions alone could support it, and it had become required reading, at least in cultured circles in Rio de Janeiro. But most of these satirical magazines lasted only a short time. By 1878 only *O Mequetrefe, Revista Ilustrada,* and *A Semana Ilustrada* were still being published.

Using new photographic techniques, cartoonists began to do pictures of the monarch and the politicians around him in hilarious settings and scenes. Paradoxically, this spread their image further and made it more familiar; the mockery became another kind of publicity. Cartoonists like Agostini and Bordalo Pinheiro were ruthless in their ridicule of the emperor's ever more frequent journeys. They showed the "itinerant monarch" obsessed with constantly demonstrating his erudition. But his journeys were not the only object of mockery. For most Brazilians, the subjects to which Dom Pedro was passionately attached—comparative literature, linguistics, human geography, ethnology, archaeology, dead languages—had nothing to do with politics or daily life. (At this time, too, the emperor became attached to Freemasonry, which displeased the Church and was disapproved of by a significant proportion of the population when it became public knowledge.)

The image of an old monarch with a long white beard—already part of his official image—dates from the 1880s, and it became even more popular through caricature. Dom Pedro, who was not yet sixty, looked tired. He slept at sessions of the Historical and Geographical Institute and during the exams in the Pedro II School, and this was lampooned—but so was his personality, his ability to dissemble, his thin legs, his squeaky voice, his travels, his obsession with learning, the empty formality of his Speeches from the Throne.

"It's said that our tireless emperor is working out how to go around the world in less than eighty days." Ângelo Agostini in *Revista Ilustrada*. CEA

(left) The emperor in Egypt. *Revista Ilustrada*, 1871. IEB

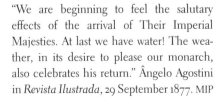

"We are beginning to feel the salutary effects of the arrival of Their Imperial Majesties. At last we have water! The weather, in its desire to please our monarch, also celebrates his return." Ângelo Agostini in *Revista Ilustrada*, 29 September 1877. MIP

"Judging by the speed with which Dom Pedro likes to travel, we have no doubt that soon His Majesty will choose this method. His illustrious retinue will have to put up with it! Poor things!" Ângelo Agostini in *Revista Ilustrada*. MIP

Dom Pedro was depicted sleeping precisely when engaging in the activities
he was proudest of. He had moved away from being represented as a superior
being, but he did not carry conviction as a citizen-monarch either, and certainly not as the great Maecenas of Brazilian Romanticism. In these changed
times, the once-popular epic novels about Indians and heroic paintings of
jungle dwellers were seen with newly jaundiced eyes.

It was Ângelo Agostini who had established the Native American as a symbol of the Brazilian people during the empire, but he was no longer a brave,
pure inhabitant of the jungle; rather, he was a figure weakened by imperial
policies who was constantly being tricked. Irony was not limited to the cartoonists. By the later years of the empire, most of the groups taking part in Carnival were abolitionist and republican, and their clubs became meeting places
where the emperor and the government were criticized. In 1864, for example,
the Euterpe Commercial Carnival Society decided to spend the money originally intended for their parade floats on freeing slaves. Then, later,

> In accordance with its aim of abolishing slavery by all valid means and
> methods, the Fenians [one of the Carnival "schools" competing in

The empire, represented by a Native
American, shows signs of exhaustion.
Ângelo Agostini, in *Revista Ilustrada*. CEA

Dom Pedro looking at the moon. In *Revista Ilustrada*. CEA

"We really must add a lyre to the imperial coat of arms. Poet-kings are rare!" *Revista Ilustrada*. CEA

Dom Pedro sleeps during a session of the Historical and Geographical Institute. CEA

"The king, our lord and master, sleeps the sleep of indifference. The papers that bring him the bad news daily seem to have a narcotic effect on His Majesty." *Revista Ilustrada*, 1887. CEA

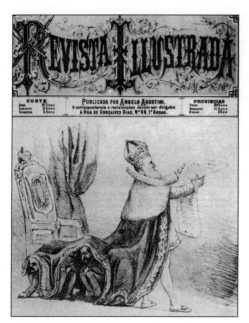

Dom Pedro, in the clouds, observes distant reality. *Revista Ilustrada.* CEA

Sheltered under the imperial mantle. *Revista Ilustrada*, 1884. CEA

Rio], . . . on the occasion of the 1881 Carnival, among the allegorical and critical floats . . . included one called "Jupiter's Stain," in which the figure of the emperor was shown as stained by slavery. Coinciding as it did with another similar caricature done by the Democrats, the Fenians' float was a great success in all the streets it passed through and provoked the anger of the much-feared Urban Guard . . . The Fenians went around distributing *The Torch of Civilization*, a little newspaper they publish, in whose pages some irreverent verses explained the criticisms being made: "Here's the slave-owning king of hearts / Of the realms of knavery / In this kingdom of humbug / Here's the slave-owning king / On his big flat butt / The idiot took a picture of himself."[12]

Thanks to their free press, Brazilians grew familiar with this entertaining way of making serious criticisms. Humor played a dual role: the cartoons generated a certain sympathy for the emperor, whose weaknesses were so cruelly exposed, but on the other hand, it was as if Dom Pedro and the imperial system were being dismantled in front of the readers' eyes. Perhaps we can say that these cartoons, though they made use of photographs, had an opposite effect to them. Photographs in an official context put over the secure, stable image of a "civilized monarchy for responsible citizens," but the cartoons stole these same features, degraded the settings, and underlined the contradictions in the imperial government. Nothing could have been worse for the image of Brazilian royalty, so well preserved until now.

Simultaneously, a deliberate policy of exposing the crown's expenses in the press arose. Amounts were listed and compared to other items in Brazil's finances, and there was a demand for transparency in the imperial household's accounts. "In a monarchy there is no check on the moneys spent for the well-being of the royal family, but in a constitutional monarchy, they should be accounted for, and excesses justified."[13] A lively polemic arose among Rio newspapers in 1873 on the topic of Dom Pedro's bill at the Hotel do Porto during his trip to Portugal the year before, which is a good example of the press alternating between preserving the monarch from criticism and subjecting his actions, as a citizen of the Brazilian Empire, to scrutiny.

Dom Pedro, with his retinue, had stayed in the Hotel do Porto, where he found the bill excessive and questioned it, lodging a legal complaint. Months later the hotel's owner, Dona Henriqueta Alvellos, came to Brazil to beg personally that the bill be paid, saying that she would go bankrupt if this did not happen. When her request was not granted, she took recourse to public opinion, writing a detailed account of the enormous expenses of the monarch and his court in the *Jornal do Commercio*. Opinions were divided: while the *Diário do Rio de Janeiro* and *A República* defended the need to preserve Dom Pedro's public image, the *Jornal do Commercio* took the line that this was a constitutional matter involving freedom of the press.

But perhaps the greatest political scandal of the time was the theft of the crown jewels. The episode in itself hardly seems to merit much attention, but its considerable repercussions are compelling evidence that criticisms and doubts about the monarchy were stronger than certainties. On the night of 17 March 1882 several of the empress's jewels disappeared from the São Cristóvão Palace. The emperor was coming back from Petrópolis at the time, and only when he got to the palace was he informed that a wardrobe in the private apartments had been forced and two small boxes, containing jewels of great value, had been stolen.

The police chief, Trigo de Loureiro, determined that someone who knew the palace intimately had carried out the robbery. Manuel Paiva and his brother Pedro, longtime servants in the palace, were the principal suspects, and it was said that the emperor protected them. They were arrested, and the jewels, valued at 40 mil-réis, were found in Manuel's house, hidden in small tins of butter. Even though they confessed their guilt, the police prosecuted neither of them, which was what most exercised the public. When the thieves were freed without being punished, the *Jornal do Commercio* said, "The return of the property may satisfy the victim of the robbery, but not society's moral demands."

Many newspapers covered the case. A running account appeared for several days in the *Gazeta de Notícias*, while the *Gazetinha* published a pamphlet entitled "The Theft from Olympus" and even accused the emperor of having raped Paiva's daughter and of having him freed out of fear of retaliation. The *Gazeta da Tarde* mounted the strongest attacks of all, while *Revista Ilustrada*, with a brilliant sense of humor, demanded that justice be done. Telegraph agencies transmitted—and somewhat exaggerated—the news for foreign countries, and some fine journalists—Raul Pompéia, Araripe Junior, Artur and Aluízio Azevedo—turned this small news item into a huge event.

Thus was the image of emperor as an institutional figure slowly demolished, and thus did his popularity, at least in the capital, diminish daily. We can say, using a parallel with Lévi-Strauss's classic analyses of the shaman in *Structural Anthropology*, that just as when too much is asked of the logic of a shaman's potions and chants, it is because their efficacy is no longer what it was, so Dom Pedro, who always had lovers, only now began to be ridiculed for them; since his childhood, he had cultivated a somewhat superficial erudition and showed it off, and now it looked absurd and superficial; his court had always had a substantial budget for its rituals, but only now did it occur to anyone to ask to see the bills.

Gilberto Freyre ventured to interpret the emperor's change from "crown to top hat" as the moment when the monarchy put its very existence at risk. "Surrounded by his books, Dom Pedro II lost sight of the Brazil that didn't want him with a top hat, but with a crown . . . a Brazil that wanted to see him with his scepter, reigning on horseback, like a real Saint George, rather than listen to his moralizing phrases and speeches, like a mediocre Marcus Aurelius, a third-rate man of letters."[14] Dom Pedro was letting go of the symbolic dimension inherent in his political power while the political state of affairs worsened: this meant he was progressively losing control. The countess of Barral, now far from Brazil, commented to her emperor friend on the journalists' daring in 1882: "As for these scandalous papers, they should be given a taste of the whip, and if libelers are not severely punished, I don't know where the monarchy will end."[15]

In the 1883 Carnival, one allegorical float showed Dom Pedro alone in a room, with the words "They've robbed him of everything." Another float made fun of his interest in the transit of the planet Venus: with telescope in hand, he continually searched for the planet lost in the heavens. (Agostini, too, made good use of the monarch's curiosity about astronomy, showing him as a comet streaking through the skies with his politicians.) Shifting between sympathetic portrayal and criticism, political caricature exposed the internal contradictions of the empire.

During the 1880s two of the empire's mainstays died, the duke of Caxias and the viscount of Rio Branco; other statesmen close to the emperor — Bernardo Pereira de Vasconcelos, Aureliano Coutinho, Paula Sousa, Eusébio de Queirós, Zacarias de Góis, and Nabuco de Araújo — had died earlier. The deaths of these men distanced Dom Pedro even more from his public role, and he increasingly gave himself over to the study of languages. He already spoke French, English, Spanish, German, and Italian; now he decided to study Greek, Latin, Hebrew, old Provençal, and Tupi-Guarani.

Meanwhile the public atmosphere became increasingly tense as pressures grew to abolish slavery and end the monarchy. In 1880 the Brazilian

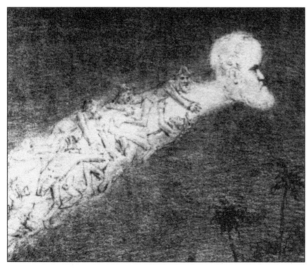

The emperor shoots through the sky with his politicians. Ângelo Agostini, in *Revista Ilustrada*. CEA

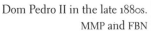

Dom Pedro II in the late 1880s.
MMP and FBN

Society Against Slavery was founded, followed by the Abolitionist Confederation in 1883, the year when Antônio de Castro Alves's and Joaquim Nabuco's
books on slavery and abolitionism were published; both authors were leaders
of the emancipation movement, and their books were crucial milestones in
literature and political science, respectively. In 1884 slavery was abolished in
Ceará and Amazonas, and on 28 September 1885 the Sexagenarian Law gave
freedom to slaves over sixty years of age while guaranteeing their masters their
work for three more years. The process of abolition was taking place at either
end of the spectrum—first the newborn, then the old.

After the Law of the Free Womb was passed in 1871, when for the first time
the government seriously tried to control slavery with a view to its eventual
and gradual abolition, slaves had to be "matriculated," or registered; this helped
to keep all slave transactions under administrative control. It became clear
that the distribution of slaves in the country had radically altered. According
to a report in 1886, since 1873 the number of slaves had dropped by 412,468 as
a result of manumissions and deaths; the estimates gave a slave population of
1,113,228, and the number of slave matriculations in 1887 as 723,419. Apart
from this general reduction, their unequal distribution was accentuated: not
only were slaves transported from northern to southern Brazil, but they were
much more likely to be freed in the north.[16] Slavery, it was clear, would soon
be at an end. The strategy was to control the process and avoid what was most

Isabel and the count d'Eu, 1887. CEA

feared: slave rebellions and agricultural chaos. Writing from Europe to Dom Pedro, the countess of Barral was fearful of how events would turn out, but the emperor, in reply to her alarmed letter, responded coolly: "Petrópolis, 28 December 1886 . . . Here it has rained quite a bit . . . The emancipation question is progressing, and I hope at last to see it completed with no great upset. My children will be leaving on 5 January . . . My life doesn't vary, and when I go past the Miranda Chalet, you have no idea how I miss you."[17]

The year 1885 brought another fright: another outbreak of cholera that weakened the population of Rio de Janeiro and stirred resentment.

Even so, the emperor—who had borrowed fifty thousand pounds from Knowler Foster, London bankers—was still determined to return to Europe, and he left on 30 June 1887. This third departure was surrounded by a storm of controversy. The press mocked his repeated desire to travel, saying that Dom Pedro suffered from "motomania, an illness characterized by constant movement,"[18] and some alleged that he was running away from the political problems plaguing Brazil. Antônio Ferreira Viana, who had called the emperor a "mock Caesar," said in a speech in the Chamber of Deputies: "He who even yesterday was the master of an empire, now is no longer even master of himself."[19] Others opined that the monarch, as well as being ill, was plainly suffering from physical decadence and old age. Like Napoleon III, at sixty-two Dom Pedro looked like an old man, his face marked by deep furrows, with a vague look in his eyes, and with his immense white beard.

Dom Pedro believed, though, that the sea air and European treatments were certain to cure his anemia. The vessel *Gironde*, which Quintino Bocaiúva called the "monarchy's funeral bier," carried the imperial retinue across the sea: the prince Pedro Augusto, the count and countess Carapebus, the count and countess Mota Maia, the viscount of Savoy, José Maria da Silva Paranhos Jr., and the emperor and empress.

The trip lasted for some months, and again it was Princess Isabel who stayed in Brazil in Dom Pedro's place, to general apprehension, for her husband, the count d'Eu, had become unpopular. There were many rumors about his avarice and shady business deals: it was said that he was the owner of "lodging houses" that in fact were grossly overcrowded tenements. Newspapers called Dom Pedro's son-in-law the "slum landlord," the "sordid speculator," and highlighted the worries brought on by the question of the succession to the throne.[20] Since the birth of Isabel's second son, when the royal family had decided that she would be attended by a French doctor, people had commented with disgust on their "foreign tendencies." And now, as Dom Pedro aged and Isabel's regency became increasingly "permanent," the count d'Eu slowly became a reviled "foreigner," an intruder; he was also the stingiest of men when it came to giving tips. Images and opinions that had been isolated and relatively unimportant took on political weight.

It is said that Dom Pedro himself had thought of preparing the succession for his grandson, Prince Dom Pedro Augusto, who since the death of his mother, Dona Leopoldina, had lived with his grandparents. The young prince talked as if he were the heir apparent. On 16 February 1888, while he watched the emperor convalesce in Cannes, he wrote,

> I say to myself that if I were the head of government I would organize a new ministry, dissolve the Chamber, and would appeal to the nation, making proclamations in all the provinces . . . Sometimes I think you have to give things a push to get them to go in the right direction. Keep this to yourself, I don't want to be called a revolutionary . . . My greatest desire is for my grandfather to be well again. But the future is hidden from us. Nobody knows anything.

He was not only showing initiative, but showing that he was more worried about the future of the nation than his grandfather was. But the dark "fate of the Braganças," which befell a good proportion of the firstborn sons in this family, was Dom Pedro Augusto's, too: already he was showing the first signs of insanity. The emperor abandoned his plan for his grandson, and the general fear of a Third Reign in the hands of a foreigner increased.*

When Dom Pedro reached Portugal on 19 July 1887, and then Paris on 22 July, not only was it a different Dom Pedro who was returning to Europe, but Europe itself had changed; his Romantic Era represented by Gobineau, Hugo, and Wagner seemed dead. After consultations and on the advice of Mota Maia, his doctors in Paris decided that the emperor should rest in the spa resort of Baden-Baden. The local population, which was used to the presence of celebrities—among them Bismarck, Queen Victoria, and the prince of Wales—could now watch the Brazilian monarch take his constitutional with his twenty-four-man-strong retinue. Silveira Martins noted that during his stay Dom Pedro had the energy to go to a concert, whose conductor dedicated the program to him. The emperor, revealing a pride that now came to him only when he was abroad, thanked him, saying, "This is a homage not to me but to Brazil."[21]

Back in Paris, Dom Pedro tried to revive his old image as a Maecenas, visiting intellectuals like Louis Pasteur and Ernest Renan, writing poems and translations that he sent to friends and relatives. After six months, he began a cruise along the Italian Riviera, returning slowly to his old traveling routine. In pictures of him, he was still a great emperor, on a par with the other monarchs of the world. Yet he was totally divorced from events at home. On 10 June 1887 the countess of Barral had written to Isabel: "I will not congratulate you on the regency you will have to exercise, but trusting in your good sense and your husband's good advice, I hope that with God's help all goes well during this absence."[22] Politically, the advance of the republican cause complicated the situation, but above all, pressure for the abolition of slavery attracted everyone's attention.

The Law of the Free Womb of 1871 had calmed abolitionist tempers somewhat, but in the 1880s both moderate abolitionists (whose great ideologue was Joaquim Nabuco) and radicals (among whom Silva Jardim, Luís Gama, and Antônio Bento stood out) again dominated the streets and the press.[23] However much the government resorted to reformist tactics like the Sexagenarian

---

*Dom Pedro Augusto lost his right of succession with the birth of Princess Isabel's son Dom Pedro de Alcântara. His signs of madness worsened after the emperor's death, when he was placed in a sanatorium in Tulln, Austria. After an attempted suicide, Pedro Augusto remained in a mental hospital until he died at the age of sixty-eight, in 1934.

Law, the result was the opposite of what it aimed for, and tensions only increased.* For Isabel and her advisers, the only solution was to anticipate the inevitable: slavery was abolished in any case in Ceará and Amazonas in 1884; elsewhere abolition was occurring in spite of the government, thanks to private initiatives and the actions of the slaves themselves, who fled from the plantations en masse and moved to the cities; the authorities were incapable of containing such large movements.

The slavery issue led to the rise and fall of several cabinets. Only in 1884 did the majority of the Liberal Party join the abolitionist movement; Conservatives did not support it until 1888. Until then the two parties agreed that abolition would disorganize the Brazilian economy and labor force and lead to the ruin of the country's credit. In 1888, however, the question rose above party politics. It led to the fall of the Liberal governments of Dantas and Saraiva, then to the appointment of the Conservative government of Cotegipe and then that of João Alfredo, who approved the measure quickly.

There was in fact no way to put the matter off. The Abolition Law was simply phrased, short and direct: "Slavery is declared abolished in Brazil from the date of this law. All measures to the contrary are revoked." On 13 May 1888 this law freed 700,000 slaves, a small proportion in a total population estimated at 15 million. Freedom had been a long time in coming, and it destroyed the monarchy's last support, for the plantation owners of the Paraíba valley, in the province of Rio de Janeiro, now split from their old ally. And once again Dom Pedro was absent, leaving the task and the "authorship" to Isabel, the regent.

Celebrated abroad as a victory for the imperial government, the abolition law was greeted in Brazil by an explosion of joy in the streets. Joaquim Nabuco, known at the time as the Prince of Abolition, was euphoric:

23 May 1888. My dear baron, abolition has happened! Nobody could have expected such a great event so soon, and never was a national event so enthusiastically celebrated in Brazil. The city has been in a state of delirium for twenty days. Everything has come to a halt, including correspondence between friends. But it is time to come back . . . Isabel is now the last person to harbor runaways: her throne

*The Sexagenarian Law favored slave owners so much that even moderate abolitionists opposed it. As well as laying down that sixty-year-old slaves had to give three years of free service to their masters, it provided for a compensation to slave owners for freed slaves and also imposed a fine of between 500 and 1,000 réis on anyone who aided runaway slaves.

has become a runaway settlement . . . The monarchy is more popular than ever.[24]

On 13 May the abolitionist leader José do Patrocínio* was spreading the image of Isabel the Redeemer, still popular in Brazil today, and the monarchy was believed to deserve rewards and laurels from the act. A new image of royalty, "Isabelism," gained in popular estimation, and the monarchy was indeed acclaimed in the streets.

But the final abolition of slavery did lead to considerable material losses for the discredited yet active minority of opponents to the measure, who were linked to the throne, and these rural landowners soon took the republican side. However much the monarchy awarded them titles and argued that abolition had been inevitable, their lack of compensation made it certain that they would oppose the empire. Rumors about a Third Reign in Princess Isabel's hands began to circulate, as did intrigues around the figure of the count d'Eu.

Two kinds of imperial image, then, came apart at this moment. The monarchy, with its decadent rituals, was regaining its imaginative power by linking itself to the empire's most popular act, the abolition of slavery, and political royalty was once again associated with mystical royalty, representing the rule of justice and security. Paradoxically, however, as it distanced itself from the plantation owners, the empire lost its support: while in official iconography the popular image was of Isabel being acclaimed in the streets, in politics things were much less simple. Abolition really did seem to be the monarchy's last great act.

In Milan, nine days after the passing of the Abolition Law, the emperor was told of the new situation: on 22 May, when his health was thought to be good enough, the empress read the telegram sent by Princess Isabel. "My good, beloved parents. I don't know where to begin today: with Mummy who has suffered so much in recent days, or Daddy; because of the occasion, I've written to both together."[25] Many of the royal biographies underline the serenity of the emperor's reply—he is supposed to have said only: "We give

---

*Patrocínio is one of the most interesting figures of the empire. A great supporter of the monarchy when the latter supported abolition, a great propagandist for "Isabelism," and a mentor of the Black Guard (see below, page 320), Patrocínio later became a fervent republican. But the republicans never forgave him for his earlier position, and he ended his days in solitude, best known as the supporter of a wonderful balloon that never flew. Another important figure is André Rebouças, an abolitionist leader who chose exile with the imperial family after 1889.

A medal of the Abolitionist
Confederation. The female
icon is close to Princess
Isabel. MMP

The Historical and
Geographical Institute
commemorated abolition
with this medal. FMLOA

A medal of the abolitionist
campaign in Bahia. The
symbol is a *jangada*, a raft
used for fishing. MMP

A medal of the abolitionist
movement in Ceará. Its
jangada fishermen brought
about abolition there in
1884. MMP

A statuette showing the
official version of the
abolition of slavery. The
act appears as a gift from
Princess Isabel and is
received with great gratitude
and servility by the former
slaves, c. 1888. MMP

thanks to God" and "A great people, a great people!" which sounds more like
a political statement than a true comment from a person who had lived with
slavery more than fifty years. Dom Pedro Augusto, who was traveling with his
grandfather, left a short note that shows a somewhat different reaction on the
family's part: "The emperor fell ill on 3 May, and we thought he was going to
die. When he got a little better, on the 22nd, they made haste to tell him
about the great Abolition Law. The telegram of congratulations was writ-

LA AVISPA

PRECIO
15
CÉNTIMOS

AÑO V   NÚM. 196.

MADRID 20 DE MAYO DE 1888

PRECIO
15
CÉNTIMOS

HOMENAJE

A.S.A.I. la Regente del Brasil, por
su decreto de abolicion de la esclavitud, felicitan
sincera y respetuosamente,

An allegorical drawing celebrating the abolition of slavery in Brazil. Isabel, with her imperial mantle, holds up the broken chains. *La Avispa*, 1888. MMP.

ten . . . 'I congratulate the princess regent on this happy measure.' I sent two telegrams. The first said: 'I hope that everything ends in general contentment.' The second: 'Best wishes on the triumph of the imperial house.'"[26]

With these salutations for the act that had sealed slavery's fate, Dom Pedro's return was set in motion. The first stop was the French resort of Aix-les-Bains, where his diabetes and heart troubles reappeared. But gradually the emperor improved, and the ship *Congo* was to take him to Brazil; his doctors recommended that he undertake only light reading. At Bordeaux, where his traveling companions Santa Anna Nery, the countess of Barral, Dr. Charcot, and members of his family bade him good-bye, the monarch opened a box of books that the Historical and Geographical Institute had sent him and said in his habitual way, "I know, I know! I mustn't get tired . . . poetry!"[27] The eulogistic accounts do not neglect the emperor's old image.

Dom Pedro's reception upon his arrival in Brazil surpassed his initial expectations, for the general tone was one of celebration over "the returning abolitionist emperor." An enormous flag with the word *Salve* on it on top of the Sugar Loaf Mountain seemed to calm fears. At that time Gusmão Lobo wrote, "The general impression is good and was excellent, but my apprehensions are beginning to be fulfilled. They can see his expressionless look and sickly face."[28]

When he left for Europe, the emperor had already been in a fragile state; he returned to Brazil an ill man. Worse, royalty as an institution was ailing, more and more thought of as backward and foreign. The diabetic Dom Pedro was a long way away from his moments of strength as the Maecenas-monarch or even citizen-monarch. He now looked like his own ghost, the ghost of a royal personage. And, like a preserved image, the monarch gradually became separate from the very institution he represented. It was as if Dom Pedro, mystically idealized as the "good father" who "had abolished slavery in an act of charity" or simply because he seemed senile, was taking a separate route from that of official royalty.

This is the only way to explain why, just as the monarchy was losing the political and ideological battle, Dom Pedro reached the highest point of his personal popularity.[29] It was time for him to appear on stage again. Only his idealized figure might hold the regime together.

SEVENTEEN

The Republic Cannot Wait
for the Old Emperor to Die

Their imperial majesties in the garden in Petrópolis; again, Dom Pedro has his book, 1889. MIP

The year 1889 seemed to begin well. For a regime increasingly dependent on pretense, the beauty and harmony of the empire seemed to allow it to float above reality in realms of its own.

On 28 February Émile Levasseur put the last touches to the long essay on the empire to be published in the *Grande Encyclopédie*. It had originally been fifteen pages long but had been increased to fifty-one, thanks to the help of the viscount of Rio Branco, who noted that "in big type, it could have had two or three hundred pages."[1] Only the entry for Germany had more pages.

Also in 1889 appeared a biography of Dom Pedro by the great Avignon rabbi Benjamin Mossé, a eulogistic homage to the New World emperor who also "cultivated the classical languages and studied Hebrew."* And as we have seen, Brazil took part in the important Paris Universal Exhibition. Cavalcanti, Rio Branco, and Eduardo Prado put a great deal of effort into its grand pavilion, built in the hybrid style typical of these fantasy palaces. Enormous pictures of tropical fruits by the Brazilian painter Estêvão da Silva decorated the cluttered rooms; and in an enormous pool there floated, romantically, a specimen of the enormous South American waterlily called

---

*Although Mossé was the official author, the biography was in fact written by the baron of Rio Branco himself.

Victoria Regia: just as Holland celebrated the French centenary with a beautiful tulip, so this exotic plant represented Brazil.[2]

On the outside, then, everything was fine, but symbols and images need more than surface if they are to have their intended effect. The use of imaginative and national emblems is particularly obvious at moments of crisis, and Brazil was no exception. Just when the Brazilian Empire was in France paying homage to the French Revolution, the republican movement was gaining strength at home and used these same celebrations as a pretext to advance its cause. The example of France, which had overthrown its aristocracy, was insistently invoked (that modern France had been a republic only for the last eighteen years was overlooked). With his eternal double-breasted coat, book in hand, and with a tropical scene in the background, Dom Pedro was powerless in the face of the republican ferment. Political positions became more radical by the day. During Ouro Preto's Liberal government (the last one of the empire) an idea that had already been mooted earlier gathered strength: to create a force parallel to that of the army, which could protect the monarchy. The mentor of this Black Guard was José do Patrocínio, which shows how complex things had become. An abolitionist and a democrat, Patrocínio had been responsible for spreading the cult of the princess Isabel. Because of the way the Black Guard was constituted—it was allegedly made up of "*carioca* riffraff and *capoeira** gangs"—and because of the polarizing of positions, it was not long before there were open conflicts.

The situation was paradoxical. Former slaves remained loyal to the monarchy and were opposed to the republicans. These *paulista* republicans—so-called because São Paulo was their bastion—were treated as if they were the real oppressors. In December 1888 members of the Black Guard invaded the headquarters of the French Gymnastic Society and interrupted the republican leader's speech; deaths and injuries resulted. It was not an isolated episode. There were many rumors about the Black Guard. Rui Barbosa called it a "gang of vagabonds cheering on the monarchy and the Liberal Party" and "legalized *capoeira.*" The group allegedly had more than eight hundred freedmen, rebellious blacks, who were marching on the city to fight against the republicans. We do not know if this figure is reliable. But it is clear that blacks and recognized abolitionists like Patrocínio were becoming loyal to the monarchy, their old opponent, and found republicans more to their taste as enemies.

Capoeira, now regarded as a kind of martial art, was originally developed by slaves as a way of fighting without arms. In the late nineteenth century, gangs of practitioners of *capoeira* developed; they were eventually repressed during the republic.

An increasingly idealized monarchy—separated off from its actual institutional function—was becoming more and more popular, and the more so with the abolition of slavery. Great popular celebrations praised both; they lasted for a week in 1888 and were repeated in the following year, five months before the proclamation of the republic. As Carvalho wrote:

> Popular enthusiasm was directed not only at Princess Isabel but at Pedro II, as was plain on the old emperor's birthday, 2 December 1888. According to Raul Pompéia, the [City] Palace was invaded by "an immense mass of people, mostly black men." The police had to intervene to convince some of the demonstrators that they should at least put on shirts to be presented to the emperor. The imposing figure of Prince Obá stood out in the midst of the crowd, a black who said he was an African king and who had adorned his honorary lieutenant's uniform with feathers. No doubt the scene occasioned laughter and mockery, and Prince Obá ended up being arrested by the police, but it was profoundly symbolic: a black king, a king of the streets and alleyways of Rio, dresses up in his uniform and his African feathers and goes forth with a multitude of poor people to salute the blue-eyed emperor.[3]

Yet while Dom Pedro as a figurehead was becoming more and more popular, tensions and criticism of the regime increased. The disaffection of the elite, who had put the emperor and empress on the throne and kept them there, was obvious.

In this tense atmosphere, on 15 June 1889, when the imperial family came out of a theater, there was heard from the crowd on the sidewalk a sudden "Long live the republic!" The emperor showed no sign of alarm and asked the policemen to "leave the people alone. People can do what they want."[4] Until that moment, the people were like an audience to be entertained by a play successfully stage-managed by the monarchy. But a few minutes later, when the emperor was already in his carriage, a shot was fired. Nobody noticed, really, but the police arrested the culprit a few hours later; he was a twenty-year-old Portuguese who had recently lost his job. The next day the newspapers published pictures of the "regicide," dramatizing the "outrage." The episode had involved no danger, but the *fact* of it nonetheless was transformed, to use Marshal Sahlin's terminology, into a culturally significant *event*, for some a symbol of the empire's fragility, for others a sign of overheated enthusiasm.

The outrage against the emperor; the insert is a portrait of Adriano do Vale. *Revista de Portugal*, 1889. MIP

The chief of the Rio police, Dr. José Basson de Miranda Osório, threatened to arrest anyone who, in violation of Article 90 of the Criminal Code, in squares, streets, and other public places shouted "Hurrah for the Republic," or "Death to the monarchy." Meanwhile, Adriano do Vale, the Portuguese suspect, lay in a cell on the Ilha das Cobras, awaiting the jury's decision. (He was freed within a month of the proclamation of the republic.) From then on passions rose daily. On 15 October, Princess Isabel's silver wedding anniversary, the Black Guard took to the streets in Rio with at least fifteen hundred men. The newspapers alternated between comments on the prevailing anarchy and rumors that the emperor would abdicate in favor of Isabel.

The Republican Party—made up mostly of *paulista* planters and members of the liberal professions, now reinforced by planters from the province of Rio who were disgusted by the abolition of slavery—began to exert pressure on the army and especially on Marshal Manuel Deodoro da Fonseca, trying to convince them that their real enemy was not the Ouro Preto ministry but the monarchy itself. And in this context the figure of the emperor himself looked stronger than, and separate from, royalty itself as an institution. It was as if Deodoro and various sectors of the armed forces wanted to wait for the "old monarch"'s death and set a republican coup in motion only then. Dom Pedro was a symbol that showed an ability to resist change in the face of a reality that was in a state of collapse. As the British ambassador had said when the emperor had first developed diabetes, "His Majesty is the single pivot on which the destiny of the empire turns."[5] He was both the antidote and the poison; the centrality of Dom Pedro's power made him the true pivot, the real aim for any coup, but he was at the same time an image with a life independent of that of the system itself.

Meanwhile, the emperor and his family, with the court, "exiled" themselves in Petrópolis and carried on their ritual existence. We can see him in photos, with his family around him and his beard now entirely white, with his old double-breasted coat (with or without his top hat), a book in one hand, and a somewhat Napoleonic pose. The images do the official work: portray-

The last image of the imperial family in Brazil: Dom Pedro II, Teresa Cristina, Princess Isabel, the count d'Eu, Dom Pedro Augusto, Dom Pedro of Orléans and Bragança, and Dom Antônio. Otto Hess, 1889. MMP

ing the united family, above the vexing world of politics. But the cartoons tell a different story: a tired monarch, worried about the possible coming of the republic, showing signs of exhaustion and fragility.

One great spectacle still remained: it was time for Dom Pedro to return from Petrópolis to the real world. On the morning of 9 November 1889 he came back to Rio to open the St. Sebastian Hospital in Caju. He presided over a meeting of the Council of Ministers and that evening went to the ball that the government was putting on for the Chilean navy on the Ilha Fiscal.

The Ilha Fiscal Ball was the first the imperial regime had ever officially laid on, and three thousand invitations were sent out. The palace on the Ilha

Cartoons making fun of the parlous situation in Brazil. *Revista Ilustrada, O Mosquito, A Vespa.* CEA

Fiscal was lit by thousands of candles. It looked as if it would be a huge opportunity for fraternization. With rivalries forgotten, Liberals and Conservatives would meet in the same room with the court and its barons and even
José Augusto Vinhaes, lieutenant of the Navy, who was to play an important
part in the coup that sealed the fate of the empire some days later.

The ball has gone down in Brazilian history as the symbol of the end
of the monarchy. There was a great deal of comment on the endless self-
indulgence of it, on its ostentation and luxury so inappropriate to the political situation; rumors circulated that military officers had been intentionally
excluded from the guest list.

Machado de Assis, in *Esau and Jacob*, remembers that at nightfall
everyone in the city ran to the beach to see "the basket of lights in the middle
of the quiet darkness of the sea." On shore, at the embarkation point where
guests left for the island, people watched the procession of elegantly dressed
women and men in gala uniforms and bemedaled jackets.

The emperor wore his usual loose black coat, and on his lapel was only his
"faithful lamb" of the Order of the Golden Fleece, seen in most of the photographs taken of him. The empress, officially in mourning, wore beaded black
Chantilly lace.[6] When he landed on the island, weak on his feet and leaning on
his doctor, Mota Maia, the emperor is supposed to have had a slight trip, but
without losing his dignity, joked: "The monarchy stumbles, but does not fall."

In the ballroom, decorated with the flags of Brazil and Chile, only Pedro
Augusto of the imperial family danced. Their imperial majesties, along with
the count d'Eu and Princess Isabel, left early, at one in the morning, "before
the colossal dinner" at which Ouro Preto toasted Chile.[7] The people, meanwhile, distanced from the great event as always, were rewarded with a police
band in gala uniform playing fandangos and *lundus* (a popular dance, pre-
cursor of the samba) in the square in front of the City Palace, right opposite
the Ilha Fiscal. Once again, the various festivals of the empire met, despite
their somewhat different styles and objectives.

At the very same time army officers were meeting at their club to plan the
last details of the coup against Dom Pedro. It was 10 November 1889: only five
days before the end of the Brazilian monarchy.

*The night of the 14th. Once this was done, Aires got into bed, prayed an ode by his favorite
Horace, and closed his eyes . . . At five-forty he was on his feet. As you know, in November it's
already light.*   —*Joaquim Maria Machado de Assis*, Esau and Jacob

Since 1874, a political abyss had opened between the Roman Catholic Church and the Brazilian state. The trouble had begun with the imprisonment that year of two bishops, Dom Vital and Dom Macedo Costa, who had attempted to curb the activities of the Freemasons in Brazil. Dom Pedro, himself a Mason, had cracked down; his subsequent amnesty for the two priests in September 1875, before he went to the United States, was not enough to calm the situation.

For their part, the coffee plantation owners of the Paraíba valley, traditional allies of the emperor, from whose ranks came some of the empire's most important politicians, had joined the republicans after slavery was abolished with no compensation to them. These "last-minute republicans" had relied on Dom Pedro to assure them that they could keep their slaves, but when the Abolition Law was passed, the ties that bound them to him were finally sundered.

But it was not only the Church and the coffee planters who were dissatisfied. The greatest discontent emerged in the army. The main proselytes of positivism came from its ranks, and it was in the army that the idea of the republic spread. The young officers had academic debates about republicanism, for they were enthusiasts for new philosophical doctrines, in particular those of Auguste Comte and his disciple Jacques Lafitte. Brazil's military leaders had been discontented ever since the end of the Paraguayan war, especially since they were prohibited from expressing opinions in the press on political matters. The situation had become tense in 1884, when army men published eulogies to Francisco do Nascimento, leader of the *jangadeiros*, the movement for abolition of slavery in Ceará; in 1886, when Marshal Deodoro da Fonseca, then commander of the army in Rio Grande do Sul, refused to punish the officers who had been responsible, the baron of Cotegipe, chief minister at the time, dismissed him. Feeling the army's growing importance on the political scene, the Conservatives tried to convert him into the "party's general" and invited him to Rio, where he was enthusiastically received by the cadets at the military school. With pressure from the *paulistas* and from officers in the discontented sectors of the army, the movement in favor of the republic was spreading. But Deodoro hesitated because of the presence of the "old man." The marshal said, "I want to accompany the emperor's coffin; he's old and I have great respect for him."

Events began to move more rapidly. In May 1889 João Alfredo resigned as president of the Council of Ministers, and there was a power vacuum until Ouro Preto took over the government. Meanwhile the republican movement was gaining still more followers, especially in the army. Then on 15 November, the key day in 1889, the rumor spread that Deodoro had been arrested. Deodoro came to headquarters to dispel it, and after shouting hurrah for his majesty the emperor, the imperial family, and the army, himself arrested Ouro Preto, saying that he would take the issue of forming a new government to the emperor personally. The republic was not proclaimed "with a shout"; nor did Deodoro echo the "Cry of Ipiranga" given by Dom Pedro I in 1822, itself a suspect tradition. "Long live the emperor" was a regimental acclamation, and all it may have meant was that the empire was united, that there was a certain caution about making any break with the past. The Brazilian republic had been not proclaimed but acclaimed.

The events that followed are the subject of controversy. According to one historian, the scene of Deodoro's impetuous arrival at the barracks, as portrayed in Henrique Bernardelli's painting, which shows him on horseback, kepi in hand, acclaiming something, is inaccurate. Interpreters say that this painting gave form to the idea that the marshal was shouting "Long live the republic," but this never happened, and they are perhaps mistaken.[8]

What we do know is that there was a hiatus between Ouro Preto's resignation and the proclamation of the republic. The emperor was waiting in Petrópolis for Marshal Deodoro to come, but this was destined never to occur since, it seems, the marshal did not want to meet the old monarch face to face. Only when Dom Pedro received Ouro Preto's telegrams informing him of the fall of the government, on 15 November, did he realize he must return to Rio de Janeiro. When he heard the empress say repeatedly that all was lost, Dom Pedro is supposed to have said, "Stuff and nonsense, my lady. When we get there, that'll be the end of it!"[9] In Rio, he met Princess Isabel and the count d'Eu at the palace and acquainted himself with the situation, which was still very confused. The cabinet had been dismissed, and there was no other government.

The Brazilian people, in their turn, in Aristides Lobo's famous words, watched everything dumbfounded with no awareness of what was happening. This was not unlike the imperial family itself, which did not comprehend Deodoro's attitude or the role of José do Patrocínio, who, his activities with the Black Guard notwithstanding, was now fomenting agitation in the streets, having returned to his old republican convictions. Deodoro was the key figure, and apart from the fact that he was ill with severe breathing difficulties, he was still hesitant. Dom Pedro did not believe that the revolution, now proceeding so slowly, could be sustained.

Marshal Deodoro at the moment of
the proclamation of the republic.
This painting by Henrique
Bernardelli, in spite of controversies
surrounding it, became the official
symbol of 15 November. Academia
Militar das Agulhas Negras.

Events speeded up. In a strategic mistake, Silveira Martins, the Liberal leader from Rio Grande do Sul, was called on to be president of the Council of Ministers, but he was away from Rio and expected back only on 17 November. (It was a double mistake, for Silveira Martins was Deodoro's political enemy in his home province.) Then, on the evening of 15 November, the situation became clearer and the republic was proclaimed. Up till then, things had been confused and the turbulence looked more like an internal quarrel within the army.*

Despite the obviously partial interpretation of Dom Pedro's biographers, the hesitant note in the revolutionary movement they describe is remarkable. The republican embarrassment vis-à-vis the emperor was such that, when the new regime was formalized, instead of sending a delegation of high-ranking officers or of traditional politicians and foreign diplomats to inform the im-

*The timetable of the proclamation of the republic is still controversial, and it involves differing interpretations of the movement's maturity. Here, I simply focus on the role of Dom Pedro himself.

perial family that they would be banished, some junior officers were sent at three in the afternoon of 16 November. Major Frederico Sólon Sampaio Ribeiro, commander of the troops surrounding the palace, handed over the document that broke the news of the government's overthrow and that of the emperor. He withdrew after having twice committed the republican gaffe of calling Dom Pedro "Your Majesty."

The official images that appeared in the newspapers showed the solemn presentation of the telegram announcing the end of the monarchy in Brazil, but the real situation was somewhat different. In the pictures, the emperor, leaning back in his chair, receives the communication from the military junta in a proud, erect pose. It was not quite like that. Even the army officers feared that the republican movement would not last. The emperor had a similar attitude: as soon as he got to the palace, all he said was, "This is a tempest in a teapot—I know my fellow Brazilians." Even Dom Pedro trusted in the notion that "monarchies don't fall that easily." But his confidence eventually collapsed. In the telegram, the provisional government communicated that the republic had been proclaimed, and gave the royal family twenty-four hours to leave the country. According to those present, the emperor stayed quite serene; the women wept, while the men tried to hold back their emotions. In his reply to the communiqué, the emperor once again placed his trust in theater and pretense. Paraphrasing Napoleon, who is supposed to have said, "I am leaving this country I have loved so much," Dom Pedro tried

The emperor and his family receive the communiqué from the provisional government on 16 November 1889. MIP

to coin a memorable phrase, which ended with the words ". . . this country which is so dear to me."[10] In both cases, a foreigner left his subjects' country without looking back, proud as only an emperor can be, a person who does not share the same emotions as common mortals.

The monarch fixed his departure for two in the afternoon of 17 November; the family was to attend eleven o'clock Mass in the Carmo church and then wait for Isabel's children, still in Petrópolis, to join them. The ghost of the monarchy still seemed so alive, however, that the provisional government, fearful of demonstrations favoring the emperor and their possible clash with republican students, told them that their departure must be immediate, at dawn on the seventeenth. On the evening of 16 November, Dom Pedro and his family went on board the vessel that was to take them to Europe, and it was then that the only tense exchange took place. The emperor reportedly asked if Deodoro was "mixed up in this" and, on hearing that he was, said, "I'm not a runaway slave. I'm not going on board at this time of night. Gentlemen, you're mad!"*

On 17 November a letter reached Rui Barbosa, the finance minister, in shaky handwriting, signed by Dom Pedro de Alcântara and dated the day before:

> In view of the information given me at three in the afternoon, I have decided to accede to the imperatives of the situation, and leave with my whole family for Europe, tomorrow, leaving this dearly beloved country, to which I have tried to show my love and dedication for the nearly half-century in which I have fulfilled the role of head of state. Leaving, then, with everyone in my family, the memory of Brazil will be strong in my heart, and I will pray for its greatness and prosperity.[11]

Calm, though betrayed by his own handwriting, the former emperor was acceding to the orders of the revolutionaries who had demanded his immediate embarkation.

On that same Saturday, 16 November, the provisional government published the following note: "Fellow citizens: the people, the army and the navy, in complete accord with the feelings of our fellow citizens in the provinces, have just decreed the overthrow of the imperial dynasty and, in

---

*A good number of Dom Pedro's biographies document this phrase. But the borders between fact and fiction are uncertain, the more so given the reverential context of most of these accounts.

consequence, the extinction of the representative monarchical system."[12]
The terms were beginning to change with the times.

A Bahian popular painter has left a testament in which Dom Pedro's departure looks more like a festival. Of course, the whole setting is imaginary,
since the imperial family did not leave from Bahia but from Rio. Everything
in the painting seems to be at the same time symbolic, imaginary, and real.
To the right, in the background, is the imperial family. In the boat are Teresa
Cristina and Isabel, weeping. Getting into the boat are the count d'Eu and
his children, who have just come from Petrópolis. Last comes the emperor,
waving his hat to the people and to the countess of Barral (who in fact was no
longer in Brazil). At the bottom of the picture, to the right, are a group of
black and mixed-blood former slaves. On the left, a female allegorical figure
symbolizes the Brazilian nation: the red skirt is the empire, the white blouse
the republic. She receives a white cap from the hand of divine providence —
which symbolizes the fact that no blood was spilled — and hands the crown to
Deodoro, Rui Barbosa, Floriano Peixoto, and Quintino Bocaiúva (whose real
features are quite well depicted). The republican flag does not show the
words *Ordem e Progresso* (Order and Progress), for the picture was actually
painted on 16 November, three days before the flag was designed.

In actual fact Dom Pedro's departure was not so colorful as the painting
suggests. Accompanied by some enforced exiles and others who chose to go
with him — the count Mota Maia, the count Aljezur, the baron and baroness
of Muritiba, the baron and baroness of Loreto, the viscountess da Fonseca
Costa, and Professor Seybold — the emperor sailed on the *Alagoas*, sealing
the end of the monarchy but not of a myth called Dom Pedro.

The republic they left behind was far from consolidated. To see its uncertainty, we could have no better guide than Machado de Assis, in *Esau and Jacob*, and in particular in the brilliant episode of the owner of the Empire
Confectionery. Custódio has hardly finished ordering a new shop sign for his
traditional "Confeitaria do Império" when he hears the news and asks the
sign-painter to stop his work: "Only some letters had been painted, the words
Confeitaria and the letter *d*; the letter *o* and the word *Império* had only been
outlined in chalk." But to Custódio's despair, the empire has ended, so he
goes to see Counselor Aires, who suggests that the name of his shop should
become "Confeitaria da República." They fear, however, that in a few
months there might be another upset, so that the name would have to be
changed again. The counselor then proposes "Confeitaria do Governo,"
which would suit any regime. Then they remember that any government has

an opposition, which might come along and smash the sign. Aires ventures that Custódio should keep the original name and simply add the words "founded in 1860." But the owner fears that this would associate him with everything old, which in this modern era doesn't sound right. So they decide to put the name of the owner himself on the sign: it will be the "Confeitaria do Custódio." And so ends this dialogue of doubters: "He would have to make a little outlay, changing one name for another, *Custódio* instead of *Empire*, but revolutions are bound to cost something."[13]

Dom Pedro's departure: valise in hand, crown on his back. *Revista Ilustrada*, November 1889. MIP

EIGHTEEN

The Emperor's Exile and Death

MARTYR TO THE NATION ONCE AGAIN

The *Alagoas*, carrying
the former emperor,
arrives in Lisbon.
L'Illustration, 1889. MMP

Dom Pedro's departure was described in contradictory ways. Some biographers say that people ran down to the harbor to wave their last good-byes to the *Alagoas* as it left Rio flying the old flag with the imperial crown. But these stories clash with journalists' accounts. Raul Pompéia, in a melancholy piece, described the emperor's last moments in Brazil in a rather different fashion:

A historic night
(From a window high up in the Palace Square)

At three on Sunday morning, as the city was sleeping, lulled by the vigilance of the provisional government, Palace Square was the setting for an extraordinary scene, which few saw, as transcendent in its meaning and as affecting as it was simple and short.

Painfully constrained by events . . . the government had to isolate the City Palace, preventing any communication from the rest of the country with the capital . . .

Many eminent personages of the empire and several families with ties of affection to the imperial family came to speak to the emperor and his august relatives, only to have to return disappointed, after a vain attempt to see them . . .

When night fell, the streets surrounding the palaces were closed to traffic . . .

An official rumor . . . spread the news that Sr. Dom Pedro de Alcântara (who, it was known, had to embark for Europe because of the revolution of the fifteenth) would only go on board on the Sunday morning . . .

Poor Dom Pedro! In homage to the rigor of the revolutionary government's decision, no one wanted to have been witness to the mysterious elimination of a sovereign . . .

At a few minutes before three in the morning, there was the sound of a carriage coming into the square. Over by the palace there was a noisy tumult of arms and horses. The watch patrols all hurried to guard the entrances to the square; in the middle, seen through the trees and gloomily lighting up the solitude, were the melancholy gaslamps. Then there appeared the procession of the exiles.

Nothing could be sadder. A black coach was slowly pulled forward by two horses with their heads lowered, as if asleep as they walked. First came two ladies in black, covered with veils, as if they were looking for the way to the grim vehicle. Ending the procession came a group of gentlemen, their profile etched on the night scene . . .

Almost at the end of the pier, the carriage stopped and Dom Pedro de Alcântara got out—indistinct among other figures—to set his feet for the last time on his country's soil . . .

The embarkation was quick. In a few minutes, a low whistle was heard, and the continuous hum of the launch's propeller echoed on the sea; the boat's internal lighting reappeared; not a single passenger could be seen. At full steam ahead, the noise of the propeller and the red glow moved away from the land.[1]

In contrast to the celebratory image of the anonymous Bahian painter, who almost makes the royal family's departure into a festival, Pompéia's text shows guilt, sadness, and even a certain shame. Instead of strong sunshine, we are in darkness; instead of a warm reception, a solitary withdrawal seen only by hidden eyes.

The first embarkation was on the *Paraíba*, and only at Ilha Grande did they board the *Alagoas*, closely followed by the *Riachuelo*, which was to escort them out of Brazilian waters. Dom Pedro, irritated, said that the convoy was unnecessary if only because the slower ship would delay their journey into exile.

Conflicting reports came to the *Alagoas*. It was said, without much certainty, that Ouro Preto had been banished, and Pedro Augusto was showing signs of emotional imbalance. A new image was developing, that of Dom Pedro as a martyr. "A martyr in his tender years," "a martyr in his marriage," "a martyr in life" (the savant who said he only wanted to be a teacher), "the martyr of an overly hasty expulsion," Dom Pedro was now an incarnation of "martyred exile." In poems he wrote onboard, the picture was completed:

> Soon I shall no longer see my beloved country
> Always, like a prayer, watched over by God,
> And passing through the deluge like a wingèd
> Dove . . .[2]

When the imperial family arrived in Portugal, the banishment was formalized. A decree of 23 December 1889 forbade them to own property in Brazil and gave them a six-month deadline to liquidate their possessions. It also gave a sum of five thousand contos to help Dom Pedro settle abroad.

On 8 January 1890 Dom Pedro rejected this assistance, saying that he "would not accept or return thanks for any favor from the hands of the general who had stripped him of everything."[3] He would receive only money to which he had a right according to preexisting laws and commitments. This reaction irritated the provisional government, which in a curt reply written by Rui Barbosa commented on his attitude:

Decree:
. . . The provisional government, in offering this boon to the deposed prince, was simply making a gesture of republican generosity, to satisfy the peaceful and conciliatory instincts of the new regime, and to pay retrospective homage to the position occupied by the former emperor in the country . . . The attitude . . . adopted by Sr. Dom Pedro de Alcântara . . . reveals whims irreconcilable with the republican system.
Decree: 1. Dom Pedro de Alcântara, and all his family, are banned from Brazilian territory.
2. He is prohibited from possessing real estate in Brazil, and must liquidate what he holds here within the space of six months.
3. The decree of 16 November 1889, which gave Sr. Dom Pedro de Alcântara five thousand contos as help in the costs of settling abroad, is hereby rescinded.

4. All endowments in favor of Sr. Pedro de Alcântara and his family are to be considered annulled. All measures to the contrary are revoked.[4]

The document reveals traces of raised tempers. Articles 1 and 2, written in different ink, were put in after 3 and 4, and so carelessly that Rui Barbosa erred with the numbers and put in two number 1s.

From then on Dom Pedro lived off favors from friends, notably the baron of Penedo, vaunting a simplicity that accorded with the martyr's role he publicly embraced; nothing could be worse for the image of the republic, which would have preferred to boast of its "generosity" and "peaceful and conciliatory instincts."

In some European newspapers, especially in France, there was a measure of incredulity. The peaceful character of the coup was commented on, and it was even said that the empire might possibly be restored—nothing more than vague ideas and rumors, of course.

It is difficult to evaluate the effect of the proclamation of the republic on Brazilian public opinion. It seems incontestable that among the elites there was "a general sense of liberation, affecting not only ideas, but feelings and attitudes."[5]

"General Boulanger and Madame de Bonnemains offer their sword for the reestablishment of an honest empire." *Le Troupier*, Paris. CRV

Yet for the black population, the monarchy strangely continued to represent freedom, if only metaphorically. The hatred of the republic harbored by Lima Barreto, Rio de Janeiro's most popular novelist, is a good example. The grandson of slaves, Barreto was seven when he saw the celebration of the Abolition Law and the welcome received by the emperor in 1888 when he returned from his last trip to Europe. His novel *Triste Fim de Policarpo Quaresma* (1915) represents the end of all naïve utopias; in his newspaper columns, he recounted how his father was summarily dismissed in 1890 from his government post because of republican policies.[6]

Still, the new republican regime eventually won the ideological battle. The republic was a turn toward modernity and rationality in human relations and a sign of new times. Hence the government had to change the symbols and eliminate any traces that might remind people of the old regime. Names and symbols were quickly altered, in the effort to validate the change of regime. Artur Azevedo ironically commented on the speedy replacement of portraits in public offices:

> Old Lima had been off sick on 14 November; on the Monday he went back to work, ignorant of the fact that the regime had fallen in the meantime. He sat down and saw that they had taken down the old lithograph of Dom Pedro de Alcântara. An errand boy happened to be passing, and he asked him:
> "Why have they taken His Majesty's portrait down?"
> The boy replied, in a slow, disdainful voice: "What do you mean, citizen? What was the point of having old Pedro Banana up there, anyway?"
> "Pedro Banana!" old Lima echoed angrily.
> Sitting down again, he thought sadly: "I'll give it three years at the outside, and this place'll be a republic."[7]

Raul Pompéia, the same journalist who years before had made fun of the scandalous "theft of the crown jewels," now mocked the meager popularity of the republican coup; it asserted itself by the imposition of new symbols, which perforce had to differ from the previous ones. Palace Square became the Fifteenth of November Square; the Pedro II Railway became the Brazilian Central Railway; the Pedro II School became the National School; the St. John the Baptist Cemetery was now the Southern Columbus Cemetery; an attractive group of houses, the Vila Ouro Preto, was renamed Vila Rui Barbosa.

A jar and a globe with the symbols of the republic. CEA

Coins, one of the most important means of spreading the image of the regime, were also altered. In Petrópolis, Emperor Street became Fifteenth of November Street; Empress Street, Seventh of September Street; Bourbon Street, Southern Cross Street; Princess Francisca, General Osório; Bom Retiro, Floriano Peixoto; Dona Januária, Marshal Deodoro; and so forth.

This fashion even affected people's names, which began to take their inspiration from North American republican models—Jefferson, Franklin, Washington—or Roman ones like Múcio (Mucius), Mário (Marius), Cornélia, and Caio (Caius). The faces and motifs printed on paper money also changed

"A republican Christmas—I've brought you all the latest novelties, everything republican I could find." *Revista Ilustrada*, 1889–90. MMP

quickly: Dom Pedro II and the monarchy were removed, and images of the Republic of the United States of Brazil replaced them.

The tidal wave of changes was not limited to names and formalities. A new list of national holidays replaced the old ones in the *Almanak Laemmert*: New Year's Day celebrated universal brotherhood; 13 May the brotherhood of the Brazilian people; 14 July the French Republic; 21 April the Precursors. This last was represented by Tiradentes, literally, the Toothpuller. This was Lieutenant José Joaquim da Silva Xavier (1746–92), who was involved in the 1789 attempt to set up an independent republic in Minas Gerais, a conspiracy known as the Inconfidência Mineira. He was the only conspirator to be executed. There was a need to rewrite Brazil's history and to create a new memory with republican motifs.

In 1892 Machado de Assis, in *A Semana*, wrote ironically about Tiradentes, the new hero of the republic, given this prominence only in 1890: "If this Tiradentes doesn't take care, he'll end up as a public enemy. Someone, whose name I don't know, wrote some lines this week to correct the general opinion of the martyr of the Inconfidência . . . Might it not be possible to imagine that, if it hadn't been for Tiradentes's indiscretion, which led to his torture and that of the other conspirators, their plan might have become a reality? This is only a short step from saying he was a police spy . . . But something will be left of the lieutenant; he can be promoted to honorary captain . . . it's better than nothing."

The cult of Tiradentes did not begin in 1890, however. The publication in 1872 of Joaquim Norberto de Sousa e Silva's *História da conjuração mineira* (History of the Conspiracy in Minas Gerais) had generated heated controversy.[8] But after the republic was proclaimed, the civic cult of Tiradentes intensified. Tiradentes, who had not often been portrayed, began to be associated with the figure of Christ. For a parade in his honor in 1890, Décio Vilares distributed a lithograph of Tiradentes's bust, with a placid calm like that of Jesus himself. In 1892 the same artist portrayed him in oils, and another artist, Aurélio de Figueiredo, finished a canvas significantly entitled *The Martyrdom of Tiradentes*. Finally, the realist version by Pedro Américo, of 1893, shows Tiradentes on the scaffold, after he was drawn and quartered. The figure of the new hero had entered political iconography. In formal pictures and satirical reviews, Tiradentes became the martyr and chief symbol of the republic.

As ever, Machado de Assis was ahead of his time with his sarcastic wit. His criticism was not limited to the new republican hero. He humorously described the daily reality of the new titles and changed vocabulary, which not everyone followed:

> Everything requires a certain tone. I once knew two estimable old gentlemen, neighbors, who had their benefit performance every day. One was a knight of the Order of the Rose, for services *connected with* the Paraguayan war; the other held the post of lieutenant in the National Guard Reserve and gave them loyal service. They played chess and slept between moves. They would wake each other up in the following manner: "Dear *Major!*" "Fine, *Commander!*" Sometimes it would vary: "Dear *Commander!*" "Here I come, *Major!*" Everything requires a certain tone.[9]

While aristocratic titles were abolished in one of the first decrees of the fledgling republic, the former barons and princes were allowed to keep their elevated names. Rio Branco, the son of the viscount of Rio Branco, one of the most illustrious members of the imperial elite, had inherited not only his father's prestige but also his name. The fact that he was a convinced monarchist did not prevent him from being called, years later, to be minister of foreign affairs by Rodrigues Alves; he kept the post until his death in 1912.

The substitution of the words *federal capital* for *court*, used until then to refer to the city of Rio de Janeiro, also caused widespread confusion. Here is Machado de Assis again:

> There is a vacancy for the post of deputy in the federal capital . . . I say federal capital, which is simply a way of referring to this city, which has no name of its own, because that is the designation adopted by the Constitution. Before 15 November the word "court" was used, though the only thing that really was the court was the emperor's palace with its respective inhabitants and employees; but it did have the name of Rio de Janeiro, which is neither pretty nor accurate, but it was a name. Guanabara and Carioca were only used in poetry* . . . The only hope we can have is that the new capital will be built; then what will happen is the return of our old name, or the decreeing of a new one.[10]

---

*The name Rio de Janeiro, literally River of January, originated with the Portuguese discovery of the bay of Guanabara, which they mistakenly thought was a huge river mouth, in January 1502. — Translator's note.

Other national symbols like the flag and the anthem were quickly modified, as we have seen. The anthem kept the imperial tune, and the flag the Bragança and Habsburg colors; only the explanations were changed. Eventually they removed the coffee and the tobacco.

While the Native American had been the favorite symbol of the empire — whether used in a spirit of praise or blame — in the republic it was the figure of the heroic woman, an obvious allusion to France's allegorical Marianne. This was a somewhat artificial choice, given that women were only beginning to appear in public. Ladies of the elite were allowed to shine in salons and balls or "in the home," the proverbial place for a woman to be. The world of politics and participation in public life were well-guarded privileges of the "gentlemen."[11]

This association of the republic with a woman, which began in classical, especially Roman, tradition, became popular in France in the period preceding the Third Republic. Though easily recognized as the image of a young woman with a tunic and a Phrygian cap — which united the ideas of freedom, happiness, and maternal fecundity — in Brazil this allegory failed, even in the Positivist version inspired by Clotilde de Vaux. Initial attempts had been made in periodicals as early as 1888 to introduce a female figure, barefoot or in sandals, carrying the flag.[12] In the early days this new female representation of Brazil shared the limelight with the Native American, consecrated by the empire, or even with Tiradentes, the new republican hero. Then, in subsequent years, alone, or with a baby, or accompanied by her French model and by the imperial Native American, or crowning the Brazilian Constitution with laurels, this new feminine symbol was seen more and more in the Brazilian satirical press.

Most Brazilian painters, except for the Positivist Décio Vilares and Henrique Bernardelli, basically ignored the new symbolism. Again, we can see that there is nothing accidental about this: when the symbolic manipulation lacks cultural backing, these figures tend to fall on stony ground. Such was the case with this frustrated attempt to impose combative and active female images, so distant from Brazilian reality at the time.

Revista Ilustrada, just as it had done with the figure of the Native American during the empire, came to use the female Brazilian figure as a way to express criticisms of and disappointment with the republic. In 1908 the magazine *Fon-Fon!* ran a debate on the topic of "the best cultural representation of Brazil," and the female figure was no longer even thought of; most of the criticisms were directed at the old figure of the Native American. Destined to

"In memory of Tiradentes."
Revista Ilustrada, 21 April
1890. MMP

Tiradentes. Lithograph by
Décio Vilares, Positivist
Church of Brazil, 1890.

*The Martyrdom of
Tiradentes*, Aurélio de
Figueiredo. MHN

On the first anniversary of Brazilian independence under
the republic, the symbols have changed: the Native American is on one side, Tiradentes on the other. Anonymous engraving. MMP

*Tiradentes Hung, Drawn,
and Quartered.* Oil on
canvas by Pedro Américo,
1893. MMP

fail as the official representative of the republic, the idealization of woman
nevertheless figured in colorful, modern advertisements in illustrated magazines. Elegant, active, and cosmopolitan, these female symbols were still far-
off images, to be admired from a distance.

Even in historiography traditional modes of analysis were being overthrown. The Historical and Geographical Institute remained faithful to its

old patron, but younger intellectuals attacked the historical image of Dom Pedro, which up to now had hardly been touched. Carlos Mendonça Süssekind, for example, wrote *Quem foi Dom Pedro II — Golpeando de frente o saudosismo* (Who Dom Pedro II Really Was — An Honest Attack on Nostalgia) (1929), not only calling the Institute "the last outpost of Sebastianism" but attacking the former emperor's self-important erudition. The poet Medeiros e Albuquerque, when he published *Dom Pedro's Complete Poems* (1932), criticized their literary quality and made fun of "Dom Pedro's flatterers . . . who said that he could speak the languages of all the savages of Brazil admirably well." Now that the monarch was far off, the symbolic battle seemed to be tak-

Allegory of the Republic. Manoel Lopes Rodrigues. Carvalho, *A construção da ordem.*

"One year old!" *Revista Ilustrada*, 15 November 1890. MMP

The woman representing the republic receives the imperial Native American in the new political scenario. *Revista Ilustrada*, 1889–90. MMP

"The French Republic recognizes the Brazilian Republic. Well done!" *Revista Ilustrada*, 1889–90. MMP

The new republican woman, militant in politics and work. Sketch by Henrique Bernardelli. MMP

The new female republican symbol. Sketch by Henrique Bernardelli. MMP

ing place with the winner already known. The Brazilian republic was creating new names, songs, heroes, symbols, memories, and monuments.

Not long after his exile, Dom Pedro received another blow. On 28 December, 1889, while he was visiting the Academy of Fine Arts in Oporto, Portugal, he was called urgently to the Grande Hotel do Porto, where the empress had had a heart attack. When he got there, accompanied by Ouro Preto and his son Afonso Celso, he found Teresa Cristina already dead; she was sixty-seven. Some biographers say that the empress, in her final moments, held on to the baroness of Japurá and whispered, "Maria Isabel, I'm dying not of sickness but of pain and sorrow." It was another page in the political culture of Brazil: "the great mother of the country had died alone and a martyr." The emperor, for his part, wrote in his diary: "I can hardly believe it. I always wanted to die before her. An emptiness has opened in my life that I do not know how to fill . . . Only study will console me." We can see how Dom Pedro II's life, even in its most affecting moments, is surrounded by elements that bolster his image. Afterward, faced with the loss of his constant companion, he took refuge in books, and Dom Pedro Augusto, bereft of his reason, was placed in a sanatorium near Vienna.

The empress's death is supposed to have inspired Dom Pedro to write this poem:

A string that breaks on a harp that's hardly touched
Thus you leave me, the sweet companion
Of my life and my exile, truly
Half of my saddened soul! . . .

How happy you were! Go to your sleep,
Mother of the people, your martyrdom is over;
Daughter of kings, you have won a great throne!

The biographers tell us that Dom Pedro became increasingly solitary, accompanied only by his books and translations. Ouro Preto and his son describe him thus, soon after the empress's death: "His Majesty, however, as soon as he heard we were there, ordered us to be let in. His room is extremely modest: on one side, his unmade bed, and a wide table covered with books and papers. A sofa and some chairs made up the rest of the furniture. Everything was cold, cheerless, and bare. With his knees covered with an old blanket, and with an old overcoat on, Dom Pedro was sitting at the table reading a large book, his head on his hand."[13]

As if to confirm that historical memory is a process of selection, the few photographs of Dom Pedro from this time—with his family, his few friends, or most often alone—are dominated by this same image: with an empty look, his face marked by time, his double-breasted coat, his books and writing desk—symbols, perhaps, of the only legend that still went with him, his erudition.

For Dom Pedro, even if the republic was transitory, his own position was irreversible. After all, "a king, once deposed, is no longer king."* He wears a distant expression, events leave him unmoved, and the old monarch keeps quiet, going back to his old routine of visiting institutions, reading and writing poetry, and meeting with intellectuals. Without financial assistance from the Brazilian government, his situation was difficult, and he could get by only with the help of wealthier friends, like Eduardo Prado, the count of Penedo, and the count Nioac, whose house in Paris he lived in for a short time after 1890.

During this time the auction of the effects of the imperial household began. "Am I bid more?" was the cry to be heard in the forty-one rooms of the São

---

*Ettore Scola, in the film La nuit de Varennes, puts these words into the mouth of Restif de la Bretonne, speaking of Louis XVI: "A king who flees is less a king by the minute."

Dom Pedro in Cannes with his friend and doctor, Count Mota Maia, 1891. MMP

Dom Pedro in Cannes. Photograph by H. Blanc and Nadar, 1890–91. MMP

Cristóvão Palace, and from its galleries, chapel, passages, and corridors during the last months of 1890, when thirteen auctions took place. Lot after lot, everything in the emperor's residence was sold off.[14] It was said that the palace had been "ransacked."[15] But by the time the auctioneer J. Dias started to catalog the family's possessions in July 1890, many things had already disappeared.

It was a delicate moment for the republican government: it had to get rid of icons reminding people of the former emperor and give a new meaning to the building that for so many decades had been at the heart of his reign. The palace itself and the vast lands of the Quinta da Boa Vista had always belonged to the state, but the additional buildings (coach houses, houses for staff, the school, hospital, et cetera); all the furniture, objects, and utensils; the large array of coaches, tilburies, victorias, calèches, and other carriages; and the animals (horses, mules, cows, and calves), were all considered — not without some disagreement — to be the emperor's private property. All this — the new buildings, the furnishings in all the buildings, and all the goods in the City Palace — was auctioned then and there. Many objects were left out, however: put in boxes, piled up and locked in one of the rooms in the palace;

five tons of them were later sent to Europe. This is not to mention the damage and disappearance of many things, like the mysterious lot 954. Even so, the list of the 2,345 lots of palace furnishings—which do not include the linen, cooking utensils, coach houses, and other outbuildings—gives a good idea of the atmosphere of the palace. It was not one of modesty: there were hundreds and hundreds of good-quality items. The auctioneer received about 400 contos for the objects and the furniture and 320 for the additional buildings, which were acquired by the government.

There was tension between the new government and the emperor's representatives at the auction, and a certain haste to get it over with, since the palace was going to be used for sessions of the Constituent Assembly. The auctioneer asked for the objects to be taken away within twenty-four hours so that the outbuildings could be handed over to the government. An official commission that was set up to expropriate the library and remove objects of historical and artistic interest—objects valuable "for the country and society in general"—intended to compensate their banished owner, but it came up against public attacks of the former emperor's lawyer. The books—except for certain volumes and the coin collection, which were sent to Dom Pedro—were finally given to the National Library and the Historical and Geographical Institute. The government, apart from buying the outbuildings, did not appear at any of the auctions. It was hinted that it sent an unofficial representative in the form of the engineer Bethencourt da Silva, director of the Lyceum of Arts and Crafts, who bought many chandeliers, costly furniture, and two magnificent Gobelin tapestries, all to decorate the future assembly building.[16]

On the appointed day not many customers appeared, for the news had got around that the objects were of interest only to monarchists. As no "citizen of the republic" wanted to be thought of in such a shameful light, many people avoided the place, and the prices dropped to ridiculous levels. The auction lasted for many days, and the last lot was only sold on 12 October. Still, many different kinds of people came:

> . . . inquisitive people, lovers of objets d'art, capitalists, friends of the imperial family, titled people, aristocrats, government spies, owners of secondhand shops and junkshops in town; all of them had their own aim in mind, some of them concerned about the security of the new regime, others in search of objects to remind them of the royal family, who had been so distinguished and magnanimous . . . A great number

of people were drawn by their desire to see the objects of unquestionable historical and artistic value that furnished the upper floors. The
atmosphere was one of great enthusiasm, although many important
people had decided not to go for fear of compromising themselves;
others, though they were hostile to the new state of affairs, did not
want to have to face the ruffians who were spying on the palace, either
on their own account or on behalf of others, often pouring scorn on
the old regime.[17]

It was not only Dom Pedro's possessions that were disappearing. "Dom Pedro's era" itself was coming to an end. The year 1891 began with the death of
the countess of Barral on 14 January in Paris. The former emperor had to live
with this sorrow at the same time as he was moving to the small Hotel Bedford in Paris, 17 rue de l'Arcade.

At this time he was concerned with writing his "Testimonial," a text two
and a half pages long, in which he summed up his life and his almost fifty-
year reign. This was after having received treatments at Vichy, and though he

The former imperial family and some of their friends sitting around a table, again with
books: Dom Pedro de Alcântara, Princes Pedro and Luís, Count Mota Maia, Dominique
(the countess of Barral's son), Princess Isabel, and the count d'Eu. CEA

was weak, Dom Pedro in Paris paid attention to what was happening in Brazil. In the last sentence of his diary, dated 1 December 1891, Dom Pedro was full of hope: "A better year than the previous one, for me and for all those I care for."[18]

A persistent cough began to plague Dom Pedro. He spent his sixty-sixth birthday confined to his room, with his friends, his daughter, and his grand-children, who did not hide their concern. On 3 December the princes Pedro Augusto and Augusto of Saxe came to say their last farewells. At half past midnight on 5 December 1891 the old monarch died, and Princess Isabel became his legal successor to the throne of the Brazilian Empire: Dom Pedro had died without abdicating. The death certificate gave the cause of death as acute pneumonia in the left lung.

In the confusion of his room, among crucifixes and notebooks, lay the emperor. They dressed him for his coffin in his imperial clothes, putting the Order of the Rose beneath his beard; near the silver crucifix from the pope was the Order of the Southern Cross, which he so esteemed. His beard, the subject of so much commentary, seemed even whiter, almost artificial because a small quantity of glue had been put on it to make it lie more smoothly on his chest. Two Brazilian flags covered his long legs. As if by accident, at the suggestion of the photographer Nadar—who was looking for a better angle for his picture—a thick book was put under the emperor's head; for the

Dom Pedro II in exile. MMP

last time, books entered into Dom Pedro's image. The count d'Eu completed the scene: he found a sealed packet containing earth brought from Brazil at the monarch's request, on it written in Dom Pedro's own hand: "This is my own country's earth; I desire that it be put in my coffin, if I should die outside my country." The former monarch was following to the letter the Oriental custom of taking a handful of one's country's earth into exile. Tradition says that "the branch does not forget the tree, and the sand is always part of the beach." In the morning a group of Brazilians resident in Paris left two bouquets at the hotel—one of coffee branches, the other of tobacco.

Again, ritual and theater invaded real life. The image of the emperor decked out in the symbols of his country—Brazilian earth, the Brazilian sky represented by the Southern Cross, the branches of coffee and tobacco—all these things took on a kind of autonomy in the imagination.

To the discomfiture of the Brazilian government, Dom Pedro received, in

Dom Pedro in his coffin; his head is raised on a book. Nadar, 1891. CPCL

A photograph of the funeral cortege. MMP

death, the treatment due a head of state: the French president, Sadi Carnot, sent an aide-de-camp to the Hotel Bedford to offer condolences. The ritual in Paris lasted three days, after which the body went to Portugal to be placed next to that of Teresa Cristina. In death a mystical king, who seemed to recover the role of an imaginary monarch, replaced the deposed emperor: his physical person seemed irrelevant. Now, "a king, once dead, becomes more a king." The exile was buried as a Brazilian emperor, adorned with the symbols of his country. The old indifference gave way once again to a great ritual, as if Dom Pedro were living up to the saying "once a king, always a king."

In photos and drawings published in the international press, the Brazilian monarch—sometimes shown as an old man, sometimes rather younger—appeared again as a picture of reliability and civic virtue. Although attacked in a few newspapers because of the belatedness of Brazil's abolition of slavery, in most instances Dom Pedro was consecrated as "a civilizing hero, unjustly treated by his people." The *Herald* said, "At another time, and in happier circumstances, he would have been idolized by his subjects and would have gone down in history as 'Dom Pedro the Good.'" The *Tribune* noted, "His reign was serene, peaceful, and prosperous." The *Chilean Press*: "Brazilians should beware of false hopes that could lead to anarchy and expose them to a dangerous horde of petty tyrants, a thousand times worse than a single despot." The *Times* of London published a long article: "Until November 1889, it was thought that the deceased Emperor and his consort were unanimously adored in Brazil, thanks to their intellectual and moral gifts and their affectionate interest in the well-being of their subjects . . . When in Rio de Janeiro, he was constantly seen in public; and twice weekly he received his subjects, as well as foreign travelers, charming them with his courtesy." The article went on to list the languages Dom Pedro spoke and the scientific institutions of which he was a member. The *Weekly Register* commented, "He seemed more of a poet or a savant than an emperor, but if he had been given the opportunity to fulfill his various projects, without a doubt he would have made Brazil one of the richest countries in the New World." The *Globe* entered this chorus of praise: "He was cultivated, he was patriotic; he was gentle and indulgent; he had all the private virtues as well as the public ones, and he died in exile." But no official expression of regret came from Brazil—merely isolated, private condolences.

With the monarch's death, the old saying "The king is dead, long live the king" took on new meaning. A certain sense of shame began to be felt in Brazil; at the same time, at the Historical and Geographical Institute, a conspiracy was afoot to have Dom Pedro's body returned. The last scene in the play, the coffin "of the emperor of Brazil," seemed to move the world, as well as many Brazilians who had thought of him as a villain. The man dies, and the myth is born, and history is again turned into a metaphor.

The republican leaders, fearful of the effect of the emperor's death, kept quiet about his desire to be buried in Brazil. The greater the interest in France and in European newspapers, the less was the reaction at home. The tone of a petition circulated by the Republican Club of Rio Grande do Sul, on 10 December 1891, is revealing (it later went through the streets of Rio, too). "The country [France] that symbolizes the republic and progress is now paying homage to the only American emperor!" it scoffed. But the republic kept quiet in the face of the strength and the widespread effect of the pro–Dom Pedro demonstrations:

> Citizens, the Republican Club of Rio Grande do Sul, considering that Brazilian republicans should not remain silent in the face of the scandalous demonstrations that the few adherents of the extinct monarchy are encouraging, with the pretext of marking the death of the former emperor, and considering that we cannot remain indifferent toward the French government's attitude, decided that it ought to take the initiative, at this moment, of calling a meeting in which a petition will be distributed, and will be sent to Paris . . .
>
> Oscar da Cunha Correia, President[19]

But this was not the end of the story. It was not yet time to bring the bodies of Dom Pedro de Alcântara and Dona Teresa Cristina back. The coffins with the mortal remains of their imperial majesties were returned to Brazil only during the celebrations of the centenary of independence, in 1922, and their funerary monument was unveiled still later. Only a strong, popular president like Getúlio Vargas (who held office both in the 1930s and in the 1950s) could transform this moment into a triumph for himself: a self-glorifying ritual in Petrópolis, the "city of Pedro" itself.

NINETEEN

A Ghost Called Dom Pedro

A card announcing the former emperor's death; it circulated in Brazil in early 1892. FMLOA

On 7 December 1891, two days after Dom Pedro's death, an article was written and signed by Dr. João Mendes de Almeida. It was not published, however; the note was later cataloged by the National Library with the documents belonging to the emperor Dom Pedro II, with the code number I.33,6,171:

> The news of the passing of H.M. the Emperor Dom Pedro II will put to the test the feelings of the Brazilian nation toward the imperial dynasty. There has been general dismay. But what is more important is that Dom Pedro II has not disappeared. "The king is dead, long live the king." The imperial dynasty is still there, with all its rights, prerogatives, rules, and privileges, as it was set up by the political Constitution of the empire on 25 March 1824. *"The Emperor is dead! Long live the Emperor!"* . . . Let us pray for the monarchy. *The king is dead! Long live the emperor!* God will take pity on the sovereign Brazilian people, whose sufferings have already brought it so close to hunger and misery.

This text must have expressed the point of view of some monarchists still faithful to the crown. But it also distributes blame, which became clearer and clearer after Dom Pedro's death. As in the story of Aukê, it is as if a new myth came to afflict the population, linking the republic's bad luck and its political and economic problems to Dom Pedro's departure. Just as Aukê's tribe was forced to become nomadic, Brazil was condemned to a "sad destiny."

It is as if the ancient structure of the medieval courts was being reproduced. When a king's death was announced, his successor immediately took his place. "The king is dead, long live the king" was a formula that gave continuity to royalty and represented the mystical, sacred body of the king. The king never dies, to use the medievalist Ralph Giesey's phrase. Although the contexts are completely different from medieval ones, Brazil's former emperor, up to that moment isolated and in exile, in death came to life as king and legend. In fact, his "return" had already been commented on and even feared. In 1891, Dom Pedro had given part of his extensive library to the Historical and Geographical Institute—it contained, it is said, fifty thousand titles—and his wonderful collection of photographs.[1] The emperor's gesture was doubtless a clear sign of his esteem for the Institute, which had been so faithful to him, but it was also a way of keeping his memory alive in the images he had collected for so many years. The Institute—which in 1890, when President Deodoro visited, would not allow him to sit in "Dom Pedro's chair," an order the president immediately obeyed—began to head a movement to preserve the image of Brazil's last monarch. It kept its doors shut for seven days in mourning after the emperor's death and had solemn mass said at the end of that time. The chair was covered with crepe, and a prize was offered for the best biography of Dom Pedro. Lastly, it tried to get authorization to bring the mortal remains of the imperial couple back to Brazil.

The first steps were thus taken in the direction of a "cult of the emperor's memory" and his posthumous "consecration": Dom Pedro was recovered not as a ruler but as a mystical, sacred king. In the years that followed, the Institute made nostalgic references to the emperor in all its anniversary sessions; since Dom Pedro's departure, it had lost its principal source of funds. Every 5 December, the date of the emperor's death, the Institute shut its doors, in an isolated gesture, in a country that was trying to create new heroes for itself. Moreover, the Institute's 1891 statute prescribed that, from that date onward, new members should give a speech in honor of Dom Pedro on their admission.[2]

In this narrow context the former emperor was increasingly honored for his virtues, while his defects were forgotten. Joaquim Nabuco, for example, when he became a member of the Institute, spoke in praise of Dom Pedro:

> To characterize the gentleness of his reign, it suffices to say that when there was a republican party in the country, strong, intelligent, and

disciplined, that same party, in deference to public feeling and giving the greatest proof of its tact, flexibility, and wisdom, had resolved to respect the emperor as long as he was alive, and that it was only by an accident that the monarchy was overthrown during Dom Pedro's lifetime.

Later Nabuco wrote:

Abolition in Brazil held my interest more than all the other events or series of events that happened in my lifetime; the expulsion of the emperor was a more profound shock to me than all the other falls of monarchs, or Brazilian national catastrophes that I had followed from a distance . . . In Brazil the monarchy was, as we all can give witness, a popular form of authority. After the reception Dom Pedro was given in the United States in 1876, there was no room for doubt that, for Brazil's cultivated intelligentsia, constitutional monarchy was a much superior form of government to those of the Latin American so-called republics. . . . *I am convinced that the black race, if consulted by a true, sincere plebiscite, would have given up its claim on liberty to spare the least displeasure to those who acted in its interest, and that at bottom, when that race thinks of the dawn of 15 November, it still regrets its 13 May . . .The fall of the empire put an end to my career.*[3] (my italics)

We know that there had never been an automatic link between abolitionists and republicans; even so, words like these, written by the most charismatic politician of the empire, make one think.[4] In memory the monarchy was still alive, and with it went a kind of remorse.

It was as if Dom Pedro had not been the monarchy at all. Monarchy had fallen, but not the monarch, who was consecrated in death. As one who had cultivated his public image and created a history for the country, the second emperor was immortalized by his own plans, by the interpretations of his historians, his painters' canvases, his composers' tunes, the projects for his scientific institutions, and even by his beautiful Petrópolis, which went on being the favorite summer residence for the republican elite.

Nor is this all. The emperor was remembered in the traditions of the people, who, leaving the distant republican heroes on one side, chose a popular emperor, reinterpreted him through their festivals, and took him up along with symbols with links to a certain familiar ideology. In popular verses—composed before and especially after the proclamation of the republic—he was the hero of the people, a true son of Brazil:

> Dom Pedro the First died
> Dom Pedro the Second stayed
> With a flicker of his eyelashes
> Ruling the world.
>
>   [Northeast, 1834]

> I threw a lemon into the water
> It was so heavy it went to the bottom.
> The little fishes replied:
> "Long live Dom Pedro the Second!"

> The tilde may be tiny,
> But it has a joy that's fecund;
> A clock for a Bahian
> Is more than Pedro the Second;
> Shiny boots and a parasol
> Are the great things of the world.
>
>   [Mato Grosso]

> Hey lightning, hey sunshine!
> Keep the moon still!
> Bravo for the Old Man
> Who walks in the street.
>
>   [Rio de Janeiro]

> Deodoro's mother said:
> "This son was once mine;
> Now he is accursed
> By me and by God."
>
>   [São Paulo]

> Dom Pedro the Second left
> For the kingdom of Lisbon
> The monarchy's ended
> And Brazil's lost its way.

These people are lost,
They've got no guide
And the one to blame
Is the head of the nation.
[Canudos, Bahia][5]

Dom Pedro, presented as a popular hero, was slowly reintroduced as an official one. The famous journalist and dandy João do Rio, in a newspaper column on "Tattooing in Rio de Janeiro" in 1904, discussed the subject first in the world at large, then in Brazil, describing the kinds of designs used, the Brazilian specialties, and noted that among Brazilian blacks, the symbols most commonly used were the crucifix and the imperial crown. "The blacks explain these tattoos in a naïve way. When it comes to the imperial crown, they scratch their heads and murmur, in words that express the whole race, in an outburst with ancient, unconscious roots: 'Heh! Heh! Didn't Pedro II own it all?'"[6] This was one of many expressions that, for some time, characterized a good proportion of the Brazilian black population's way of linking the end of slavery to the monarchy, to "Isabel the Redeemer," and her father, getting older and older, with his white beard.

For the first years, however, the rehabilitation of Dom Pedro's image was limited to restricted circles. Only in 1892, when the Historical and Geographical Institute decided to start a campaign to transfer the mortal remains of its late patron, did the question get taken up nationwide. In 1906 a proposal was again put to the Chamber of Deputies,* and in 1916 the campaign reached President Venceslau Brás, who approved it, saying that it should be carried out on the centenary of Brazil's independence, in 1922. And until then members of the imperial family were still prohibited from setting foot on Brazilian territory.

While these legal maneuvers were going on, in 1909 a rather revealing struggle developed. The heirs of Dom Pedro sued the republic, whose representative was the minister João Pedro, demanding that it hand over Dom Pedro II's personal effects—a gold crown set with diamonds, the royal scepter, and the mantle—which were said to have remained in the São Cristóvão Palace on 25 July 1887 when the emperor left on his last official journey, and

---

*Article 1: "The federal government is authorized to effect the transfer of the bodies of Dom Pedro de Alcântara and Teresa Cristina, former emperor and empress of Brazil." Article 2: "It is authorized to have a pantheon constructed where the mortal remains shall be laid, twenty-five years after their death."

then, with the coming of the republic, had been removed to the Treasury (document number 42 of 29 November 1889). The terms of the complaint were plainly provocative: "If there is a desire to hide the theft of many of the diamonds, which were not found on the said crown, the government should pay for them. What is not so easily understood is that a republic should insist on retaining a symbol that was acquired by the late monarch and that represents only the monarchy."*

More interesting than the incident itself, which had its shady side, was the fact that these symbols of monarchy still had the power to provoke a public fight of this sort. In any case the Brazilian republic refused to relinquish insignia that were, in its own estimation, out of date and "foreign." Only with decree number 4120 (of 3 September 1920) was the question resolved. In the terms of the decree: "Articles 1 and 2 of decree number 78 of 21 December 1889 are revoked, and the transfer to Brazil of the mortal remains of the former emperor Dom Pedro II and his wife Teresa Cristina is permitted, as well as the presence of the imperial family in the country."

It was a while before the transfer took place, however. For the republican regime the moment was not a good one. Since the federalist rebellion of 1893–95, when a state of siege had been declared in four of Brazil's federated states, further conflicts had broken out. In 1897 the settlement of Canudos was destroyed, believed at the time to be a monarchist canker but in fact revealing unknown aspects of considerable disaffection and alienation from the modernizing aims of the ruling elites in the south of the country.† Here, too, the monarchy in question was a mythical, idealized entity, albeit having nothing to do with the exiled Bragança dynasty. And other episodes showed up the contradictions in Brazilian society, still in the process of formation: the vaccine revolt against compulsory vaccination for yellow fever in 1904, and the general strike of 1917. In the satirical press, the heroic female figure had been showing signs of fatigue for some time.

The break with Brazil's monarchical past, decreed in the first years of the republican regime, began to be attenuated. The same presidential decree revoking the banishment of the imperial family announced the creation of the

---

*There were two crowns, in fact: the first had been Dom Pedro I's and was the property of the nation; it was said that the imperial family itself had paid for the second. Both can be seen today in the Imperial Museum in Petrópolis.
†Canudos—or Belo Monte, as Antônio Conselheiro, the leader of the revolt, liked to call it—in a few years had become the second biggest city in the state of Bahia, with a population estimated at between twenty and thirty thousand.

Princess Isabel, the count d'Eu, and the family in exile. Photographs of them were kept in Brazil like talismans. MMP

National Historical Museum, whose collection was basically concerned with the empire or, rather, dedicated to a "nostalgic cult of the past," in the words of its first director, Gustavo Barroso.[7] The distinction of the Brazilian nobility as a social group, and of the empire as a historical period, inspired many articles for the *Anais do Museu Histórico Nacional*, giving evidence of a new fashion in the country.[8] Even titles abolished at the beginning of the republic began to figure again as symbols of distinction.

Rui Barbosa, who twenty years previously had drawn up the decree banishing the imperial family, on 14 December 1920 in the headquarters of the National Defense League gave a speech in praise of the former emperor, calling him Dom Pedro II once more:

> The banishment of Dom Pedro II and his family was not an act of proscription. It was a measure taken for the security of the chief figures of

the late regime . . . It was not right, however, to remove him from the country, except when the new regime was in the process of consolidation. It has been consolidated now for a long time. This reparation should have been made a long time ago, therefore. It has been late in coming . . . The political parties and politicians have refused to do it, and so have removed from their king the most glorious of crowns.[9]

The official rehabilitation of Dom Pedro as a national hero, alongside several other famous figures, began in 1922, with the centenary of Brazil's independence. Several statues were unveiled: in the Savings Bank, in the 15 November School (paradoxically), in the Benjamin Constant School for the Blind, in the Brazilian Society for the Fine Arts, and in the National Museum.[10] Both republican and imperial names were used, and even the section of railroad going to Petrópolis was again called Pedro II. The long-established Casa Silva ordered a large tapestry to be made, "with two national heroes on horseback": Marshal Deodoro with his uniform on the left, and Dom Pedro with his frock coat and top hat on the right. The elaborate wood frame was made by the Lyceum of Arts and Crafts.

The Historical and Geographical Institute took on the responsibility of receiving the remains of the imperial couple, after being assured that the count d'Eu and Princess Isabel could return to the country. It was decided that a mausoleum should be built in Petrópolis and suitable public homage made. Just as in a myth, however, Princess Isabel, now quite elderly, did not have the strength to come back: she died on 14 November 1921, in her château in France. And the count d'Eu died in 1922 on board the *Massilia* as it was bringing him back to Brazil with their son Pedro, who became the only member of the imperial family to attend events and take part in the centenary of independence. Thus Dom Pedro joined a strange new pantheon of heroes in a country so short of them. With Tiradentes, Deodoro, and Rui Barbosa, Dom Pedro was rehabilitated as a great national figure.

After thirty-three years the "body of the king" was returned, surrounded by a sea of conflicting sentiments. On the one hand, there was an "outburst of patriotic joy" appropriate to the date; on the other, discomfort at seeing the king's ghost again. This, at least, is the sensation one feels in an article by Humberto de Campos, published in *A Semana* in September 1922: "*The ghost.* Brought back to us now, to his native land, Dom Pedro II . . . provokes a cry of alarm in the soul of some republicans: 'What is this ghost doing here again?' It is a gesture of Shakespearean terror, when faced by the ghost of the

Material for the celebration of the centenary of independence. Imperial and republican heroes appear in the same pantheon. MIP

brother whose crown he has taken. It is, in fact, a gesture of fear and re-morse."[11] The parallel is with the figure of Richard II, only this time it was the nation, not the monarch, that was tormented with guilt.

Yet the setting was right for reconciliation. The whole episode was de-scribed as if the emperor himself were making his triumphal return: "They took him slowly off the ship. As they brought him down, the cannons thun-dered and the fusillades sounded, until finally these relics returned to the sa-cred earth of Brazil. *He was dead, but his great figure, thirty-three years after the catastrophe, dominated the public imagination.* The atmosphere seemed electric with the arrival of these remains, still surrounded by nostalgia, but over which there shone the indestructible halo of a century of glory."[12] The king who "towered over the imagination of the people" had nothing to do with the deposed emperor, however. The "body of the king," "mystical and sacred," was a medium through which many other ideas were expressed. For the republican elite, he figured beside other heroes in a newly formed pan-theon. In the streets and parades, it was a king of accomplishments and pub-lic celebrations who was returning.

The departure of the bodies from Lisbon and their arrival in Brazil. MMP

There were many discordant voices, it is true, but the general atmosphere was favorable. In 1925 in *A Semana* President Artur da Silva Bernardes, attired in republican emblems, posed beside an old photo of Dom Pedro II in military uniform. In the revealing text accompanying this montage, we can see how the about-face happened: "We republicans of today feel strong enough to turn to the past . . . and not to deny the emperor the justice due to him. He loved Brazil, and while he had the strength and energy, he tried to serve it, surrounding himself with the best people of the time." With the symbols of monarchy and republic thus united, Bernardes's note betrays republican fears: the republic had to show that it felt strong enough to confront the now invisible, ghostly enemy, to look at the past without fear of making mistakes.

But 1925 was not just any year, especially for the construction of a mythical "memory" of Dom Pedro. At that time, in the middle of a serious republican crisis, there took place an important debate that caught the attention of the city of Rio de Janeiro. The polemic surrounded the celebrations of the centenary of Dom Pedro's birth, on 2 December. Could the republic celebrate a hero whom it had banished?

The "coffee and milk" republic was showing clear signs of unpopularity. The elites of the states of São Paulo and Minas Gerais, the chief producers of these two commodities, respectively, were manipulating the political system to keep their hold on power. But changes that had occurred since the First World War had altered the face of Brazil and the carefully constructed mechanisms by which the *paulistas* and *mineiros* shared power and shut others out. Industrial growth and urbanization were beginning to bring other social groups to the fore—middle-class groups, an industrial haute bourgeoisie and proletariat—who until then had been excluded from power.[13] In São Paulo working-class groups virtually paralyzed the city in 1917, and the same thing happened in Rio in 1919. In 1922 the Brazilian Communist Party was founded in Rio, and in São Paulo a Modern Art Week celebrating the centenary of independence amounted to a frontal attack on conventional aesthetic values. Meanwhile, the so-called *Tenentista* revolts shook Brazil in a number of places: in Rio de Janeiro (1922), in Rio Grande do Sul (1923), and in São Paulo (1924). President Bernardes governed for four years (1922–26) in a state of siege.

It was in this tense atmosphere that, in 1925, the commemoration of the centenary of Dom Pedro II's birth was considered. The disparity between the enthusiasm generated by this and by the thirty-sixth anniversary of the republic (on 15 November) was striking. A cartoon by Storni—"Echoes of the Anniversary"—published in the newspaper A *Noite* on 18 November showed a dialogue between a traditional republican (represented by an old man) and the republic (no longer a lovely young woman but a blowzy matron): "See where you were celebrated this year?" says the man. "Celebrated? Where?" asks the republic. "Abroad!" says the old republican.

In the Chamber of Deputies, Wanderley Pinho drew up a bill proposing that 2 December, Dom Pedro's birthday, be made into a national holiday. There was a speedy reaction: a group of deputies headed by Ranulfo Bocaiúva Cunha, Simões de Lopes, and Joaquim Mello alleged that the project was a monarchist provocation and suggested instead a "permanent" civic cult of the republic. The most interesting thing about the polemic over the question of who ought to be "celebrated" is that, although the quarrel centered on Dom Pedro and the monarchy, it was the republic that was at stake.

Meanwhile, the images of the late monarch were going in a new direction: Dom Pedro was, paradoxically, becoming a model of republican ideals. Francisco de Assis Chateaubriand, for example, in a 1925 article, described the "Tupi Brazil" over which Dom Pedro ruled and called him "the most luminous and purest incarnation of a republican we have yet had."[14] Debates

"Echoes of the Anniversary." Storni in *A Noite*, 18 November 1925. A fat, aging republic. From Silva, "A República comemora o Império."

continued in the press, polarizing attitudes favorable or hostile to the "new cult" of Dom Pedro; the Brazilian Academy of Letters began a series of lectures about Dom Pedro II; and *Estado de São Paulo* published articles with the title "Dom Pedro II the Magnanimous."

Pinho's project was not approved in the Chamber. Even so, on 2 December 1925 Rio de Janeiro was in festival mood. President Bernardes declared a national holiday; shops, pavilions, ships, and monuments were hung with flags; and the celebrations were enlivened by the presence of the emperor's grandchildren and great-grandchildren: Prince Dom Pedro de Alcântara, Princess Elisabete, and their children. The Historical and Geographical Institute sponsored several Masses, and celebrations were held in several places, such as the Pedro II School, the Geographical Society, and the Brazil Central Railway.

There was no lack of locations: even traditional republicans were rehabilitating the emperor. The idea was, again, to separate the emperor from the empire. For republicans, Dom Pedro was the best republican of all; monarchists, of course, praised him for different reasons. One way or another, the centenary was given support: it was a strange alliance of old and new. The dethroned king was celebrated, but not his defunct regime. Popular memory selected the kind of royalty it wanted to celebrate.

It seemed there was no real danger the monarchy would return; the republic was less worried about the old regime coming back than about its own weaknesses. In this context, it was the man, now turned into a myth, who was the object of adulation. In commemorative medallions, in various homage ceremonies held all over the country, the late monarch appeared as the "magnanimous emperor." Not surprisingly, the festival in Petrópolis was the most splendid one, with processions, bands, receptions, and other solemnities, and

a large statue that summed it all up: the "citizen-monarch" and the "intellectual king." Simultaneously, a new statue of Dom Pedro was unveiled in the
Quinta da Boa Vista: the emperor appears as a citizen, right in the middle of
the square. With his beard, calm expression, and the bald head of a mature
man, Dom Pedro is again "father of the country." (And in Paris in 1927 the
Hotel Bedford, which was being renovated, noted the growing popularity of
its most illustrious guest and joined some Brazilian monarchist sympathizers
in France in putting up a plaque in which Dom Pedro's distinctions and the
scientific associations he had belonged to were listed. When the hotel was re-
opened, there was a small ceremony "in memory of Dom Pedro II, Emperor
of Brazil.")

It was as if the official iconography of the republic could no longer leave
the emperor's image out. In one illustration a female allegorical figure says:
"May your mortal remains come to their final resting place, in this country
that you loved so much." The icon of the young republic welcomes Dom Pedro; now only a symbol, he is removed from the context of the regime he in
fact presided over.

On 5 December 1939, in the presence of President Getúlio Vargas, the
mortuary chapel in Petrópolis was dedicated. A tomb sculpted by Leão Veloso
showed the effigies of Pedro II and the empress in marble. Opposite them
stained-glass windows designed by Carlos Osvald represented the rise and fall
of the emperor's reign; at one side Dom Pedro's poem of complaint is shown,

The statue of Dom Pedro in
Petrópolis, with its pensive look
and worn coat. MMP

Another statue of Dom Pedro as enlightened citizen-monarch, at its installation and inauguration. MMP

"The Republic welcomes Dom Pedro II." MMP

in which he asks for "God's justice in History's voice." In this ideal setting for a consecration, and under the eye of a strong republican president, Dom Pedro returned as a king of the people, free of time and place.

Petrópolis again became, in a certain sense, Pedro's city. The Imperial Museum, created with the explicit object of "portraying the history of Brazilian life under the monarchy," was opened in 1940, again by decree of President Vargas.[15] Only then did memory find a place to settle, and the last emperor returned to Brazil, which in one sense he had barely left.

Dom Pedro never knew Getúlio Vargas, much less the farewell letter he composed before his suicide in 1954, but he too, as Vargas's concluding line put it, "went out of life, to enter History." In Dom Pedro's case, it is hard to tell if it was history or myth that redeemed him, or, better, if history became myth and vice versa. In this history, so hemmed in by the theater and ritual of the tropical court, it is difficult to see where life ends and image begins, or if sometimes the two of them go forward hand in hand.

> The water's mad! Even the little fishes flee from it!
> Even the stones tremble!
> Even Dom Pedro II is afraid of the waterfall.
>
> [1927]

> On the seats in the park lively conversation,
> Handshakes, kisses, maybes.
> Dom Pedro II peeps down from above,
> His beard so white,
> I can't even say how white,
> And the parents are walking, it seems they're dancing,
> They're dancing a round-dance, all round the king.
>
> ["Retreta do Vinte," 1930]

> Land of God! Land of my great-grandmother
> Who danced a waltz with Dom Pedro the Second.
>
> [Northeast, anonymous, 1930]

"If the People Are the Body, the King Is the Head"

An illustration by Dom João Solórzano from Francisco Antônio de Novais Campos, *The Perfect Prince—A Pedagogical Manual for the Education of a Prince* (1790), given to Dom João before his arrival in Brazil. FBN

"Without miracles, there can be no real kings."
—*Marc Bloch*, The Royal Touch

In 1890 the Portuguese writer Eça de Queirós visited the former emperor in Paris and defined in a few words the strange distance that existed between the monarch and his former subjects: "Studying Phoenician monuments and Hebrew texts is not enough to attract, in Brazil, a useful current of intellectual sympathy; the emperor would be popular only if he had published a collection of songs . . . He seemed the least Brazilian of all Brazilians; and a king really achieves the love of his people only when he incarnates their qualities and defects."[1]

It was a long time since Dom Pedro, so far removed from his Brazilian subjects, had been anything like them. He was no longer the king "who had been born Brazilian" and who had engaged in a dialogue with his national context. The Dom Pedro in his cape of toucan breast-feathers who had linked himself with the figure of the jungle-dwellers, who had distributed indigenous titles to his nobility, who had helped promote national literature and a Brazilian artistic and musical style, whose greatest ideal was the Romantic Native American of the forests: this king no longer existed. The monarch who had participated in popular events, who had had his Friday receptions with

King Obá, who encouraged the slave singers of the Fazenda de Santa Cruz, who surrounded himself with palm trees and local fruits and animals, was gone. Even "citizen Pedro de Alcântara," the likable character who traveled around Europe with his valise, who cut down the expenses spent on ritual but worked hard at spreading news of his exotic kingdom, was distant from his subjects' imagination.

Yet however superficial they might have been thought to be, the symbolic signs of Dom Pedro's royalty were powerful and enduring, beyond the end of the monarchical system and even beyond Dom Pedro's changes of personality. Paradoxically, after his exile, the imagined representation of the king seemed to impose itself on his actual physical person. In 1922 on the centenary of independence or in 1939 with the opening of the mortuary chapel, different interpretations of royalty lived side by side: the official and practical one, and its mythic aspect, in which Dom Pedro became a sacred and religious king alongside other kings and queens in popular festivals. As the historian Marc Bloch says, "The royal miracle stands out above all as the expression of a certain concept of supreme political power."[2] Here were symbols and images that outlived the socioeconomic structure they were conceived in and that were collectively shared, in differing ways and in different contexts.

Once again we can let Machado de Assis tell the story. Bentinho, the narrator and central character of *Dom Casmurro* (1900), is talking to José Dias, who lives as a dependent with Bentinho's family, within which he exercises some influence. The young man is trying to persuade José Dias that "he is not cut out for the seminary," to which his mother has promised God to send him with the idea of his becoming a priest. Suddenly, the emperor appears:

> We met the emperor, who was coming from the School of Medicine. The bus we were in stopped, as did all the other vehicles; the passengers got out and removed their hats until the imperial coach had passed. When I went back to my seat, I had a fantasy, nothing less than the idea of going to see the emperor, telling him everything, and asking him to intervene . . . *If His Majesty asks, Mamma will give way*, I thought to myself.
>
> Then I saw the emperor listening to me, reflecting and in the end saying yes, he would go and speak to my mother; and I kissed his hand with tears in my eyes. Next thing I was at home waiting, until I heard the outriders and the cavalry escort: It's the emperor! It's the emperor! Everybody came to the window to see him pass by, but he didn't pass

by. The coach stopped at our door, the emperor got out and came in. Great excitement in the neighborhood: "The emperor has gone into Dona Glória's house! What on earth can be happening?" Our family came out to receive him; my mother was the first to kiss his hand. Then the emperor, all smiles, whether he came into the living room or not—I don't remember, dreams are often confused—asked my mother not to make me a priest, and she, flattered and obedient, promised she would not.

"Medicine—why don't you send him to study medicine?"

"If such is Your Majesty's pleasure . . ."

"Send him to study medicine; it's a fine career, and we've got good teachers here. Haven't you ever been to our school? It's splendid. We've got first-class doctors, who can match the best in other countries.". . .

Then the emperor held out his hand to be kissed and went out, accompanied by all of us, with the street full of people and the windows crammed. There was an astonished silence. The emperor entered the coach, bowed, and said good-bye with his hand, still repeating: "Medicine, our school." And the coach left, amid envy and humble thanks . . .

For some moments—minutes, even—I consoled myself with this vision, until the plan collapsed and I returned to the dreamless faces of my fellow passengers.[3]

The emperor, a character in a novel or, more exactly, in a site of invention and allusion within a fiction, is a locus where depiction and imagination meet. He is the wise Maecenas who looks after Brazil's schools, an intimate friend of the household who gives advice about life's choices, a crutch to lean on in times of uncertainty.

Machado's text offers food for thought on the many and varied ways in which the public image of royalty is constructed, penetrates the minds of the people, and takes root there. The emperor was at one and the same time the creator of the symbolic games surrounding him and their chief feature (as an object of praise or criticism). The figure of a king occupied more and more space in the national imagination and, like a fetish, was in the end separable from his actions. His image became greater than his person, and an idealization prevailed over reality.

There was a certain cultural circularity in the understanding of the

Brazilian monarchy, a process of exchange that cannot be reduced to any Machiavellian intentions on the emperor's part, which in any case it is not for us to judge. A universe of common meaning permitted several groups of people to identify themselves within it in differing ways but using similar structures. Popular festivals might be the other side of the coin to the court manuals of etiquette, but in both spaces royalty was an essential point of reference. The kings and queens of Carnival went out of their way to pass by the City Palace. And we should not forget the delegation who communicated this request to the police, who gave the following decision: "It is necessary that Your Excellency send to this department a noncommissioned officer of the cavalry . . . to accompany a certain group of Indians who wish to have the honor of kissing the hand of His Majesty."[4]

Thus, while the political discourse of Brazil's elites found an echo among some parts of the people at large and a certain political culture was deliberately constructed during Dom Pedro's reign, it is still reductive to explain the monarch's success only by virtue of his own personal, conscious intentions. To link the dissemination of the image simply to the initiatives of the emperor and the ruling groups surrounding him limits the possibilities of reinterpretation present in any process of communication. The popular imagination fed on royalty and to a certain degree was thereby "Europeanized," but the obverse was also true: the Brazilian monarchy was imbued with elements of local culture.

This is the reason I have focused on the memory of Dom Pedro rather than on his biography, which has already been the subject of a series of more or less eulogistic volumes. As the historian Robert Darnton says, we must "ask new questions of old topics and questions."[5] Unless we do so, how can we explain that a monarch like Dom Pedro, an old man with a white beard, should have remained in Brazil's public memory for so long? How can we understand why official historical memory paid so much attention to his father's mistresses but not to his own? How can we interpret the fact that an emperor who dissembled so much has gone down in history only as a wise and curious Maecenas? The answer is to be found less in Dom Pedro's "story," in documented, biographical fact, than in the way certain images were developed in Brazil's memory, to the detriment of others. We move from history toward myth, looking at the way memory appropriates history to neutralize it or make it into a myth in its own right.

For a long time, the production of myths was associated with archaic societies opposed to the pursuit of science and history that supposedly characterized modern societies. To frame the debate this way separated the two concepts as if they were equivalent and opposite. Claude Lévi-Strauss denied the implicit hierarchy in the terms and showed that they in fact belong to different domains: mythical narrative has an unconscious, signifying structure, while historical discourse is linked more immediately to its context, its meaning changing daily by practice and action. In other words, while history is in the realm of the diachronic, myth has its synchronic logic, witnessed in repetition and reiteration.*

How are we to introduce this distinction into the context of societies with a history? How are we to think about contemporary political myths entering into a dialogue with their context, but also reiterating past structures? How can we see that "representations are historically produced by the interaction of political, social and discursive practices," as one scholar puts it, and at the same time analyze images that go on being repeated out of context? Perhaps the answer is to recognize the existence of values that have a mental *longue durée*, that survive their immediate structural causes and take on new meanings in new contexts. It is in the articulation between the "social structure" and the "cultural structure" that we must look for this "order of permanencies," as Braudel puts it, corresponding neither to a simple reflection in a mirror nor to a mechanical process empty of meaning. To take seriously the symbolic universes a society produces is to insist in some manner not exclusively on the social foundations of symbolic life, as Émile Durkheim proposed, but on the symbolic foundations of social life, on the relevance of symbolic structures in uncovering the constructions of political power.

Of contemporary thinkers who have studied this question of historical structure, Marshall Sahlins has perhaps come closest to overcoming the dichotomy between "event" and "structure." He uses the notion of "conjunctural structure" to delineate a series of historical relationships that, at the same time as they reproduce old cultural categories, give them new life drawn from their immediate context. In his book *Islands of History*, Sahlins shows that each society carries its own cosmologies along with it: it transforms

---

*Mythic structure rearticulates the contradictions of society, in spiraling fashion, working with fundamental binary oppositions that escape the understanding of the individual in his own context, since they are always universal. Lévi-Strauss does not use the Freudian concept of the unconscious, with its structure and its meaningful symbols, but something closer to the Lacanian model of a structure that is empty of signified meaning. He links this concept of structure to his theoretical aim, which is to consider, from a humanist perspective, the unity of the human species, and to postulate the existence of a universal "human spirit." In our context, we consider his theory only in its most general terms; the debate here is about myths undergoing changes in *modern* society.

only certain happenings charged with meaning into "events." He goes further: he analyzes how any meeting between two cultures, notwithstanding any political power exercised by the one over the other, alters both. The cultural dynamics show a continual process of re-creation between sender and receiver, and a constant surmounting of the problems resulting from this. Culture turns out to be a two-way street, in which reception is always reciprocal. Structures, then, are always permanent and historical, as "each reproduction implies its own transformation."

It is in this sense that, as the anthropologist Franz Boas said, "the eye that sees is the organ of tradition"[6]; no one sees exactly what he wants to, alters the content of what he sees at will, or engages exclusively with new situations. Each context brings possible and shared categories along with it, which correspond "not to the audacity of the past, but to the limits of what can be thought," as one scholar has put it. In other words, each culture carries with it meanings that antecede it and that refer back to pre-existing classifications and orders.[7]

What comes into being, then, is not a process of evolution from lower to higher forms of cultural expression but a complementary relationship between myth and history. We can then see that contemporary political myths are perhaps a little like sacred myths, carrying with them matter from the past and preserving levels of meaning that can help to explain the present. They may tell us something about how a given society understands itself and its history, and they may also bring a society's understanding up to date—bringing back to life its images of itself, or its values, or its customs.

It is not enough to eradicate these myths or show their potential for domination and manipulation. "Historicizing culture" means, in some way, linking culture to history, but it would be better to explain how both are interpretable material and symbolically inseparable.[8]

In the case of Dom Pedro, we have to understand the way elites imposed the monarchy on Brazil, intentionally and from the outside, and also which elements favored giving welcome to the Portuguese court in Brazil, even at a moment of crisis in the colonial system. As the historian Rodrigo Bentes Monteiro has shown, in Portuguese America, "the myth of the king functioned as a vital catalyst, bringing social forces into action. Immensely charismatic as it was, royal power in its divine form was given a new importance by the objectification of the power of the colonizers, in the legitimacy of the festivals and ceremonies they put on."[9]

Along with Dom João's baggage, there arrived in Brazil, literally, a representation of the king's dual body. In 1790 the *bacharel* Francisco Antônio de Novais Campos offered the prince regent a manuscript entitled *The Perfect Prince—A Pedagogical Manual for the Education of a Prince*. The manuscript was put into the collection of the Royal Library, which was brought to Brazil in 1807 and opened to the public in 1814.[10] In it we can see the doctrine of the king's two bodies in a new version with a new interpretation: the people are the body, the king the head.

But in the tropics, this doctrine changed: conforming to local ritual, the people often enough were the body and the king the head, but at other times the king was the body and the people the head. In Brazil the externalization of authority combined with elaborate festivals that were moments in which royalty played out its theater. Through the *congadas* with their "king of the Congo," or the Festival of the Divine Holy Spirit, when a new "emperor" was elected every year, crowns and scepters from the Western European tradition mixed with elements that recalled an African aesthetic. Brazil's tropical monarchy also combined with the influence of Sebastianism and the mystique of the absent king[11]; or, in the words of Fernando Pessoa, "It is in the Atlantic that he remains, even symbolically, in his place. And where there is an emperor, there is always an empire."[12]

In the "country of festivals," the monarch was incorporated into the calendar of celebrations and holidays. Dom Pedro is a recurrent figure, sometimes chosen because of his halo of royalty, sometimes as the "child of the country," sometimes recalled by a portrait, sometimes officially, and sometimes pitched into a time with no fixed dates or owners:

> When Dom Pedro the Second
> Played for Brazil
> A fine upstanding gambler
> In the lottery of life
> His election agent,
> Mr. Mané Raimundo, told me
> That he danced at carnival
> With Princess Isabel
> In the times of Colonel
> Pedro Álvares Cabral.[13]

Thus, while monarchical power is surely at one level an instrument of dynasties, its popularity is nevertheless linked to the way it is received. The fun-

Zé Limeira. Booklet of popular (cordel) poetry by J. Barros, 1996. Private collection.

damental problem is to understand how a phenomenon elaborated in restricted circles at the top of the social and cultural hierarchy (not only Dom Pedro's elites but the circle of intellectuals and artists surrounding him) can reach, or did reach, the masses. On the one hand, we have the elites' theories and practices and on the other popular beliefs and mentalities. The relation between these two lies at the heart of "royal miracles" and the effectiveness of their power. The same sacred objects and political instruments—scepter, crown, sword, ring—are retranslated by local structures and groups and acquire new historical identities. Tradition, folklore, and symbols are "transported into history," the history the elites fashion but also a history that antedates official chronology.

Linked in its magical and historical origins to both spheres since earliest times, royalty makes ritual and ceremony into political gestures, and as it does so, it locates itself in a sacred dimension, in a history that precedes these rituals.

Whether through the Festival of the Divine Holy Spirit, or the Day of the Three Kings; congadas and the king of the Congo; cavalcades with the presence of King Arthur; King Bamba and the Festival of Ticumbi; the Quilombo festival in Alagoas, in which the mixed-blood caboclos abduct the queen of the blacks; or the Maracatu in Recife, when the queen of Maracatu parades beside the lady of the palace and Dom Henrique—the numerous images and figures surrounding royalty reappear, newly translated by so many black, mulatto, and mestizo kings and queens. We must understand these "habits of thought" and the mentalities that preceded the arrival of the Portuguese court, and we must engage with the "machinations of the elite," which re-translated Dom Pedro and fit him in a modern context.

In privileged moments, on the one hand power with its pomp, its rituals, and the charisma of the royal figure is reaffirmed and made visible, and on the other the journey to popular reinterpretation begins. In official celebrations, the calculated pretense and the aspect of show were present, but ritual was not limited to mere pretense and the play of appearances. True, the affirmation of monarchy in a hemisphere filled with republics was difficult to handle, just as it is clear that the brilliance of Brazilian ritual hid great contradictions in the system and that royalty was fertile in the production of symbols with political effect.

In his meetings with King Obá and other popular personalities of the Rio de Janeiro of the time, in his support for and presence in a series of popular festivals, we can see both how Dom Pedro constructed his reign and how it was constructed for him. As a "man," Dom Pedro fell from power, but he came back as a myth. His story seems to restate the theory developed by Ralph Giesey, who studied the burial ceremonies of French kings in the Re-

Whites and blacks in the traditional costumes of Rio de Janeiro and Serra do Frio celebrating the Festival of the Divine Holy Spirit. Carlos Julião, 1795. FBN

The elegant king Obá, as seen in the streets of Rio. From Moraes Filho, *Festas e tradições populares*, 1946. CGJM

naissance, that "the dead king seems to live through his realistic effigy, while the living king seems to exist no longer." History tells of a drama, and it is through myth that the history is recounted. Perhaps monarchy was more than a "happy accident," as Rui Barbosa defined it.

The king was overthrown and exiled when he died, but the "ghost" or popular idealization of the deposed king perturbed the social imagination until his return. In the latter, Dom Pedro is still the "father of the whites" but is also "lord of all festivals" and, together with Isabel, the "eternal redeemer." Silvio Romero, with a large dose of irony, summed up the destiny of monarchy in Brazil. Brazil would one day turn into a truly mulatto empire, he said: "The first emperor fell because he wasn't born here; the second will fall because he isn't mulatto."[14]

It is not only exceptions that prove the rule. In Brazil royalty seemed to contend with multiple, changing realities. Long before he was born, Dom Pedro was a king. Still present today in handkerchiefs and all kinds of keepsakes, in schoolbooks and even on telephone cards, the national hero Dom Pedro is almost like a distant relative. On the wall of the *beato* Pedro Batista, in Santa Brígida, Bahia, our king shares space with Getúlio Vargas, his brother in "popular memory." And in the church of Nossa Senhora da Conceição da Praia, in Salvador, Bahia, his image is near the altar, right above that of the powerful Bahian politician Antônio Carlos Magalhães.

As a myth, Dom Pedro is *bon à penser*, useful to think about, to parody Lévi-Strauss's famous words, and he is still eternally old in popular imagination. In a reinterpretation by an anonymous painter in the 1930s, the same official scene, so often reproduced in the newspapers of 1889, is shown again. It is the dramatic moment when the telegram was handed over announcing the end of the empire. This time Dom Pedro is even older, and behind the soldiers a female angel observes the event. The wings of the popular imagination hover over the scene. They show that "the king is dead, long live the king."

A vision of the famous scene from November 1889, with an angel hovering over the monarch. Anonymous, oil on canvas, 1930s. CEA

CHRONOLOGY

ARCHIVAL SOURCES AND
THEIR ABBREVIATIONS

NOTES

BIBLIOGRAPHY

INDEX

ILLUSTRATION CREDITS

Chronology

1825 2 December. Birth of Pedro de Alcântara João Carlos Leopoldo Salvador Bibiano Francisco Xavier de Paula Leocádio Miguel Gabriel Rafael Gonzaga, called Pedro de Alcântara.

     10 December. Dom Pedro's baptism.

     Portugal and Great Britain recognize Brazil's independence.

     Cisplatine war between Brazil and Argentina for control of the Cisplatine province (present-day Uruguay) begins.

1826 11 May. Death of Dom Pedro de Alcântara's mother, Dona Leopoldina.

     2 August. Solemn thanksgiving for Pedro de Alcântara.

1828 End of the Cisplatine war.

1829 16 October. Arrival in Rio of Dom Pedro I's second wife, Dona Amélia de Leuchtenberg.

     11 December. Collapse of the Banco do Brasil.

1831 7 April. Abdication of Dom Pedro I. Provisional three-man regency chosen.

     8 April. José Bonifácio de Andrada e Silva becomes Dom Pedro's tutor.

     9 April. Acclamation of Dom Pedro II.

     13 April. Dom Pedro I leaves for Europe.

     17 June. Permanent three-man regency chosen.

1833 15 December. The marquis of Itanhaém replaces José Bonifácio as Dom Pedro's tutor.

1834 24 September. Death of Dom Pedro I in Lisbon.

     Reform of Dom Pedro I's Constitution: the Additional Act.

1835 Outbreak of Cabanagem revolt in Pará, Farroupilha revolt in Rio Grande do Sul, and slave revolt of the Malés in Bahia.

     12 October. Padre Diogo Feijó elected regent.

1837 19 September. Feijó resigns and is replaced temporarily by Pedro de Araújo Lima, marquis of Olinda.

     November. Outbreak of the Sabinada revolt in Bahia.

     2 December. Pedro II school founded.

1838 Brazilian Historical and Geographical Institute founded.

     6 April. Death of José Bonifácio.

     22 April. Olinda elected regent.

     End of the Sabinada revolt.

1840 End of the Cabanagem revolt.

     23 July. Coup establishing that Dom Pedro is to reach his majority early.

24 July. The "majority cabinet" chosen, with Aureliano Coutinho as foreign minister. The daguerreotype is introduced to Brazil.

1841 23 March. Fall of the majority cabinet and formation of a replacement.
18 July. Consecration and coronation of Dom Pedro II.
Balaiada revolt in Maranhão defeated.

1842 10 May. Liberal rebellion in São Paulo.
20 May. Bento Lisboa signs marriage contract between Dom Pedro and Princess Teresa Cristina of Naples.
10 July. Liberal rebellion in Minas Gerais.

1843 20 January. Cabinet headed by Honório Hermeto Carneiro Leão, marquis of Paraná.
1 May. Marriage of Dona Francisca to the prince of Joinville, François d'Orléans, in Rio de Janeiro.
30 May. Marriage in Naples, by proxy, of the emperor to Teresa Cristina Maria of Bourbon, princess of the Two Sicilies.
3 September. Arrival of the empress in Rio de Janeiro, on board the frigate *Constituição*.

1844 28 April. Marriage of Dona Januária and the count of Áquila, Luigi of Bourbon of the Two Sicilies, in Rio de Janeiro.
22 October. Departure of the count and countess of Áquila for Europe.

1845 23 February. Birth of imperial prince Dom Afonso.
1 March. End of the Farroupilha war.
6 August. Departure of the emperor for the southern provinces.
8 August. The British Parliament passes the Aberdeen Bill, a unilateral measure giving the British Navy the right to stop and search ships involved in the slave trade.

1846 26 April. The emperor returns to Rio de Janeiro.
29 July. Birth of Princess Isabel.

1847 11 June. Death of Prince Dom Afonso.
13 June. Birth of Princess Leopoldina.
20 July. Creation of the post of president of the Council of Ministers.
Arrival of the first immigrants to work on Senator Vergueiro's coffee plantation.
The emperor travels to the interior of Rio de Janeiro province.

1848 19 July. Birth of Prince Dom Pedro Afonso.
29 September. Conservatives take power; first ministry of the marquis of Olinda.
Outbreak of Praieira revolt in Pernambuco.
Fall of King Louis Philippe in France and end of the July Monarchy.

1849 6 October. Fall of the marquis of Olinda; Monte Alegre becomes President of the Council.
End of Praieira revolt.

1850 10 January. Death of Prince Dom Pedro Afonso.
4 September. End of the transatlantic slave trade (Eusébio de Queirós Law).
Yellow fever epidemic.
Passage of the Land Law.
Publication of the Commercial Code.

1851 The Uruguayan leader Oribe is defeated by Brazilian troops.

1852 5 February. Defeat of Rosas at Monte Caseros.

First Brazilian telegraph.

First gas lighting in Rio de Janeiro.

1853 The marquis of Paraná organizes the Conciliation cabinet.

1854 Varnhagen's *General History of Brazil* published.

1855 17 October. Death of the countess of Belmonte, Dom Pedro II's governess.

1856 Caxias becomes head of the Conciliation cabinet on the death of the marquis of Paraná.

31 December. The countess of Barral is invited to be the empress's lady-in-waiting and governess to the princesses.

Rebellion of immigrant sharecroppers on Vergueiro's plantation.

1857 4 May. Olinda's second postmajority cabinet.

1858 Opening of the Dom Pedro II railroad.

12 December. Abaeté cabinet (Conservative).

1859 10 August. End of the Conciliation cabinet; cabinet of Ângelo Ferraz, baron of Uruguaiana.

2 October. Dom Pedro visits the northern provinces.

1860 11 February. The emperor returns to Rio de Janeiro.

25 February. British ambassador W. D. Christie presents his credentials.

1861 2 March. Caxias organizes his first cabinet.

The Christie Question.

1862 24 May. First cabinet headed by Zacarias de Góis (Liberal).

30 May. Third Olinda cabinet (Liberal).

30 December. British Navy attacks Brazilian shipping.

Brazil participates in the Universal Exhibition in London.

1863 11 March. Christie returns to England.

5 July. Diplomatic relations with Britain severed.

Maximilian, Dom Pedro's cousin, becomes emperor of Mexico.

1864 15 January. Second Zacarias cabinet (Liberal).

4 August. Ultimatum to the Montevideo government.

31 August. Furtado cabinet (Liberal).

2 September. The count d'Eu (Gaston of Orléans) and the duke of Saxe (August von Saxe-Coburg-Gotha), suitors of the imperial princesses, arrive in Rio de Janeiro.

15 October. Marriage of Princess Isabel and the count d'Eu.

1 December. Beginning of military operations against Uruguay.

15 December. Marriage of Princess Leopoldina and the duke of Saxe.

27 December. Paraguayan army of Solano López invades Mato Grosso.

1865 Surrender of Montevideo.

1 May. The Treaty of the Triple Alliance: Uruguay, Brazil, and Argentina.

12 May. Fourth Olinda cabinet (Liberal).

11 June. Battle of Riachuelo.

10 July. Dom Pedro leaves Rio for the theater of war.

11 September. The emperor reaches Uruguaiana.

23 September. Resumption of diplomatic relations with Britain.

9 November. The emperor returns to Rio de Janeiro.

1866 24 May. Battle of Tuiuti.

3 August. Third Zacarias cabinet (Liberal).

November. Caxias arrives in Paraguay.

1867 June. Execution of Maximilian in Mexico.

Opening of the Santos-Jundiaí railroad.

Cholera outbreak.

Brazil participates in the Universal Exhibition in Vienna.

1868 13 January. Caxias takes over command of the army.

19 February. Passage of Humaita.

16 July. Itaboraí cabinet (Conservatives return to power).

11 December. Battle of Avaí.

1869 1 January. Asunción is occupied.

19 January. Caxias withdraws from the war.

16 April. The count d'Eu becomes commander-in-chief.

Gobineau arrives in Rio as French minister.

1870 1 March. Solano López is killed at Cerro Corá; end of the Paraguayan war.

29 September. São Vicente cabinet (Conservative).

3 December. Liberal Republicans' manifesto is published in A República.

The Society for Liberation and the Society for the Emancipation of the Slaves are founded in Rio de Janeiro.

Carlos Gomes finishes his opera O Guarani.

1871 7 February. Death of Dom Pedro's daughter Dona Leopoldina, duchess of Saxe.

7 March. Rio Branco cabinet (Conservative).

25 May. The emperor leaves for Europe and the Middle East.

28 September. Law of the Free Womb.

10 November. The emperor receives the news of the law in Alexandria.

1872 17 January. Republican Party established.

30 March. The emperor returns to Brazil.

1873 July. First Republican Party congress, in Itu.

Death in Lisbon of the duchess of Bragança, former empress Dona Amélia de Leuchtenberg.

The bishops of Olinda and Pará prohibit brotherhoods linked to Freemasonry.

1874 22 June. A submarine cable links Brazil to Europe.

The bishops of Olinda and Pará are arrested and imprisoned.

Rebellion and riots (quebra-quilos [smash-kilos]) in Pernambuco and Paraíba.

1875 25 June. Second Caxias cabinet (Conservative).

15 October. Birth of the emperor's grandson, Dom Pedro, prince of Grão-Pará.

Failure of Mauá Bank and National Bank.

The Caxias cabinet gives an amnesty to the imprisoned bishops.

The newspaper A Provincia de São Paulo is established.

1876 26 March. Dom Pedro leaves for his second journey abroad: to Europe, the Middle East, and the United States.

First publication of the satirical *Semana Ilustrada*, edited by Ângelo Agostini.

Brazil participates in Universal Exhibition in Philadelphia.

1877 Drought in the northeast.

26 September. Dom Pedro returns to Brazil.

12 December. Death of José de Alencar.

Electoral reform.

1878 Sinimbu cabinet; Liberals return to power.

29 June. Death of Varnhagen in Vienna.

1880 Vintém revolt in Rio de Janeiro.

7 March. Death of the duke of Caxias.

28 March. First Saraiva cabinet.

9 August. Birth of Prince Dom Antônio, son of Princess Isabel.

1 November. Death of the viscount of Rio Branco.

First telephones installed in Brazil.

Brazilian Society Against Slavery founded.

1882 21 January. Martinho Campos cabinet (Liberal).

The affair of the "theft of the crown jewels."

Death of Gobineau.

1883 3 July. Paranaguá cabinet (Liberal).

Abolitionist Confederation established.

Castro Alves's *Os escravos* and Joaquim Nabuco's *O abolicionismo* published.

1884 March. Slavery abolished in Ceará.

6 June. Dantas cabinet (Liberal).

July. Slavery abolished in Amazonas.

1885 6 May. Saraiva cabinet (Liberal).

20 August. Cotegipe cabinet; Conservatives return to power.

Another outbreak of cholera in Rio de Janeiro.

1886 Society for the Promotion of Immigration founded.

1887 30 June. The emperor leaves on his third journey abroad; Princess Isabel is regent.

Brazil's first railroad, in Espírito Santo.

The Roman Catholic Church announces that it favors the abolition of slavery.

1888 10 March. João Alfredo cabinet (Conservative).

13 May. Slavery is abolished in Brazil.

22 August. Dom Pedro returns to Brazil.

1889 Brazil participates in the Universal Exhibition in Paris.

7 June. The Liberals return to power. Ouro Preto cabinet.

15 June. Attempt made on Dom Pedro II's life.

9 November. The ball on the Ilha Fiscal.

15 November. Proclamation of the republic.

17 November. The imperial family is banished.

7 December. The imperial family arrives in Portugal.

28 December. Death of the empress Teresa Cristina.

1890 Official decree of banishment.

20 January. Competition for a republican national anthem.

Missões treaty between Brazil and Argentina.

Constituent Assembly is convened.

15 September. Elections for federal constituent assemblies.

15 November. Constituent Assembly opens.

1891 14 January. Death of the countess of Barral.

20 January. Crisis in the government of Marshal Deodoro da Fonseca; resignation of the first Republican cabinet.

14 February. Constitution of the United States of Brazil is promulgated.

25 February. Deodoro is elected president and Floriano Peixoto vice president.

3 November. Deodoro decrees the congress closed.

5 December. Death of Dom Pedro in Paris.

1892 22 August. Death of Deodoro da Fonseca.

1893 Outbreak of Federalist rebellion in Rio Grande do Sul.

3 September. Prudente de Morais becomes candidate to the presidential succession.

6 September. The naval revolt in Rio de Janeiro.

25 September. A state of siege is proclaimed in four states of the federation and in the Federal District (Rio de Janeiro).

1894 Brazil breaks off diplomatic relations with Portugal.

1 March. Prudente de Morais is elected president.

1895 Prudente de Morais gives an amnesty to members of the army.

29 June. Death of Floriano Peixoto.

First expedition against Canudos.

1897 Brazilian Academy of Letters founded.

Second and third expedition against Canudos.

Destruction of Canudos.

1898 Campos Sales elected president of Brazil.

1900 Start of the *Política dos Governadores*, of the "Coffee-and-Milk Republic," in which the most powerful state oligarchies monopolize power.

1902 1 March. Rodrigues Alves elected president.

1904 November. The Vaccine Revolt.

1905 15 November. Afonso Pena elected president.

1908 Death of Machado de Assis.

1909 14 June. Death of Afonso Pena; Nilo Peçanha becomes president.

1910 End of the monarchy in Portugal.

November. *Revolta da chibata* (Whip Revolt, against corporal punishment in the navy).

15 November. Hermes da Fonseca becomes president.

1914 Hermes da Fonseca asks for a state of siege in Rio de Janeiro.

Venceslau Brás becomes president.

1916 Venceslau Brás approves the Historical and Geographical Institute's proposal that Dom Pedro's and Teresa Cristina's bodies be returned to Brazil in 1922.

1917 Brazil enters the world war.

General strike in São Paulo.

1918 17 January. Death of president-elect Rodrigues Alves.

25 February. Epitácio Pessoa becomes president.

1920 3 September. Royal family allowed to enter Brazil.
1922 Centenary of Brazil's independence.
      Arrival of the bodies of the emperor and empress.
      1 March. Artur da Silva Bernardes is elected president.
      5 July. Insurrections of the Copacabana Fort and the Military School.
1925 2 December. Centenary of Dom Pedro II's birth is celebrated.
1939 5 December. The mortuary chapel in Petrópolis is opened, in the presence of
      Getúlio Vargas.

Archival Sources and Their Abbreviations

ACRJ   City of Rio de Janeiro Archive
AN   National Archive
APESP   São Paulo State Public Archive
BM   Mazarine Library (Paris)
BMMA   Mário de Andrade Municipal Library
BNP   National Library, Paris
CAT   André de Toral Collection
CCABL   Caio Augusto P. Lucchesi Collection
CEA   Emanoel Araújo Collection
CEJH   Ambassador João Hermes Collection
CGJM   Guita and José Mindlin Collection
CGMS   Gilda de Mello e Sousa Collection
CMPR   Manuel Paula Ramos Collection
CPCL   Pedro Correa do Lago Collection
CPGOB   Dom Pedro Gastão de Orléans e Bragança Collection
CRV   Roger Viollet Collection (Paris)
FBN   National Library Foundation (Brazil)
FMCM   Castro Maya Museums Foundation (Rio de Janeiro)
FMLOA   Maria Luísa and Oscar Americano Collection
IEB   Brazilian Studies Institute of the University of Sãn Paulo
IHGB   Brazilian Historical and Geographic Institute
IPHAN   Institute of the National Historical and Artistic Heritage (Rio de Janeiro)
MASP   São Paulo Art Gallery
MB   British Museum (London)
MHN   National Historical Museum (Brazil)
MI   Museum of the Itamaraty
MIP   Imperial Museum of Petrópolis
MIS   Museum of Image and Sound (São Paulo)
MMP   Mariano Procópio Museum
MNBA   National Gallery of Fine Art
MP   São Paulo Museum, University of São Paulo
MR   Museum of the Republic
NPG   National Portrait Gallery (London)
RGPL   Royal Portuguese Reading Room
RMM   Roberto Menezes de Moraes Collection

Notes

PREFACE

1. From the several variants of this myth, I have chosen the Canela tribe's version, collected by Nimuendaju and J. Schultz and quoted in DaMatta, *Ensaios de antropologia estrutural*, and have somewhat rewritten and abridged it. For an analysis of the myth, see DaMatta, 20–23.

2. Manuela Carneiro da Cunha, in her essay "Lógica do mito e da ação — O movimento messiânico canela de 1963," in *Antropologia do Brasil*, takes up Lévi-Strauss's debate about the relationship between myths and rituals. In the 1963 uprising involving the Ramkokumekra-Canela tribes in the state of Maranhão, a version of this same myth about the origin of the white man was reenacted as events unfolded. In this case, Aukê's sister was at the center of the story. Lévi-Strauss himself, in *The Story of Lynx*, takes up the Aukê myth and shows how all the versions, no matter what the variations, insist on "the marvelous aspect of a pregnancy during which the child in the womb talks with his mother, the son of Maíra-Ata amongst the Tupinambás; or, better still, comes out of his mother's womb and returns to it when he wants to"(59). The frightening aspect of the character recurs in the various narratives, and he returns in the guise of several animals. Lévi-Strauss says: "Thanks to his magical powers, whose origins we do not know, Aukê revives or, apparently untouched by the fire, reappears as the lord of the white man's treasures" (59).

3. See Reis, "Quilombos e revoltas escravas no Brasil," 24.

4. Avé-Lallemant, *Viagens*, 22.

5. Silva, "O Brasil," 197.

6. Verger, *Fluxo e refluxo*, 8. Manuela Carneiro da Cunha analyzes another case of freed Brazilian slaves going back to Africa during the nineteenth century and setting up a community in Lagos, where they were known as "the Brazilians." Cunha, *Negros estrangeiros*.

7. Reis, "Quilombos e revoltas escravas no Brasil," 32.

8. Freyre, "Dom Pedro II, imperador cinzento."

9. See Madariaga, *Bolívar*. According to Francisco Iglésias, Bolívar, who began as openly republican, little by little adopted monarchist measures. See Iglésias, *Trajetória política*. This was also the case of the constitution proposed for Bolivia in May 1862, which advocated an almost hereditary form of continuity in power.

10. Ibid., 121.

11. Bonifácio, José, *Notas íntimas*, 93.

12. Eric Hobsbawm, in *The Invention of Tradition*, notes that at moments of rupture "new traditions are invented, sufficiently widespread and speedy changes occur, either on the side of supply or that of demand," p. 11. Arno Mayer makes the point about the power of imperial symbols in *The Force of Tradition*. It was only at the end of World War I that a new society less tied to the system of court privileges and etiquette began to be glimpsed in Europe.

13. Candido, "O romantismo," 53. Carvalho, in *A formação das almas*, calls attention to these same elements of Brazilian patriotic symbolism. He points out that the flag raised on 15 November 1889, the day of the proclamation of the Brazilian Republic, was inspired by the United States' model. It had green and yellow horizontal stripes and, at top left, a square with a black background sprinkled with white stars. It had been made by members of the Lopes Trovão Club, named after a Republican. The Positivists questioned its political origins, arguing in favor of links between past and present. Green and yellow were therefore kept, as well as forms and elements like the stars and the cross.

14. Candido, "O romantismo," 54.

15. Holanda, *Raízes do Brasil*, 132.

16. See Sahlins, *Historical Metaphors*.

17. This book has benefited from material gathered and interpretations offered by students who have been working with me since 1994. Alessandra El Far (with a Fundação de Apoio à Pesquisa do Estado de São Paulo scholarship, 1994) analyzed the newspapers of the time. Luciana Cestari (FAPESP scholarship, 1994) worked on the reviews of the Instituto Histórico e Geográfico Brasileiro. Stélio Marras (Conselho Nacional de Pesquisa scholarship, 1995) studied the society of the court. Valéria Mendonça de Macedo (CNPq scholarship, 1995–96) did research on the world of popular festivals and celebrations. Fernando Frochtengarten (CNPq scholarship, 1996) analyzed the personality of Dom Pedro II. Paula Miraglia (FAPESP scholarship, 1996) worked on the Universal Exhibitions. Ângela Marques da Costa (CNPq scholarship, 1995–96) studied the Brazilian nobility and the royal palaces and houses. And Paula Pinto e Silva, in a recent study entitled "Entre tampas e panelas" (Among Pots and Pans), has been carrying out an original survey on colonial cookery and standards of conduct. Finally, Inês de Castro, of the Laboratory of Social Anthropology of the University of São Paulo, provided continuous, fundamental help in the reproduction of photos and images.

1. "THE EMPEROR'S NEW CLOTHES"

1. This version of Hans Christian Andersen's famous story, probably written in about 1835, is in Andersen, *The Complete Fairy Tales and Stories*.

2. See Elias, *The Court Society*, 38, 85, 88.

3. See Kantorowicz, *King's Two Bodies*, 37; and Candido, *Ética*, 92.

4. Bloch, *The Royal Touch*, 242, 243.

5. Barbey, *Âtre roi*, 10.

6. Lévi-Strauss, *Structural Anthropology*, 193–214.

7. See Geertz, *Local Knowledge*, 124, and Geertz, *Negara*, 139. Other scholars have also underlined the importance of the theatrical aspect of rituals, notably Johan Huizinga in *Homo Ludens*.

8. Ribeiro, A *última razão dos reis*, 9.

9. Burke, *Fabrication of Louis XIV*, 19. Although he says that the construction of a king's public image by the prince, his court, and the larger community is a widespread phenomenon, he understands the reception of the public image merely as consumption by an audience of onlookers. For example, he says that "the communicators of the time had three targets in particular: the French upper classes, posterity and foreigners," and he does an important survey of those with access to the crown's messages. The challenge remains to understand how a people as a whole absorbed these messages.

2. AN EMPIRE IS BORN IN THE TROPICS

1. According to Raymundo Faoro in *Os donus do poder*, prominent among the administrative services created in Brazil after 1808 were the Council of State, superior councils for the armed forces and judiciary, a police department for Rio and one for Brazil, as well as the Royal Exchequer, the Council of the Treasury, and the Brazilian Military Archive.

2. "At the beginning of the nineteenth century the Spanish colonies were administratively divided into four viceroyalties; four captaincies-general by midcentury had been transformed into seventeen independent countries. By contrast, the eighteen captaincies-general of the Portuguese colony of 1820 . . . already formed a single independent country in 1825, once the Confederation of the Equator [a separatist movement in the northeast] had been defeated." Carvalho, A *construção da ordem*, 11, 20.

3. Salles, "Nostalgia imperial," 74.

4. Naves, A *forma difícil*, 35, 44.

5. Debret, *Viagem pitoresca e histórica ao Brasil*, 326. Debret was criticized some years later by members of the Brazilian Historical and Geographical Institute, who agreed with the official iconography but disliked the way he had represented slavery. The official image of an empire that was "indigenous," not African, was already beginning.

6. Ibid., 327–29.

7. Salles, "Nostalgia imperial," 74.

8. It was not the first time that a Native American figure was associated with Brazil. The whole continent had been represented in this manner in the sixteenth century. In Chinese fans sent to Portugal's constituent assemblies in 1820, the then Brazilian colony was linked to the image of its indigenous population. Some years later, in the 2 July 1823 uprising in Bahia, the empire was portrayed as a Native American. Naves, 37.

9. Karasch, *Slave Life*, 335.

3. THE NATION'S ORPHAN

1. DaMatta, *Carnavais, malandros*, 191. A poem published in *A Luz da Verdade* (The Light of Truth) on the occasion of Dom Pedro II's sixtieth birthday, 2 December 1885, is interesting in this context: "The second of December is wondrous / for D. Pedro was born and is the sacred pledge / of his beloved people."

2. Celso, *Oito anos*, 197.

3. From a letter to Bom Schaffer, quoted in Calmon, *História de D. Pedro II*, 14.

4. Dona Amélia, letter of 25 April 1831. The same idea was put across in newspapers: "The innocent imperial child, sustained by the Love and Honor of Brazilians," *Aurora Fluminense* called him, 18 July 1831. "The orphan emperor, beloved child of the nation," said *Correio Paulistano*, 26 October 1832.

5. *Aurora Fluminense*, 11 April 1831.

6. *Cultura Política*, 1942.

7. Tobias Montero Collection, Brazilian National Library.

8. Tobias Montero Collection, 1834, Brazilian National Library.

9. Caldeira, *Mauá*, p. 148.

4. THE LITTLE BIG KING

1. *Aurora Fluminense*, 18 January 1838.

2. *A Regeneração*, 18 August 1840.

3. *A Phenix*, 19 August 1840.

4. An excellent summary of the electoral process can be found in Graham, *Patronage and Politics*.

5. *Disposições para a sagração de S. M. o imperador*. Ângela Marques da Costa ("Pedra e poder") assisted in the research on this "ritual of the majority."

6. Quoted in Calmon, *História do Brasil na poesia do povo*, 191.

7. Papers concerning the consecration and coronation of Dom Pedro II, Fundo Casa Imperial, National Archive.

8. "Descrição do edifício construído para a solenidade da coroação e sagração de S.M. o imperador o senhor D. Pedro II," in *Publicações do Arquivo Nacional*, 1925.

9. Conde de Valença Collection, Museu Paulista.

10. Newspapers of the time all described the ceremony in minute detail. See the *Jornal do Commercio*, 15 July 1841.

11. Ms. I, 1, 19, 28, National Library.

12. Cited in Lyra, *História de Dom Pedro II*, 740.

5. THE GREAT EMPEROR

1. Letters from Dom Pedro II to Paulo Barbosa, n.d., 1842, and 26 February 1863, National Library.

2. Paulo Barbosa, Tobias Montero Collection, National Library.

3. *A Phenix*, 13 April 1843.

4. Tobias Montero Collection, National Library.

5. Lyra, *História de D. Pedro II*, 2:109; Soublin, *O defensor*, 54.

6. Sodré, *Abrindo um cofre*, 11.

7. Caldeira, *Mauá*, 194.

6. LIFE AT COURT

1. Alencastro, "Le commerce," 494.

2. Ibid., 502.

3. Attitudes of specialists on these topics vary. For Luiz Felipe de Alencastro, the object of the Land Law was to expel small subsistence farmers and prevent the acquisition of land by future immigrants. "Le commerce," 530. José Murilo de Carvalho argues, in *A construção da ordem* and *Teatro de sombras*, that on the contrary the point was to sell public land to attract immigrants and slowly substitute free for slave labor. He shows how the Land Law approved on 18 September 1850 dragged along until the end of the empire, with the government unable to overcome resistance to it, and, as a consequence, how the main aim of the law, bringing immigrants to Brazil who were more attracted to the United States, failed. *A construção da ordem*, 303–22.

4. See Caldeira, *Mauá*, 241.

5. See Carvalho, *A construção da ordem*, 316. A future of immigrant labor was assured only in the 1870s, when the government started to finance it, taking the exclusive responsibility for this away from the plantation owners. See Holanda's introduction to Davatz, *Memórias de um colono no Brasil*.

6. Alencastro, "Le commerce," 515.

7. Caldeira, *Mauá*, 262.

8. Lyra, *História de D. Pedro II*, vol. III, p. 12.

9. One can get a better idea of the high prices in Rio if one contrasts them with the daily earnings of street saleswomen in São Paulo, which varied in the second half of the century, between 280 and 350 réis; male carpenters, tailors, and soldiers got 600 réis a day. See Dias, *Quotidiano e poder em São Paulo do século XIX*, 73.

10. Lyra, *História de D. Pedro II*, 63.

11. Alencar, *A pata da gazela*, 13, 17.

12. Assis, *Histórias sem data*, 118, 120.

13. Pinho, *Salões e damas*, 125.

14. Alencar, *O tronco do ipê*, 14, 114, 133.

15. Mattos, *O tempo saquarema*, 51.

16. Pinho, *Salões e damas*, 96.

17. Pena, *Comédias*, 73–74.

18. Ibid., 45, 78, 255, 44.

19. Ibid., 25, 141.

20. Pinho, *Salões e damas*, 5, 10.

21. Tobias Montero Collection, National Library.

22. Pena, *Comédias*, 46.

23. Assis, *Relíquias de Casa Velha*, 17, 27.

24. Alencastro, *História da vida privada*, 2:13. According to Alencastro, other Brazilian cities had an even larger proportion of slaves. In Niterói, in 1833, four-fifths of the population were slaves; in Campos 59 percent.

25. *Life and Times*, 103.

26. See Carvalho, *A construção da ordem*, 104, 84.

27. Ibid., 210.

28. Ibid., 56.

29. Ibid., 77.

30. Ibid., 49.

31. Lyra, *História de D. Pedro II*, 1:78.

32. Celso, *Oito anos*, 21.

33. Assis, *The Psychiatrist and Other Stories*, 120.

34. Mattos, *O tempo saquarema*, 103, 105.

35. Carvalho, *A construção da ordem*, 186. The Progressive Party came into being around 1864, made up of dissident conservatives and traditional liberals; it dissolved in 1868 when one section of its representatives formed the new Liberal Party.

36. Carvalho, *A construção da ordem*, 374.

37. From 1858 on, the two parties governed alternately: Dom Pedro II manipulated the situation, using the pendulum swings to maintain his authority over everybody. Dom Pedro ruled from 1858 to 1862 with the ministries of the viscount of Abaeté (12 December 1858), Ferraz (10 August 1859), and Caxias (2 March 1861). During this last ministry, several Conservatives allied themselves to the Liberal Party and assured its rise to power: Zacarias, Olinda, Nabuco, Saraiva, and others. The Liberals governed from 1862 to 1868 with the ministries of Zacarias de Góis e Vasconcelos (24 May 1862), marquis of Olinda (31 May 1862), Zacarias (15 January 1864), Furtado (31 August 1864), Olinda (12 May 1865), and Zacarias (3 August 1866). The Conservatives returned in 1868–78 with the ministries of the viscount of Itboraí (16 July 1868), marquis of São Vicente (21 September 1870), viscount of Rio Branco (7 March 1871), and duke of Caxias (25 March 1875). The Liberals governed in 1878–85 with the ministries of Sinimbu (5 January 1878), Saraiva (28 March 1880), Martinho de Campos (21 January 1882), Lafayette (24 March 1883), Paranaguá (3 July 1883), Dantas (6 June 1884), and Saraiva (6 May 1885). From 1885 to 1889, there were two Conservative ministries: those of the baron of Cotegipe (20 August 1885) and of Councilor João Alfredo (10 March 1888). On 7 June 1889, the Liberals returned, with the ministry of the viscount of Ouro Preto. In Richard Graham's opinion, clientelism began with the emperor himself: "He took a place atop the 'great pyramid,' as one jurist called it, by appointing the Cabinet . . . From 1840 to 1889 Pedro II, always with the advice of the Council of State, dismissed Parliament eleven times; and seven Parliaments served their full four-year terms. A total of eighteen national elections thus took place during his reign." *Patronage and Politics in Nineteenth-Century Brazil*, 79.

38. Celso, *Oito anos*, 114.

39. In his observations, Afonso Arinos de Melo Franco described the inside of the building: "The main chamber was a large room with an arcade, supported by pillars reach-

ing to the ceiling, and capable of holding 200 or 300 people. In each corner were four special tribunes, and below them four more, with a table for stenographers, who could see and hear everything that happened. The deputies sat on two semicircular rows of benches . . . At the back, high up, one could see the throne, with the arms of the empire above it. When the emperor was not there, as he usually was not, it was kept covered by curtains of the canopy. In front of and below the throne was the table where the president of the council sat, flanked by the secretaries." A Câmara dos Deputados, 63.

40. Celso, Oito anos, 123.

41. This copy of Magalhães's poem was in Dom Pedro's personal library; it is now in the Museu Mariano Procópio.

7. "A MONARCH IN THE TROPICS"

1. A Ilustração Luso-Brasileira (1858), 258.

2. Revista do Instituto Histórico e Geográfico Brasilicero, vol. 1 (1839), 68.

3. Revista do Instituto Histórico e Geográfico Brasilicero, vol. 2 (1839), 561, 574–82.

4. See Candido, "O romantismo," 12. The intellectual context was certainly characterized by ambiguity. An early emphasis in Revista Niterói on the question of slavery was replaced by official statements about Indianism. This is an important clue to how a "literary policy" was constructed.

5. See Amoroso, "Mudanças de hábito"; Cunha, "Política indigenista" and "Legislação indigenista"; and finally Miriam Dolhnikoff, "O projeto nacional de José Bonifácio."

6. See Puntoni, "Gonçalves de Magalhães e a historiografia do império."

7. Magalhães, A Confederação dos Tamoyos, 76.

8. Ibid., 180–81, 181, 183.

9. Ibid., 197.

10. Ibid., 325.

11. Ibid., 328.

12. Dias, Poesias completas, 522.

13. Ibid., 525.

14. Alencar, Iracema, 84. On Alencar's position on slavery, see Carvalho, Pontos e bordados, 54.

15. Alencar, Iracema, 175.

16. Alencar, Ubirajara, 11.

17. Ibid., 12.

18. Alencar, O Guarani, 27. A stimulating analysis of O Guarani can be found in Carvalho, Pontos e bordados, 91.

19. Alencar, O Guarani, 97, 45, 218, 280, 285.

20. Ibid., 157.

21. Puntoni, "Gonçalves de Magalhães e a história do império," 129.

22. Magalhães, A Confederação dos Tamoyos, 353, 353–54.

23. Alencastro, "L'Empire du Brésil," 307.

24. Recent specialized treatments of this subject disagree with this dichotomy of academicism and the Baroque. But what happened above all, with the coming of the

Academy, was the imposition of a new model in which the individual was given more importance. See, among others, Montes, O universo mágico do barroco brasileiro.

25. Caldeira, Mauá, 20.

26. Cited in Revista da Semana, 28 November 1925.

27. Pedro II, Diario de 1861.

8. HOW TO BE BRAZILIAN NOBILITY

1. The number of titled people in the Brazilian Empire is still the subject of discussion. In 1918 the subject was dealt with by Baron Smith de Vasconcellos in Arquivo nobi- liárquico brasileiro, where he gives the figure of 1,029. This pioneering calculation was revised twice: in volume 6 of Anuário do Museu Imperial in 1945, and in Revista do Ar- quivo Municipal de São Paulo in 1939. In 1960 Carlos Rheingantz carried out another survey: he claims that 1,221 noble titles were given out by the two emperors and the princess as regent. Zuquete, Nobreza de Portugal e do Brasil, lists 1,200; in Exposição de Modelos de Brasão e Cartas de Fidalguia, 960. Tostes, Princípios de heráldica (120) writes of 1,211 nobles: three dukes, forty-seven marquises, fifty-one counts, one hun- dred forty-six viscounts with grandeza, eighty-nine viscounts without grandeza, 135 barons with grandeza, and 740 barons without grandeza. Here we follow the survey by the National Archive in Rio de Janeiro.

2. Castro, Memória sobre a nobreza no Brasil, 93.

3. Elias, The Court Society, 85.

4. Silva, O Chalaça—Memórias, 96.

5. Quoted in Lyra, História de D. Pedro II, 1:82.

6. In Portugal there were three kings at arms, for Portugal, Algarve, and India; in 1814 kings at arms for America, Asia, and Africa were introduced.

7. Félix José da Silva, who had been a sweeper in the royal palaces and was a master car- penter, was passavante under Dom João VI and was present when he was acclaimed: he was also chief herald at the coronations of Dom Pedro I and Dom Pedro II. He was followed by José Maria da Silva Rodrigues, Manuel dos Santos Carramona, and Ernesto Aleixo Boulanger (appointed on a temporary basis but lasting until the end of the empire).

8. Decree 7540 of 15 November 1879.

9. Criminal Code of 1830 (Law of 16 December), IV, VII, Articles 301 and 302: ten to sixty days' imprisonment and a fine corresponding to half that time. Law 2033 of 20 Sep- tember 1871.

10. Tostes, "Estrutura familiar e simbologia na nobreza brasonada," 101.

11. Holanda, Raízes do Brasil, 122.

12. Lago, Nobiliarquia brasileira, 7.

13. Ibid., 16.

14. Assis, Esaú e Jacó, 59–60.

15. Lyra, História de D. Pedro II, 1:152.

16. Tostes, Princípios de heráldica, 83.

17. Data compiled from Zuquete, Nobreza de Portugal e do Brasil.

18. According to Lacombe, *Uma cerimônia na corte*, 62, the rules were not widely known, there were no official or private publications on the subject, and officials in the department of heraldry at the nobility registry were few and badly informed. The *Almanak Laemmert* in 1888 advertised the services of Leopoldo Heck, heraldic painter and engraver to the imperial house, with premises at the Rua da Assembléia, 36.

19. The use of symbols exclusive to the emperor was prohibited: coffee branches and tobacco leaves embracing the shield, the scepter, and the hand of Justice. Even so, a gentleman of the imperial household, Teodoro Teixeira Gomes, got permission in 1878 to put a new quarter on his escutcheon with the branches inverted. The same branches also appeared in the arms of Manuel Luís Ribeiro, baron of Castelo, in 1882.

20. Holanda, *Raízes do Brasil*, 32.

21. Carvalho, *A construção da ordem*, 238.

22. Holanda, *O Brasil monárquico*, 4:332.

23. Silva, *Life and Times*, 40.

24. Roquete, *Código do bom-tom*, 69.

25. Ibid., 36, 203, 205.

26. Ibid., 110.

27. Horace, *Code de la conversation*, 68.

28. Roquete, *Código do bom-tom*, 79.

29. Horace, *Code de la conversation*, 212.

30. Ibid., 284.

31. Roquete, *Código do bom-tom*, 285–87.

9. DOM PEDRO'S RESIDENCES

1. Elias, *The Court Society*, 54.

2. Articles 114 and 115, Chapter III, *Constituição política do Império do Brasil* (25 March 1824).

3. In 1743 the work carried out by the engineer José Fernandes Alpoim, on the orders of the governor of the captaincy of Rio de Janeiro, Gomes Freire de Andrade, the count of Bobadela, was finished: this was the new Governors' House, which had the look of a Portuguese aristocratic mansion. In 1763, when the seat of government moved from Bahia to Rio de Janeiro, this house became the Palace of the Viceroys. At this time, the construction of the quay, all of hewn stone, with three flights of steps going down to the water, was undertaken, as well as the new public fountain, the work of Mestre Valentim da Fonseca e Silva, which supplied the ships and nearby houses and is still there in the present-day Praça Quinze de Novembro. After the proclamation of the republic, the palace was used as the headquarters of the postal and telegraph service. In 1938 it was made a listed building by Brazilian National Heritage. Restored between 1982 and 1985, it is now a cultural center.

4. Coaracy, *Memórias da cidade do Rio de Janeiro*, 18.

5. A report by Carlos Schlichthorst, who lived in Brazil between 1824 and 1826.

6. Decree of 24 August 1840, Articles 2, 3 and 4. Doc. 50, pc. 3, box 12, National Archive.

7. Doc. 60, pc. 6, box 12, National Archive.

8. Dom Pedro II Collection, I–35, 10, 41, National Library.

9. Doc. 34, pc. 1, box 13, National Archive.

10. Doc. 87A, pc. 6, box 12, Fundo Casa Imperial, National Archive.

11. Doc. 25, pc. 1, box 13, Fundo Casa Imperial, National Archive.

12. Doc. 871, pc. 6, box 12, National Archive.

13. I–35, 6, 76, National Library.

14. *Inventário do imperial Paço da Cidade e Tesouro em 1854.* This document belongs to Dom Pedro Gastão de Orléans e Bragança and is cited in Ferrez, *O Paço da cidade do Rio de Janeiro.* A similar document, predating Dom Pedro II's reign, is the inventory done in 1831, which also describes each of the rooms of the palace, its function and use, the furniture, objets d'art, and utensils. Code 572, doc. 42, National Archive.

15. The data on the changes and remodelings of the palace are contradictory and incomplete, but I have tried to provide a chronological outline of the best-known alterations. The data given here have been taken principally from Lima and Auler, *Paço de São Cristóvão,* and Lyra, *História de Dom Pedro II.*

16. Dória, "Reminiscências do palácio de São Cristovam."

17. Santos, *O leilão do Paço de São Cristóvão.*

18. "Alegrias e tristezas" (Joys and Sorrows), quoted in Lyra, *História de Dom Pedro II,* vol. 1.

19. The details of the imperial calendar come from Barros, "Reminiscências de há 50 annos."

20. See Gama, "História da imperial Fazenda de Santa Cruz."

21. "Priests should not be forced to undress in the Refectory to be beaten, since this is against decency; if it has to be done, it should be done in their cells, by the order of the Provincial." Freitas, *Santa Cruz,* 1:34.

22. Gama, "História da imperial Fazenda de Santa Cruz," 211.

23. Ibid.

24. Lyra, *História de Dom Pedro II,* 1:287.

25. *O Paiz,* 10 October 1908, quoted in Freitas, *Santa Cruz,* 1:140.

26. Graham, *Diário de uma viagem ao Brasil.*

27. Freitas, *Santa Cruz,* 1:129, 130.

28. The most famous of the teachers were Father José Maurício and the Portuguese brothers Marcos and Simão Portugal. Afterward, when the band was reorganized, other directors stood out: Inácio Pinheiro da Silva, who carried out the reorganization, Carlos José Maria, João Targine das Chagas (1849), Francisco de Sant'Ana (1852), José Joaquim Goiano, and Joaquim de Araújo Cintra (1856). From 1860 to 1862 a so-called master slave conducted the band; in 1864 the conductor was José Martins Leandro Filgueiras. In 1872 Joaquim Antônio da Silva Gandres was in charge: he was also the conductor of the orchestra and staged Carlos Gomes's opera *O Guarani* at the Fazenda de Santa Cruz. Manuel dos Santos Ventura took over in 1875.

29. M. D. Horner (1841–42), quoted in Ferrez, *O Paço da cidade do Rio de Janeiro.*

30. Freitas, *Santa Cruz,* 1:151.

31. Alencar, *O tronco do ipê,* 100.

32. Marquis of Itanhaém, *Contas dadas à Assembléia Geral.*

33. *Relatório da Comissão de Contas—1837,* National Library.

34. *Registro de escravos da imperial Fazenda de Santa Cruz alugados a diversos e a si, que devem seus aluguéis*—1862–1868, National Archive.

35. Cited in Fernandes, "Petrópolis em 1844."

36. Cited in Lacombe, *Paulo Barbosa e a fundação*, 39. Barbosa held the chief stewardship of the imperial household from 1833 to 1846, then, as we have seen, took a diplomatic post in Europe; he became chief steward again in 1855 and held the post until his death in 1868.

37. *Representação feita à Assembléia Constituinte e Legislativa do Império em 1823.*

38. Lacombe, *Paulo Barbosa e a fundação*, 58.

39. "Príncipe Dom Pedro diz que enfiteuse não é privilégio," *Jornal do Brasil*, 7 September 1975.

40. Cited in Rabaço, *História de Petrópolis*, 93.

41. Auler, *A construção do Palácio de Petrópolis*.

42. Paupério, "O governo municipal."

43. Elias, *The Court Society*, 42–43.

44. Dom Pedro II, letter to Paulo Barbosa, 1866, drawer 4, National Library.

45. Tobias Montero Collection, National Library.

46. Magalhães letter to Barbosa, 8 April 1851, Tobias Montero Collection, National Library.

47. Minutes of the 6th Ordinary Session of the Town Council of Petrópolis, 16 March 1872.

48. *O Futuro* [literary periodical], 1867, Museu Mariano Procópio.

49. Newspapers cited in Sodré, *Aspectos da vida municipal*, 87, 89.

50. *O Mercantil*, 1889.

51. Pinho, *Salões e damas*, 121.

10. THE EMPIRE OF FESTIVALS AND THE FESTIVALS OF THE EMPIRE

1. Koster, *Travels in Brazil*, 4–5.

2. For a wider view of the work of Spix and Martius, see Lisboa, "A nova Atlântida."

3. Spix and Martius, *Viagem pelo Brasil*, 1:248.

4. Ibid.

5. Seidler, *Dez anos no Brasil*, 223.

6. Ibid., 304, 306.

7. Kidder, *Sketches of Travels and Residence*, 1:55–56, 61.

8. Coaracy, *Memórias da cidade do Janeiro*, 49–50.

9. Kidder, *Sketches of Travels and Residence*, 2:372.

10. Ibid., 2:145.

11. Koseritz, *Imagens do Brasil*, 176–77.

12. Fletcher and Kidder, *Brazil and the Brazilians*, 100–101.

13. Kidder, *Sketches of Travels and Residence*, 2:127–28.

14. Spix and Martius, *Viagem pelo Brasil*, 1:152.

15. Fletcher and Kidder, *Brazil and the Brazilians*, 146, 151–52.

16. Kidder, *Sketches of Travels and Residence*, 2:184–85.

17. Koster, *Travels in Brazil*, 410–11.

18. Kidder, *Sketches of Travels and Residence*, 2:96.

19. Ibid., 184.

20. Andrade, *Danças dramáticas do Brasil*, 19.

21. Koster, *Travels in Brazil*, 35.

22. Fletcher and Kidder, *Brazil and the Brazilians*, 107–8.

23. Koster, *Travels in Brazil*, 242–43.

24. Spix and Martius, *Viagem pelo Brasil*, 1:66.

25. Koster, *Travels in Brazil*, 174.

26. Ibid., 202–3.

27. Seidler, *Dez anos no Brasil*, 45–46.

28. Koster, *Travels in Brazil*, 226–27.

29. Moraes, *Festas e tradições*, 47, 49–50.

30. Fletcher and Kidder, *Brazil and the Brazilians*, 74.

31. Seidler, *Dez anos no Brasil*, 42.

32. Habsburg, *Bahia 1860*, 128–31.

33. Spix and Martius, *Viagem pelo Brasil*, 1:152.

34. Koseritz, *Imagens do Brasil*, 69–70.

35. Fletcher and Kidder, *Brazil and the Brazilians*, 156–57.

36. Moraes, *Festas e tradições*, 69.

37. Luis da Câmara Cascudo, introduction to Moraes, *Festas e tradições*, 43.

38. Coaracy, *Memórias da cidade do Rio de Janeiro*, 149–50.

39. Fletcher and Kidder, *Brazil and the Brazilians*, 155.

40. Moraes, *Festas e tradições*, 39–40, 42–44.

41. Ibid., 117–18, 126.

42. Spix and Martius, *Viagem pelo Brasil*, 2:46–47.

43. Ibid., 2:188–89.

44. Avé-Lallemant, *Viagens pelas províncias da Bahia*, 108–109.

45. Koster, *Travels in Brazil*, 332–33.

46. Romero, *Cantos populares do Brasil*, 1:53–54, quoted in Rabaçal, *As congadas do Brasil*, 64–65.

47. A note in Koster, *Travels in Brazil*, 331–32.

48. Seidler, *Dez anos no Brasil*, 204.

49. Spix and Martius, *Viagem pelo Brasil*, 1:160.

50. Seidler, *Dez anos no Brasil*, 237.

51. Fletcher and Kidder, *Brazil and the Brazilians*, 30.

52. Spix and Martius, *Viagem pelo Brasil*, 2:67.

53. Coaracy, *Memórias da cidade do Rio de Janeiro*, 132.

54. Koster, *Travels in Brazil*, 203.

55. Ibid., 203–5.

56. Fletcher and Kidder, *Brazil and the Brazilians*, 148–49.

57. Moraes, *Festas e tradições*, 34.

58. Cunha, "Você me conhece."

59. Dom Pedro II and Countess of Barral Collection, National Library.

60. Koster, *Travels in Brazil*, 273.
61. According to Cascudo, there are innumerable references in Portugal to this festival: "Teófilo Braga (*O povo português nos seus costumes, crenças e tradições*, Lisbon 1885, 2:313) tells us of the election of a king of the Congo in a popular festival in Portugal. João Pedro Ribeiro tells of a festival of Our Lady of the Rosary, popular in Oporto." Câmara Cascudo, in Koster, *Travels in Brazil*, 365.
62. Spix and Martius, *Viagem pelo Brasil*, 2:46, 48.
63. Moraes, *Festas e tradições*, 226, 228.
64. Avé-Lallemant, *Viagens pelas províncias da Bahia*, 48.
65. Rabaçal, *As congadas do Brasil*, 80–81, citing Artur Ramos, *Folclore negro no Brasil* (Rio de Janeiro/São Paulo: Livraria Casa do Estudante do Brasil, 1954). Ramos found the documents in the Angolan Archives in Luanda, in the Museu de Angola, and in the Office of the National Press, October 1944, 2d Series, vol. 2, no. 8, 142.
66. Andrade, *Danças dramáticas do Brasil*, 20.
67. Koseritz, *Imagens do Brasil*, 150.
68. Moraes, *Festas e tradições*, 311–12.
69. Ibid., 301. King Obá is the subject of an excellent study by Eduardo Silva, *Prince of the People: The Life and Times of a Brazilian Free Man of Colour*, trans. Moyra Ashford (Verso, 1993).
70. Ibid., 301.
71. Fletcher and Kidder, *Brazil and the Brazilians*, 135.
72. Koster, *Travels in Brazil*, 411.
73. Coaracy, *Memórias da cidade do Rio de Janeiro*, 371.
74. Kidder, *Sketches of Travels and Residence*, 2:148–50.
75. Spix and Martius, *Viagem pelo Brasil*, 1:248.
76. Carvalho, *Os bestializados*, 38.

II. THE PARAGUAYAN WAR

1. I am especially grateful for suggestions and criticisms from André Toral on this chapter. His studies of the Paraguayan war give a great deal of importance to the caricatures produced in newspapers and magazines in all the countries involved in the conflict. See *Adiós, chamigo brasileiro*.
2. Doratioto, *O conflito do Paraguai*, 7.
3. Lyra, *História de Dom Pedro II*, 1:207.
4. Nabuco, *Um estadista do império*, 98.
5. Lima, *O império brasileiro*, 69.
6. See the work of Júlio José Chiavenatto, among others.
7. For a more detailed analysis of these three interpretations see Doratioto, *O conflito do Paraguai*, and Brun, "La guerra de la Triple Alianza."
8. Lyra, *História de Dom Pedro II*, 1:235.
9. Doratioto, *O conflito do Paraguai*, 22.
10. See Salles, *Guerra do Paraguai*.
11. Assis, *Iaiá Garcia*, 27, 28.

12. Assis, *Relíquias da Casa Velha*, 56–68.

13. Assis, *Histórias sem data*, 127.

14. Tobias Montero Collection, National Library.

15. Dom Pedro II, letter to Paranaguá, National Library.

16. Imperial Museum of Petrópolis.

17. Ibid.

18. Doratioto, *O conflito do Paraguai*, 94.

19. Rosa, *La Guerra del Paraguay*, 216.

20. Tobias Montero Collection, National Library.

21. Sodré, *História militar do Brasil*, 137.

22. Lyra, *História de Dom Pedro II*, 2:164.

23. Besouchet, *Dom Pedro II e o século XIX*, 127.

24. The illustrated magazines and reviews, especially all the *Revista Ilustrada* of Ângelo Agostini, changed their posture during the war, following the popular mood. In the first year the *Revista* was jingoistic; later it criticized and made ironic comments on the Brazilian generals; finally, it praised the "brave Brazilian combatants." See Toral, *Adiós, chamigo brasileiro*.

25. Beards seem to have been a fundamental part of political culture. In 1881 a book appeared entitled *A barba em Portugal — Estudo de etnografia comparativa*, based on research about the forms and uses of beards.

12. A CITIZEN-MONARCH

1. Carvalho, *A construção da ordem*, 347.

2. Ibid., 290.

3. *Correio Paulistano*, 28 August 1870.

4. Ibid., 15 October 1869.

5. Morel, "Le roi, le peuple et la nation," 75.

6. Holanda, *O Brasil monárquico*, 5:78.

7. Cited in Torres, *A democracia coroada*, 102.

8. See Holanda, *O Brasil monárquico*, 5:69.

9. *Jornal do Commercio*, 19 March 1870.

10. Gilberto Freyre, "Dom Pedro II, imperador cizento de uma terra de sol tropical," in *O perfil de Euclides da Cunha e outros perfis*, 86.

11. Abreu, *A fabricação do imortal*, 62.

13. THE DAGUERREOTYPE REVOLUTION IN BRAZIL

1. See Vasquez, *Dom Pedro II e a fotografia*, 14.

2. Cited in Trachtenberg, *Classic Essays on Photography*, 37.

3. Ibid., 11.

4. On photography during Dom Pedro II's reign, see, among others, Vasquez, *Dom Pedro II e a fotografia*, and Mauad, "Imagem e auto-imagem."

5. Mauad, "Imagem e auto-imagem."

6. Besouchet, *Dom Pedro II e o século XIX*, 445.
7. Mauad, "Imagem e auto-imagem."

14. A MONARCH ON HIS TRAVELS

1. *Programma para o recebimento de Sus Majestades Imperiais no regresso de sua viagem às provincias de São Pedro, São Catarina e São Paulo*. Typographia Nacional 18 March 1846. Cód. 572, doc. 85, National Archive.
2. Eça de Queirós, *As Farpas*, February 1872, 72.
3. For detailed accounts of the journey, see Besouchet, *Dom Pedro II e o século XIX*, and Calmon, *História de Dom Pedro II*.
4. Cited in Besouchet, *Dom Pedro II e o século XIX*, 203.
5. Raeders, *Dom Pedro II e conde Gobineau*, 106. For more information on Gobineau's relationship with Brazil and Dom Pedro, see also Raeders, *Dom Pedro II e os sábios franceses*.
6. Gobineau, *Les Pléiades*, 303, 308.
7. Cited in Calmon, *História de Dom Pedro II*, 2:1072.
8. Besouchet, *Dom Pedro II e o século XIX*, 287. Telephones came to Brazil very early, in the 1880s.
9. Magalhães, *O selvagem*, 13.
10. Machado, "Para uma história da sensibilidade."
11. *New York*, 10 July 1876, Tobias Montero Collection, National Library.
12. *Etnofilax*, 20 September 1876.
13. Lyra, *História de Dom Pedro II*, 1:174.
14. Pinho, *Salões e damas*, 173.
15. Tobias Montero Collection, National Library.
16. Ibid.
17. 18 November 1883, National Library.
18. 22 November 1884, National Library. Barral's correspondence is in both the National Library and the private collection of Guita and José Mindlin. On the relationship between the monarch and the countess, see Monteiro, *Os timbres nos brasões*, and Sodré, *Abrindo um cofre*.
19. Magalhães, *Dom Pedro II e a condessa de Barral*, 326.
20. Elias, *The Court Society*, 19–20.

15. UNIVERSAL EXHIBITIONS

1. Koseritz, *Imagens do Brasil*, 117–18.
2. This chapter owes a great deal to research into Brazilian participation in the universal exhibitions carried out by Paula Miraglia under my supervision and financed by FAPESP.
3. Experts differ as to whether Brazil took part in the Great Exhibition. Hardman, in *Trem fantasma*, says that Brazil took part for the first time in 1862, in London; Benedict, in *The Anthropology of World's Fairs*, and Greenhalgh, in *Ephemeral Vistas*, record Brazil's participation in 1851.

4. *Guide Bleu et du Petit Journal*, 1889 Paris exhibition.

5. Hamburger, "Representação brasileira nas feiras mundiais," p. 3.

6. *Guide Bleu et du Petit Journal*.

7. 2 December 1862, Museu Mariano Procópio.

8. 1867, Museu Mariano Procópio.

9. This document, along with a good proportion of the works produced for the 1889 exhibition, is in the Museu Mariano Procópio.

10. *Revista Ilustrada*, no. 552 (1889).

11. This display was the subject of dispute among the directors of the Brazilian museums, for other establishments (like the Museu Paulista and the Goeldi Museum) complained about the improper use of objects and documents.

12. *Journal Exposition de Paris*, no. 23 (3 October 1889), Museu Mariano Procópio, 178–79.

16. THE MONARCHY WILL FALL

1. Assis, *The Psychiatrist and Other Stories*, 59, 60, 63.

2. Koseritz, *Imagens do Brasil*, 32–34.

3. Ibid., 29.

4. Tobias Montero Collection, National Library.

5. Habsburg, *Bahia 1860*, 123.

6. Binzer, *Os meus romanos*, 52.

7. Geertz, *Local Knowledge*, 125.

8. Nabuco, *Minha formação*, 28.

9. Carvalho, *A construção da ordem*, 212

10. Ibid., 214; Nabuco, *O abolicionismo*, 184.

11. Carvalho, *A construção da ordem*, 214.

12. Efegê, *Figuras e coisas do carnaval carioca*, 71.

13. *Correio Paulistano*, 28 January 1872. On this subject, see El Far, "Entre a coroa e a cartola."

14. Freyre, "Dom Pedro II, imperador cinzento," 123.

15. 19 May 1882, Tobias Montero Collection, National Library.

16. Carvalho, *A construção da ordem*, 291.

17. Tobias Montero Collection, National Library.

18. *Província de São Paulo*, March 1888.

19. 20 June 1888, Tobias Montero Collection, National Library.

20. *O Diário*, 3 August 1889. See also Besouchet, *Dom Pedro e o século XIX*, 495.

21. Tobias Montero Collection, National Library.

22. Cited in Calmon, *O rei filósofo*, 1398.

23. Antislavery newspapers included *Jornal do Commercio*, *A Onda*, *Oitenta e Nove*, *A Redenção* (edited by Antônio Bento), *A Vida Semanária*, *Vila da Redenção*, *A Liberdade*, *O Alliot*, *A Gazeta da Tarde* (published by José do Patrocínio), *A Terra da Redenção*, *O Amigo do Escravo*, *A Luta*, and *O Federalista*, as well as dozens of pamphlets and lampoons.

24. Tobias Montero Collection, National Library.

25. Quoted in Calmon, *História de Dom Pedro II*, 4:1415.

26. Tobias Montero Collection, National Library.

27. Quoted in Calmon, *História de Dom Pedro II*, 4:1435.
28. Quoted in Besouchet, *Dom Pedro II e o século XIX*, 502.
29. Carvalho defends this point of view in *Os bestializados*, 29.

17. THE REPUBLIC CANNOT WAIT FOR THE OLD EMPEROR TO DIE

1. Calmon, *História de Dom Pedro II*, 4:1504.
2. Oliveira, *Impressão de viagem*.
3. Carvalho, *Os bestializados*, 29.
4. Quoted in Lyra, *História de Dom Pedro II*, 3:387.
5. Cited in Carvalho, *A construção da ordem*, 384.
6. *Gazeta de Notícias*, 12 November 1889.
7. Calmon, *História de Dom Pedro II*, 5:1562.
8. Lyra, *História de Dom Pedro II*, 3:281.
9. Quoted in Calmon, *O rei filósofo*, 203.
10. Quoted in Besouchet, *Dom Pedro II e o século XIX*, 542.
11. Dom Pedro II, letter to Rui Barbosa, 16 November 1889; Casa de Rui Barbosa.
12. *Gazeta de Notícias*, 16 November 1889.
13. Assis, *Esaú e Jacó*, 158, 164.

18. THE EMPEROR'S EXILE AND DEATH

1. *Revista Sul Americana*, vol. 1, no. 2, 15 November 1889.
2. Quoted in Calmon, *História de Dom Pedro II*, 5:1644.
3. Quoted in ibid., 5:1728.
4. Casa de Rui Barbosa.
5. Carvalho, *Os bestializados*, 26.
6. Ibid., 30.
7. Azevedo, *Vidas alheias*, 273.
8. The subject is dealt with fully in Carvalho, *A formação das almas*.
9. *A Semana*, 24 April 1892.
10. Ibid.
11. Eleutério, in "Esfinges e heroínas," analyzes the formation of a female literary universe, at the same time as female suffrage was beginning to be discussed. But this was still a very small group.
12. See Carvalho, *A formação das almas*, 80.
13. Lyra, *História de Dom Pedro II*, III, 279.
14. All the data about the 1890s auctions are taken from Santos, *O leilão do Paço*, where the objects auctioned, along with the prices and the buyers' names, are listed. Ângela Marques da Costa assisted me in my research on these auctions.
15. *Jornal do Brasil*, 22 June 1924.
16. "Bethencourt da Silva, professor of architecture at the Academy of Fine Arts, who had retired in April 1888, was the engineer in charge of the Interior Ministry building and

he prepared the lavish provisional room, on the model of the Versailles Chamber, for the meetings of the Constituent Assembly. This salon, magnificent in appearance . . . cost more than three hundred contos; it was of painted cardboard, with beams and columns in the classical style made of papier mâché. It was made of temporary materials because it had to be done cheaply; but considering how absurd and precarious is everything that is not supposed to be permanent, it was very dear. What was ugly and cheaper was rejected, and they succumbed to a seductively false good taste, a showy, empty stage decoration." Santos, *O leilão do Paço*, 177.

17. Santos, *O leilão do Paço*, 178, 180, 192.
18. Lyra, *História de Dom Pedro II*, IV, 164.
19. Parreiras Museum, Niterói.

19. A GHOST CALLED DOM PEDRO

1. According to Tobias Montero, a large part of the emperor's collection was made up of books that he was given and never read. Many of them were sent in the hope that the donor would get some recognition, even a noble title. In Dom Pedro's correspondence, kept in the National Library, there are innumerable references to the donation of both Brazilian and foreign books to the Brazilian emperor.
2. I owe these observations on the Historical and Geographical Institute to Luciana Cestari, who during 1994 researched Dom Pedro's role there.
3. Nabuco, *Minha formação*, 29, 129, 173–74, and 210.
4. Celso, in *Oito anos*, comments that Nabuco was a great exception in the empire's dull legislature. It is interesting to note that three of the great names of abolitionism, André Rebouças, José do Patrocínio, and Joaquim Nabuco, ended their careers distanced from the republic. When Nabuco took an ambassadorial post, it represented a kind of voluntary exile.
5. Quoted in Souza, *Inferno atlântico*.
6. *Kosmos*, no. 11, November 1904.
7. Abreu, in *A fabricação do imortal*, offers an interesting analysis of the museum and other collections.
8. Ibid., 187.
9. Rui Barbosa, speech of 14 December 1920; Casa de Rui Barbosa.
10. *O Globo*, 2 December 1925.
11. Tobias Montero Collection, National Library.
12. Fernando Pessoa, Tobias Montero Collection, National Library.
13. See Silva, "A República comemora o Império."
14. Chateaubriand, in *O Jornal*, 17 November 1925.
15. Maria Horta, in *Museo Imperial*, says that the idea for the museum originated with Alcindo Sodré in 1922. In 1938 the Museum of the History of Petrópolis was created and provisionally installed in the Crystal Palace; the City Palace was also made a listed building at this time. Decree-law 2096, on 29 March 1940, turned the palace into a museum.

FINAL CONSIDERATIONS

1. Cited in Besouchet, *Dom Pedro II e o século XIX*, 573.
2. Bloch, *The Royal Touch*, 28.
3. Assis, *Dom Casmurro*, 54–55.
4. This strange request was found and described in Malerba, "A corte no exílio."
5. Darnton, *The Great Cat Massacre*, 64.
6. Boas, *Anthropology and Modern Life*, 89.
7. Cunha, *Antropologia do Brasil*, 14.
8. See Montes, "'Complexo de Zé Carioca.'"
9. Monteiro, "História e mito," 24.
10. This lavishly illustrated manuscript is in the manuscript section of the National Library (I.14,1,11); in 1985 a facsimile was printed by the National Library.
11. Vieira, in *História do futuro*, added to this Sebastianist mystique by commenting that a human king, elevated to the status of emperor of the Fifth Empire, would rule in a New World.
12. Pessoa, *Mensagem e outros poemas afins*, 155.
13. Barros, *Zé Limeira, livro de cordel*.
14. Romero, *O evolucionismo e o positivismo no Brasil*, xxxix.

Bibliography

Abreu, Regina. *A fabricação do imortal—Memória, história e estratégias de consagração no Brasil*. Rio de Janeiro: Rocco, 1996.

Aimone, Linda. *Les expositions universelles—1851–1900*. Paris: Belin, 1993.

Alencar, José de. *O Guarani*. 1857. Reprint, São Paulo: Ática, 1995.

———. *Iracema*. 1865. Reprint, São Paulo: Ática, 1996.

———. *A pata da gazela*. 1870. Reprint, São Paulo: Ática, 1995.

———. *O tronco do ipê*. 1871. Reprint, São Paulo: Ática, 1995.

———. *Ubirajara*. 1874. Reprint, São Paulo: Ática, 1990.

Alencastro, Luiz Felipe de. "L'Empire du Brésil." In Maurice Duverger, ed. *Le concept d'empire*. Paris: PUF, 1980.

———. "Le commerce des vivants—Traites d'esclaves et 'pax lusitana' dans L'Atlantique Sud." Ph.D. diss., University of Paris x, 1986.

———, ed. *História da vida privada no Brasil*. Vol. 2: *Império: a corte e a modernidade nacional*. São Paulo: Companhia das Letras, 1997.

Almanaque brasileiro ilustrado. Rio de Janeiro: Editora Antônio Manuel dos Reis, 1881.

Amaral, Leo do. *O imperador*. São Paulo: Editora O Pensamento, 1913.

Andersen, Hans Christian. *The Complete Fairy Tales and Stories*. Garden City: Doubleday, 1974.

Andrade, Ana Maria. "Crônica fotográfica do Rio de Janeiro." In Antonio Candido et al., *A crônica*. Campinas: Editora da Unicamp, 1992.

Andrade, Mário de. *Danças dramáticas do Brasil*. São Paulo: Martins, 1959.

Antonil, André João. *Cultura e opulência do Brasil*. 1711. Belo Horizonte; São Paulo, Itatiaia: EDUSP, 1982.

Apostolides, Jean-Marie. *O rei-máquina—Espetáculo e política no tempo de Luis XIV*. Rio de Janeiro: José Olympio, 1993.

Araújo, Emanoel. *Rafael Bordalo Pinheiro—O português tal e qual. O caricaturista*. São Paulo: Pinocoteca do Estado de São Paulo, 1996.

Araujo, Joaquim Aurélio Barreto. *O erro do imperador*. Rio de Janeiro: G. Leuzinger, 1886.

Araujo, Roberto Assumpção. *Retratos da família imperial do Brasil em Viena*. Rio de Janeiro: MEC, 1956.

Assis, Joaquim Maria Machado de. *Iaiá Garcia*. 1878. Reprint, Rio de Janeiro and Belo Horizonte: Garnier, 1988.

———. *Papéis avulsos*. 1882. Reprint, Rio de Janeiro and Belo Horizonte: Garnier, 1989.

———. *Histórias sem data*. 1884. Reprint, Rio de Janeiro and Belo Horizonte: Garnier, 1989.

———. *Dom Casmurro*. 1899. Reprint, Rio de Janeiro and Belo Horizonte: Garnier, 1988.

———. *Esaú e Jacó*. 1904. Reprint, Rio de Janeiro and Belo Horizonte: Garnier, 1988.

———. *The Psychiatrist and Other Stories.* Translated by Helen Caldwell and William Grossman. Berkeley: University of California Press, 1973.

———. *Relíquias da Casa Velha.* 1906. Reprint, Rio de Janeiro and Belo Horizonte: Garnier, 1990.

———. *Crônicas escolhidas.* São Paulo, *Folha de São Paulo;* Ática, 1994.

Ata da 6a sessão ordinária aos 16 dias de mês de março de 1872, sob a presidência do sr. coronel Bernardo Ferraz de Abreu. Petrópolis: Câmara Municipal; Museu Imperial.

Auler, Guilherme. *A construção do Palácio de Petrópolis.* Petrópolis: Vozes, 1952.

———. "O mobiliário do Palácio de Petrópolis." *Jornal do Brasil.* 28 July 1857.

Avé-Lallemant, Robert. *Viagens pelas províncias da Bahia, Alagoas, Pernambuco e Sergipe (1859).* Belo Horizonte: São Paulo: Itatiaia; EDUSP, 1980.

Avila, Carmem. *Boas maneiras—Manual de civilidade.* 3d ed. N.p., 1936.

Azambuja, Gabriel d'. *Les contemporains—Dom Pedro II, empereur du Brésil.* N.p., n.d.

Azeredo, Carlos Magalhães. "Dom Pedro II—traços de sua phisionomia." In Ruiz Galvão, ed., *Contribuições para a biographica de Dom Pedro II.* Rio de Janeiro: Imprensa Nacional, 1925.

Baczo, Bronislaw. *Les imaginaires sociaux.* Paris: Payot, 1984.

Bakhtin, Mikhail. *Rabelais and His World.* Bloomington: Indiana University Press, 1988.

Barbey, Jean. *Âtre roi—Le roi et son gouvernement en France de Clovis à Louis XVI.* Paris: Fayard, 1992.

Bardi, Pietro Maria, ed. *Arte no Brasil.* São Paulo: Abril, 1982.

Barros, João Rego. "Reminiscências de há 50 annos, de um cadete do 1º regimento de cavalaria." *Revista do Instituto Histórico e Geográfico Brasileiro,* vol. 152 (1925), 98.

Barroso, Gustavo. *Ao som da viola.* 1921. Reprint, Rio de Janeiro: Imprensa Nacional, 1949.

Belluzzo, Ana Maria de Moraes, ed. *O Brasil dos viajantes.* São Paulo, Fundação Odebrecht; Metalivros, 1994.

Benedict, Burt. *The Anthropology of World's Fairs.* Berkeley: University of California Press, 1992.

Besouchet, Lídia. *Dom Pedro II e o século XIX.* Rio de Janeiro: Nova Fronteira, 1993.

Binzer, Ina von. *Os meus romanos.* 1881. Reprint, Rio de Janeiro: Paz e Terra, 1994.

Bloch, Marc. *The Royal Touch.* London: Routledge & Kegan Paul, 1973.

Bosi, Alfredo. *História concisa da literatura brasileira.* São Paulo: Cultrix, 1972.

Boulanger, Ernesto Aleixo. *Armorial brasiliense.* Rio de Janeiro: n.p., 1860.

Brandão, Carlos Rodrigues. *O que é folclore.* São Paulo: Brasiliense, 1982.

Brandão, Théo. *Folguedos natalinos.* Vol. 1, *Cavalhada.* Vol. 2, *Maracatu.* Vol. 3, *Quilombo.* Maceió: Universidade Federal de Alagoas; Museu Théo Brandão, n.d.

Brun, Diego Abente. "La guerra de la Triple Alianza—Tres modelos explicativos." *Revista Paraguaya de Sociologia,* vol. 26, no. 74 (1989).

Buarque, Felicio. *Origens republicanas.* Recife: Francisco Soares Quintas, 1894.

Burke, Peter. *The Fabrication of Louis XIV.* New Haven: Yale University Press, 1992.

Caldeira, Jorge. *Mauá—Empresário do Império.* São Paulo: Companhia das Letras, 1995.

Calmon, Pedro. *O rei filósofo.* São Paulo: Nacional, 1938.

———. *História do Brasil na poesia do povo.* Rio de Janeiro: Bloch, 1973.

———. *História de Dom Pedro II.* Rio de Janeiro: José Olympio, 1975.

Câmara, Gerardo Brito Raposo da. *A cidade imperial—Elevação de Petrópolis a cidade; o papel do coronel Veiga. Geopolítica dos municípios: Petrópolis, 100 anos da cidade.* Rio de Janeiro: n.p., 1957.

Campos, Joaquim Pinto de. *O senhor Dom Pedro II, imperador do Brasil.* Porto: Typographia Pereira, 1871.

Candido, Antonio. *Formação da literatura brasileira.* São Paulo: Martins, 1959.

————. "A literatura durante o Império." In Sérgio Buarque de Holanda, *História geral da civilização brasileira,* vol. 7. São Paulo: Difel, 1976.

————. *O método crítico de Silvio Romero.* São Paulo: EDUSP, 1988.

————. "O romantismo." São Paulo, 1990. Photocopy.

————. "A culpa dos reis—mando e transgressão no *Ricardo II.*" In Adauto Novaes, ed. *Ética.* São Paulo: Companhia das Letras, 1992.

Carvalho, José Murilo de. *A construção da ordem—A elite política imperial.* Rio de Janeiro: Campus, 1980.

————. *Os bestializados—O Rio de Janeiro e a República que não foi.* São Paulo: Companhia das Letras, 1987.

————. *Teatro de sombras—A política imperial.* Rio de Janeiro, Vértice; IUPERJ, 1988.

————. *A formação das almas—O imaginário da República no Brasil.* São Paulo: Companhia das Letras, 1990.

————. "República-mulher: Entre Maria e Mariane." In Antonio Candido et al., *A crônica.* Campinas: Editora da Unicamp, 1992.

————. *A construção da ordem—A elite política imperial; Teatro de sombras—A política imperial.* 2d ed. Rio de Janeiro; UFRJ; Relume-Dumará, 1996.

————. *Pontos e bordados—Escritos de história e política.* Belo Horizonte: Editora da UFMG, 1998.

Castro, José da Gama e. *Memória sobre a nobreza no Brasil por hum brasileiro.* Rio de Janeiro: Typographia Nacional, 1841.

Castro, Zaíde M., and Aracy do P. Couto. *Folias de reis. Cadernos de Folclore,* vol. 16. Rio de Janeiro: MEC, 1977.

Catálogo da Exposição dos Modelos dos Brasões de Armas da Nobreza e Fidalguia. Rio de Janeiro: Arquivo Nacional, 1965.

Celso, Afonso. *Oito anos de Parlamento—Poder pessoal de Dom Pedro II.* São Paulo: Melhoramentos, 1928.

Cestari, Luciana. "D. Pedro e o Instituto Histórico e Geográfico Brasileiro." São Paulo: FAPESP, 1994.

Chalhoub, Sidney. *Trabalho, lar e botequim.* São Paulo: Brasiliense, 1986.

Chartier, Roger. "Distinction et divulgation: La civilité et ses livres." In *Lectures et lecteurs dans la France d'Ancien Régime.* Paris: Seuil, 1987.

————. "Novos caminhos da historiografia francesa." São Paulo: Instituto de Estudos Avançados, 1993. Photocopy.

Chateaubriand, Francisco de Assis. "Um professor de elites." *Revista do Instituto Histórico e Geográfico Brasileiro,* vol. 152 (1928), 98.

Chiavenatto, Júlio José. *Genocídio americano—A Guerra do Paraguai.* São Paulo: Brasiliense, 1979.

Clarke, Graham, ed. *The Portrait in Photography*. London: Reaktion Books, 1992.

Coaracy, Vivaldo. *Memórias da cidade do Rio de Janeiro*. 3d ed. São Paulo: EDUSP, 1988.

Conrad, Robert. *Os últimos anos da escravatura*. 2d ed. Rio de Janeiro: Civilização Brasileira, 1978.

Contribuição para a biografia de Dom Pedro II. Rio de Janeiro: Instituto Histórico e Geográfico Brasileiro, 1925.

Costa, Ângela Marques da. "Pedra e poder—Os palácios de d. Pedro II." Relatório de aperfeiçoamento. São Paulo: CNPq, 1997.

Costa, Emilia Viotti da. *Da monarquia à República—Momentos decisivos*. São Paulo: Grijalbo, 1977.

Costa, Wilma Peres. *A espada de Dâmocles—O Exército, a Guerra do Paraguai e a crise do Império*. São Paulo: Hucitec, 1996.

Cristiano Junior, José. *Escravos brasileiros do século XIX*. São Paulo: Ex-Libris, 1988.

Cunha, Joaquim Pedro. *Elogio histórico de sua magestade o imperador d. Pedro II*. Lisbon: Typographia Universal, 1893.

Cunha, Lygia da Fonseca Fernandes da. "Fisionotipo e fisionotraço—Métodos práticos para desenhar retratos." *Revista do Instituto Histórico e Geográfico Brasileiro*. Rio de Janeiro: 1984, sep.

Cunha, Manuela Carneiro da. *Negros estrangeiros*. São Paulo: Brasiliense, 1985.

———. *Antropologia do Brasil*. São Paulo: Brasiliense, 1986.

———. "Política indigenista no século XIX." In *História dos índios no Brasil*. São Paulo: FAPESP; Companhia des Letras, 1992.

———. "Legislação indigenista no século XIX." São Paulo: Comissão Pró-Índio; EDUSP, 1992.

Cunha, Maria Clementina Pereira da. "Você me conhece." *Projeto História*, vol. 16. São Paulo: PUC, 1997.

Cunha, Rui Vieira da. *Figuras e fatos da nobreza brasileira*. Rio de Janeiro: Ministério da Justiça; Arquivo Nacional, 1975.

DaMatta, Roberto. *Ensaios de antropologia estrutural*. Petrópolis: Vozes, 1973.

———. *Carnavais, malandros e heróis*. 1978. Reprint, Rio de Janeiro: Guanabara, 1990.

Darnton, Robert. *The Kiss of Lamourette: Reflections in Cultural History*. New York: W. W. Norton, 1991.

Davatz, Thomas. *Memórias de um colono no Brasil*. 1870. Reprint, São Paulo: EDUSP, 1980.

Debret, Jean-Baptiste. *Voyage pittoresque et historique au Brésil*. Paris: F. Didot Frères, 1835. Translation: *Viagem pitoresca e histórica ao Brasil*. 1823. Reprint, São Paulo: EDUSP, 1978.

Decretos da Casa Real e Imperial—1809–1889. Rio de Janeiro: Arquivo Nacional, n.d.

Delgado, Alexandre Miranda. *O imperador magnânimo*. Rio de Janeiro: n.p., 1992.

Descripção do edifício construido para solemnidade de coroação e sagração de S. M. O Imperador o senhor Dom Pedro II. Rio de Janeiro: Arquivo Nacional, 1825.

Dias, Antônio Gonçalves. *Poesias completas*. 2d ed. São Paulo: Saraiva, 1957.

Dias, Maria Odila Leite da Silva. "A interiorização da metrópole." In Carlos Guilherme Mota, ed., *1922—Dimensões*. São Paulo: Perspectiva, 1982.

———. *Quotidiano e poder em São Paulo do século XIX*. São Paulo: Brasiliense, 1984.

Diesbach, Guislain. *Les secrets du Gotha*. Paris: René Julliard, 1964.

Dolhnikoff, Miriam. "O projeto nacional de José Bonifácio." *Novos Estudos-Cebrap*, vol. 146. São Paulo: n.p., 1996.

Doratioto, Francisco Fernando Monteoliva. *O conflito do Paraguai—A grande guerra do Brasil*. São Paulo: Ática, 1996.

Dore, Helen. *A arte dos retratos*. Rio de Janeiro: Ediouro, 1996.

Dória, Escragnolle. "Reminiscencias do Palácio de São Christovam." *Revista do Instituto Histórico e Geográfico Brasileiro*, vol. 152 (1925), 96.

———. "A fazenda de Santa Cruz." *Revista da Semana*, 22 April 1933.

Dornas Filho, João. "D. Pedro II e o inventor do telefone." *Diário de Notícias*. Rio de Janeiro, 1951.

Dubois, Philippe. *O ato fotográfico*. Campinas: Papirus, 1994.

Duquesne, Jacques. *Exposition Universelle—1900*. Paris: Les Éditions, 1991.

Durand, José Carlos. *Arte, privilégio e distinção*. São Paulo: Perspectiva: EDUSP, 1989.

Durkheim, Émile. *The Elementary Forms of Religious Life*. New York: Oxford University Press, 2001.

Duverger, Maurice. "Le concept d'empire." In *Le concept d'empire*. Paris: PUF, 1980.

Edwards, Elizabeth, ed. *Anthropology and Photography: 1860–1920*. New Haven: Yale University Press, 1992.

Efegê, João Francisco Gomes. *Figuras e coisas do carnaval carioca*. Rio de Janeiro: Funarte, 1982.

Eleutério, Maria de Lourdes. "Esfinges e heroínas—A condição da mulher letrada na transição do fim de século." Ph.D. diss., São Paulo: USP, 1997.

El Far, Alessandra. "Entre a coroa e a cartola—A representação de d. Pedro II nos jornais paulistas e cariocas de 1825 a 1891." Relatório de iniciação cientifica. São Paulo: FAPESP, 1994.

Elias, Norbert. *The Court Society*. New York: Pantheon, 1983.

Ender, Thomas. *Brasilien expedition*. N.p., 1817.

Eulalio, Alexandre. *Remate de males*. Campinas: Editora da Unicamp, 1993.

Ewbank, Thomas. *Life in Brazil, or A Journal of a Visit to the Land of the Cocoa and the Palm*. Detroit: Blaine Ethridge Books, 1971.

Faoro, Raymundo. *Os donos do poder*. 4th ed. Porto Alegre: Globo, 1977.

Fausto, Boris. *História do Brasil*. São Paulo: EDUSP, 1995.

Fernandes, João. "Petrópolis em 1844." *Tribuna de Petrópolis*, 6 August 1933.

Fernandes, Juvenal. *Carlos Gomes—Do sonho à conquista*. São Paulo: IMESP, 1994.

Ferrez, Gilberto. *A fotografia no Brasil (1840–1900)*. Rio de Janeiro: Funarte, 1985.

———. *O Paço da cidade do Rio de Janeiro*. Rio de Janeiro: Fundação Pró-Memória, 1985.

Fialho, Anfrisio. *Dom Pedro II empereur du Brésil*. Brussels: Thyp. de Mlle. Weissenbruch, 1876.

Fleiuss, Max. "D. Pedro II: Seu nascimento, seus irmãos." *Revista do Instituto Histórico e Geográfico Brasileiro*, vol. 152 (1928), 98.

———. "Nascimento, primeiros anos e educação." In *Contribuições para a biographia de Dom Pedro II*. Rio de Janeiro: Imprensa Nacional, 1928.

Fletcher, James Cooley, and D. P. Kidder. *Brazil and the Brazilians*. Boston: Little, Brown, 1866.

Fonseca, Rubem. *O selvagem da ópera*. São Paulo: Companhia das Letras, 1994.

Foucault, Michel. *Discipline and Punish: The Birth of the Prison*. New York: Pantheon, 1977.

Fradique, Mendes. *História do Brasil pelo método confuso*. Rio de Janeiro: Editora e Livraria Leite Ribeiro, 1927.

Francastel, Pierre. *A realidade figurativa*. São Paulo: Perspectiva, 1993.

Franco, Afonso Arinos de Melo. *A Câmara dos Deputados—Síntese histórica*. Brasília: n.p., 1978.

Frazer, James George. *The Golden Bough*. New York: Macmillan, 1940.

Freire, Laudelino de Oliveira. *Pedro II e a arte no Brasil*. Rio de Janeiro: Imprensa Nacional, 1917.

Freitas, Benedicto. *Santa Cruz—Fazenda jesuítica, real, imperial*. Rio de Janeiro: n.p., 1985–87.

Freitas, Newton. *Los Braganza*. Buenos Aires: Emecê, 1943.

Freyre, Gilberto. *The Masters and the Slaves: A Study in the Development of Brazilian Civilization*. New York: Knopf, 1946.

———. "Dom Pedro II julgado por alguns estrangeiros seus contemporâneos." In *Conferências do Museu Imperial*. Petrópolis: n.p., 1970.

———. "Dom Pedro II, imperador cinzento de uma terra de sol tropical." In *O perfil de Euclides da Cunha e outros perfis*. 1944. Reprint, Rio de Janeiro: Record, 1987.

Funchal, marquis of. *Títulos nobiliárquicos*. 1859.

Galbreath, D. L., and Léon Jéquier. *Manuel du blason*. Lausanne: Spes, 1977.

Gama, José de Saldanha da. "História da imperial Fazenda de Santa Cruz." *Revista do Instituto Histórico e Geográfico Brasileiro* (1875), 38.

Garcia, Antônio José Nunes. *O senhor dom Pedro Segundo*. Rio de Janeiro: n.p., 1985.

Geertz, Clifford. *Interpretation of Cultures*. New York: Basic Books, 1973.

———. *Local Knowledge: Further Essays in Interpretative Anthropology*. New York: Basic Books, 1983.

———. *Negara: The Theatre State in Nineteenth-Century Bali*. Princeton, N.J.: Princeton University Press, 1980.

Giesey, Ralph E. *Le roi ne meurt jamais*. Paris: Flammarion, 1987.

———. *Mitos, emblemas, sinais—Morfologia e história*. São Paulo: Companhia das Letras, 1989.

Ginzburg, Carlo. *Indagações sobre Piero*. Rio de Janeiro: Paz e Terra, 1989.

———. *História noturna—Decifrando o sabá*. São Paulo: Companhia das Letras, 1991.

Gobineau, Arthur de. *Les Pléiades*. Paris: n.p., 1875.

Gomes, Plínio Freire. "Notas sobre a mediação entre o erudito e o popular—contribuições para uma história dialógica." São Paulo: 1991.

Graham, Maria. *Diário de uma viagem ao Brasil—Segunda visita, 1822*. São Paulo: Nacional, 1956.

Graham, Richard. *Patronage and Politics in Nineteenth-Century Brazil*. Palo Alto: Stanford University Press, 1990.

Greenhalgh, Paul. *Ephemeral Vistas: The Expositions Universelles, Great Exhibitions and World's Fairs, 1851–1939*. Manchester, Eng.: Manchester University Press, 1988.

Guimarães, Argeu de Segadas Machado. *Pedro II na Escandinávia e na Rússia*. Rio de Janeiro: J. Leite, n.d.

———. *Em torno do casamento de Dom Pedro II*. Rio de Janeiro: Zelio Valdeverde, 1942.

———. *Dom Pedro II nos Estados Unidos*. Rio de Janeiro: Civilização Brasileira, 1961.

Gurgel, Amaral. *O neto de Marco Aurélio (d. Pedro II)*. São Paulo: Empresa Editora, 1994.

Habsburg, Ferdinand Maximilian of. *Bahia 1860—Esboços de viagem*. 1861. Reprint, Rio de Janeiro: Tempo Brasileiro, and Salvador: Fund. Cultural do Est. da Bahia, 1982.

Hamburger, Ester Império. "Representação brasileira nas feiras mundiais—1862/1939." São Paulo, 1990. Photocopy.

Hardman, Francisco Foot. *Trem fantasma—A modernidade na selva*. São Paulo: Companhia das Letras, 1988.

———. "Os negativos da história." In Antonio Candido et al., *A crônica*. Campinas: Editora da Unicamp, 1992.

Haskell, Francis. *History and Its Images*. New Haven: Yale University Press, 1993.

Hirsch, Irene. "A baleia traduzida—Traduções de Herman Melville." In *Cadernos de literatura em tradução*. São Paulo: Humanitas, 1997.

Hobsbawm, Eric, and Terence Ranger, eds. *The Invention of Tradition*. Cambridge, Eng.: Cambridge University Press, 1992.

Holanda, Sérgio Buarque de. *O Brasil monárquico*, vols. 4 and 5: *O Império e a República*. 2d ed. São Paulo: Difel, 1977.

———. *Raízes do Brasil*. 1936. Reprint, Rio de Janeiro: José Olympio, 1979.

Horace, Napoleon Raisson. *Code de la conversation—Manuel complet du langage, élégant et polides*. Paris: J. P. Ronet, 1829.

Howard, Maurice. *The Tudor Image*. London: Tate Gallery, 1995.

Hugo, Victor. *Choses vues—1870–1885*. Paris: Gallimard, 1972.

Iglésias, Francisco. *Trajetória política do Brasil—1500–1964*. São Paulo: Companhia das Letras, 1993.

Infância e adolescência de d. Pedro II—Documentos interessantes publicados para comemorar o primeiro centenário de nascimento. Rio de Janeiro: Arquivo Nacional, 1925.

Itanhaém, marquis of. *Contas dadas á Assemblea Geral pelo marques de Itanhaém, encarregado da tutela de SMI e de suas augustas irmãs, precedidas de um relatório explicativo*. Rio de Janeiro: 1834.

Japur, Jorge. *Manual de boas maneiras*. 2d ed. N.p., 1914.

Joubert, Pierre. *Nouveau guide de l'héraldique*. Rennes: Ouest-France, 1985.

Kantorowicz, Ernst. *The King's Two Bodies: A Study in Medieval Political Theology*. Princeton, N.J.: Princeton University Press, 1957.

Karasch, Mary. *Slave Life in Rio de Janeiro: 1808–1850*. Princeton, N.J.: Princeton University Press, 1987.

Kidder, Daniel Parish. *Sketches of Travels and Residence in Brazil, Embracing Historical and Geographical Notices of the Empire and Its Several Provinces*. Philadelphia: Sorin and Ball, 1845.

Koseritz, Carl von. *Imagens do Brasil*. 1883. Reprint, São Paulo: Martins; Edusp, 1972.

Koster, Henry. *Travels in Brazil.* 1816. Reprint, Carbondale: Southern Illinois University Press, 1966.

Lacombe, Américo Jacobina. *Paul Barbosa e a fundação de Petrópolis.* Petrópolis: Ypiranga, 1939.

———. *Nobreza brasileira—Notas prévias aos "Apontamentos" de Silva Maia.* Petrópolis: Anuário do Museu Imperial, 1940.

———. *O mordomo do imperador.* Rio de Janeiro: Biblioteca do Exército, 1994.

Lacombe, Lourenço L. *Uma cerimônia na corte em 1864.* Vol. 2. Petrópolis: Anuário do Museu Imperial, 1941.

Ladurie, Emmanuel Le Roy. *O Estado monárquico—França: 1460–1610.* São Paulo: Companhia das Letras, 1994.

Lago, Colonel Laurênio. *Nobiliarquia brasileira—Titulares do sexo feminino.* Rio de Janeiro: Imprensa Militar, 1949.

Langer, Madame de. *Le protocole mondaine.* Paris: Montgredien et C. Librairie, 1887.

Le Goff, Jacques, and Pierre Nora. *História—Novas abordagens.* Rio de Janeiro: Francisco Alves, 1976.

Leclerc, Max. *Cartas do Brasil (1889–1890).* São Paulo: Nacional, 1942.

Leite, Miriam Moreira. "Documentação fotográfica, potencialidades e limitações." In Antonio Candido et al., *A crônica.* Campinas: Editora da Unicamp, 1992.

Lemoine, Bertrand. *La tour de Monsieur Eiffel.* Paris: Gallimard, 1989.

Levasseur, E. *Album de viés du Brésil.* Paris: n.p., 1889.

Lévi-Strauss, Claude. *Structural Anthropology.* New York: Basic Books, 1963.

———. *The Story of Lynx.* Chicago: University of Chicago Press, 1995.

Lima, Alberto, and Guilherme Auler. *Paço de São Cristóvão—Rio de Janeiro: 1817–1880.* Vol. 2. Petrópolis: Vitor P. Brumlik, 1965.

Lima, Oliveira. *O império brasileiro.* São Paulo: Melhoramentos, 1927.

———. *Dom João VI no Brasil.* 3d ed. Rio de Janeiro: Topbooks, 1996.

Lima, Rossini Tavares de. *Folguedos populares do Brasil.* São Paulo: Ricordi, 1962.

———. *Abecê do folclore.* 5th ed. São Paulo: Ricordi, 1972.

Lisboa, Karen M. "A nova Atlântida ou o gabinete naturalista dos doutores Spix e Martius." Master's thesis. São Paulo: USP, 1995.

———. *A nova Atlântida de Spix e Martius—Natureza e civilização na "Viagem pelo Brasil (1817–1820)."* São Paulo: Hucitec, 1997.

Lyra, Heitor. *História de Dom Pedro II.* 1938–40. Reprint, São Paulo: EDUSP; and Belo Horizonte: Itatiaia, 1977.

Macedo, Gervasio do Rego. "A sociedade do Rio de Janeiro." *Gazeta da Tarde.* Rio de Janeiro, 1886.

Macedo, Valéria Mendonça de. "O Brasil do XIX: entre santos e cetros—O imaginário da realeza nas festas brasileiras do século XIX." São Paulo: CNPq, 1996.

Machado, Julio Cesar. *O outro Dom Pedro II.* Rio de Janeiro: Bramante Editora, 1996.

Machado, Maria Helena P. T. "Para uma história da sensibilidade—Couto Magalhães e a trajetória privada de um personagem público do Império." *Revista Eclética.* São Paulo: USP, 1997, 2.

————. "Um mitógrafo no Império—A construção de mitos da história nacionalista do XIX." São Paulo: n.p., 1997.

————. "Um país em busca de moldura—O pensamento de Couto de Magalhães, *O selvagem e Os sertões.*" In John Manuel Monteiro and Francisca L. Nogueira Azevedo, eds., *Confronto de culturas—Conquista, resistência, transformação.* São Paulo: Edusp. 1997.

————. ed. *José Vieira Couto de Magalhães—Diário íntimo.* São Paulo: Companhia das Letras, 1998.

Madariaga, Salvador de. *Bolívar.* 2d ed. Mexico City: Editorial Hermes, 1953.

Magalhães, Couto de. *O selvagem.* 1913. Reprint, Belo Horizonte: Itatiaia; and São Paulo: EDUSP, 1975.

Magalhães, Domingos José Gonçalves de. *A Confederação dos Tamoyos.* 3d ed. Rio de Janeiro: Garnier, 1864.

Magalhães Jr., Raimundo. *Dom Pedro II e a condessa de Barral.* Rio de Janeiro: Civilização Brasileira, 1956.

————. *O Império em chinelos.* Rio de Janeiro: Civilização Brasileira, 1957.

Malerba, Jurandir. "A corte no exílio—Interpretação Brasil joanino (1808–1821)." Ph.D. diss. São Paulo: USP, 1997.

Manual da civilidade brasileira, contendo as leis da decência e do bom-tom; máximas e preceitos de bem viver na sociedade e regras para bem escrever cartas. Rio de Janeiro: Livros de Agostinho de Freitas Guimarães, 1848.

Mappa da totalidade da escravatura da Imperial Fazenda de Santa Cruz, 30 de junho de 1849. Rio de Janeiro: Instituto Histórico e Geográfico Brasileiro.

Marinho, José Antonio. *A declaração de maioridade.* Rio de Janeiro: Typographia da Associação do Despertador, 1840.

Marques, A. H. de Oliveira. *História de Portugal.* Portugal: Imprensa Nacional, 1991.

Marques, Maria Eduarda C. M., ed. *A Guerra do Paraguai.* Rio de Janeiro: Relume-Dumará, 1995.

Marras, Stélio A. "Sobre a boa sociedade de Machado de Assis." São Paulo: CNPq, 1996.

Mathias, Herculano Gomes. *D. Pedro II.* São Paulo: Ediouro, 1984.

Matoso, Ernesto. *Cousas do meu tempo.* Bordeaux: Gounouilhou, 1916.

Mattos, Ilmar Rohloff de. *O tempo saquarema.* São Paulo: Hucitec, 1987.

Mattoso, José. *A nobreza portuguesa.* Lisbon: Presença, 1976.

Mauad, Ana Maria. "Imagem e auto-imagem do Segundo Reinado." In Luiz Felipe de Alencastro, ed., *História da vida privada no Brasil.* Vol. 2: *Império: A corte e a modernidade nacional,* ed. Fernando A. Novais. São Paulo: Companhia das Letras, 1997.

Mauro, Frédéric. *O Brasil no tempo de dom Pedro II—1831–1889.* São Paulo: Companhia das Letras, 1991.

Medeiros e Albuquerque, ed. *Poesias completas de d. Pedro II.* Rio de Janeiro: Guanabara, 1932.

Meghreblian, Caren Ann. "Art, Politics and Historical Perception in Imperial Brazil—1854–1884." Master's thesis. University of Michigan, 1994.

Mendes, Oscar. *Quem foi d. Pedro II.* Rio de Janeiro: Artes Gráficas, 1930.

Mendonça, Carlos Süssekind de. *Quem foi d. Pedro II—Golpeando de frente o "saudo-sismo."* Rio de Janeiro: Imprensa Nacional, 1929.

Menezes, Paulo Braga de. Introduction to *Catálogo da Exposição dos Modelos dos Brasões de Armas da Nobreza e Fidalguia.* Rio de Janeiro: Arquivo Nacional, 1965.

Montagu, James Augustus. *A Guide to the Study of Heraldry.* London: Pickering, 1840.

Montaigne, Michel de. *Os canibais.* São Paulo: Abril, 1980.

Monteiro, Aristides. *Os timbres nos brasões de armas brasileiros dos 1º e 2º reinados,* vols. 42–43. Petrópolis: Anuário do Museu Imperial, n.d.

Monteiro, John Manuel, and Francisca L. Nogueira de Azevedo. *Confronto de culturas—Conquista, resistência, transformação.* Rio de Janeiro: Expressão e Cultura; and São Paulo: EDUSP, 1997.

Monteiro, Mozart. "A infância do imperador." *Revista do Instituto Histórico e Geográfico Brasileiro,* vol. 152 (1928), 98.

———. "A vida amorosa de d. Pedro II." *O Cruzeiro.* Rio de Janeiro, 1962.

Monteiro, Rodrigo Bentes. "História e mito—O príncipe perfeito chega ao Brasil." São Paulo, apost., 1995.

Montero, Paula. *O V Centenário—Entre o mito e a história.* Petrópolis: Vozes, 1996.

Monteverde, Emilio. *Manual encyclopedico.* Lisbon: Imprensa Nacional, 1879.

Moraes Filho, Alexandre José de Mello. *Festas e tradições populares do Brazil.* 1893. Reprint, Rio de Janeiro: Garnier, 1946.

———. *Festas e tradições populares.* 3d ed. Rio de Janeiro: F. Briguiet, 1946.

Morel, Marco. "Le roi, le peuple et la nation." In Katia M. de Queirós Mattoso, ed., *Cahiers du Brésil contemporain.* Paris: Hérault, 1994.

Mossé, Benjamin. *Dom Pedro II empereur du Brésil.* Paris: Librairie de Firmin-Didot, 1889.

Motivos, fins e systemas da obra. São Paulo: n.p., 1865.

Moura, Carlo Eugênio Marcondes. *Retratos quase inocentes.* São Paulo: Nobel, 1983.

Museu Histórico Nacional. São Paulo: Banco Safra, 1989.

Museu Imperial. São Paulo: Banco Safra, 1992.

Museu Nacional de Belas-Artes. São Paulo: Banco Safra, 1985.

Nabuco, Joaquim. *O abolicionismo.* 1883. Reprint, São Paulo: Nacional, 1938.

———. *Um estadista do império.* Rio de Janeiro: Nova Aguilar, 1975.

———. *Minha formação.* 1949. Reprint, Porto Alegre: Editora Paraula, 1995.

Nava, Pedro. *Balão cativo—Memórias 2.* Rio de Janeiro: José Olympio, 1973.

Naves, Rodrigo. *A forma difícil—Ensaios sobre arte brasileira.* São Paulo: Ática, 1996.

Needell, Jeffrey D. *Belle Époque tropical—Sociedade e cultura de elite no Rio de Janeiro.* São Paulo: Companhia das Letras, 1993.

Neves, Guilhermina de Azambuja. *Entretenimentos sobre os deveres de civilidade cole-cionados para uso da puericia brasileira de ambos os sexos.* Rio de Janeiro: Typo-graphia Cinco de Março, 1875.

Nicoulin, Martin. *A gênese de Nova Friburgo—Emigração e colonização no Brasil: 1817–1827.* Rio de Janeiro: Fundação Biblioteca Nacional, 1995.

Novais, Fernando A., and Carlos Guilherme Mota. *A independência política do Brasil.* 2d ed. São Paulo: Hucitec, 1996.

Oliveira, Filinto. *Impressão de viagem*. Lisbon: n.p., 1890.

Paço Imperial: Roteiro para visita histórica. MEC; IPHAN, 1995.

Palácio Itamaraty. São Paulo: Banco Safra, 1993.

Panofsky, Erwin. *Significado nas artes visuais*. 3d ed. São Paulo: Perspectiva, 1995.

Parecer. Comissão de Contas—1837. Deputado Rafael de Carvalho. Rio de Janeiro: Arquivo Nacional, Seção de Obras Raras.

Parr, Catherine. *L'usage et le bon ton de nos jours*. 2d ed. Paris: Reuff Éditeurs, 1892.

Patrocínio, José do. *Campanha abolicionista—Coletânea de artigos*. Rio de Janeiro: FBN, 1996.

Paulino, Roseli Figaro. "Entre um rei, queijos e gatos: Um estudo de recepção." São Paulo, 1995. Photocopy.

Paupério, Artur Machado. "O governo municipal e a monarquia." In *Geopolítica dos municípios: Petrópolis, 100 anos da cidade*. Rio de Janeiro, 1957.

Pedro II, Dom. *Conselhos à regente por dom Pedro II*. Rio de Janeiro: Livros São José, n.d.

———. *Diário do imperador no. 4*. (n.d.). Petrópolis: Museu Imperial.

———. *Diário do imperador (1840–41)*. Petrópolis: Museu Imperial.

———. *Diário da viagem ao Alto Nilo (1856)*. In *Revista do Instituto Histórico e Geográfico Brasileiro*. 2 (1909), 72.

———. *Diário do imperador Dom Pedro II (1860)*. Petrópolis: Museu Imperial, ms.

———. *Diário da viagem ao Espírito Santo (1860)*. Vol. 17. Petrópolis: Anuário do Museu Imperial, 1956.

———. *Digressão a Santa Cruz—1860. Diário no. 17*. Petrópolis: Museu Imperial.

———. *Diário de viagem de 1861*. Petrópolis: Museu Imperial.

———. *Diário do imperador (1862)*. Vol. 17. Petrópolis: Anuário do Museu Imperial, 1956.

———. *Conselhos políticos de Dom Pedro II a sua filha Isabel*. 1871.

———. *Diários da década de 1880*. Petrópolis: Museu Imperial.

———. *Sonetos do exílio*. Paris: n.p., 1898.

———. *Poesias e traduções—Homenagem de seus netos*. Petrópolis: Tipographia do Correio Imperial, 1939.

———. *Viagem a Pernambuco em 1859*. Recife: Arquivo Público Estadual, 1952.

———. *Diário da viagem ao Norte do Brasil*. Salvador: Universidade da Bahia; Progresso Editora, 1953.

———. *Poemas completos de Dom Pedro II*. Rio de Janeiro: Guanabara, 1953.

Pena, Luís Carlos Martins. *Comédias*. São Paulo: Ediouro, n.d.

Pereira, Leonardo Affonso de Miranda. *O carnaval das letras*. Rio de Janeiro: Biblioteca Carioca, 1994.

Pessoa, Fernando. *Mensagem e outros poemas afins seguidos de Fernando Pessoa e a idéia de Portugal*. Sintra: Publicações Europa-América, n.d.

"Petrópolis e a proclamação da República." *Tribuna de Petrópolis*, 15 November 1944.

Picchio, Luciana Stegagno. *La letteratura brasiliana*. Milan: Sansoni, 1972.

Pierre, Boitard. *Novo manual do bom-tom, contendo modernismos, preceitos de civilidade, política, conduta e maneiras em todas as circunstâncias da vida indispensáveis à mocidade e adultos para serem benquistos e caminharem sem tropeço pela carreira do mundo*. 2d ed. Rio de Janeiro: E. H. Laembert, 1872.

Pimentel, João Maria Pereira Botelho do Amaral. *A sciencia da civilização — Curso elementar de educação religiosa, individual e cultural.* Porto: Livros Internacional de E. Chardon, 1877.

Pimentel, Mesquita. *Dom Pedro II.* Petrópolis: Papel Silva, 1925.

Pinacoteca do Estado. São Paulo: Banco Safra, 1994.

Pinheiro, Rafael Bordalo. *Apontamento da viagem do imperador na Europa.* Lisbon: n.p., 1872.

———. *Apontamentos sobre a picaresca viagem do imperador de Rasilb pela Europa.* Lisbon, 1872. Facsimile, Pinacoteca, 1996.

Pinho, José Wanderley de Araujo. *Cartas do imperador.* São Paulo: Nacional, 1933.

———. *Salões e damas do Segundo Reinado.* São Paulo: Revista dos Tribunais, 1942.

———. "Dom Pedro II em Petrópolis." *Geopolítica dos municípios: Petrópolis, 100 anos da cidade.* Rio de Janeiro, 1957.

Poliano, Luiz Marquês. *Ordens Honoríficas no Brasil.* Rio de Janeiro: Imprensa Nacional, 1943.

Pomian, Krzysztof. "Coleção." In *Memória — História.* Portugal: Imprensa Nacional, 1984.

Pompéia, Raul. *Obras.* Rio de Janeiro: Civilização Brasileira, 1982.

Prado Jr., Caio. *Evolução política do Brasil.* 1933. 11th ed. São Paulo: Brasiliense, 1979.

Puntoni, Pedro. "Gonçalves de Magalhães e a historiografia do império." *Novos Estudos-Cebrap.* São Paulo: 1996, no. 45.

Rabaçal, Alfredo João. *As congadas do Brasil.* São Paulo: Secretaria da Cultura, Ciência e Tecnologia, Conselho Estadual de Cultura, 1976.

Rabaço, Henrique José. *História de Petrópolis — Antecedentes históricos e a povoação.* Petrópolis: Instituto Histórico, 1985.

Raeders, Georges Pierre Henri. *Dom Pedro II e conde Gobineau — Correspondências inéditas.* São Paulo: Nacional, 1938.

———. *Dom Pedro II e os sábios franceses.* Rio de Janeiro, Atlântica Editora, s.d.

Raffard, Henri. "Jubileu de Petrópolis." *Revista Trimestral do Instituto Histórico e Geográfico Brasileiro* (1895), 58.

Rangel, Alberto do Rego. *A educação do príncipe.* Rio de Janeiro: Agir, 1945.

RCM. *O cozinheiro imperial.* São Paulo: Best-Seller, 1996.

Real, José Alberto Homem da Cunha Corte. *Viagem dos imperadores do Brasil em Portugal.* Coimbra: Imprensa da Universidade, 1872.

Registro de escravos da Imperial Fazenda de Santa Cruz alugados a diversos e a si, que devem seus aluguéis — 1862–1868. Rio de Janeiro: Arquivo Nacional, cód. 1122, vol. 9.

Reis, João José. "Quilombos e revoltas escravas no Brasil." *Revista da USP, Dossiê Povo Negro — 300 anos.* São Paulo: USP, 1996, no. 28.

Reis, Letícia Vidor de Sousa. "O domínio da imaginação — Reflexões sobre a dimensão simbólica do poder." São Paulo, 1995. Photocopy.

Relatório e sinopse dos trabalhos da Cámara dos Senhores Deputados, 1869–1889. Rio de Janeiro: Imprensa Nacional, 1869–89.

Revel, Jacques. "Os usos da civilidade." In *História da vida privada.* São Paulo: Companhia das Letras, 1991, vol. 3.

Ribeiro, Maria Euridice de Barros. *Os símbolos do poder.* Brasília: Editora da UnB, 1995.

Ribeiro, Renato Janine. *A etiqueta no Antigo Regime — Do sangue à doce vida.* São Paulo: Brasiliense, 1983.

———. *A última razão dos reis.* São Paulo: Companhia das Letras, 1993.

Ribeyrolles, Charles. *Brasil pittoresco.* Rio de Janeiro: Typographia Nacional, 1859.

Rieusseyroux, L. Alquiré. *La science des circonstances de la vie.* 5th ed. Paris: F. Ebhart, 1901.

Rio Branco, Miguel. *Correspondências entre d. Pedro e o barão de Rio Branco.* São Paulo: Nacional, 1957.

Rodriguez, Francisco. *O retrato brasileiro.* Rio de Janeiro: Fundaçao Joaquim Nabuco, 1983.

Romero, Silvio. *O evolucionismo e o positivismo no Brasil.* Rio de Janeiro: n.p., 1888.

———. *Doutrina contra doutrina.* Rio de Janeiro: Livraria Clássica de Álvares, 1895.

———. *Cantos populares do Brasil.* Rio de Janeiro: José Olympio, 1954.

Roquete, J. I. *Código do bom-tom ou Regras da civilidade e de bem viver no século XIX.* São Paulo: Companhia das Letras, 1997.

Rosa, José Maria. *La Guerra del Paraguay.* Buenos Aires: n.p., 1974.

Rugendas, J. Moritz. *Voyage pittoresque dans le Brésil.* Paris: Engelman, 1834.

Saboia, Vicente Candido Figueiredo. *O senhor Dom Pedro II Imperador do Brasil.* London: Livros Nacional, 1871.

———. *O senhor Dom Pedro II.* Rio de Janeiro: Litho-typographia, 1896.

Sahlins, Marshall. *Cultura e razão prática.* Rio de Janeiro: Zahar, 1979.

———. *Historical Metaphors and Mythical Realities.* Ann Arbor: University of Michigan Press, 1981.

Salles, Ricardo. "Nostalgia imperial." Rio de Janeiro, n.d. Photocopy.

———. *Guerra do Paraguai — escravidão e cidadania na formação do Exército.* Rio de Janeiro: Paz e Terra, 1990.

Santos, Francisco Marques dos. *O leilão do Paço de São Cristóvão.* Vol. 1. Petrópolis: Anuário do Museu Imperial, 1940.

———. *As duas últimas festas da monarquia.* Vol. 2. Petrópolis: Anuário do Museu Imperial, 1941.

Schneider, Norbert. *The Art of the Portrait.* London: Benedikt Tashen, 1994.

Schnoor, Eduardo, and Hebe Maria Mattos de Castro, eds. *Resgate — Uma janela para o Oitocentos.* Rio de Janeiro: Topbooks, 1995.

Schorske, Carl G. *Fin-de-Siècle Vienna: Politics and Culture.* New York: Vintage, 1981.

Schwarcz, Lilia Moritz. "Entre amigas: relações de boas vizinhanças." *Revista da USP,* no. 23 (1994).

———. "Complexo de Zé Carioca: Notas sobre uma identidade mestiça e malandra." *Revista Brasileira de Ciências Sociais,* vol. 10, no. 29 (1995).

Schwarz, Roberto. *Que horas são?.* São Paulo: Companhia das Letras, 1987.

Seidler, Carl. *Dez anos no Brasil.* 1835. Reprint, Rio de Janeiro: Martins, 1942.

Sevcenko, Nicolau. *Literatura como missão: tensões sociais e criação na Primeira República.* São Paulo: Brasiliense, 1983.

Silva, Alberto da Costa e. "O Brasil, a África e o Atlântico." *Revista STVDIA* [Lisbon], no. 52 (1994).

Silva, Eduardo. *Barões e escravidão—Três gerações de fazendeiros e a crise da estrutura escravista.* Rio de Janeiro: Nova Fronteira, 1984.

———. "A República comemora o Império—Um aspecto ideológico da crise dos anos 20." *Revista Rio de Janeiro.* Niterói: UFF, 1986.

———. *The Life and Times of a Brazilian Free Man of Colour.* London: Verso, 1993.

Silva, Francisco Gomes da. *O Chalaça—Memórias.* Rio de Janeiro: n.p., 1939.

Silva, João Manuel Pereira da. *Le Brésil sous l'empereur Dom Pedro II.* Paris: n.p., 1858.

Sisson, S. A. *Galeria dos Brasileiros Ilustres.* São Paulo: Martins Editora, 1859.

Sodré, Alcindo de Azevedo. *Aspectos da vida municipal—Crônicas petropolitanas.* Vol. 2. Petrópolis: Prefeitura. Municipal, Comissão do Centenário, 1939.

———. *Abrindo um cofre—Cartas de Dom Pedro II à condessa de Barral.* Rio de Janeiro: Livros de Portugal, 1956.

Sodré, Nelson Werneck. *História militar do Brasil.* Rio de Janeiro: Civilização Brasileira, 1965.

———. *As razões da Independência.* Rio de Janeiro: Civilização Brasileira, 1978.

Sontag, Susan. *On Photography.* New York: Farrar, Straus and Giroux, 1977.

Soublin, Jean. *O defensor perpétuo do Brasil—Memórias imaginárias do último imperador do Brasil.* Rio de Janeiro: Paz e Terra, 1996.

Sousa, Otávio Tarqüínio de. *A vida de Dom Pedro I.* São Paulo: EDUSP; and Belo Horizonte: Itatiaia, 1988.

Souza, Laura de Mello e. *Inferno atlântico—Demonologia e colonização: séculos XVI–XVIII.* São Paulo: Companhia das Letras, 1993.

Spix, Johann Baptist von, and Carl Friedrich Phillipp von Martius. S. a. *Brasil—Histórias, costumes e lendas.* São Paulo: Editora Três, n.d.

———. *Viagem pelo Brasil.* 1823, 1828. Reprint, Belo Horizonte: Itatiaia, 1981.

Starobinski, Jean. *The Invention of Liberty, 1700–1789.* New York: Rizzoli, 1987.

Suetônio. *O antigo regime—Homens e coisas.* Rio de Janeiro: Cunha e Irmãos, 1896.

Taunay, Alfredo d'Escragnolle. *O grande imperador.* São Paulo: Melhoramentos, 1932.

———. *Pedro II.* São Paulo: Nacional, 1933.

Távora, Araken. *Dom Pedro II e seu mundo através da caricatura.* Rio de Janeiro: Editora Documenta, 1976.

Toral, André. *Adiós, chamigo brasileiro.* São Paulo: Companhia das Letras, 1998.

Torres, João Camilo de Oliveira. *A democracia coroada.* Rio de Janeiro: Nacional, 1957.

Tostes, Vera Lúcia Bottrel. "Estrutura familiar e simbologia na nobreza brasonada—Províncias do Rio de Janeiro e São Paulo, século XIX." Master's thesis. São Paulo: USP, 1989.

———. *Princípios de heráldica.* Rio de Janeiro: n.p., 1993.

Trachtenberg, Alan, ed. *Classic Essays on Photography.* New Haven: Leete's Island Books, 1980.

Varnhagen, Francisco Adolfo de. *História geral do Brasil.* São Paulo: EDUSP; and Belo Horizonte: Itatiaia, 1981.

Vasconcellos, Luiz Smith de. *Archivo nobiliarchico brasileiro.* Lausanne: La Concorde, 1918.

Vasconcelos, J. Leite. *A barba em Portugal—Um estudo de etnografia comparativa*. Lisbon: Imprensa Nacional, 1881.

Vasquez, Pedro. *Dom Pedro II e a fotografia*. Rio de Janeiro: Internacional de Seguros, n.d.

———. *Fotógrafos pioneiros no Rio de Janeiro*. Rio de Janeiro: Dazibao, 1990.

Ventura, Roberto. *Estilo tropical—História cultural el polêmicas literárias no Brasil: 1870–1914*. São Paulo: Companhia das Letras, 1991.

Verardi, C. *Novo manual do bom-tom*. 6th ed. Rio de Janeiro: Laemmert, 1900.

Verger, Pierre. *Fluxo e refluxo—Do tráfico de escravos entre o golfo do Benin e a Bahia de Todos os Santos: Dos séculos XVII e XIX*. Salvador: Corrupio, 1987.

Vianna, Helio. *Letras imperiais*. Rio de Janeiro: MEC, n.d.

———. *Dom Pedro I e Dom Pedro II—Acréscimos às suas biografias*. São Paulo: Nacional, 1966.

Vieira, Antônio. *História do futuro*. 1718. Reprint, Lisbon: Imprensa Nacional, 1982.

Wheatcroft, Andrew. *The Habsburgs*. London: Viking, 1995.

Williams, Mary. *Dom Pedro the Magnanimous, Second Emperor of Brazil*. Chapel Hill: University of North Carolina Press, 1937.

Wolff, Egon. *Dom Pedro II e os judeus*. Rio de Janeiro: B'nai B'rith, 1983.

Woodford, Susan. *Looking at Pictures*. Cambridge, Eng.: Cambridge University Press, 1995.

Zanini, Walter. *História geral da arte no Brasil*. São Paulo: Instituto Moreira Salles, 1983.

Zuquete, Afonso Eduardo Martins, coord. *Nobreza de Portugal e do Brasil*. Lisbon and Rio de Janeiro: Editorial Enciclopédia, 1960.

Index

434

INDEX

Pedro II, emperor of Brazil (*cont.*)
319, 343, 345, 368; liberal support for,
42–43, 45–46, 84, 235, 240, 251, 320,
325, 328; literature inspired by, 48, 89,
97–98, 99, 355–57, 369–70; love affairs
of, 278–81, 308; marriage of, 63–67,
273–74, 297; maturity of, 36–37, 43–
45, 58, 62–63, 68, 232; as military
leader, 232–48, 249, 254, 255–57;
"moderating power" of, 86, 89, 91,
114, 119, 251–52, 301; mythology of,
xi-xiii, xxii-xxiv, 43, 60–62, 331, 335,
342–43, 353–78; nobility and, 30–31,
33, 42, 51, 118–52, 253–54, 340, 359,
368; old age of, 311–12, 344–45, 378;
palaces of, 56–57, 60, 120, 153–83,
189, 254, 298–99, 321, 345–48, 371;
Pedro I compared with, 40, 57, 280,
282; personality of, 36–37, 43–45, 58,
189, 247–48, 280–82, 302, 369; poetry
written by, 343, 344–45, 365–67; political influence of, xxiii, 42–43, 59–60,
64, 68–69, 84, 85, 89, 91, 112–13,
142–46, 184, 245, 247, 251–52, 273,
274, 282, 296, 298, 300, 301, 315–18,
322–23; popular support for, 30–31,
46, 73, 132, 190–94, 232, 240–45, 247,
249–50, 253, 272–73, 296–309, 318,
320–21, 336–37, 355–57, 368–70,
374–78; portraits of, 28, 36, 37–41, 44,
60–63, 65, 67–68, 105–106, 108, 153,
192, 254–66, 374; Portugal visited by,
269–71, 307, 313; posthumous rehabilitation of, 358–67; press coverage of,
31–32, 42, 43–45, 63, 67, 90, 180–82,
241, 247–48, 251, 253, 282, 301–309,
321–22, 329, 336, 337, 351, 352,
363–64; private life of, 81, 169, 280–82;
public appearances of, 46–58, 73, 91,
156–60, 208, 219–20, 283–301, 317–18,
324–25, 368–69; regency of, 30–46, 58,
83, 86, 88, 90–91, 188, 191; as religious
leader, 19, 208, 302, 326; robes of,

52–55, 58, 105–106, 108; Romantic
movement supported by, xxii-xxiii,
91, 92–113, 116, 275–77, 304, 313,
368; scepter of, 52, 55, 60, 108,
297, 375; as slave owner, 168–71,
174–75, 179–80, 183, 241; sovereign
power of, 53–54, 59–60, 64, 73, 105–
106, 272–73; stability established by,
44–46, 48, 82, 90; sword of, 47, 55,
60, 298, 375; "Testimonial" of,
348–49

Pedro II School, 109, 113–15, 116, 302,
337

Pereira de Vasconcelos, Bernardo, 42, 86,
88

Perfect Prince, The (Novais Campos), 374

Petrópolis, 171–83, 220, 233, 299, 307,
323–24, 327, 330, 331, 338, 352, 355,
360, 364–67

Pezerat, Pierre Joseph, 161

Philadelphia Exhibition (1876), 275, 277,
290

Philip II, king of France, 124–25

Pinheiro, Rafael Bordalo, 270–71, 302

Pinho, José Wanderley de Araújo, 81, 363,
364

Pinto Duarte, Francisco (baron of Tinguá), 140

Plancher, Pedro, 25

Pléiades, Les (Gobineau), 273–74

Poe, Edgar Allan, 261

Pompéia, Raul, 333–34, 337

Portugal: aristocracy of, 118–19; Brazil as
colony of, xviii, xix, 15–22, 27, 30, 118–
19, 126, 187, 373–74, 376; cultural
influence of, 91, 93, 183, 253; economy
of, 143; empire of, 185–86, 192; monarchy of, 29–30, 122–24, 148, 190, 209,
373–74, 376; slave trade by, 70; visited
by Pedro II, 269–71, 307, 313

Praieira revolt (1849–50), 83–84, 87

Preto, Ouro, 320, 322, 325, 326, 327, 335,
344, 345

Illustration Credits

The images from the Brazilian National Library, which belong to that institution, were acquired in microfilm form and developed by Inês de Castro, of the Anthropology Laboratory of the University of São Paulo. She also developed reproductions of images from the private collections of Emanoel Araújo, Pedro Correa do Lago, and the collection of the Maria Luísa and Oscar Americano Foundation; some of the reproductions from the Museu Paulista are also of her doing.

Vicente de Mello photographed the images belonging to the Brazilian Historical and Geographical Institute, some of the images from the Museum of Fine Arts in Rio de Janeiro, and the images of the Roberto Menezes de Moraes collection in Rio.

Ivson reproduced some documents taken from private collections.

The images from the Museu Imperial were made by Raul Lopes and Rômulo Fialdini.

The illustrations belonging to the Museu Mariano Procópio were produced by that institution's own laboratory.

The photographs from the Museu do Itamaraty are by Rômulo Fialdini.

Luiz Hossaka reproduced the work from the Assis Chateaubriand São Paulo Museum of Art.

All this wealth of material was reproduced thanks to the support and finance of the Fundaçao de Apoio à Pesquisa de Estado de São Paulo, and later of the Conselho Nacional de Pequisa.